UNITED
ARAB EMIRATES

BUSINESS LAW HANDBOOK
VOLUME 1
STRATEGIC INFORMATION AND BASIC LAWS

International Business Publications, USA
Washington DC, USA- United Arab Emirates

UNITED ARAB EMIRATES
BUSINESS LAW HANDBOOK
VOLUME 1 STRATEGIC INFORMATION AND BASIC LAWS

UPDATED ANNUALLY

We express our sincere appreciation to all government agencies and international organizations which provided information and other materials for this handbook

Databases & Information: International Business Publications, USA
Cover Design: International Business Publications, USA

International Business Publications, USA. has used its best efforts in collecting, analyzing and preparing data, information and materials for this unique handbook. Due to the dynamic nature and fast development of the economy and business environment, we cannot warrant that all information herein is complete and accurate. IBP does not assume and hereby disclaim any liability to any person for any loss or damage caused by possible errors or omissions in the handbook.
This handbook is for individual use only. Use this handbook for any other purpose, included but not limited to reproducing and storing in a retrieval system by any means, electronic, photocopying or using the addresses or other information contained in this handbook for any commercial purposes requires a special written permission from the publisher.

**2019 Edition Updated Reprint International Business Publications, USA
ISBN 1-5145-0219-4**

For additional analytical, business and investment opportunities information,
please contact Global Investment & Business Center, USA
at (703) 370-8082. Fax: (703) 370-8083. E-mail: ibpusa3@gmail.com
Global Business and Investment Info Databank - www.ibpus.com

Printed in the USA

For additional analytical, marketing, investment and business opportunities
information, please contact
Global Investment & Business Center, USA
(202) 546-2103. Fax: (202) 546-3275. E-mail: rusric@erols.com

UNITED
ARAB EMIRATES
BUSINESS LAW HANDBOOK
VOLUME 1
STRATEGIC INFORMATION AND BASIC LAWS

TABLE OF CONTENTS

**For additional analytical, marketing, investment and business opportunities
information, please contact
Global Investment & Business Center, USA
(202) 546-2103. Fax: (202) 546-3275. E-mail: rusric@erols.com**

For additional analytical, marketing, investment and business opportunities information, please contact
Global Investment & Business Center, USA
(202) 546-2103. Fax: (202) 546-3275. E-mail: rusric@erols.com

**For additional analytical, marketing, investment and business opportunities
information, please contact
Global Investment & Business Center, USA
(202) 546-2103. Fax: (202) 546-3275. E-mail: rusric@erols.com**

**For additional analytical, marketing, investment and business opportunities
information, please contact
Global Investment & Business Center, USA
(202) 546-2103. Fax: (202) 546-3275. E-mail: rusric@erols.com**

**For additional analytical, marketing, investment and business opportunities
information, please contact
Global Investment & Business Center, USA
(202) 546-2103. Fax: (202) 546-3275. E-mail: rusric@erols.com**

For additional analytical, marketing, investment and business opportunities
information, please contact
Global Investment & Business Center, USA
(202) 546-2103. Fax: (202) 546-3275. E-mail: rusric@erols.com

BUSINESS AND DEVELOPMENT PROFILES

STRATEGIC PROFILE

Capital	Abu Dhabi 24°28′N 54°22′E24.467°N 54.367°E
Largest city	Dubai
Official language(s)	Arabic
Ethnic groups	16.6% Emirati 23% Other Arabs and Iranian 60.5% South Asian, Indian, Pakistani, Bangladeshi, Chinese, Filipino, Thai, Westerners (2009)
Demonym	Emirati
Government	Constitutional federation of absolute monarchies with an executive president elected by Emir Council amongst themselves
- President	Khalifa bin Zayed Al Nahyan
- Vice President and Prime Minister	Mohammed bin Rashid Al Maktoum
Legislature	Federal National Council
Sovereignty	End of special treaty with the United Kingdom
- Constitution	December 2, 1971
Area	
- Total	83,600 [1] km^2 (116th) 32,278 sq mi
- Water (%)	negligible
Population	
- 2010 estimate	8,264,070 (93rd)
- 2005 census	4,106,427
- Density	99/km^2 (110th) 256/sq mi
GDP (PPP)	2011 estimate
- Total	$258.825 billion
- Per capita	$48,158
GDP (nominal)	2011 estimate
- Total	$360.136 billion
- Per capita	$67,008
Gini (2008)	36
HDI (2011)	▲0.846 (very high) (30th)
Currency	UAE dirham (AED)
Time zone	GMT+4 (UTC+4)
- Summer (DST)	not observed (UTC+4)
Date formats	dd/mm/yyyy
Drives on the	right
ISO 3166 code	AE
Internet TLD	امارات. ,ae.
Calling code	971

For additional analytical, marketing, investment and business opportunities information, please contact
Global Investment & Business Center, USA
(202) 546-2103. Fax: (202) 546-3275. E-mail: rusric@erols.com

The **United Arab Emirates** (**UAE**), sometimes simply called the **Emirates**, is a country situated in the southeast of the Arabian Peninsula in Western Asia on the Persian Gulf, bordering Oman to the east and Saudi Arabia to the south, as well as sharing sea borders with Qatar to the west and Iran to the north.

The UAE is a federation of seven emirates (equivalent to principalities), each governed by a hereditary emir, with a single national president. The constituent emirates are Abu Dhabi, Ajman, Dubai, Fujairah, Ras al-Khaimah, Sharjah, and Umm al-Quwain. The capital is Abu Dhabi, which is also the state's center of political, industrial, and cultural activities.

Prior to independence in 1971, the UAE was known as the Trucial States or Trucial Oman, in reference to a 19th-century truce between the local sheikhs, hereditary rulers of the territories, and the United Kingdom. The term *Pirate Coast* was also used by some to refer to the emirates from the 18th to the early 20th century, owing to the preponderance of pirates operating from Emirati ports.

The UAE's political system is based on its 1971 Constitution, which is composed of several intricately connected governing bodies. As a federation of seven monarchies, whose rulers retain absolute power within their emirates, but with a UAE president, it is neither a constitutional monarchy nor a republic. The *emirs* choose one of their members to be the president of the federation, but this does not alter the monarchical character of the government of the individual emirates. The constitution is concerned solely with the relations between the emirates as members of the federation, and does not prescribe a constitutional system of government. Islam is the official religion of the UAE, and Arabic is the official language.

UAE oil reserves are ranked as the world's sixth-largest and it possesses one of the most developed economies in West Asia. It is the thirty-fifth-largest economy at market exchange rates, and ranks among the world's wealthiest nations with per capita GDP (PPP) of US$48,597. It is 15th in purchasing power per capita and has a relatively high Human Development Index for the Asian continent, ranking thirtieth globally. The UAE is classified as a high-income developing economy by the IMF

GEOGRAPHY

Location: Middle East, bordering the Gulf of Oman and the Persian Gulf, between Oman and Saudi Arabia
Geographic coordinates: 24 00 N, 54 00 E
Map references: Middle East

Area:
total: 82,880 sq km *land:* 82,880 sq km *water:* 0 sq km

Area—comparative: slightly smaller than Maine
Land boundaries:
total: 867 km *border countries:* Oman 410 km, Saudi Arabia 457 km

Coastline: 1,318 km

Maritime claims:
contiguous zone: 24 nm *continental shelf:* 200 nm or to the edge of the continental margin
exclusive economic zone: 200 nm
territorial sea: 12 nm

For additional analytical, marketing, investment and business opportunities information, please contact
Global Investment & Business Center, USA
(202) 546-2103. Fax: (202) 546-3275. E-mail: rusric@erols.com

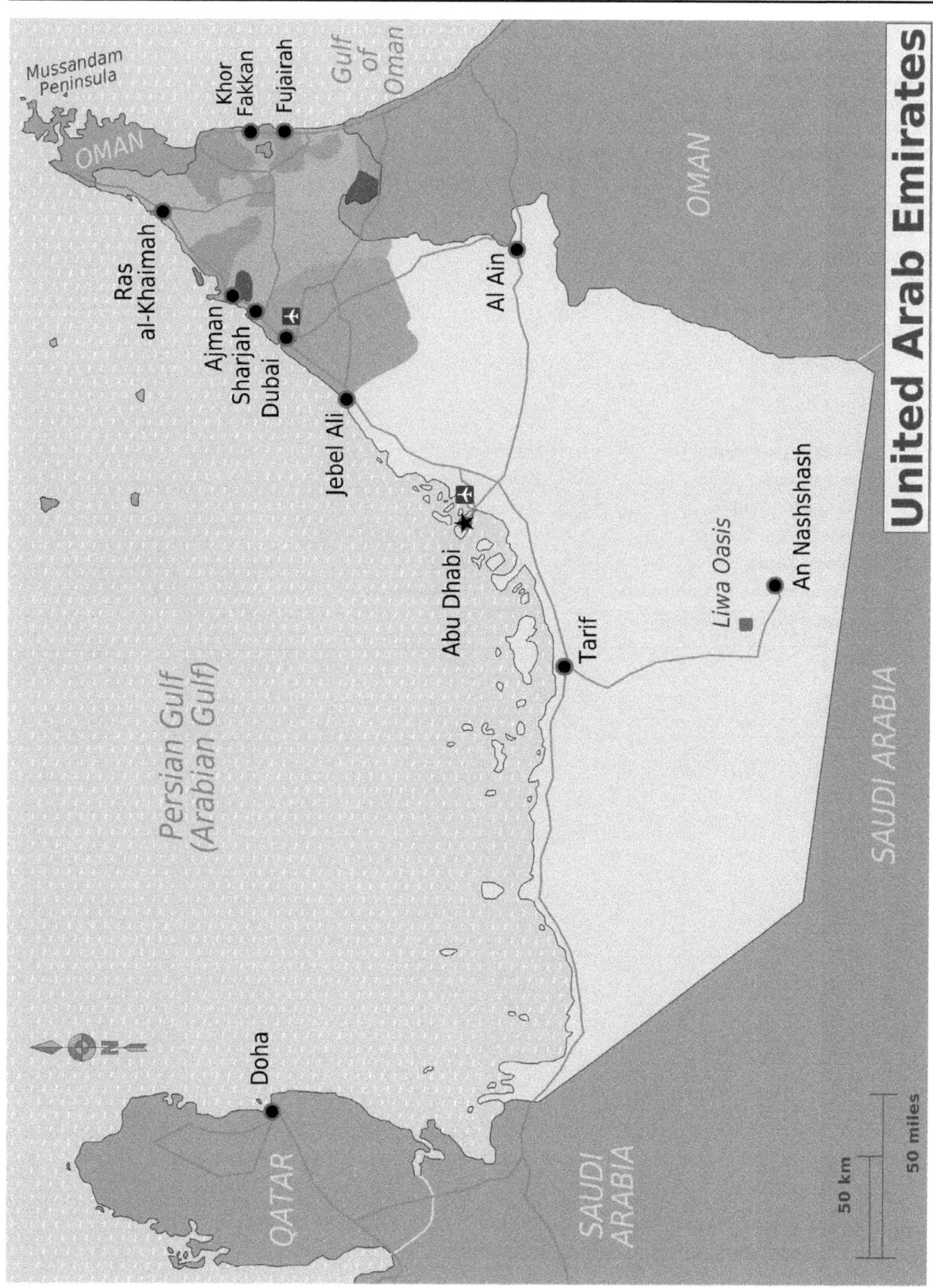

Climate: desert; cooler in eastern mountains

For additional analytical, marketing, investment and business opportunities
information, please contact
Global Investment & Business Center, USA
(202) 546-2103. Fax: (202) 546-3275. E-mail: rusric@erols.com

Terrain: flat, barren coastal plain merging into rolling sand dunes of vast desert wasteland; mountains in east

Elevation extremes:
lowest point: Persian Gulf 0 m
highest point: Jabal Yibir 1,527 m
Natural resources: petroleum, natural gas

Land use:
arable land: 0%
permanent crops: 0%
permanent pastures: 2%
forests and woodland: 0%
other: 98%

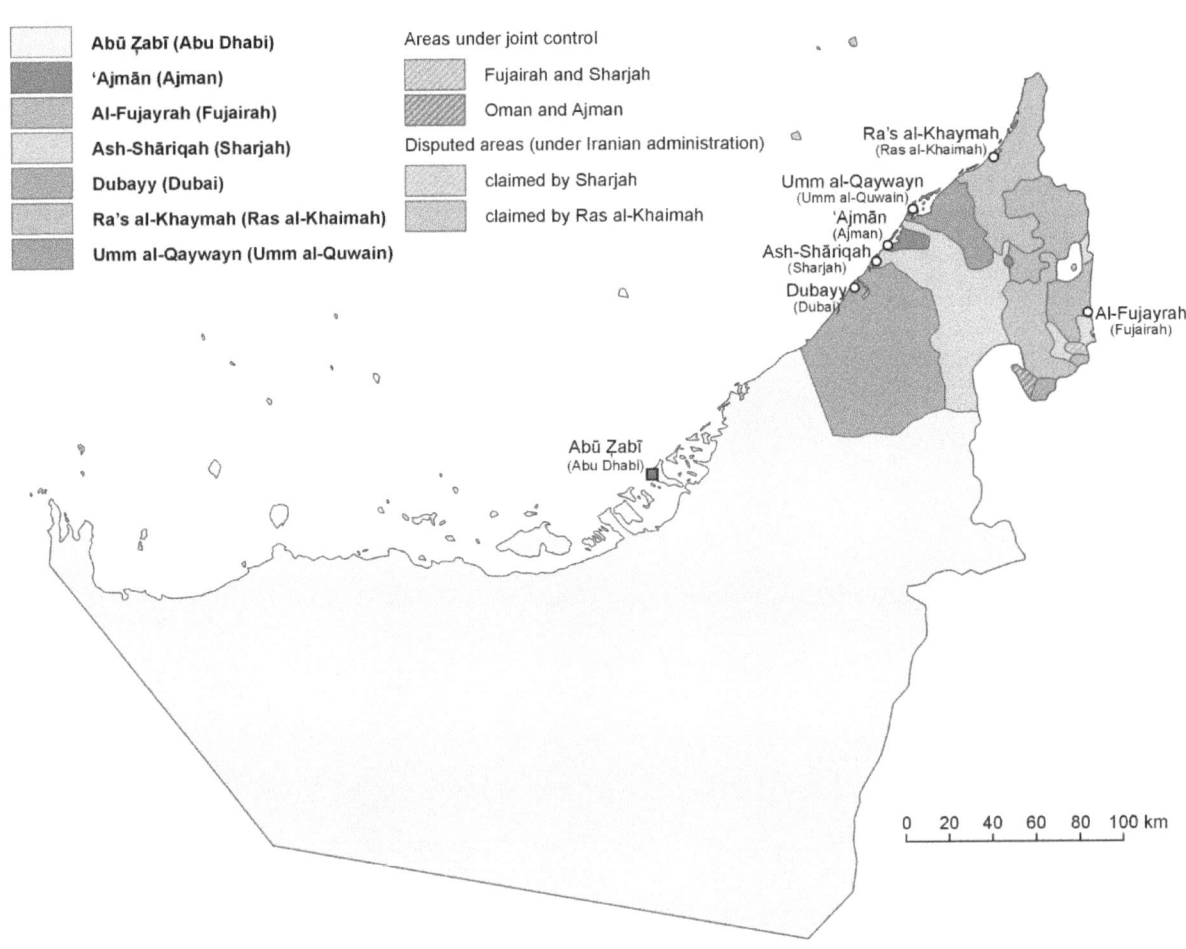

Irrigated land: 50 sq km
Natural hazards: frequent sand and dust storms

For additional analytical, marketing, investment and business opportunities
information, please contact
Global Investment & Business Center, USA
(202) 546-2103. Fax: (202) 546-3275. E-mail: rusric@erols.com

Environment—current issues: lack of natural freshwater resources being overcome by des
Environment—international agreements:
party to: Climate Change, Desertification, Endangered Species, Hazardous Wastes, Marine Dumping, Ozone Layer Protection
signed, but not ratified: Biodiversity, Law of the Sea

Geography—note: strategic location along southern approaches to Strait of Hormuz, a vital transit point for world crude oil alination plants; desertification; beach pollution from oil spills

PEOPLE

Population: 2,344,402
note: includes 1,576,589 non-nationals

Age structure:
0-14 years: 31% (male 368,844; female 353,183)

15-64 years: 67% (male 1,015,690; female 558,902)
65 years and over: 2% (male 32,935; female 14,848)

Population growth rate: 1.78%
Birth rate: 18.86 births/1,000 population
Death rate: 3.13 deaths/1,000 population
Net migration rate: 2.03 migrant(s)/1,000 population

Sex ratio:
at birth: 1.05 male(s)/female
under 15 years: 1.04 male(s)/female
15-64 years: 1.82 male(s)/female
65 years and over: 2.22 male(s)/female
total population: 1.53 male(s)/female

Infant mortality rate: 14.1 deaths/1,000 live births

Life expectancy at birth:
total population: 75.24 years
male: 73.83 years
female: 76.72 years
Total fertility rate: 3.5 children born/woman
Nationality:
noun: Emirian(s)
adjective: Emirian
Ethnic groups: Emiri 19%, other Arab and Iranian 23%, South Asian 50%, other expatriates (includes Westerners and East Asians) 8%
note: less than 20% are UAE citizens
Religions: Muslim 96% (Shi'a 16%), Christian, Hindu, and other 4%
Languages: Arabic (official), Persian, English, Hindi, Urdu

For additional analytical, marketing, investment and business opportunities information, please contact
Global Investment & Business Center, USA
(202) 546-2103. Fax: (202) 546-3275. E-mail: rusric@erols.com

Literacy:
definition: age 15 and over can read and write
total population: 79.2%
male: 78.9% *female:* 79.8%

GOVERNMENT

Country name:
conventional long form: United Arab Emirates
conventional short form: none
local long form: Al Imarat al Arabiyah al Muttahidah
local short form: none
former: Trucial States
abbreviation: UAE

Data code: TC
Government type: federation with specified powers delegated to the UAE federal government and other powers reserved to member emirates
Capital: Abu Dhabi

Administrative divisions: 7 emirates (imarat, singular—imarah); Abu Zaby (Abu Dhabi), 'Ajman, Al Fujayrah, Ash Shariqah (Sharjah), Dubayy (Dubai), Ra's al Khaymah, Umm al Qaywayn

Independence: 2 December 1971 (from UK)
National holiday: National Day, 2 December (1971)
Constitution: 2 December 1971 (made permanent in 1996)

Legal system: federal court system introduced in 1971; all emirates except Dubayy (Dubai) and Ra's al Khaymah have joined the federal system; all emirates have secular and Islamic law for civil, criminal, and high courts

Suffrage: none

Executive branch:

chief of state: President KHALIFA bin Zayid Al-Nuhayyan (since 3 November 2004), ruler of Abu Zaby (Abu Dhabi) (since 4 November 2004); Vice President and Prime Minister MUHAMMAD BIN RASHID Al-Maktum (since 5 January 2006)

head of government: Prime Minister and Vice President MUHAMMAD BIN RASHID Al-Maktum (since 5 January 2006); Deputy Prime Ministers SAIF bin Zayid Al-Nuhayyan (since 11 May 2009) and MANSUR bin Zayid Al-Nuhayyan (since 11 May 2009)

cabinet: Council of Ministers appointed by the president

note:there is also a Federal Supreme Council (FSC) composed of the seven emirate rulers; the FSC is the highest constitutional authority in the UAE; establishes general policies and sanctions federal legislation; meets four times a year; Abu Zaby (Abu Dhabi) and Dubayy (Dubai) rulers have effective veto power

For additional analytical, marketing, investment and business opportunities information, please contact
Global Investment & Business Center, USA
(202) 546-2103. Fax: (202) 546-3275. E-mail: rusric@erols.com

elections: president and vice president elected by the FSC for five-year terms (no term limits) from among the seven FSC members; election last held 3 November 2004 upon the death of the UAE's Founding Father and first President ZAYID bin Sultan Al Nuhayyan (next election NA); prime minister and deputy prime minister appointed by the president

election results: KHALIFA bin Zayid Al-Nuhayyan elected president by a unanimous vote of the FSC; MUHAMMAD bin Rashid Al-Maktum unanimously affirmed vice president after the 2006 death of his brother Sheikh MAKTUM bin Rashid Al-Maktum

Legislative branch:

description: unicameral Federal National Council or Majlis al-Ittihad al-Watani (40 seats; 20 members appointed by the rulers of the 7 constituent states and 20 indirectly elected by an electoral college whose members are selected by each emirate ruler proportional to its FNC membership; members serve 4-year terms)
elections: last held on 3 October 2015 (next to be held in 2019); note - the electoral college was expanded from 129,274 electors in the December 2011 election to 224,279 in the October 2015 election; elections for candidates rather than political parties; 347 candidates including 78 women ran for 20 contested seats in the 40-member FNC; 80,000 voters, or 35% of eligible voters, turned out to vote and 19 men and one woman were elected
election results: elected FNC seats by emirate - Abu Dhabi 4, Dubai 4, Sharjah 3, Ras al-Khaimah 3, Ajman 2, Fujairah 2, Umm al-Quwain 2; note - only 1 woman (from Ras Al Khaimah) won an FNC seat

Judicial branch: Union Supreme Court, judges appointed by the president
Political parties and leaders: none
Political pressure groups and leaders: NA

International organization participation: ABEDA, AfDB, AFESD, AL, AMF, CAEU, CCC, ESCWA, FAO, G-77, GCC, IAEA, IBRD, ICAO, ICRM, IDA, IDB, IFAD, IFC, IFRCS, IHO, ILO, IMF, IMO, Inmarsat, Intelsat, Interpol, IOC, ISO (correspondent), ITU, NAM, OAPEC, OIC, OPCW, OPEC, UN, UNCTAD, UNESCO, UNIDO, UPU, WHO, WIPO, WMO, WTrO

chief of mission: Ambassador Yusif bin Mani bin Said al-UTAYBA (since 28 July 2008)
chancery: 3522 International Court NW, Suite 400, Washington, DC 20008
telephone: [1] (202) 243-2400
FAX: [1] (202) 243-2432
consulate(s) general: Boston, Los Angeles, New York

Diplomatic representation from the US:
chief of mission: Ambassador (vanant); Charge d'Affaires Steven C. BONDY (since 22 March 2018)
embassy: Embassies District, Plot 38 Sector W59-02, Street No. 4, Abu Dhabi
mailing address: P. O. Box 4009, Abu Dhabi
telephone: [971] (2) 414-2200
FAX: [971] (2) 414-2603
consulate(s) general: Dubai

Flag description: three equal horizontal bands of green (top), white, and black with a thicker vertical red band on the hoist side

For additional analytical, marketing, investment and business opportunities information, please contact
Global Investment & Business Center, USA
(202) 546-2103. Fax: (202) 546-3275. E-mail: rusric@erols.com

ECONOMY

The UAE has an open economy with a high per capita income and a sizable annual trade surplus. Successful efforts at economic diversification have reduced the portion of GDP from the oil and gas sector to 30%.

Since the discovery of oil in the UAE nearly 60 years ago, the country has undergone a profound transformation from an impoverished region of small desert principalities to a modern state with a high standard of living. The government has increased spending on job creation and infrastructure expansion and is opening up utilities to greater private sector involvement. The country's free trade zones - offering 100% foreign ownership and zero taxes - are helping to attract foreign investors.

The global financial crisis of 2008-09, tight international credit, and deflated asset prices constricted the economy in 2009. UAE authorities tried to blunt the crisis by increasing spending and boosting liquidity in the banking sector. The crisis hit Dubai hardest, as it was heavily exposed to depressed real estate prices. Dubai lacked sufficient cash to meet its debt obligations, prompting global concern about its solvency and ultimately a $20 billion bailout from the UAE Central Bank and Abu Dhabi Government that was refinanced in March 2014.

The UAE's dependence on oil is a significant long-term challenge, although the UAE is one of the most diversified countries in the Gulf Cooperation Council. Low oil prices have prompted the UAE to cut expenditures, including on some social programs, but the UAE has sufficient assets in its sovereign investment funds to cover its deficits. The government reduced fuel subsidies in August 2015, and introduced excise taxes (50% on sweetened carbonated beverages and 100% on energy drinks and tobacco) in October 2017. A five-percent value-added tax was introduced in January 2018. The UAE's strategic plan for the next few years focuses on economic diversification, promoting the UAE as a global trade and tourism hub, developing industry, and creating more job opportunities for nationals through improved education and increased private sector employment.

GDP (purchasing power parity):

$696 billion (2017 est.)
$690.5 billion (2016 est.)
$670.5 billion (2015 est.)
note: data are in 2017 dollars
country comparison to the world: 32

GDP (official exchange rate):
$382.6 billion (2017 est.) (2017 est.)

GDP - real growth rate:
0.8% (2017 est.)
3% (2016 est.)
5.1% (2015 est.)
country comparison to the world: 188

GDP - per capita (PPP):
$68,600 (2017 est.)
$70,100 (2016 est.)

For additional analytical, marketing, investment and business opportunities
information, please contact
Global Investment & Business Center, USA
(202) 546-2103. Fax: (202) 546-3275. E-mail: rusric@erols.com

$70,000 (2015 est.)
note: data are in 2017 dollars
country comparison to the world: 13

Gross national saving:
28.5% of GDP (2017 est.)
30.9% of GDP (2016 est.)
30.7% of GDP (2015 est.)
country comparison to the world: 39

GDP - composition, by end use:
household consumption: 34.9% (2017 est.)
government consumption: 12.3% (2017 est.)
investment in fixed capital: 23% (2017 est.)
investment in inventories: 1.8% (2017 est.)
exports of goods and services: 100.4% (2017 est.)
imports of goods and services: -72.4% (2017 est.)

GDP - composition, by sector of origin:
agriculture: 0.9% (2017 est.)
industry: 49.8% (2017 est.)
services: 49.2% (2017 est.)

Agriculture - products:
dates, vegetables, watermelons; poultry, eggs, dairy products; fish

Industries:
petroleum and petrochemicals; fishing, aluminum, cement, fertilizer, commercial ship repair, construction materials, handicrafts, textiles

Industrial production growth rate:
1.8% (2017 est.)
country comparison to the world: 138

Labor force:
5.344 million (2017 est.)
note: expatriates account for about 85% of the workforce
country comparison to the world: 78

Labor force - by occupation:
agriculture: 7%
industry: 15%
services: 78% (2000 est.)

Unemployment rate:
3.6% (2014 est.)
country comparison to the world: 14

Population below poverty line:
19.5%

Budget:
revenues: 110.2 billion (2017 est.)

For additional analytical, marketing, investment and business opportunities information, please contact
Global Investment & Business Center, USA
(202) 546-2103. Fax: (202) 546-3275. E-mail: rusric@erols.com

expenditures: 111.1 billion (2017 est.)
note: the UAE federal budget does not account for emirate-level spending in Abu Dhabi and Dubai

Taxes and other revenues:
28.8% (of GDP) (2017 est.)
country comparison to the world: 90

Budget surplus (+) or deficit (-):
-0.2% (of GDP) (2017 est.)
country comparison to the world: 51

Public debt:
19.7% of GDP (2017 est.)
20.2% of GDP (2016 est.)
country comparison to the world: 190

Fiscal year:
calendar year

Inflation rate (consumer prices):
2% (2017 est.)
1.6% (2016 est.)
country comparison to the world: 108

Commercial bank prime lending rate:
6% (31 December 2017 est.)
5.7% (31 December 2016 est.)
country comparison to the world: 126

Stock of narrow money:
$134 billion (31 December 2017 est.)
$129.1 billion (31 December 2016 est.)
country comparison to the world: 32

Stock of broad money:
$134 billion (31 December 2017 est.)
$129.1 billion (31 December 2016 est.)
country comparison to the world: 32

Stock of domestic credit:
$395.5 billion (31 December 2017 est.)
$396 billion (31 December 2016 est.)
country comparison to the world: 31

Market value of publicly traded shares:
$195.9 billion (31 December 2015 est.)
$201.6 billion (31 December 2014 est.)
$180.3 billion (31 December 2013 est.)
country comparison to the world: 33

Current account balance:
$26.47 billion (2017 est.)

For additional analytical, marketing, investment and business opportunities information, please contact
Global Investment & Business Center, USA
(202) 546-2103. Fax: (202) 546-3275. E-mail: rusric@erols.com

$13.23 billion (2016 est.)
country comparison to the world: 13

Exports:
$308.5 billion (2017 est.)
$298.6 billion (2016 est.)
country comparison to the world: 18

Exports - partners:
India 10.1%, Iran 9.9%, Japan 9.3%, China 5.4%, Oman 5%, Switzerland 4.4%, South Korea 4.1% (2017)

Exports - commodities:
crude oil 45%, natural gas, reexports, dried fish, dates (2012 est.)

Imports:
$229.2 billion (2017 est.)
$226.5 billion (2016 est.)
country comparison to the world: 21

Imports - commodities:
machinery and transport equipment, chemicals, food

Imports - partners:
China 8.5%, US 6.8%, India 6.6% (2017)

Reserves of foreign exchange and gold:
$95.37 billion (31 December 2017 est.)
$85.39 billion (31 December 2016 est.)
country comparison to the world: 27

Debt - external:
$237.6 billion (31 December 2017 est.)
$218.7 billion (31 December 2016 est.)
country comparison to the world: 32

Stock of direct foreign investment - at home:
$129.9 billion (31 December 2017 est.)
$134.8 billion (31 December 2016 est.)
country comparison to the world: 41

Stock of direct foreign investment - abroad:
$124.4 billion (31 December 2017 est.)
$114.6 billion (31 December 2016 est.)
country comparison to the world: 32

Exchange rates:
Emirati dirhams (AED) per US dollar -
3.673 (2017 est.)
3.673 (2016 est.)
3.673 (2015 est.)
3.673 (2014 est.)
3.673 (2013 est.)

For additional analytical, marketing, investment and business opportunities
information, please contact
Global Investment & Business Center, USA
(202) 546-2103. Fax: (202) 546-3275. E-mail: rusric@erols.com

ENERGY

Electricity access:
population without electricity: 177,824 (2012)
electrification - total population: 98% (2012)
electrification - urban areas: 99% (2012)
electrification - rural areas: 93% (2012)

Electricity - production:
121.8 billion kWh (2016 est.)
country comparison to the world: 31

Electricity - consumption:
113.2 billion kWh (2016 est.)
country comparison to the world: 31

Electricity - exports:
0 kWh (2016 est.)
country comparison to the world: 213

Electricity - imports:
1.141 billion kWh (2016 est.)
country comparison to the world: 66

Electricity - installed generating capacity:
28.91 million kW (2016 est.)
country comparison to the world: 33

Electricity - from fossil fuels:
99% of total installed capacity (2016 est.)
country comparison to the world: 26

Electricity - from nuclear fuels:
0% of total installed capacity (2017 est.)
country comparison to the world: 204

Electricity - from hydroelectric plants:
0% of total installed capacity (2017 est.)
country comparison to the world: 210

Electricity - from other renewable sources:
1% of total installed capacity (2017 est.)
country comparison to the world: 170

Crude oil - production:
3.174 million bbl/day (2017 est.)
country comparison to the world: 8

Crude oil - exports:
2.552 million bbl/day (2015 est.)
country comparison to the world: 5

For additional analytical, marketing, investment and business opportunities information, please contact
Global Investment & Business Center, USA
(202) 546-2103. Fax: (202) 546-3275. E-mail: rusric@erols.com

Crude oil - imports:
0 bbl/day (2015 est.)
country comparison to the world: 210

Crude oil - proved reserves:
97.8 billion bbl (1 January 2018 est.)
country comparison to the world: 7

Refined petroleum products - production:
943,500 bbl/day (2017 est.)
country comparison to the world: 19

Refined petroleum products - consumption:
896,000 bbl/day (2016 est.)
country comparison to the world: 24

Refined petroleum products - exports:
817,700 bbl/day (2015 est.)
country comparison to the world: 10

Refined petroleum products - imports:
392,000 bbl/day (2015 est.)
country comparison to the world: 23

Natural gas - production:
62.01 billion cu m (2017 est.)
country comparison to the world: 14

Natural gas - consumption:
74.48 billion cu m (2017 est.)
country comparison to the world: 12

Natural gas - exports:
7.504 billion cu m (2017 est.)
country comparison to the world: 25

Natural gas - imports:
20.22 billion cu m (2017 est.)
country comparison to the world: 16

Natural gas - proved reserves:
6.091 trillion cu m (1 January 2018 est.)
country comparison to the world: 6

Carbon dioxide emissions from consumption of energy:
289.4 million Mt (2017 est.)
country comparison to the world: 24

COMMUNICATIONS

Telephones - main lines in use:
1.825 million
country comparison to the world: 61

**For additional analytical, marketing, investment and business opportunities
information, please contact
Global Investment & Business Center, USA
(202) 546-2103. Fax: (202) 546-3275. E-mail: rusric@erols.com**

Telephones - mobile cellular:
11.727 million
country comparison to the world: 66

Telephone system:
general assessment: modern fiber-optic integrated services; digital network with rapidly growing use of mobile-cellular telephones; key centers are Abu Dhabi and Dubai
domestic: microwave radio relay, fiber optic and coaxial cable
international: country code - 971; linked to the international submarine cable FLAG (Fiber-Optic Link Around the Globe); landing point for both the SEA-ME-WE-3 and SEA-ME-WE-4 submarine cable networks; satellite earth stations - 3 Intelsat (1 Atlantic Ocean and 2 Indian Ocean) and 1 Arabsat; tropospheric scatter to Bahrain; microwave radio relay to Saudi Arabia (2011)

Broadcast media:
except for the many organizations now operating in Dubai's Media Free Zone, most TV and radio stations remain government-owned; widespread use of satellite dishes provides access to pan-Arab and other international broadcasts (2007)

Internet country code:
.ae

Internet hosts:
337,804 (2012)
country comparison to the world: 61

Internet users:
3.449 million
country comparison to the world: 61

TRANSPORTATION

Railways: 0 km
Highways:
total: 4,835 km
paved: 4,835 km
unpaved: 0 km
Pipelines: crude oil 830 km; natural gas, including natural gas liquids, 870 km
Ports and harbors: 'Ajman, Al Fujayrah, Das Island, Khawr Fakkan, Mina' Jabal 'Ali, Mina' Khalid, Mina' Rashid, Mina' Saqr, Mina' Zayid, Umm al Qaywayn
Merchant marine:
total: 74 ships (1,000 GRT or over) totaling 1,093,795 GRT/1,757,189 DWT
ships by type: bulk 4, cargo 20, chemical tanker 4, container 8, liquefied gas tanker 1, livestock carrier 1, oil tanker 28, refrigerated cargo 1, roll-on/roll-off cargo 7
Airports: 41
Airports—with paved runways:
total: 21
over 3,047 m: 8 2,438 to 3,047 m: 3 1,524 to 2,437 m: 3 914 to 1,523 m: 3
under 914 m: 4
Airports—with unpaved runways: *total:* 20
over 3,047 m: 1 2,438 to 3,047 m: 1
1,524 to 2,437 m: 4 914 to 1,523 m: 9
under 914 m: 5
Heliports: 2

For additional analytical, marketing, investment and business opportunities information, please contact
Global Investment & Business Center, USA
(202) 546-2103. Fax: (202) 546-3275. E-mail: rusric@erols.com

MILITARY

Military branches: Army, Navy, Air Force, Air Defense, paramilitary (includes Federal Police Force)

Military manpower—military age: 18 years of age

Military manpower—availability: *males age 15-49:* 791,097

note: includes non-nationals

Military manpower—fit for military service:

males age 15-49: 425,248

Military manpower—reaching military age annually:

males: 23,358

Military expenditures—dollar figure: $2.118 billion

Military expenditures—percent of GDP: 5%

TRANSNATIONAL ISSUES

Disputes—international: location and status of boundary with Saudi Arabia is not final, de facto boundary reflects 1974 agreement; no defined boundary with most of Oman, but Administrative Line in far north; claims two islands in the Persian Gulf occupied by Iran: Lesser Tunb (called Tunb as Sughra in Arabic by UAE and Jazireh-ye Tonb-e Kuchek in Persian by Iran) and Greater Tunb (called Tunb al Kubra in Arabic by UAE and Jazireh-ye Tonb-e Bozorg in Persian by Iran); claims island in the Persian Gulf jointly administered with Iran (called Abu Musa in Arabic by UAE and Jazireh-ye Abu Musa in Persian by Iran)—over which Iran has taken steps to exert unilateral control since 1992, including access restrictions and a military build-up on the island; the UAE has garnered significant diplomatic support in the region in protesting these Iranian actions

Illicit drugs: growing role as heroin transshipment and money-laundering center due to its proximity to southwest Asian producing countries and the bustling free trade zone in Dubai

For additional analytical, marketing, investment and business opportunities information, please contact
Global Investment & Business Center, USA
(202) 546-2103. Fax: (202) 546-3275. E-mail: rusric@erols.com

IMPORTANT INFORMATION FOR UNDERSTANDING UAE

The **United Arab Emirates** (also the **UAE** or the **Emirates**) is a Middle Eastern country situated in the southeast of the Arabian Peninsula in Southwest Asia on the Persian Gulf, comprising seven emirates: Abu Dhabi, Ajmān, Dubai, Fujairah, Ras al-Khaimah, Sharjah, and Umm al-Quwain. Before 1971, they were known as the **Trucial States** or **Trucial Oman**, in reference of a nineteenth-century truce between Britain and several Arab Sheikhs. It borders Oman and Saudi Arabia. The country is rich in oil.

Few nations on earth have experienced more complete and far-reaching change over the past few decades than the United Arab Emirates. Today a land of six-lane highways and glittering streams of motorcars, where space-age cities of ivory-white and crystal glass emerge like a mirage from the haze of desert and sea, this federation of seven ancient Emirates - Abu Dhabi, Dubai, Sharjah, Ras a]-Khaimah, Umm al Qawain, Ajman and Fujairah - is not only the world's fourth largest oil-producer, but also its richest state per head of population, and the new commercial hub of the Middle East

Yet only fifty years ago, when oil-exploration started, there was no electricity, no plumbing or telephone system, not a single public hospital nor modern school, no bridges, no deep-water harbor, no metalloid roads, no more than a handful of cars and scarcely a building more impressive than the crumbling mud-brick forts and watchtowers of Abu Dhabi and Dubai, where now high-rise stacks, gilded domes and minarets tower over wide boulevards, where cascades of water are flaunted with conspicuous opulence, and where acres of shrubs burgeon on the desert shore, stood sleepy settlements of reed, coral and mud-brick houses, sweltering on sand spits and islands in the most ferocious summer heat.

Life on the Trucial Coast - as it was known until the 1970s - and in its hinterland, was one of considerable hardship. In the towns, fresh water was scarcely available and often had to be drawn by oxen from deep wells, or even brought in barrels from neighboring islands by dhow.

Tribesmen would harvest the unreliable winter rains by stretching a sail with a hole in its center between two poles, and in the merciless heat of the Arabian summer would trap the cooling winds by the ingenious use of wind-towers made of sackcloth or cotton. On the sun-blasted terraces of the Hajar Mountains, subsistence farmers eked out a bitter existence, and in the interior the hardy Bedouin scoured the dunes of the great Empty Quarter for pasture. In the hot months, members of these various groups would come together to work as divers in the pearl-yielding oyster beds which flourished in the warm, shallow waters of the Gulf For almost three millennia the economy of this region was bound up with the pearling fleet, culminating in a boom that was only ended by the invention, in the 1920s of the cultured pearl.

Despite its harsh climate, civilization has flourished in this region since the earliest times. At Jebel Hafit, near al-Ain, lie the remains of a settlement dating back more than five thousand years;

at Hili, not far away, have been found pillbox-shaped tombs of dressed masonry so finely wrought that archaeologists believe they may be connected with the ancient land of Magan, mentioned in ancient Sumerian texts as a land of fabulous wealth, the source of copper, minerals and semi-precious stones.

COUNTRY

For additional analytical, marketing, investment and business opportunities information, please contact
Global Investment & Business Center, USA
(202) 546-2103. Fax: (202) 546-3275. E-mail: rusric@erols.com

United Arab Emirates, federation of seven independent states lying along the east central coast of the Arabian Gulf.

The states which include Abu Dhabi (capital of the UAE), Dubai, Al Sharjah, Ras Al Khaimah, Ajman, Umm Al Quwain, and Al Fujairah, bounded on the north by the Arabian Gulf, on the east by Sultanate of Oman, and on the west by Qatar and Saudi Arabia. The total area of the UAE is about 83,600 sq. km (with a total of 200 islands) .The area of the U.A.E. excepting the islands is about 77,700 square kilometers and among the G.C.C. states it is the third largest after Saudi Arabia & Oman. United Arab Emirates is a member of the Gulf Co-operation Council (G.C.C.).

HISTORY

On December 2, 1971, the seven states became independent as the United Arab Emirates. President, His Highness Sheikh Zayed Bin Sultan Al Nahyan who is also Ruler of Abu Dhabi has devoted much of his attention in the intervening years to the development of the federation of the United Arab Emirates.

Each of the states has its own ruler, together they comprise the highest body of the federal government, the Supreme Council of Rulers. The council elects from its members a president and vice president. The federation is also governed by a prime minister and a 40 member consultative assembly called the Federal National Council.

CLIMATIC CONDITIONS

The UAE lies in the arid tropical zone extending across Asia and northern Africa, however the Indian Ocean has a strong influence on the climatic conditions in the area, since the country borders both the Arabian Gulf and the Gulf of Oman. This explains why high temperatures in summer are always accompanied by high humidity along the coast.
Noticeable variations in climate occur between the coastal regions, the deserts of the interior and mountainous areas.

Between the months of November and March a moderate, warm climate prevails during the day at an average temperature of 26°C, and a slightly cooler climate prevails throughout the night at an average temperature of 15°C. The humidity tends to rise in the summer months, between June and August. Prevailing winds, influenced by the monsoons, vary between south or southeast, to west or north to northwest depending upon the season and location. Average rainfall is low at less than 6.5 centimeters annually and more than half of the average rainfall occurs in December and January.

UAE CURRENCY

Dirhams and fils are the units of currency with 100 fils to the Dirham (Dh). The Dirham is tied to the US Dollar at a steady exchange rate of $US 1= Dh 3.671. Banks usually give the best rates on foreign currency exchange

but hotels and airports are often quicker and are open outside banking hours. Money changers tend to have a wider range of currencies but their rates may be higher. Exchange rates are published daily.

TELEPHONE

Telecommunications throughout the UAE	International areas codes of UAE 00971 +

For additional analytical, marketing, investment and business opportunities information, please contact
Global Investment & Business Center, USA
(202) 546-2103. Fax: (202) 546-3275. E-mail: rusric@erols.com

are modern and efficient. International Direct Dialing is available to most countries. Local telephone calls are free. Local and international dialing codes may be obtained by dialing the operator on 181.	Abu Dhabi	02
	Dubai	04
	Al Sharjah	06
	Ras al Khaimah	07
	Ajman	06
	Umm al Quwain	06
	Al Fujairah	09

BASIC DATA

Geography
Area: 82,880 sq. km. (30,000 sq. mi.); about the size of Maine.
Cities (est.): *Capital*--Abu Dhabi (pop. 1,000,000); Dubai (pop. 860,000).
Terrain: Largely desert with some agricultural areas.
Climate: Hot, humid, low annual rainfall.

People
Nationality: *Noun and adjective*--U.A.E., Emirati.
Population : 4.4 million.
Population growth rate : 4.0%.
Ethnic groups: Indian, Pakistani, Bangladeshi, Egyptian, Jordanian, Iranian, Filipino, other Arab; (15-20% of residents are U.A.E. citizens).
Religions: Muslim (96%), Hindu, Christian.
Languages: Arabic (official), English, Hindi, Urdu, Persian.
Education: *Years compulsory*--ages 6-12. *Literacy* (U.A.E. citizens)--about 80%.
Health: *Life expectancy*--about 76 yrs.
Work force 2.968 million (93% foreign in 15-64 age group): *Agriculture*--2.3%; *industry*--61.9%; *services*--35.8%.

Government
Type: Federation of emirates.
Independence: December 2, 1971.
Provisional constitution: December 2, 1971.
Branches: *Executive*--7-member Supreme Council of Rulers, which elects president and vice president. *Legislative*--40-member Federal National Council (consultative only). *Judicial*--Islamic and secular courts.
Administrative subdivisions: Seven largely self-governing city-states.
Political parties: None.
Suffrage: State-nominated electors chose half of the Federal National Council seats in 2006.
Central government budget: $7 billion.

Economy
Natural resources: Oil and natural gas.
Agriculture (est., 2.0% of GDP): *Products*--vegetables, dates, dairy products, poultry, fish.
Petroleum : 36%.
Manufacturing : 13%.
Services (44% of GDP): Trade, government, real estate.
Trade : *Exports*--$157 billion: petroleum, gas, and petroleum products. *Major markets*--Japan,

For additional analytical, marketing, investment and business opportunities information, please contact
Global Investment & Business Center, USA
(202) 546-2103. Fax: (202) 546-3275. E-mail: rusric@erols.com

South Korea, Thailand, India. *Imports*--$126.6 billion: machinery, chemicals, food. *Major suppliers*--Western Europe, Japan, U.S., China, India.
Foreign economic aid (2007): In excess of $5.25 billion.

PEOPLE

Nationality: Noun and adjective--UAE, Emirian, or Emiri. Population (est.): 1.8 million. Annual growth rate: 2.8%. Ethnic groups: Arab, Pakistani, Indian, Iranian, Filipino (15-20% of residents are UAE citizens). Religions: Muslim (90%), Hindu, Christian. Languages: Arabic (official), English, Hindi, Urdu, Persian. Education: Years compulsory--ages 6-12. Literacy (UAE citizens)--about 60%. Life expectancy: About 63 yrs. Work force 650,000 (90% foreign): Agriculture--6%. Industry and commerce--65%. Services--16%. Government--13%.

Only 15-20% of the total population of 1.8 million are UAE citizens. The rest include significant numbers of other Arabs--Palestinians, Egyptians, Jordanians, Yemenis, Omanis--as well as many Iranians, Pakistanis, Indians, Filipinos, and West Europeans.

The majority of UAE citizens are Sunni Muslims with a small Shia minority. Most foreigners also are Muslim, although Hindus and Christians make up a portion of the UAE's foreign population.

Educational standards among UAE citizens population are rising rapidly. Citizens and temporary residents have taken advantage of facilities throughout the country. The UAE University in Al Ain had roughly 10,000 students in 1990. A network of technical-vocational colleges opened in 1989.

HISTORY

The UAE was formed from the group of tribally-organized Arabian Peninsula shaikhdoms along the southern coast of the Persian Gulf and the northwestern coast of the Gulf of Oman. This area was converted to Islam in the 7th century; for centuries it was embroiled in dynastic disputes. It became known as the Pirate Coast as raiders based there harassed foreign shipping, although both European and Arab navies patrolled the area from the 17th century into the 19th century. Early British expeditions to protect the India trade from raiders at Ras al-Khaimah led to campaigns against that headquarters and other harbors along the coast in 1819.

The next year, a general peace treaty was signed to which all the principal shaikhs of the coast adhered. Raids continued intermittently until 1835, when the shaikhs agreed not to engage in hostilities at sea. In 1853, they signed a treaty with the United Kingdom, under which the shaikhs (the "Trucial Shaikhdoms") agreed to a "perpetual maritime truce." It was enforced by the United Kingdom, and disputes among shaikhs were referred to the British for settlement.

Primarily in reaction to the ambitions of other European countries, the United Kingdom and the Trucial Shaikhdoms established closer bonds in an 1892 treaty, similar to treaties entered into by the UK with other Gulf principalities. The shaikhs agreed not to dispose of any territory except to the United Kingdom and not to enter into relationships with any foreign government other than the United Kingdom without its consent. In return, the British promised to protect the Trucial Coast from all aggression by sea and to help out in case of land attack.

In 1955, the United Kingdom sided with Abu Dhabi in the latter's dispute with Saudi Arabia over the Buraimi Oasis and other territory to the south. A 1974 agreement between Abu Dhabi and Saudi Arabia would have settled the Abu Dhabi-Saudi border dispute;

For additional analytical, marketing, investment and business opportunities
information, please contact
Global Investment & Business Center, USA
(202) 546-2103. Fax: (202) 546-3275. E-mail: rusric@erols.com

however, the agreement has yet to be ratified by the UAE Government and apparently is not recognized by the Saudi Government. The border with Oman also remains unsettled.

In 1968, the UK announced its decision, reaffirmed in March 1971, to end the treaty relationships with the seven Trucial Shaikhdoms which had been, together with Bahrain and Qatar, under British protection. The nine attempted to form a union of Arab emirates, but by mid-1971 they were unable to agree on terms of union, even though the termination date of the British treaty relationship was the end of 1971. Bahrain became independent in August and Qatar in September 1971. When the British-Trucial Shaikhdoms treaty expired on December 1, 1971, they became fully independent. On December 2, 1971, six of them entered into a union called the United Arab Emirates. The seventh, Ras al-Khaimah, joined in early 1972.

GOVERNMENT

Principal Government Officials

Pres.	KHALIFA bin Zayid Al Nuhayyan
Vice Pres.	MUHAMMAD BIN RASHID Al Maktum
Prime Min.	MUHAMMAD BIN RASHID Al Maktum
Dep. Prime Min.	MANSUR bin Zayid Al Nuhayyan
Dep. Prime Min.	SAIF bin Zayid Al Nuhayyan
Min. of Cabinet Affairs	Muhammad Abdallah al-GERGAWI
Min. of Culture, Youth, & Community Development	Abd al-Rahman Muhammad al-UWAIS
Min. of Defense	MUHAMMAD BIN RASHID Al Maktum
Min. of Development & Intl. Cooperation	LUBNA al-Qasimi
Min. of Economy	Sultan bin Saeed al-MANSURI
Min. of Education	Humaid Muhammad Ubayd al-QATAMI
Min. of Energy	Suhail bin Muhammad al-MAZROUI
Min. of Environment & Water	Rashid Ahmed bin FAHD
Min. of Finance	HAMDAN bin Rashid Al Maktum
Min. of Foreign Affairs	ABDALLAH bin Zayid Al Nuhayyan
Min. of Health	Hanif bin Hassan ALI
Min. of Higher Education & Scientific Research	NUHAYYAN bin Mubarak Al Nuhayyan
Min. of Interior	SAIF bin Zayid Al Nuhayyan
Min. of Justice	Hadef bin Juaan al-DHAHERI
Min. of Labor	Saqr Ghobash Saeed GHOBASH
Min. of Presidential Affairs	MANSUR bin Zayid Al Nuhayyan
Min. of Public Works	Abdullah Belhaif Al-NUAIMI
Min. of Social Affairs	Mariam bint Muhammad Khalfan al-RUMI
Min. of State for Federal National Council Affairs	Anwar Muhammad GARGASH
Min. of State for Financial Affairs	Obaid Humaid al-TAYER
Min. of State for Foreign Affairs	Anwar Muhammad GARGASH
Min. of State Without Portfolio	ABDULLAH bin Muhammad Ghobash
Min. of State Without Portfolio	Reem Ibrahim al-HASHEMI
Min. of State Without Portfolio	Sultan Ahmed Al JABER
Min. of State Without Portfolio	Maitha Salem al-SHAMSI
Governor, Central Bank	Sultan bin Nasir al-SUWAYDI
Ambassador to the US	Yusif bin Mani bin Said al-UTAYBA

For additional analytical, marketing, investment and business opportunities
information, please contact
Global Investment & Business Center, USA
(202) 546-2103. Fax: (202) 546-3275. E-mail: rusric@erols.com

Permanent Representative to the UN, New York   Ahmad Abd al-Rahman al-JARMAN

Ambassador to the United States--Saqr Ghobash
Ambassador to the United Nations--Abd al-Aziz Bin Nasir al-Shamsi

The U.A.E. maintains an embassy in the United States at 3522 International Court, NW, Washington, DC8 (tel. 202-243-2400). The U.A.E. Mission to the UN is located at 747 3rd Avenue, 36th Floor, New York, NY 10017 (tel. 212-371-0480).

POLITICAL CONDITIONS

The relative political and financial influence of each emirate is reflected in the allocation of positions in the federal government. The ruler of Abu Dhabi, whose emirate is the U.A.E.'s major oil producer, is president of the U.A.E. The ruler of Dubai, which is the U.A.E.'s commercial center, is vice president and prime minister.

Since achieving independence in 1971, the U.A.E. has worked to strengthen its federal institutions. Nonetheless, each emirate still retains substantial autonomy, and progress toward greater federal integration has slowed in recent years. A basic concept in the U.A.E. Government's development as a federal system is that a significant percentage of each emirate's revenues should be devoted to the U.A.E. central budget.

The U.A.E. has no political parties. The rulers hold power on the basis of their dynastic position and their legitimacy in a system of tribal consensus. Rapid modernization, enormous strides in education, and the influx of a large foreign population have changed the face of the society. In December 2006, the U.A.E. held its first-ever limited elections to select half the members of the FNC. Ballots were cast by electors selected by the emir of each emirate. One woman was elected to the FNC and seven additional women were appointed to be council members.

DEFENSE

The Trucial Oman Scouts, long the symbol of public order on the coast and commanded by British officers, were turned over to the U.A.E. as its defense forces in 1971. The U.A.E. armed forces, consisting of 48,800 troops, are headquartered in Abu Dhabi and are primarily responsible for the defense of the seven emirates.

Although small in number, the U.A.E. armed forces are equipped with some of the most modern weapon systems, purchased from a variety of outside countries. The military has been reducing the number of foreign nationals in its ranks, and its officer corps is composed almost entirely of U.A.E. nationals. The U.A.E. air force has about 4,000 personnel. The Air Force has advanced U.S. F-16 BLOCK 60 multi-role fighter aircraft. Other equipment includes French Mirage 2000-9 fighters, British Hawk trainer aircraft, 36 transport aircraft and U.S. Apache and French Puma helicopters. The Air Defense Force is linked into a joint air defense system with the other six Gulf Cooperation Council (GCC) nations aimed at protecting the airspace of the allied states. The U.A.E. Navy is small--about 2,500 personnel--and maintains 12 well-equipped coastal patrol boats and 8 missile boats. Although primarily concerned with coastal defense, the Navy is constructing a six-unit class of blue water corvettes in conjunction with French shipbuilder CMN. The U.A.E.'s Land Forces are equipped with several hundred French LeClerc tanks and a similar number of Russian BMP-3 armored fighting vehicles. The U.A.E. Special Operations Command (SOC) is a small but effective force centered on the counter-terrorism mission within the country. SOC is well-financed, trained, and equipped and is capable of executing its mission with a level of expertise equal to, or above, the rest of the GCC.

For additional analytical, marketing, investment and business opportunities
information, please contact
Global Investment & Business Center, USA
(202) 546-2103. Fax: (202) 546-3275. E-mail: rusric@erols.com

The U.A.E. contributes to the continued security and stability of the Gulf and the Straits of Hormuz. It is a leading partner in the campaign against global terrorism, providing assistance in the military, diplomatic, and financial arenas since September 11, 2001

ECONOMY

Currency	United Arab Emirates dirham
Trade organisations	OPEC and WTO
Statistics	
GDP	$405 Billion
GDP growth	4%
GDP per capita	$48,158 (7th)
GDP by sector	Agriculture (0.8%), industry (56.1%), services (43.1%)
Inflation (CPI)	1.4%
Population below poverty line	19.5%
Labour force	4.34 million
Labour force by occupation	Agriculture (7%), industry (15%), services (78%)
Unemployment	4.6%
Main industries	Petroleum and petrochemicals, fishing, aluminium, cement, fertilizers, commercial ship repair, construction materials, some plane building, handicrafts, textiles.
Ease-of-doing-business rank	26th
External	
Exports	$314 billion
Export goods	Crude oil, natural gas, reexports, dried fish, dates
Main export partners	Japan 15.4% India 13.4% Iran 10.7% Thailand 5.5% Singapore 5.5% South Korea 5.3%
Imports	$273.5 billion
Import goods	Machinery and transport equipment, chemicals, food
Main import partners	India 17.0% China 13.7% United States 10.5% Germany 5.1% Japan 4.2%
Gross external debt	$151.8 billion
Public finances	
Public debt	40.4% of GDP
Revenues	$130.3 billion
Expenses	$99 billion

The **economy of the United Arab Emirates** is the second largest in the Arab world (after Saudi Arabia), with a gross domestic product (GDP) of $377 billion (AED1.38 trillion) in 2012. The United Arab Emirates has been successfully diversifying its economy. 71% of UAE's total GDP comes from non-oil sectors.

For additional analytical, marketing, investment and business opportunities information, please contact
Global Investment & Business Center, USA
(202) 546-2103. Fax: (202) 546-3275. E-mail: rusric@erols.com

Although UAE has the most diversified economy in the GCC, the UAE's economy remains extremely reliant on oil. With the exception of Dubai, most of the UAE is dependent on oil revenues. Petroleum and natural gas continue to play a central role in the economy, especially in Abu Dhabi. More than 85% of the UAE's economy was based on the oil exports in 2009. While Abu Dhabi and other UAE emirates have remained relatively conservative in their approach to diversification, Dubai, which has far smaller oil reserves, was bolder in its diversification policy. In 2011, oil exports accounted for 77% of the UAE's state budget.

Dubai suffered from a significant economic crisis in 2007-2010 and was bailed out by Abu Dhabi's oil wealth. Dubai's current prosperity has been attributed to Abu Dhabi's petrodollars. Dubai is currently in extreme debt. Tourism is one of the main sources of revenue in the UAE, with some of the world's most luxurious hotels being based in the UAE. Although the UAE is now less dependent on natural resources as a source of revenue, petroleum and natural gas exports still play an important role in the economy, especially in Abu Dhabi. A massive construction boom, an expanding manufacturing base, and a thriving services sector are helping the UAE diversify its economy. Nationwide, there is currently $350 billion worth of active construction projects.

The UAE is a member of the World Trade Organization and OPEC

Prior to the first exports of oil in 1962, the U.A.E. economy was dominated by pearl production, fishing, agriculture, and herding. Since the rise of oil prices in 1973, however, petroleum has dominated the economy, accounting for most of its export earnings and providing significant opportunities for investment. The U.A.E. has huge proven oil reserves, estimated at 98.8 billion barrels in 2003, with gas reserves estimated at (212 trillion cubic feet); at present production rates, these supplies would last well over 150 years. In 2006, the U.A.E. produced about 2.8 million barrels of oil per day.

Major increases in imports occurred in manufactured goods, machinery, and transportation equipment, which together accounted for 70% of total imports. Another important foreign exchange earner, the Abu Dhabi Investment Authority--which controls the investments of Abu Dhabi, the wealthiest emirate--manages an estimated $600 billion in overseas investments.

More than 6,000 companies from more than 120 countries operate at the Jebel Ali complex in Dubai, which includes a deep-water port and a free trade zone for manufacturing and distribution in which all goods for re-export or transshipment enjoy a 100% duty exemption. A major power plant with associated water desalination units, an aluminum smelter, and a steel fabrication unit are prominent facilities near the complex.

Except in the free trade zone, the U.A.E. requires at least 51% local citizen ownership in all businesses operating in the country as part of its attempt to place Emiratis into leadership positions.

As a member of the Gulf Cooperation Council (GCC), the U.A.E. participates in a wide range of GCC activities that focus on economic issues. These include regular consultations and development of common policies covering trade, investment, banking and finance, transportation, telecommunications, and other technical areas, including protection of intellectual property rights.

FOREIGN RELATIONS

The UAE joined the United Nations and the Arab League and has established diplomatic relations with more than 60 countries, including the US, Japan, the Soviet Union, the People's Republic of China, and most Western European countries. It has played a moderate role in the Organization

For additional analytical, marketing, investment and business opportunities information, please contact
Global Investment & Business Center, USA
(202) 546-2103. Fax: (202) 546-3275. E-mail: rusric@erols.com

of Petroleum Exporting Countries, the Organization of Arab Petroleum Exporting Countries, the United Nations, and the GCC.

Substantial development assistance has increased the UAE's stature among recipient states. Most of this foreign aid (in excess of $15 billion) has been to Arab and Muslim countries.

Following Iraq's 1990 invasion and attempted annexation of Kuwait, the UAE has sought to rely on the GCC, Syria, Egypt, the US, and other Western allies for its security. The UAE believes that the Arab League needs to be restructured to become a viable institution.

US-UAE RELATIONS

The United States has enjoyed friendly relations with the UAE since 1971. Private commercial ties, especially in petroleum, have developed into friendly government-to-government ties which include security assistance. The breadth, depth, and quality of US-UAE relations are increasing dramatically as a result of the US-led coalition's campaign to end the Iraqi occupation of Kuwait. The United States was the third country to establish formal diplomatic relations with the UAE and has had an ambassador resident in the UAE since 1974.

PRINCIPAL US OFFICIALS

Ambassador-- Barbara A. Leaf

Barbara A. Leaf was confirmed as the U.S. Ambassador to the United Arab Emirates on November 17, 2014. Prior to that, she served as Deputy Assistant Secretary of State for the Arabian Peninsula in the Bureau of Near Eastern Affairs from 2013-2014, and as Deputy Assistant Secretary for Iraq from 2011-2013.

Deputy Chief of Mission--Martin Quinn
Political Officer--Al Magleby
Economic Officer--Oliver John
Consular Officer--Robert Dolce
Public Affairs Officer--Steven Pike
Management Officer--Stewart Devine
Commercial Officer--Christian Reed

Mailing Address--PO Box 4009, Abu Dhabi; tel: 336691, USIS: 336567, Commercial Office: 345545; fax: 318441, Chancery: 213771, US Labor
Office: 391604, Commercial Office: 331374.

Consul General in Dubai--Joseph Le Barron; PO Box 9343; tel: (04) 371115; fax: 379043, Commercial Office: 375121).

TRAVEL

The U.S. Department of State's Consular Information Program advises Americans traveling and residing abroad through Country Specific Information, Travel Alerts, and Travel Warnings. **Country Specific Information** exists for all countries and includes information on entry and exit requirements, currency regulations, health conditions, safety and security, crime, political disturbances, and the addresses of the U.S. embassies and consulates abroad. **Travel Alerts** are issued to disseminate information quickly about terrorist threats and other relatively short-term conditions overseas that pose significant risks to the security of American travelers. **Travel**

For additional analytical, marketing, investment and business opportunities information, please contact
Global Investment & Business Center, USA
(202) 546-2103. Fax: (202) 546-3275. E-mail: rusric@erols.com

submitted to the National Assembly before presenting to the President. The Council of Ministers also drafts decrees and various decisions. The Prime Minister and fellow members of the Council are responsible for their work under the supreme control of the President of the Federation and the Supreme Council.

RELATIONSHIP BETWEEN FEDERAL AND LOCAL GOVERNMENTS

The powers of the various federal institutions and their relationship with the separate institutions in each emirate, laid down in the constitution, have evolved and changed since the establishment of the state.

Under the terms of the Constitution, Rulers may, if they wish, relinquish certain areas of authority prescribed as being the responsibility of individual emirates to the federal government. One significant such decision being that to unify the Armed Forces in the mid-1970s. The 1971 Constitution also permitted each emirate to retain or to take up membership in the Organization of Petroleum Exporting Countries and the Organization of Arab Petroleum Exporting Countries, although none have done so; the only emirate to be a member in 1971, Abu Dhabi, having chosen to relinquish its memberships in favour of the Federation.

Over the course of the 25 years since the Federation was established, the United Arab Emirates has grown dramatically as a result of a sustained development programme, which has not only seen the completion of a modern infrastructure that reaches into the remotest mountain villages, but has also seen population rise more than ten fold. With such a pace of growth, the organs of government, both federal and local, have also developed impressively, and their influence now affect almost all aspects of life, for both UAE citizens and expatriates. As with other relatively young states, new institutions that were created for the first time, have derived their legitimacy and status from the extent of their activities and achievements, and from acknowledgement and appreciation of their role by the people.

The relationship between the new systems of government, federal and local, has itself evolved in a constructive manner. As the smaller emirates have benefited from development in terms of, for example, education, so they have been able to find the personnel to extend the variety of services provided by their own local governments, which had once been handled on their behalf by federal institutions, such as tourism.

At the same time, in other areas, such as the judiciary, there has been an evolving trend towards a further voluntary relinquishment of local authority to the federal institutions. These new systems of government have not, however, replaced the traditional forms. which coexist and evolve alongside them.

UAE GOVERNMENT STRATEGY 2011-2013

The UAE Government Strategy 2011-2013 lays the foundations to achieve the UAE Vision 2021, launched by HH Sheikh Mohammed Bin Rashid Al Maktoum, Vice President and Prime Minister of the UAE and Ruler of Dubai. It forms the basis upon which the Federal Entities develop their strategic and operational plans, and consists of seven general principles, seven strategic priorities and seven strategic enablers.

The strategic priorities and enablers are not fully comprehensive but comprise the major focus areas for the government. Each strategic priority and enabler includes general main directions and specific sub-directions - which combined lead to the fulfillment of the relevant main direction - and which the government will work to achieve during this strategy cycle.

GENERAL PRINCIPLES THAT GUIDE THE UAE GOVERNMENT STRATEGY

The UAE Government Strategy 2011-2013 strives to ensure that all Government work is conducted according to a set of guiding principles that puts citizens first and promotes an

For additional analytical, marketing, investment and business opportunities information, please contact
Global Investment & Business Center, USA
(202) 546-2103. Fax: (202) 546-3275. E-mail: rusric@erols.com

accountable, lean, innovative, and forward-looking Government.

The seven general principles that will steer Government work are as follows:

- Enhance the role of Federal Entities in devising effective regulations and integrated policies by successful planning and enforcement
- Enhance effective coordination and cooperation among Federal Entities and with Local Governments
- Focus on delivering high-quality, customer-centric and integrated government services
- Invest in human resource capabilities and develop leaders
- Promote efficient resource management within Federal Entities and leverage dynamic partnerships
- Pursue a culture of excellence through strategic thinking, continuous performance improvement, and superior results
- Enhance transparency and accountable governance mechanisms throughout Federal Entities

STRATEGIC PRIORITIES OF THE UAE GOVERNMENT

The seven strategic priorities are the themes that define the priorities of the UAE Government over the coming three years:

- Cohesive Society and Preserved Identity
- First-Rate Education System
- World-Class Healthcare
- Competitive Knowledge Economy
- Safe Public and Fair Judiciary
- Sustainable Environment and Infrastructure
- Strong Global Standing

STRATEGIC ENABLERS OF THE UAE GOVERNMENT

The seven strategic enablers direct how the machinery of the UAE Government must operate in order to fulfill its strategic priorities:

- Skilled Human Capital
- Customer-Centric Service
- Efficient Financial Management
- Good Institutional Governance
- Dynamic Government Networks
- Effective Legislative Process and Integrated Policy-Making
- Effective Government Communication

For additional analytical, marketing, investment and business opportunities information, please contact
Global Investment & Business Center, USA
(202) 546-2103. Fax: (202) 546-3275. E-mail: rusric@erols.com

STRATEGIC INFORMATION FOR CONDUCTING BUSINESS

ECONOMIC TRENDS

Rank	30th
Currency	United Arab Emirates dirham aed
Fiscal year	1864
Trade organisations	OPEC and WTO
	Statistics
GDP	$360 billion (
GDP growth	4%(est.)
GDP per capita	$48,158 ((7th)
GDP by sector	Agriculture (0.8%), industry (56.1%), services (43.1%)(est.)
Inflation (CPI)	1.4%(est.)
Population below poverty line	19.5% (2003 est.)
Labour force	4.34 million (2010 est.)
Labour force by occupation	Agriculture (7%), industry (15%), services (78%) (2000 est.)
Unemployment	4.6% (
Main industries	Petroleum and petrochemicals, fishing, aluminium, cement, fertilizers, commercial ship repair, construction materials, some plane building, handicrafts, textiles.
Ease of Doing Business Rank	26th
	External
Exports	$300.6 billion(est.)
Export goods	Crude oil, natural gas, reexports, dried fish, dates
Main export partners	Japan 15.6% India 13.4% Iran 10.5% Thailand 5.6% Singapore 5.5% South Korea 5.3%(est.)
Imports	$220.3 billion(est.)
Import goods	Machinery and transport equipment, chemicals, food
Main import partners	India 17.0% China 13.8% United States 10.5% Germany 5.2% Japan 4.2%(est.)
Gross external debt	$151.8 billion (31 December 2010 est.)
	Public finances
Public debt	40.4% of GDP(est.)
Revenues	$130.3 billion
Expenses	$99 billion(est.)

At $360 billion in 2012, the GDP of the UAE ranks second in the CCASG (after Saudi Arabia), third in the Middle East—North Africa (MENA) region (after Saudi Arabia and Iran), and 30th in the world. There are various inaccurate estimates regarding the actual growth rate of the nation's

For additional analytical, marketing, investment and business opportunities information, please contact
Global Investment & Business Center, USA
(202) 546-2103. Fax: (202) 546-3275. E-mail: rusric@erols.com

GDP, however all available statistics indicate that the UAE currently has one of the fastest growing economies in the world. According to a recent report by the Ministry of Finance and Industry, nominal GDP rose by 20.8% in 2012 to $360 billion, compared with $298 billion in 2011.

Tourism is one of the main sources of revenue in the United Arab Emirates. Although the UAE is less dependent on natural resources as a source of revenue, petroleum and natural gas exports still play an important role in the economy, especially in Abu Dhabi. A massive construction boom, an expanding manufacturing base, and a thriving services sector are helping the UAE diversify its economy. Nationwide, there is currently $350 billion worth of active construction projects. The UAE is a member of the World Trade Organization.

Recently, the Emirate of Dubai has started to look for other sources of revenue. High-class tourism and international finance are the new sectors starting to be developed. In line with this initiative, the Dubai International Financial Centre was announced, offering 55.5% foreign ownership, no withholding tax, freehold land and office space and a tailor-made financial regulatory system with laws taken from best practice in other leading financial centres like New York, London, Zürich and Singapore. A new stock market for regional companies and other initiatives were announced in DIFC. Dubai has also developed Internet and Media free zones, offering 100% foreign ownership, no tax office space for the worlds leading ICT and media companies, with the latest communications infrastructure to service them.

Many of the world's leading companies have now set up branch offices, and even changed headquarters to, there. Recent liberalisation in the property market allowing non citizens to buy freehold land has resulted in a major boom in the construction and real estate sectors, with several signature developments such as the 2 Palm Islands, the World (archipelago), Dubai Marina, Jumeirah Lake Towers, and a number of other developments, offering villas and high rise apartments and office space. Mean wages were $45.61 per manhour in 2009.

Emiratisation (or **Emiratization**) is an initiative by the government of the United Arab Emirates to employ its citizens in a meaningful and efficient manner in the public and private sectors.

While the program has been in place for more than a decade and results can be seen in the public sector, the private sector is still lagging behind with citizens only representing 0.34% of the private sector workforce.

While there is general agreement over the importance of Emiratisation for social, economic and political reasons, there is also some contention as to the impact of localization on organizational efficiency. It is yet unknown whether, and the extent to which, employment of nationals generates returns for MNEs operating in the Middle East. Recent research cautions that localization is not always advantageous for firms operating in the region, and its effectiveness depends on a number of contingent factors.

In December 2009 however, a positive impact of UAE citizens in the workplace was identified in a newspaper article citing a yet unpublished study, this advantage being the use of networks within the evolving power structures.

Overall, however, uptake in the private sector remains low regardless of significant investments in education, which have reached record levels with education now accounting for 22.5% – or $ 2.6 billion – of the overall budget planned for 2010. Multiple governmental initiatives are actively promoting Emiratisation by training anyone from highschool dropouts to graduates in a multitude of skills needed for the - essentially Western - work environment of the UAE, these initiatives include Tawteen UAE, ENDP or the Abu Dhabi Tawteen Council.

For additional analytical, marketing, investment and business opportunities
information, please contact
Global Investment & Business Center, USA
(202) 546-2103. Fax: (202) 546-3275. E-mail: rusric@erols.com

Beyond directly sponsoring educational initiatives, the Emirates Foundation for Philanthropy is funding major research initiatives into Emiratisation through competitive research grants, allowing universities such as United Arab Emirates University or Dubai School of Government to build and disseminate expertise on the topic.

Academics working on various aspects of Emiratisation include *Paul Dyer* and *Natasha Ridge* from Dubai School of Government, *Ingo Forstenlechner* from United Arab Emirates University, *Kasim Randaree* from the British University of Dubai and Paul Knoglinger from the FHWien.

The UAE rulers are striving to make their country's economy free from dependence on oil exports by 2030

The United Arab Emirates (UAE) is a federation of seven emirates located on the Arabian Peninsula. The UAE has a coastline and seaports inside, as well as outside, the Strait of Hormuz, which is the entrance to the Arabian Gulf. The seven emirates are Abu Dhabi, Dubai, Sharjah, Ajman, Umm Al Qaiwain, Fujairah and Ras Al Khaimah. The total area of the UAE is about the size of Maine, with a population of approximately 3.1 million, of which approximately 85% are expatriates. Each emirate has its own ruler and retains a high degree of autonomy within the federal system. The President of the UAE is chosen by the Supreme Council, which is composed of the rulers of the seven emirates. The Abu Dhabi ruler, Sheikh Zayed Bin Sultan Al Nahyan, has been President of the UAE since the country's foundation in 1971. In addition to the Supreme Council, the federal structure includes the Council of Ministers, a Federal Judiciary, and the Federal National Council (FNC), a consultative body of 40 members representing the seven emirates. The FNC does not have the power to legislate, but it can summon ministers and it performs an oversight function. There are no political parties or elections in the UAE.

A high degree of political and economic power resides in the individual emirates. Under the UAE constitution, each ruler retains control over natural resources, including oil, within his emirate, and regulates commercial activity. Because hydrocarbon reserves, and thus revenues, are not equally distributed, wealth, political and economic power, and the level of economic development are disproportionate among the seven emirates. Abu Dhabi, the nation's second largest commercial center and largest oil producer, is the wealthiest and most powerful emirate, followed by Dubai, the federation's commercial center and second largest oil producer. The other emirates, with little to no oil reserves, rely heavily on federal funds.

The terrain is mostly sandy desert, barren mountains, and salt flats. Before the exploitation of petroleum deposits, beginning in the 1960's, the UAE had a subsistence economy, which consisted of fishing, dates, livestock, small-scale trading and pearling. Now, the UAE is a prosperous country of global economic significance. Nominal GDP in 2000 totaled 223 billion dirhams (about US $ 59 billion). Per capita GDP in 2000 was roughly US $ 19,700.

GDP has historically been highly dependent on oil prices and has therefore followed a roller coaster pattern over the past 20 years, soaring during the 1970's and declining precipitously during the 1980's. These swings in national income have caused the authorities to look for ways to diversify the economy, particularly in Dubai, where oil reserves are dwindling. These attempts at diversification have met with considerable success. Government spending of past, present, and future oil revenues, along with proceeds of overseas investments derived from oil revenues, remains the engine that powers the economy. Oil revenues provide approximately 70%-80% of fiscal revenue and account for roughly 30% of export earnings.

As a result of sustained higher oil prices throughout 2000, UAE GDP last year rose by 17.3%, according to Central Bank statistics. These figures demonstrate that while diversification continues apace, the UAE remains heavily dependent upon oil revenue as the main engine of the

For additional analytical, marketing, investment and business opportunities information, please contact
Global Investment & Business Center, USA
(202) 546-2103. Fax: (202) 546-3275. E-mail: rusric@erols.com

economy. In 2000, it was reported that the oil sector of the economy accounted for 34% of GDP. This larger than usual figure reflects continued high oil revenues across the year, which totaled US $ 20.6 billion.

The UAE, with the second largest economy in the Gulf Cooperation Council (GCC), is in better financial condition than its immediate neighbors. Generally, the government is not delaying payments to contractors or borrowing from foreign commercial banks to pay its debts to the degree that most of its neighbors are. The UAE's modest 2001 budget expansion reflects a desire to reduce the fiscal deficit and to increase investment holdings.

The UAE maintains an extensive cradle-to-grave welfare system for UAE nationals, comprised of numerous subsidies, grants, loans and free services. Most employed UAE nationals work for federal or emirate governments. The government also provides many subsidized services for foreigners, who constitute more than 85% of the population and 93% of the labor force. While some efforts have been made to increase fees charged for some services, such as health, water and electricity, the increases do not cover costs, and nationals still receive many services free of charge. Abu Dhabi's ambitious privatization of the power/water sector is continuing, but outside of this initiative, privatization efforts have been minimal. The establishment in 2000 of stock exchanges in Dubai and Abu Dhabi, however, has allowed for the regularization of trading of shares in private and semi-private firms, and has created limited opportunities for foreign investors. The unemployment rate appears to be holding steady. Observers have noted that unemployment among UAE nationals may be an issue in the future.

Economic analysis in the UAE is difficult because of delays by the federal and emirate governments in publishing comprehensive and accurate statistics in a timely manner. Moreover, private sector institutions, including banks and foreign oil companies, are not allowed to disseminate statistics to the public. Information on oil and gas pricing, overseas investments and government budgets is generally only available from external sources. Despite criticisms from the IMF concerning the lack of reliable data, no steps have been taken to remedy this problem.

GOVERNMENT ROLE IN THE ECONOMY

The UAE has a mixed economy, with the most productive assets owned by the governments of the individual emirates. Considerable scope is given to private enterprise; however, the legal regime favors UAE nationals over foreigners. In both Abu Dhabi and Dubai, international oil companies maintain equity interests in their operations.

UAE federal government steps toward privatization have been tentative. Abu Dhabi Emirate, however, has initiated and maintained an ambitious program to privatize the emirate's power and water sector. In April 1997 the Abu Dhabi government gave the go-ahead for power and desalination projects to be carried out as independent power projects (IPP), which have significantly widened investment opportunities for domestic and foreign investors. (See Chapter 7, Investment Climate)

Some banks are privately owned. They are amongst the few forums where stock is sold to the public. Only UAE nationals are permitted to own stock in UAE joint stock companies. Foreigners are permitted to own up to 49% of a limited liability company (LLC) partnership. UAE nationals must own the remaining 51%. Foreign companies can market their products in the UAE either through these LLCs or through 100% UAE national-owned distributorships. Foreign contractors or service businesses require UAE national sponsors, one for each emirate in which they operate. Foreign ownership of land is presently extremely restricted.

The UAE federal government is attempting to establish a legal framework covering all aspects of doing business in the UAE. The most recent additions to this framework were the intellectual

For additional analytical, marketing, investment and business opportunities information, please contact
Global Investment & Business Center, USA
(202) 546-2103. Fax: (202) 546-3275. E-mail: rusric@erols.com

property rights protection laws, passed in 1992 but not enforced until 1994, and the commercial code, passed in 1993 and containing, for the first time in the UAE, provisions for bankruptcy.

There are no restrictions on the import or export of either the UAE dirham or foreign currencies, by foreigners or UAE nationals, with the exception of Israeli currency and the currencies of those countries subject to United Nations sanctions. Since 1981, the UAE dirham has been pegged to the US dollar at an exchange rate of 3.671 in an effort to stabilize the dirham and control inflation. Periodically there are calls to peg the dirham to a basket of currencies, including the Euro.

The government sector includes the accounts of the federal government as well as accounts of the seven individual emirate governments. Only the federal budget, a small part of the total, is published. In general, UAE fiscal deficits amount to a whopping 10%-12% of GDP. Even with higher oil revenues, that figure in 2000 was 12.6%. However, since 96% of the deficit was met by transfers from the Government's huge investment income (holdings in the Government-owned Abu Dhabi Investment Authority are conservative estimated to be in excess of US $ 200 billion), only US $ 300 million of the fiscal deficit was financed through the domestic banking system. Outside observers and UAE government sources project continued fiscal deficits for the next several years, assuming current policies remain unchanged.

There is no income tax in the UAE. Foreign banks pay a 20% tax on their profits. Foreign oil companies with equity in concessions pay taxes and royalties on their proceeds. There are no consumption taxes. A 4% customs duty is imposed on almost all imports except tobacco products and alcoholic beverages. According to Federal Law no. 2 of 1998, customs duties were increased from 50% to 70% on imported tobacco items, and will reach 100% on July 1, 2000. However, like other items imported for re-export, tobacco products imported for re-export purposes are tax exempt. The period given for the importer to re-export the items which are imported for re-export has been reduced from one year to six months. There is no minimum wage.

BALANCE OF PAYMENTS SITUATION

In 2000, the UAE ran a current account surplus of US $ 9.2 billion. This represented 15% of GDP - largely a result of much higher oil prices.

Total UAE exports (including re-exports for which accounting is imprecise) in 2000 increased by 23%. In 2000 the United States provided 6% of UAE imports. US exports to the UAE in 2000 totaled US $ 2.3 billion, according to Commerce Department data. The UAE consistently ranks among the US's top 10 trading partners in terms of trade balance.

The UAE maintains a booming re-export trade. In 2000, 24% of all exports were re-exports. Traditional re-export markets are the GCC states and Iran, but Iran has sharply restricted imports in an attempt to come to grips with a deteriorating economy and mounting debts. UAE traders have therefore aggressively sought out new markets in such areas as Russia, the newly independent states (NIS) of central Asia, and East and South Africa.

A serious problem affecting compilation of the UAE's balance of payments statistics is that the government does not provide statistics for many transactions. The major gaps are workers' remittances, investment income, oil and gas export revenues, foreign direct investment transactions, and capital transactions.

INFRASTRUCTURE SITUATION

The UAE has a fairly well developed and modern infrastructure. Land transportation is by road. An asphalt highway network links all major cities. Authorities in Abu Dhabi and Dubai are busily engaged in widening existing roads and replacing worn stretches. There is no rail system in the

For additional analytical, marketing, investment and business opportunities information, please contact
Global Investment & Business Center, USA
(202) 546-2103. Fax: (202) 546-3275. E-mail: rusric@erols.com

UAE, nor any domestic air transportation network, despite the fact that all the emirates, with the exception of Ajman and Umm Al Quwain, have modern airports.

All emirates have modern seaports. The port of Jebel Ali in Dubai is the largest manmade port in the world. Goods are imported by sea and distributed by truck within the UAE and to nearby locations in neighboring GCC countries. As part of its drive to diversify its economy away from oil to regional trade, Dubai has developed free zones at the two main seaports and its international airport. At these sites it handles re-export cargo with considerable expertise and precision.

Other ports in the region, including in the UAE, have noticed Dubai's success and are seeking a share of the re-export business for themselves. While they may never be able to match Dubai for volume, efficiency and expertise, Khor Fakkan and Fujairah, both in the UAE, possess something Dubai does not - they are located on the Gulf of Oman outside the entrance to the Arabian Gulf. An international cargo ship can cut 24 hours off the sailing time from Europe to the Far East by not joining the queue to pass through the busy straits; by-passing the Gulf also means lower insurance rates. Port operations at Salalah in Oman could in future begin to cut into Dubai's cargo volume.

In an effort to attract business, Dubai recently inaugurated two new free zones: Dubai Media City, and Dubai Internet City. In Abu Dhabi, plans for the Saadiyat Island Free Zone, an estimated US $ 3 billion project, have stalled indefinitely.

The UAE has well-developed water and electricity utilities and is aggressively expanding output to keep up with increasing demand. Overall, the growth in water demand is greater than for power. Both Abu Dhabi and Dubai expect to double electric power output between 1997 and 2010. The commercial value of the UAE's planned water and power projects is more than US $ 10 billion. Expansion projects, including Shuweihat in Abu Dhabi Emirate, and a massive water and power project in Fujairah managed by the UAE Offsets Group, are currently underway, and the government is considering additional projects. The UAE has the highest per capita consumption of desalinated water in the world. Ground water levels have dropped significantly as a result of over-consumption; wells have gone dry, and much remaining ground water has become unusable because of increased salinity from salt leeching into underground reservoirs.

INVESTMENT AND BUSINESS CLIMATE - STRATEGIC INFORMATION AND CONTACTS FOR STARTING BUSINESS IN UAE

The United Arab Emirates is located in the Middle East region of Asia, at the tip of the Arabian Peninsula. The Government of the United Arab Emirates (UAE) is pursuing an economic agenda that focuses on diversification and seeks to promote the development of the private sector as a complement to the historical economic dominance of the state. There have been numerous initiatives, laws and regulations throughout the seven emirates of the UAE that aim to develop a more conducive environment for foreign investment. However, the regulatory and legal framework in the UAE continues to favor local over foreign investors.

The UAE maintains a position as the major trade and investment hub for a large geographic region, which includes not only the Middle East and North Africa, but also South Asia, Central Asia, and Sub-Saharan Africa. The country ranked 12th of 143 economies in the World Economic Forum's 2014-2015 overall Global Competitiveness Index, and 22nd of 189 on the World Bank's 2015 Ease of Doing Business report, moving up seven places and one place respectively from the previous year. Multinational companies cite the UAE's political and economic stability, rapid population and Gross Domestic Product (GDP) growth, fast growing capital markets, an absence of corporate and personal taxes, and the absence of evidence of systematic corruption, were all positive factors contributing to the UAE's attractiveness to foreign investors. Despite regional

For additional analytical, marketing, investment and business opportunities information, please contact
Global Investment & Business Center, USA
(202) 546-2103. Fax: (202) 546-3275. E-mail: rusric@erols.com

headwinds attracting Foreign Direct Investment (FDI), UAE's inward FDI held at USD 10.1 billion in 2014 according to the United Nations Conference on Trade and Development (UNCTAD), slightly down from USD 10.5 billion in 2013.

While foreign investment continued to grow, the regulatory and legal framework in the UAE favors local over foreign investors. There is no national treatment for investors in the UAE and foreign ownership of land and stocks remains restricted. The UAE maintains non-tariff barriers to investment in the form of restrictive agency, sponsorship, and distributorship requirements. In order to do business in the UAE outside one of the free zones, a foreign business in most cases must have a UAE national sponsor, agent or distributor, with at least a 51 percent ownership interest of the business. Foreign investors also expressed concern over weak dispute resolution mechanisms and insolvency laws, spotty intellectual property rights protection, and a lack of regulatory transparency. Labor rights and conditions, although improving, continue to be an area of concern as the UAE prohibits both labor unions and worker strikes.

The UAE government (UAEG) is, however, opening up trade sectors in line with its World Trade Organizations (WTO) obligations. Investment laws and regulations are slowly evolving with the goal of making the UAE more conducive to foreign investment. The UAEG recently passed a new Companies Law. There is an additional eighteen draft laws which are meant to address a number of concerns that have discouraged foreign investment in the UAE. These laws include insolvency and arbitration laws, in addition to a draft foreign investment law. The UAEG has publicly declared its commitment to cutting red tape for foreign investors with the intent of becoming the most competitive economy in the Gulf as well as one of the top economies globally.

1. OPENNESS TO, AND RESTRICTIONS UPON, FOREIGN INVESTMENT

Attitude toward Foreign Direct Investment

The UAE generally is open to foreign direct investment (FDI) citing it as a key part of its long term economic plans. The UAE Vision 2021 strategic plan aims to achieve FDI flows to the UAE of five percent of Gross National Product (GNP), a number one rank for the UAE in the global index for ease of doing business, and a place among the top 10 countries worldwide in the Global Competitiveness Index. UAE investment laws and regulations are evolving in support of the goal of creating an environment more conducive to foreign investment. However, current frameworks still favor local over foreign investors. While recently updated UAE laws validate the practice of foreign owned free zone companies operating "onshore," and permit majority GCC ownership of public joint stock companies, there remains no national treatment for investors in the UAE and foreign ownership of land and stocks is restricted. Non-tariff barriers to investment persist in the form of restrictive agency, sponsorship, and distributorship requirements.

Other Investment Policy Reviews

During 2014, the UAEG hosted the IMF for an Article IV Consultation, but has not conducted an investment policy review through the Organization for Economic Cooperation and Development (OECD), the WTO, or the United Nations Conference on Trade and Development (UNCTAD).

Laws/Regulations of Foreign Direct Investment

There are four major federal laws affecting foreign investment in the UAE: the Companies Law, the Commercial Agencies Law, the Industry Law, and the Government Tenders Law. In 2011, the Ministry of Economy announced that 19 federal laws were in draft status to address a number of concerns historically discouraging foreign investment in the UAE. Today, the laws include an

For additional analytical, marketing, investment and business opportunities information, please contact
Global Investment & Business Center, USA
(202) 546-2103. Fax: (202) 546-3275. E-mail: rusric@erols.com

updated commercial agencies law, an insolvency law, an arbitration law, and a drafted foreign investment law under review.

The Federal Commercial Companies Law (Law No. 02, 2015) was issued on April 2015 and applies to all commercial companies established in the UAE and to branch offices of foreign companies operating in the UAE. The new law, with which all companies must come into compliance by July 1, 2016, will provide a stronger, more up to date basis for corporate regulation in the UAE. Companies established in the UAE are currently required to have a minimum of 51 percent UAE national ownership. Regardless, profits and management control may be apportioned differently and often are negotiated at fixed amounts. Branch offices of foreign companies are required to have a national agent with 100 percent UAE national ownership unless the foreign company has established its office pursuant to an agreement with the federal or an emirate-level government. The new commercial law allows companies to offer between 30 and 70 percent of shares upon undertaking an initial public offering (IPO) and eliminates the requirement to issue new shares at the time of IPO. The law also eases the process for forming a limited liability company by requiring between 1 to 75 shareholders (the prior requirement was between 2 to 50 shareholders). Under the new law, when a public joint stock company lists, 51 percent UAE ownership is not required, although there is a 51 percent Gulf Cooperation Council (GCC) ownership requirement. UAE nationals must chair and be the majority of board members of any public joint stock company.

Provisions in the new commercial law which would have relaxed the foreign ownership limit, were rejected by the UAE Federal National Council (FNC) and will be addressed in a separate investment law that is currently still in draft form, according to the FNC spokesperson. A provision to allow 100 percent foreign ownership outside of free zones would reportedly be restricted to certain sectors, such as high technology projects, and would require Cabinet approval on a case-by-case basis.

Foreign investors may purchase 105 of the 138 issues on the UAE stock markets, the Abu Dhabi Securities Market (ADX) and Dubai Financial Market (DFM). The remaining 33 issues are primarily those of government-related entities (GREs), such as the national telecommunications and oil companies. Companies on the exchanges are subject to the Federal Commercial Companies Law, thus foreign investors are allowed to own up to 49 percent of a company. The Emirates Securities and Commodities Authority (SCA), the UAE's regulator, introduced a new minimum level of capital for brokerages in July 2014.

The Commercial Agencies Law's provisions are collectively set out in Federal Law No. 18 of 1981 on the Organization of Commercial Agencies as amended by Federal Law No. 14 of 1988 (the Agency Law), and applies to all registered commercial agents. Federal Law No. 18 of 1993 (Commercial) and Federal Law No. 5 of 1985 (Civil Code) govern unregistered commercial agencies. The Commercial Agencies Law requires that foreign principals distribute their products in the UAE only through exclusive commercial agents that are either UAE nationals or companies wholly owned by UAE nationals. The foreign principal can appoint one agent for the entire UAE or for a particular emirate or group of emirates. The Ministry of Economy handles registration of commercial agents. It remains difficult, if not impossible, to sell in UAE markets without a local agent. Only UAE nationals or companies wholly owned by UAE nationals can register with the Ministry of Economy as local agents.

The Federal Industry Law stipulates that industrial projects must have 51 percent UAE national ownership. The law also requires that projects either be managed by a UAE national or have a board of directors with a majority of UAE nationals. Exemptions from the law are provided for projects related to extraction and refining of oil, natural gas, and other raw materials. Additionally, projects with a small capital investment or projects governed by special laws or agreements are exempt from the industry law.

There have been no confirmed reports of government interference in the court system that could affect foreign investors.

To obtain an investor number from the Abu Dhabi Securities Exchange, go to:
http://www.adx.ae/FormsAndApplications/InvestorNumberApplication.pdf

To obtain an investor number for trading on the Dubai Exchanges, go to:
http://www.nasdaqdubai.com/assets/docs/NIN-Form.pdf

Industrial Promotion

The Abu Dhabi Government in early 2015 formed the Abu Dhabi Investment Attraction Committee to achieve sustainable economic development and develop an attractive investment environment. The committee started the process of forming a foreign investment attraction strategy in March 2015 focusing on the sectors that Abu Dhabi's strategic plan—Abu Dhabi Economic Vision 2030—identified and targeted as engines for non-oil sector growth. These sectors include industry, tourism, transport and logistics, financial services, insurance, media, energy, construction, real estate, telecommunications, information technology, health and education.

In February 2009, the Higher Corporation for Specialized Economic Zones (ZonesCorp), which operates an industrial zone based in Abu Dhabi, signed Memoranda of Understanding with the Ministry of Economy (MoE) and the Abu Dhabi Chamber of Commerce and Industry (ADCCI) to develop an industrial environment in Abu Dhabi and facilities, transactions and services for local, regional and international investors. Through the electronic exchange of data and information, the MoU gives ZonesCorp the authority to issue, amend and renew Chamber of Commerce certificates for industrial businesses operating in the industrial cities, as well as collect fees on the Chamber's behalf, streamlining the process and saving time for investors. ZonesCorp has also established a one-stop-shop for investors.

In 2008, the Abu Dhabi Chamber of Commerce and Industry also created a one-stop shop for investors, with the exception of investors dealing in Israeli currency and the currencies of those countries subject to United Nations sanctions.

In 2006, the UAE Cabinet amended the law regarding ownership of insurance companies to state that insurance companies must be 75 percent owned by a UAE national or 100 percent by UAE legal persons, i.e., a UAE corporation. No new insurance companies or new branches have been authorized since 2008. Any new company entering the market is required to meet high level international rating criteria and must complete a viability study to prove that it will be offering new products to the market.

Limits on Foreign Control

Foreign companies or individuals are limited to 49 percent ownership/control in any parts of the UAE not in a free trade zone, pursuant to law. There have been reports of waivers of the application of this law by decree of the ruler of an individual emirate. There have also been reports that companies owned by primarily GCC citizens have been de facto permitted to operate

For additional analytical, marketing, investment and business opportunities information, please contact
Global Investment & Business Center, USA
(202) 546-2103. Fax: (202) 546-3275. E-mail: rusric@erols.com

in the UAE outside of free trade zones. This was codified recently in the updated Commercial Companies Law.

Privatization Program

There has been no privatization program in the UAE. There have been several listings of portions of state owned enterprises (SOEs), which are referred to locally as government related entities (GREs), on local UAE stock exchanges, as well as some "greenfield" IPOs that are focused on priority government projects.

Screening of FDI

The UAE does not have a formal FDI review process; however, as noted elsewhere in this report, there is no national treatment for investors in the UAE and restrictions on foreign ownership of land and stocks are common. Non-tariff barriers to investment persist in the form of restrictive agency, sponsorship, and distributorship requirements.

Competition Law

The Ministry of Economy reviews transactions for competition-related concerns.

Investment Trends

The UAE continued to attract foreign direct investments, with inflows of FDI reaching USD 10.5 billion in 20s and USD 10.1 billion in 2014, largely focused on construction, finance and wholesale and retail trade. FDI outflows from the UAE reached USD 2.9 billion in 2013. The FDI recovery coincided with economic growth driven by both oil and non-oil activities (including manufacturing), led by aluminum and petrochemicals; tourism and transportation; and real estate.

According to UNCTAD, the overall economy received a further boost in November 2013, when Dubai gained the right to host the World Expo 2020. As a result, investors in the UAE are among the most confident of all those surveyed in the Schroders Global Investment Trends Report 2014. More than 72 percent said they were more confident about investment prospects in 2014 versus 2013, with 61 percent saying they intended to increase the amount they invested within the next 12 months.

Table 1

Measure	Year	Index or Rank	Website Address
TI Corruption Perceptions index	2014	25 of 175	transparency.org/cpi2014/results
World Bank's Doing Business Report "Ease of Doing Business"	2015	22 of 189	doingbusiness.org/rankings
Global Innovation Index	2014	36 of 143	globalinnovationindex.org/content.aspx?page=data-analysis
World Bank GNI per capita	2012	USD 38,360	data.worldbank.org/indicator/NY.GNP.PCAP.CD

**For additional analytical, marketing, investment and business opportunities information, please contact
Global Investment & Business Center, USA
(202) 546-2103. Fax: (202) 546-3275. E-mail: rusric@erols.com**

2. CONVERSION AND TRANSFER POLICIES

Foreign Exchange

The UAE has no restriction on the making of payments and transfers for current international transactions, according to the IMF, except for those restrictions for security reasons that have been notified by authorities. There are no restrictions on the transfer of funds into or out of the UAE and currencies are traded freely at market-determined prices. Further, free zone entities are generally expressly permitted to repatriate 100 percent of their profits from the UAE in accordance with regulations in place in their respective free zones. In the free zones, foreigners may: i) own up to 100 percent of the equity in an enterprise; ii) have 100 percent import and export tax exemption; iii) have 100 percent exemption from commercial levies; iv) repatriate 100 percent of capital and profits.

The UAE dirham has been de jure pegged to the dollar since February 2002. The mid-point between the official buying and selling rate for the dirham (AED or Dhs) is fixed at AED 3.6725 per 1 USD.

The UAE has recently amended its anti-money laundering (AML) law, expanding the list of AML predicate offenses, among other improvements. The various free zones, including the Dubai International Financial Center (DIFC), are subject to the federal AML law. Free zone licensing authorities have the ability to set their own AML rules and regulations as long as they are consistent with the federal law, resulting in variance among the free zones. Federal authorities continue to examine ways to expand their regulatory reach on AML/CFT. The UAE is a member of the Middle East and North Africa Financial Action Task Force, a Financial Action Task Force (FATF)-style regional body.

Remittance Policies

The UAE Central Bank initiated the creation of the Foreign Exchange & Remittance Group (FERG), made of up of various exchange companies, which is registered with Dubai Chamber of Commerce & Industry. The unique feature of the industry is that, unlike its counterparts across the world which deal mainly in money exchange, exchange companies in the UAE are the primary channels for transferring large volumes of remittances through official channels. It is estimated that more than USD 30 billion (AED 110 billion) is transferred annually by expatriate workers in the UAE to home markets. Exchange companies are also important partners in a unique Wages Protection System of the UAE Government. They also handle various ancillary services ranging from credit card payments, national bonds, and travelers checks.

3. EXPROPRIATION AND COMPENSATION

To Post's knowledge, foreign investors have not been involved in any expropriations in the UAE for at least the last five years. There are no set federal rules governing compensation if expropriations were to occur, and individual emirates would likely treat expropriations differently. In practice, authorities in the UAE would be unlikely to expropriate unless there were a compelling development or public interest need to do so, and in such cases compensation would likely be generous in order to maintain foreign investor confidence.

4. DISPUTE SETTLEMENT

Legal System, Specialized Courts, Judicial Independence, Judgments of Foreign Courts

For additional analytical, marketing, investment and business opportunities
information, please contact
Global Investment & Business Center, USA
(202) 546-2103. Fax: (202) 546-3275. E-mail: rusric@erols.com

The UAE follows the civil law system, inspired by the Roman and French legal systems and the Egyptian civil codes of law. The primary source of law is legislation. The legal system of the country is generally divided between off shore free trade zones, which have a British-based system of common law, and domestic law, which is governed by a Sharia civil law system. The mechanism for enforcing ownership of property through either court system is generally considered to be both predictable and fair.

The judiciary does not form its own branch of government. The Ministry of Justice, as part of the executive branch, appoints judges to the federal courts, while judges in other emirates such as Abu Dhabi, Dubai and Ras Al Khaimah are appointed by the respective rulers of those emirates. Each emirate applies federal law in its judicial system. While there is some variation, each system generally consists of the courts of first instance, courts of appeal, and a court of cassation. The federal Supreme Court sits in Abu Dubai. The court of first instance consists of civil, criminal, and Sharia (Islamic law) courts.

Sharia law is technically applicable to both Muslims and non-Muslims. UAE's Sharia courts primarily focus on domestic relations, inheritance and personal status matters. In April 2015, DIFC courts announced a wills and probate registry which made it the first jurisdiction in the region where a non-Muslim individual can register a will under internationally recognized common law principles. The United States District Court for the Southern District of New York recently signed a memorandum with the DIFC courts that provides companies operating in Dubai and New York with procedures for the mutual enforcement of money judgments. A properly executed last will and testament will take precedence over Sharia law, however, and is recommended by local attorneys as the best way for expatriates to ensure that the default inheritance laws of the UAE are not applied unless so desired.

Judgments of foreign civil courts are generally recognized and enforceable under the local courts.

Bankruptcy

There have been reports that a bankruptcy (insolvency) law is under consideration. However, at present, a chapter in the UAE federal commercial code, promulgated in 1993, is the only comprehensive legal guidance on the subject. In the judgment of Western legal experts, the commercial code chapter on bankruptcy governs the procedures and effects of bankruptcy in the UAE, but does not provide a mechanism for the orderly evaluation and distribution of assets of a bankrupt entity. Monetary judgments in bankruptcy cases are made in the local currency, and UAE courts enforce the judgments of foreign courts if there is reciprocity based on bilateral or international treaties. A debtor may be sent to jail for failure to make payments.

Investment Disputes

The Embassy is aware of a few substantial investment disputes during the past few years involving U.S. or other foreign investors and government and/or local businesses. There have also been several contractor/payment disputes, with the government as well as local businesses. Dispute resolution can be difficult and uncertain. In December 2009, the Ruler of Dubai signed Decree No. 57 bringing into effect bespoke insolvency protection regulations to govern any future formal reorganization and restructuring of Dubai World and its subsidiaries. The Decree was used to reach a deal with creditors to amend and extend terms for USD 14.6 billion of Dubai World debt by establishing an independent tribunal of three judges of the DIFC courts.

Disputes generally are resolved by direct negotiation and settlement between the parties themselves, recourse to the legal system, or arbitration. Small, medium, and some larger

For additional analytical, marketing, investment and business opportunities
information, please contact
Global Investment & Business Center, USA
(202) 546-2103. Fax: (202) 546-3275. E-mail: rusric@erols.com

enterprises continue to fear being frozen out of the UAE market for escalating payment issues through civil or arbitral courts, particularly when politically influential local parties are involved. Some firms may feel compelled to exit the UAE market as they are unable to sustain pursuit of legal or dispute resolution mechanisms that can add months or years to the dispute resolution process. Arbitration may commence by petition to the UAE federal courts on the basis of mutual consent (a written arbitration agreement), independently (by nomination of arbitrators), or through a referral to an appointing authority without recourse to judicial proceedings.

International Arbitration

The UAEG's accession to the UN Convention on the Recognition and Enforcement of Foreign Arbitral Awards became effective in November 2006. An arbitration award issued in the UAE is now enforceable in all 138 states that have acceded to the Convention, and any award issued in another member state is directly enforceable in the UAE. The Convention supersedes all incompatible legislation and rulings in the UAE, and should be welcomed by many businesses that consider arbitration the most advantageous form of dispute resolution. The Mission does not yet have any experience with U.S. firms attempting to use arbitration under the UN convention on the recognition and enforcement of foreign arbitral awards. A 2010 case in the emirate of Fujairah was the first reported recognition of a foreign arbitral judgment but its collection status is unknown. Concerns have been raised about delays and other obstacles encountered by firms seeking to enforce their arbitration awards in the UAE despite the recognition of progress in compliance with this convention. An appeal on a foreign arbitration award in the Dubai Court of First Instance was upheld within the last few years.

ICSID Convention and New York Convention

The United Arab Emirates is a contracting state to the International Centre for the Settlement of Investment Disputes (ICSID convention) and since 1982, and a signatory to the convention on the Recognition and Enforcement of Foreign Arbitral awards (1958 New York Convention).

Duration of Dispute Resolution

Enforcing arbitration judgments rendered in the UAE requires court certification and can be a lengthy process. Judicial proceedings may continue for several years and can be invalidated for procedural considerations.

5. PERFORMANCE REQUIREMENTS AND INVESTMENT INCENTIVES

WTO/TRIMS

According to the WTO, UAE procurement gives preference to local companies and suppliers, as foreign participation is limited by nationality requirements. However, there is a strong reliance on foreign companies, particularly with major projects for which local expertise is not always available. An offset program is in place for defense contracts.

Foreign insurance companies in Abu Dhabi are not permitted to tender for certain government projects, e.g. roads, oil and gas. Because of these restrictions, foreign insurance companies in Abu Dhabi focus mainly on auto insurance, medical and life insurance.

Government tendering is not conducted according to generally accepted international standards, and re-tendering is the norm. To bid on federal projects, a supplier or contractor must be either a

For additional analytical, marketing, investment and business opportunities information, please contact
Global Investment & Business Center, USA
(202) 546-2103. Fax: (202) 546-3275. E-mail: rusric@erols.com

UAE national or a company in which UAE nationals own at least 51 percent of the capital or have a local agent or distributor. Federal tenders must be accompanied by a bid bond in the form of an unconditional bank guarantee for five percent of the value of the bid. UAE federal government entities can tender internationally since foreign companies sometimes are the only suppliers of specialized goods or services that are not widely available.

The UAE's offset program requires that defense contractors awarded contracts valued at more than USD 10 million in any five-year period establish a commercially viable joint venture with local business partners, which yields profits equivalent to 60 percent of the contract value within a specified period.

Investment Incentives

Incentives are given to foreign investors in the free zones. Outside the free zones, no incentives are given, although the ability to purchase property as freehold in certain favored projects in Dubai would appear to be an incentive aimed at attracting foreign investment. The federal government and the governments of the individual emirates promote a business environment largely free of taxation and exchange controls.

Research and Development

Post is unaware of any formal restrictions on investment or involvement with official research and development projects.

Performance Requirements

There is a federal incentive program called Emiratization was made to increase the number of jobs available for Emirati citizens within the private sector. Most Emirati citizens are employed by the UAE government or one of its many government related enterprises (GREs). There is a guest worker system in place, which generally guarantees transportation back to country of origin at conclusion of employment. There have been no reports of excessively onerous visa, residence, work permit, or similar requirements inhibiting mobility of foreign investors and their employees. There are government/authority-imposed conditions on permission to invest, in the form of a general 49 percent limitation of ownership/control by foreign individuals or corporations.

Data Storage

The UAE does not force foreign investors to use domestic content in goods or technology or compel foreign IT providers to turn over source code. Press reports indicated that UAE officials threatened in August 2010 to ban certain services for Research in Motion's BlackBerry devices if the company did not comply with federal regulatory requirements on data availability. The two sides reached an agreement several months later.

6. RIGHT TO PRIVATE OWNERSHIP AND ESTABLISHMENT

Except as detailed elsewhere in this report, there are no restrictions on the right of private entities to establish and own business enterprises and engage in all forms of remunerative activity.

7. PROTECTION OF PROPERTY RIGHTS

Real Property

For additional analytical, marketing, investment and business opportunities information, please contact
Global Investment & Business Center, USA
(202) 546-2103. Fax: (202) 546-3275. E-mail: rusric@erols.com

The UAE allows each individual emirate to decide on the form in which ownership of land may be transferred within its borders. Generally, Abu Dhabi has limited ownership to Emirati or other GCC citizens, who may then lease out the land to foreigners. The property reverts back to the owner at the conclusion of the lease. Although Dubai has identified such restricted areas within its borders, traditional freeholds, also known as outright ownership, are also available. Freeholders of land own the land. Subject to very few regulations, freehold owners may sell on the open market. The contract rights of lienholders, as well as ownership rights of freeholders, are generally respected and enforced throughout the UAE, which in some cases has employed specialized courts for this purpose. Mortgages and liens are permitted, with restrictions. Each emirate has its own system of recordkeeping. In Dubai, for example, the system is considered extremely reliable, being mainly centralized within the Dubai Land Department. Land not otherwise allocated or owned is the property of the emirate, and may be disposed of at the will of its ruler, who generally consults with his advisors prior to disposition.

Intellectual Property Rights

The legal regime of the UAE with respect to intellectual property rights (IPR) is generally considered fair and in compliance with international obligations. Enforcement of IPR takes place generally at the emirate level. During 2014, a Dubai government agency, the Commercial Compliance and Consumer Protection (CCCP) office, reported that it had been granted the power to search and seize counterfeit goods within the emirate of Dubai, a power that the Dubai Police, Dubai Customs, and the Dubai Department of Economic Development also hold. A draft of a new anti-commercial fraud law is still pending. Interested stakeholders are watching the draft law closely, especially due to a potential conflation of counterfeit goods with substandard and defective goods. Each emirate works with individual stakeholders regarding counterfeits of its brands, and the government publicly reports only the largest seizures of counterfeit goods. Dubai Customs reported several hundred seizures of counterfeit goods in 2014, which Post has been unable to verify. The UAE is not currently listed in the United States Trade Representative's (USTR) Special 301 report, or in its Notorious Markets report.

The two main challenges IPR holders face in the UAE are in the areas of counterfeit goods, and enforcement of rights to music. The practice of fining shippers of counterfeit goods and permitting re-exportation of those goods subjectively deemed too hazardous to destroy has occurred regularly in the UAE during the reporting period, primarily in the emirate of Dubai. It is important to note that recently, Dubai Customs officials reported that negotiations were underway to outsource destruction of counterfeit goods. As to enforcement of rights to music, although the UAE has generally been responsive when encountering pirated physical CDs, DVDs, and software, the lack of a copyright collecting society, which is allowed for under UAE's existing copyright law, is a major obstacle to adequate protection of IPR.

Officers with responsibility for IPR at Embassy Abu Dhabi: Mark Motley, +971-2-414-2595, motleyme@state.gov; at Consulate Dubai: Joseph Giblin, +971-4-309-4034, giblinjp@state.gov; and the Department of Commerce Middle East/North Africa Regional IP Attaché at Embassy Kuwait: Aisha Salem, +965-2259-1455, aisha.salem@trade.gov. The website of the American Chamber of Commerce in Abu Dhabi can be found at http://www.amchamabudhabi.org/ and the American Business Council of Dubai and the Northern Emirates at http://www.abcdubai.com/. The website of the U.S.-UAE Business Council is located at http://usuaebusiness.org/

Resources for Rights Holders
Embassy Abu Dhabi:
Mark Motley, +971-2-414-2595, motleyme@state.gov
Consulate Dubai:

**For additional analytical, marketing, investment and business opportunities
information, please contact
Global Investment & Business Center, USA
(202) 546-2103. Fax: (202) 546-3275. E-mail: rusric@erols.com**

Joseph Giblin, +971-4-309-4034, giblinjp@state.gov

U.S. Dept. of Commerce Middle East/North Africa Regional IP Attaché at Embassy Kuwait:
Aisha Salem, +965-2259-1455, aisha.salem@trade.gov.
American Chamber of Commerce in Abu Dhabi: www.amchamabudhabi.org
American Business Council of Dubai and the Northern Emirates: www.abcdubai.com
U.S.-UAE Business Council: usuaebusiness.org

8. TRANSPARENCY OF THE REGULATORY SYSTEM

UAE legislation is only published when it has been enacted into law and before that it is not available for public comment, although the press will occasionally report on some details of high-profile legislation. Final bills are published in an official register, usually only in Arabic, although there are private companies that specialize in translating laws into English.

The fundamental instrument by which all of the emirates regulate business activity is the requirement that any place of business must acquire and maintain a proper license. The procedures for obtaining a license, which are publicly available, vary from emirate to emirate.

A license is not required unless a place of business is set up in the UAE. In other words, foreign businesses exporting to the UAE but without a regular or continuing business presence in the UAE do not need a license. Licenses available include trade licenses, industrial licenses, service licenses, professional licenses, and construction licenses. Several federal regulations govern business activities in the UAE outside free trade zones. Activities within the free zones are governed by special by-laws.

9. EFFICIENT CAPITAL MARKETS AND PORTFOLIO INVESTMENT

The UAEG is focused on building infrastructure to create an environment conducive to economic growth and outside investment. It is also collaborating with its partners in the GCC to support ventures in the region. UAEG efforts to create such an environment for investments resulted in: i) no taxes or restrictions on the repatriation of capital; ii) free movement of labor and low barriers to entry (effective tariffs are five percent for most goods); and an emphasis on diversifying the economy away from oil, which offers a broad array of investment options for FDI. Drivers for the economy include real estate, tourism, manufacturing, and financial services.

The UAE issued new investment funds regulations in September 2012, known as the "twin peak" regulatory framework. The framework is designed to further govern the marketing of investment funds established outside the UAE to investors in the UAE and the establishment of local funds domiciled inside the UAE. This regulation set forth several key changes such as giving the SCA (rather than the Central Bank) authority over the licensing, regulation and oversight of the marketing of investment funds. The marketing of a foreign fund (including "offshore" UAE-based funds, such as those domiciled in the DIFC) now require the appointment of a locally licensed placement agent. Other restrictions contained in the regulations, such as limitations on funds investing more than 15 percent in any one underlying issuer, have led fund managers to question whether the UAE is seeking to attract international or regionally focused investment funds to be domiciled in the country. The federal government has also encouraged certain high-profile projects to be undertaken via a public joint stock company in order to allow the issue of shares to the public. Further, any company carrying out banking, insurance or investment for a third party must be a public joint stock company.

Money and Banking System, Hostile Takeovers

For additional analytical, marketing, investment and business opportunities information, please contact
Global Investment & Business Center, USA
(202) 546-2103. Fax: (202) 546-3275. E-mail: rusric@erols.com

The UAE has accepted the obligation of IMF Article VIII, Sections 2, 3, and 4. There are no restrictions on the making of payments and transfer for current international transactions, except for those restrictions for security reasons that have been notified to the Fund, by the authorities, in accordance with Executive Board Decision No. 144 (52/51).

In September 2003, the UAE Central Bank announced that it would allow more foreign banks to operate on a reciprocal basis and in 2008, the Central Bank allowed several foreign banks operating in the UAE to set up new branches. According to Central Bank statistics, there have been no new foreign bank branches licensed since 2009. As of October 2014, the Central Bank listed 28 foreign banks with 115 branches in the UAE.

In 2010, the Central Bank issued Regulations for Classification of Loans and Determining Provision, furthering its oversight of lending policies in response to the 2008 financial crisis. In April 2012, an IMF report said the UAE had made significant progress in recapitalizing banks and strengthening capital adequacy ratios, and that despite continuing debt recovery concerns and spillover from European and global credit concerns, the banking system showed significant increases in profitability. However, the IMF noted that the UAE financial system is highly integrated and still remains exposed to global vulnerabilities, primarily for its risk concentration in a few banks in the UAE system, and called for increased regulation and oversight of the sector. In its July 2013 Article IV Consultation with the UAE, the IMF noted that "the banking system maintains significant capital and liquidity buffers, and non-performing loans may finally have peaked at 8.7 percent in December 2012," suggesting a significant turnaround in the UAE banking sector's post-crisis health. During 2014, Emirati banks experienced healthy increases in profits, and improved asset quality. Dubai's largest bank, Emirates NBD—which was exposed to the debt crisis at the parastatals Dubai Holding and Dubai World in 2009—reported a 51 percent year-on-year rise in net profits for the first nine months of 2014, to Dh3.9bn (USD 1.1bn). The largest Abu Dhabi bank, National Bank of Abu Dhabi (NBAD), posted a 14.7 percent increase in net profits to Dh4.2bn (USD 1.14 billion). Abu Dhabi Commercial Bank reported a similar rise, of 16 percent, to Dh3.18bn (USD 0.87billion).

Foreign investors may purchase 105 of the 138 issues on the UAE stock markets, the ADX and the DFM. The remaining issues are primarily those of GREs, such as the oil and national telecommunications companies. Companies on the exchanges are subject to the Federal Companies Law, thus foreign investors are allowed to own up to 49 percent of a company. However, some company by-laws prohibit foreign ownership, and others limit it to less than the legally allowable 49 percent. Several major companies raised their foreign ownership limits in 2013, in anticipation of an increase in foreign investment generated by announcements that ratings agencies MSCI and Standard & Poor's would upgrade the UAE from "frontier" to "emerging" market status. The international financial crisis and foreign speculation contributed to significant declines in local equity valuations since 2008, but the markets rebounded strongly in 2013. UAE's regulatory body, the SCA, raised capital requirements to operate a brokerage house from AED 20 million (USD 5.5 million) to AED 30 million (USD 8.2 million) and in July 2014 classified brokerages into two groups: "those which engage in trading only while the clearance and settlement operations are conducted through clearance members" and "those which engage in trading clearance and settlement operations for their clients." Under the regulations, trading brokerages require paid-up capital of AED 3 million (USD 820k), whereas trading and clearance brokerages will need AED 10 million (USD 2.7 million). Bank guarantees required for brokerages to trade on the bourses will be AED 1 million (USD 367k).

10. COMPETITION FROM STATE-OWNED ENTERPRISES

For additional analytical, marketing, investment and business opportunities
information, please contact
Global Investment & Business Center, USA
(202) 546-2103. Fax: (202) 546-3275. E-mail: rusric@erols.com

Some SOEs such as Emirates National Oil Company (ENOC) are strategically important companies and a major source of fiscal revenues. Mubadala Development Company established Masdar in 2006 to develop renewable energy and sustainable technologies industries. A number of Dubai's SOEs such as Emirates Airlines and Etisalat have in recent years emerged as internationally recognized brands. Some, but not all of these companies, compete, and in a number of cases against other state-owned firms (Emirates against Fly Dubai or Etisalat against Du). While they are not granted full autonomy, they are integrated in a system where the state leverages synergies among entities it controls to foster national economic development. Perhaps the best example of such an economic ecosystem is Dubai, where SOEs have been used as a motor of diversification and are present in a number of sectors, including construction, hospitality, transport, banking and telecommunications.

The central bank in 2012 required local financial institutions to limit their exposure to the governments of the seven-member UAE federation and related entities to a maximum of 100 percent of their capital base, and exposure to individual public sector borrowers to 25 percent. This measure was adopted as a reaction to the Dubai crisis, during which several SOEs and government-related entities defaulted on loans, creating significant liquidity problems in the local banking market. Creditors to these companies assumed that in providing funding to large SOEs they would benefit from a blanket state guarantee. The fact that many UAE banks are themselves partially state-owned – sometimes through holding entities that are related to the SOEs they lend to – exacerbated the situation. In October 2012, the government of Abu Dhabi issued a new decree requiring SOEs to apply for an explicit sovereign guarantee prior to issuing debt. Sectoral regulations also in some cases address governance structures and practices of state-owned companies. For example, the Dubai Real Estate Regulatory Agency (RERA) developed a code of corporate governance for real estate developers in 2011. In doing so, RERA has considered that the peculiarity of the real estate sector, which includes many actors such as developers and promoters, merits specific guidelines.

OECD Guidelines on Corporate Governance of SOEs

Corporate governance of most SOEs is largely comprised of ruling family members, the merchant class, and a variety of advisors. While the selection and allocation of board seats remains vague, the UAEG states it strives to follow guidelines consistent with OECD's guidelines for SOEs, with the state acting as an owner, and equitable treatment of shareholders. In 2009, the UAEG government established the Emirates Competitiveness Council (ECC) to address issues related to optimizing the efficiency and governance of SOEs, recognizing some SOEs are a fiscal burden while others can be a source of economic competitiveness. Another ECC objective is to engage the private sector to identify and communicate their needs in order to become competitive.

Sovereign Wealth Funds

Abu Dhabi is home to four sovereign wealth funds—the Abu Dhabi Investment Authority (ADIA), the Abu Dhabi Investment Council (ADIC), the International Petroleum Investment Company (IPIC), and Mubadala Development Company (Mubadala)—with total assets of about USD 990 billion. Emirates Investment Authority, the UAE's federal sovereign wealth fund, has assets of about USD 15 billion. Each Abu Dhabi fund is comprised of a chair and board members who are appointed by a decree of the Ruler of Abu Dhabi. President Khalifa Bin Zayed Al Nahyan is the chair of ADIA and ADIC, and Abu Dhabi Crown Prince Mohammed Bin Zayed Al Nahyan is the chair of IPIC and Mubadala. The Investment Corporation of Dubai (ICD) is the emirate's sovereign wealth fund, with an estimated USD 70 billion of assets.

For additional analytical, marketing, investment and business opportunities information, please contact
Global Investment & Business Center, USA
(202) 546-2103. Fax: (202) 546-3275. E-mail: rusric@erols.com

UAE funds are involved in their investments to varying degrees. ADIA does not actively seek to manage or take an operational role in the public companies in which it invests, while Mubadala tends to take a more active role in particular sectors, including oil and gas, aerospace, and infrastructure, among others. ADIA exercises its voting rights as a shareholder in certain circumstances to protect its interests or to oppose motions that may be detrimental to shareholders as a body. According to ADIA, the fund carries out its investment program independently and without reference to the government of Abu Dhabi.

ADIA in 2008 agreed to act alongside the IMF as co-chair of the International Working Group of sovereign wealth funds, which eventually became the International Forum of Sovereign Wealth Funds (IFSWF). The IFSWF, which is comprised of representatives from 28 countries, was created to demonstrate that sovereign wealth funds had robust internal frameworks and governance practices and that their investments were made only on an economic and financial basis.

11. CORPORATE SOCIAL RESPONSIBILITY

Many companies in the UAE maintain corporate social responsibility (CSR) offices and participate in CSR initiatives, including mentorship and employment training; philanthropic donations to UAE-licensed humanitarian and charity organizations; and initiatives to promote environmental sustainability. The UAE's rulers actively support such efforts through official government partnerships, as well as their own private foundations. The UAE's resident population actively takes part in such CSR activities.

OECD Guidelines for Multinational Enterprises

The UAEG has stated broadly that corporate good governance and social responsibility are priorities. The UAEG has Governance Rules and Corporate Discipline Standards (Ministerial Resolution No. 518 of 2009) in which it encourages companies to apply social policy towards local society. In 2012 the Dubai Chamber of Commerce and Industry presented Corporate Social Responsibility Label certificates to honor Dubai-based companies for best practices. In April 2015, the Pearl Initiative and the United Nations Global Compact (UNGC) held their inaugural Forum in Dubai, with Reem Al Hashimy, UAE Minister of State, giving the keynote address. The Pearl Initiative is an independent private sector-led not-for-profit organization working across the Gulf region to encourage better business practices

12. POLITICAL VIOLENCE

There have been no reported instances of politically motivated property damage in recent years.

13. CORRUPTION

The UAE has stiff laws, regulations and enforcement against corruption, and has pursued several high profile cases. There is no evidence that corruption of public officials is a systemic problem. However, in February 2012 (the most recent public announcement of bribery cases), the UAE's anti-corruption body said it uncovered 10 cases in which more than 1 billion dirhams of public funds were misappropriated. The State Audit Institution (SAI) said that the cases had been referred to the public prosecution. It said irregularities were discovered during audits that took place over the prior two years, including acts of forgery, bribery and fraud. No verdicts have been rendered so far in these investigations. During 2008-2010, UAE authorities investigated several high-profile embezzlement cases, including three cases involving two former ministers and the

For additional analytical, marketing, investment and business opportunities information, please contact
Global Investment & Business Center, USA
(202) 546-2103. Fax: (202) 546-3275. E-mail: rusric@erols.com

former governor of the DIFC. Several senior Emirati and foreign nationals were dismissed and detained, though none were convicted or jailed.

Ahmed Abdullah Al Hammadi, Chief of Public Funds Prosecution told media outlets that the number of bribery cases registered in all federal courts in UAE between 2012 and 2013 was 47. Numerous bribery cases at the junior level were also reported in 2010. The law stipulates that a public servant convicted of embezzlement shall be subject to imprisonment for a minimum of five years if the crime is connected to counterfeiting.

Article 237 imposes a minimum term of one year for accepting a bribe, while anyone convicted of attempting to bribe a public servant may be imprisoned for up to five years. In August 2005, the UAE signed the UN Anticorruption Convention and ratified it in February 2006.

UN Anticorruption Convention, OECD Convention on Combatting Bribery

The UAE signed and ratified the UN Anticorruption Convention in 2005 and 2006, respectively. The UAE is not party to the OECD Convention on Combating Bribery of Foreign Public Officials in International Business Transactions.

Resources to Report Corruption

Resources to Report Corruption: Dr. Harib Al Amimi, President, State Audit Institution, 20th Floor, Tower C2, Aseel Building, Bainuna (34th) Street, Al Bateen, Abu Dhabi, United Arab Emirates; +971 2 635 9999; info@saiuae.gov.ae

14. BILATERAL INVESTMENT AGREEMENTS

UNCTAD lists the UAE as currently having 46 bilateral investment treaties, of which 31 are in force, and 14 other international investment agreements (IIAs), of which seven are in force. There is currently no bilateral investment treaty between the United States and the UAE.

In March 2004, the U.S. signed a Trade and Investment Framework Agreement (TIFA) with the UAE to provide a formal framework for dialogue on economic reform and trade liberalization; https://ustr.gov/sites/default/files/uploads/agreements/tifa/asset_upload_file305_7741.pdf. TIFAs promote the establishment of legal protection for investors, improvements in intellectual property right protection, more transparent and efficient customs procedures, and greater transparency in government and commercial regulations. As a member of the Gulf Cooperation Council (GCC), the UAE is also party to the U.S. - GCC framework agreement for trade, economic, investment, and technical cooperation, signed in September 2012.

The United States began negotiating an FTA with the UAE in March 2005. In early 2007, the United States and the UAE announced that despite considerable progress in a number of areas under negotiation, they would not be able to complete FTA negotiations under the existing time frame for trade promotion authority. The United States and the UAE have since initiated a "TIFA Plus" consultative process under the existing bilateral TIFA; this process is intended to advance trade liberalization in as many areas as possible - building where appropriate on progress made during the FTA negotiations. Incorporating a broader range of issues, the State Department negotiated and signed a Memorandum of Understanding creating an Economic Policy Dialogue (EPD) with the UAE Ministry of Foreign Affairs on January 15, 2012. The EPD establishes semi-annual high-level meetings to address a variety of topics, including but not limited to trade, investment, sector-specific cooperation, competitiveness, and entrepreneurship. A CEO Summit

For additional analytical, marketing, investment and business opportunities information, please contact
Global Investment & Business Center, USA
(202) 546-2103. Fax: (202) 546-3275. E-mail: rusric@erols.com

process for the EPD was established in 2013, bringing recommendations from the private sector directly into the EPD discussions.

Bilateral Taxation Treaties

There is currently no double taxation treaty between the United States and the UAE.

UAE has ratified 45 bilateral agreements for the promotion and protection of investments and 55 double taxation avoidance agreements.

15. OPIC AND OTHER INVESTMENT INSURANCE PROGRAMS

The UAE does not have a bilateral agreement with OPIC after having its agreement suspended in 1995 for not meeting statutory "taking steps" standards on worker rights grounds.

16. LABOR

The UAE economy is robust, with low unemployment among the country's citizen population. Expatriates, who represent over 85 percent of the country's 9.3 million residents, account for over 98 percent of private sector workers.

UAE citizens overwhelmingly work in the public sector, although the federal and emirates-level governments aim to incentivize greater Emirati participation in the private sector through Emiratization quotas. Private sector hiring quotas for Emiratis vary by sector, ranging from 2-15 percent of annual hires. The National Human Resource Development and Employment Authority (Tanmia) oversees Emiratization efforts nationally, while emirate-level entities - such as the Abu Dhabi Tatween Council and Dubai's Emirates National Development Program – similarly work to place increasing numbers of UAE citizens into private sector positions.

A significant portion of the country's expatriate population is comprised of low-skill workers, primarily from South Asia, who work in manual labor industries such as construction. In addition, several hundred thousand domestic workers, primarily from South and Southeast Asia, work in the homes of both Emirati and expatriate families. The 2014 Trafficking in Persons Report (**http://www.state.gov/documents/organization/226849.pdf**) details the UAE government's efforts to combat human trafficking.

Under UAE labor law, severance pay is required for workers who have completed one year or more of service; however, no severance pay shall be provided to employees terminated under certain conditions described in Article 120 of the Federal Labor Law.

Federal Law No. 8 of 1980 prohibits both labor unions and worker strikes. There are no legally mandated minimum wages.

Mediation plays a central role in resolving labor disputes in the UAE. The federal Ministry of Labor and local police forces actively maintain telephone hotlines and other venues for labor dispute and complaint submissions; the Ministry of Labor alone fields tens of thousands of such complaints each year, the majority of which are settled between the employer and employee(s) before reaching the formal judicial system. Labor protests are rare, in part due to employers' ability to cancel contracts of striking workers, which can lead to immediate deportation.

For additional analytical, marketing, investment and business opportunities information, please contact
Global Investment & Business Center, USA
(202) 546-2103. Fax: (202) 546-3275. E-mail: rusric@erols.com

The Ministry of Labor, in conjunction with local police forces, also inspects company workplaces as well as low-skill worker accommodations to ensure labor rights are upheld according to UAE law and employer-employee contractual agreements. The Ministry of Labor conducted tens of thousands of such inspections in 2014. The UAE federal government also enacted legislation to protect workers' health, including a June 15-September 15 ban on outdoor work between 12:30 pm and 3:00 pm; though companies could be exempted from this legislation. Companies found in violation of this ban were fined over USD 4,000 per employee in 2014. In place since 2009, the federally mandated Wage Protection System electronically transfers wages to nearly 4 million private sector workers.

The multi-agency National Committee to Combat Human Trafficking is the federal body tasked with monitoring and preventing human trafficking, including forced labor. The UAE government is party to the "Palermo Convention" (Protocol to Prevent, Suppress and Punish Trafficking in Persons, Especially Women and Children), and has made increasing efforts in recent years to prevent forced labor, and punish those who perpetrate it. Child labor is illegal and rare in the UAE.

A new federal law governing domestic worker contracts came into effect in 2014; under the law, the UAE government provided a standard employer-employee contract. In early 2015, the FNC, the UAE's quasi-legislative body, passed amendments to 2006 Federal Law 51 (which governs human trafficking, including forced labor) to more specifically prescribe protection for human trafficking victims, and punishment for human trafficking perpetrators.

The UAE is home to nearly 40 free zones, all of which offer incentives to expatriate workers and investors. Specifically, free zone regulations permit 100 percent foreign ownership – compared to the 51 percent UAE citizen ownership required outside of free zones under federal law – as well as tax, salary, and customs incentives for foreign investment and industry.

17. FOREIGN TRADE ZONES/FREE PORTS/TRADE FACILITATION

There are numerous duty-free import zones throughout the UAE. Foreign companies generally enjoy the same investment opportunities within those zones as Emirati citizens. Free zones in the UAE are home to more than 17,000 companies. By one government report in November 2010, total FDI is estimated at USD 73 billion in the 36 free zones. These free zones form a vital component of the local economy, and serve as major re-export centers to the Gulf region.

Since UAE tariffs are low and not levied against numerous imports, the chief attraction of the free zones is the waiver of the requirement for majority local ownership. In the free zones, foreigners may own up to 100 percent of the equity in an enterprise. All free zones provide 100 percent import and export tax exemption, 100 percent exemption from commercial levies, 100 percent repatriation of capital and profits, multi-year leases, easy access to sea and airports, buildings for lease, energy connections (often at subsidized prices), and assistance in labor recruitment. In addition, free zone authorities provide significant support services, such as sponsorship, worker housing, dining facilities, recruitment, and security.

Free zones have their own independent authority with responsibility for licensing and helping companies establish their business. Investors can register new companies in a free zone, or license branch or representative office. Free zones have limited liability and are governed by the laws and regulations of free zones. Companies in free trade zones seeking to operate within the UAE may be governed by the new Commercial Companies Law, if the laws of the relevant free zone permit companies to operate outside of the free zones.

For additional analytical, marketing, investment and business opportunities information, please contact
Global Investment & Business Center, USA
(202) 546-2103. Fax: (202) 546-3275. E-mail: rusric@erols.com

18. FOREIGN DIRECT INVESTMENT AND FOREIGN PORTFOLIO INVESTMENT STATISTICS

Table 2: Key Macroeconomic Data, U.S. FDI in Host Country/Economy

	Host Country Statistical source*		USG or international statistical source		USG or International Source of Data: BEA; IMF; Eurostat; UNCTAD, Other
Economic Data	Year	Amount	Year	Amount	
Host Country Gross Domestic Product (GDP) ($M USD)	2013	402,300	2013	402,000	www.worldbank.org/en/country
Foreign Direct Investment	Host Country Statistical source*		USG or international statistical source		USG or international Source of data: BEA; IMF; Eurostat; UNCTAD, Other
U.S. FDI in partner country ($M USD, stock positions)	2012	3,100	2012	8,335	BEA, Haver Analytics
Host country's FDI in the United States ($M USD, stock positions)	N/A		2013	1,804	BEA, Haver Analytics
Total inbound stock of FDI as % host GDP	NA		NA		

*UAE National Bureau of Statistics; UAE Ministry of Economy public statements.

Table 3: Sources and Destination of FDI

Direct Investment from/in Counterpart Economy Data						
From Top Five Sources/To Top Five Destinations (US Dollars, Millions)						
Inward Direct Investment			Outward Direct Investment			
Total Inward	73,107	100%	Total Outward	N/A	100%	
United Kingdom	9,688	13.3%				
India	4,258	5.8%				
France	4,084	5.6%				
Japan	3,991	5.5%				
United States	3,110	4.3%				

"0" reflects amounts rounded to +/- USD 500,000.

Source: IMF Coordinated Direct Investment Survey. Figures are from 2012.

For additional analytical, marketing, investment and business opportunities information, please contact
Global Investment & Business Center, USA
(202) 546-2103. Fax: (202) 546-3275. E-mail: rusric@erols.com

IMPORTANT CONTACTS

CONTACT FOR MORE INFORMATION

Please direct any questions regarding Mission UAE's Investment Climate Statement to:

Judith E. Baker
Vice Consul, Economic Affairs Officer
U.S. Consulate General Dubai
PO Box 121777
First Street, Umm Hurair-1
Dubai, UAE
+971.4.309.4857
BakerJE@State.gov
The alternate point of contact is:
Kevin J. Su
Economic Officer
U.S. Embassy Abu Dhabi
PO Box 4009
Abu Dhabi, UAE
+971.2.414.2449
SuKJ@State.gov

ABU DHABI ADVOCATE & LEGAL CONSULTANCY

Hamdan St, Al Ain Ahlia Insurance Building, 7th Floor PO Box 127547, Abu Dhabi, United Arab Emirates Tel: 02-627-0888 Fax: 02-627-1201 Website: www.advocateshakir.ae Mr. Shakir Matouq Marzouqi
Languages: E-mail :
Arabic - English- Urdu advshaki@eim.ae
Afridi & Angell

PO Box 3961, Abu Dhabi, United Arab Emirates Specialties Tel: 02-627-5134 Fax: 02-627-2905 • Insurance • Foreign Investments Email: abudhabi@afridi-angell.com • Banking / Financial • Marketing Agreements

aaadh@emirates.net.ae • Commercial / • Civil Law Web site www.afridi-angell.com Business Law • Damages

Mr. Charles S. Laubach • Commercial Law • Contracts Languages: English - Arabic - French - Urdu • Transportation Law • Corporations E-mail : claubach@ afridi-angell.com • Foreign Claims • Aeronautical / Maritime

Mr. Gregory Mayew • Labor • Immigraton Languages: English • Government Relations E-mail : gmayew@ afridi-angell.com

Specialties • Family Law • Adoptions • Marriage / Divorce • Child custody
• Parental Child Abduction • Child Protection • Insurance • Banking/Finance
• Commercial/Business Law
Foreign Investments
• Marketing Agreements
•   Patents/Trademarks/ Copyrights

For additional analytical, marketing, investment and business opportunities information, please contact
Global Investment & Business Center, USA
(202) 546-2103. Fax: (202) 546-3275. E-mail: rusric@erols.com

- Civil Law Damages Narcotics Collections
- Commercial Law Transportation Law Corporations Aeronautical/Maritime
- Foreign Claims
- Estates
- Taxes
- Government Relations
- Labor Relations Immigration Auto/Accidents

Al-Bawardi & Mahmoud

PO Box 46891, Abu Dhabi, United Arab Emirates
Tel: 02-626-3325
Fax: 02-626-4840
Website: www.albawardiadvocates.com

Mr. Juma Butti Al Bawardi

Languages:
Arabic - English
E-mail :
jumaa@albawardiadvocates.com
Mr. Ali Ahmed Hassan Ali

Languages:
Ar abic - English

Specialties

• Family Law	• Child Protection	• Aeronautical /
• Marriage / Divorce	• Insurance	Maritime
• Banking / Financial	• Foreign Investments	• Foreign Claims
• Commercial /	• Marketing Agreements	• Estates
Business Law	• Civil Law	• Taxes
• Patents / Trademarks / Copyrights	• Criminal Law	• Government Relations
	• Damages	• Labor
• Narcotics	• Collections	• Immigration
• Commercial Law	• Contracts	• Auto / Accidents
• Transportation Law	• Corporations	

Ali H. Ghosheh Law Office
PO Box 767, Abu Dhabi, United Arab Emirates
Tel: 02-627-2323   Fax: 02-627-2979
E-mail: ghosheh@eim.ae
Specialties: Commercial law

PO Box 45628, Abu Dhabi, United Arab Emirates Specialties

For additional analytical, marketing, investment and business opportunities
information, please contact
Global Investment & Business Center, USA
(202) 546-2103. Fax: (202) 546-3275. E-mail: rusric@erols.com

Tel: 02-626-9050 Fax: 02-626-9040 • Insurance • Civil Law E-mail : jabriauh@emirates.net.ae • Banking / Financial • Aeronautical / Maritime Website: www.aljabrilegal.com • Estates • Corporations

Mr. Salem Al-Jabri • Commercial / Business Law • Labor Languages: Arabic - English • Criminal Law

Al Mannaei Advocates

PO Box 33432, Abu Dhabi, United Arab Emirates Tel: 02-62704484 Fax: 02-627-3393 E-mail : mannaei1@emirates.net.ae

Mr. Ali Al Mannaei

Al Masaood & Associates

Advocates & Legal Consultants Specialties Alternative Dispute

P.O Box : 53288, Abu Dhabi, United Arab Emirates • Resolution • Labor and Employment Tel :02-676-1133 Fax : 02-676-4477 • Banking / Financial • Litigation Email : masadvlc@emirates.net.ae • Debt Recovery • Maritime

Website : www.masaoodlegal.com • Government Regulations • Real Estate Mr. Abdulqader Ismail • Health Care • Intellectual Property

• Insurance

Al Modharreb Law Offices & Legal Consultants

P.O. Box 2894, Abu Dhabi, United Arab Emirates
Tel: 02-626-7671 02-626-7670

Mr. Melhem Fayes Sharrouf
Languages: Arabic -English-French
Mobile: 050-661-3942
Mr. Mahmoud Azmeh
Languages: English
E-mail :   m_azmeh_law@yahoo.com
Al Rowaad Advocates & Legal Consultancy

Specialties
• Aeronautical / Maritime
• Auto / Accidents
• Banking / Financial
• Child Custody
• Civil Law
• Collections
• Commercial / Business
• Corporations
• Criminal Law
• Damages

For additional analytical, marketing, investment and business opportunities information, please contact
Global Investment & Business Center, USA
(202) 546-2103. Fax: (202) 546-3275. E-mail: rusric@erols.com

- Estates
- Family Law
- Immigration
- Insurance
- Labor
- Marketing Agreements
- Marriage / Divorce
- Transporation Law

One Sheikh Zayed Road Monarch Office Tower, 6th Floor, Office No. 602 PO Box 40073, Dubai, United Arab Emirates Specialties Tel: 04-325-4000 Fax: 04-358-9494 • Family Law • Narcotics E-mail: awf@awfuae.com • Marriage / Divorce • Contracts Web site www.awf.ae • Insurance • Corporations

- Commercial / Business • Estates

Mr. Hassan Mohsen Elhais • Civil Law • Labor Relations Mrs. Awatif Mohd Khouri • Criminal Law • Auto / Accidents
- Damages Languages: French-Arabic-English
Al-Tamimi Bureau
Abu Dhabi, United Arab Emirates Tel: 02-626-5050 Fax: 02-627-0705
Mr. Ibrahim Al-Tamimi
Avacato Advocates and Legal Consultants

Office Number 1501 PO Box 110600, Abu Dhabi, United Arab Emirates Specialties Tel: 02-633-7677 Fax: 02-633-7688 • Family Law Email: info@ezz4law.com • Adoptions

- Marriage/Divorce Web site www.ezz4law.com

Mr. Ezz Eldin Othamn • Marketing Agreements Languages: Arabic - English • Contracts

- Taxes

Mr. Saeed Al Menhaly

City International Advocates & Legal Consultants

Languages: English - Arabic - French
Emirates Tower, Hamdan Street
P.O. Box 53847, Abu Dhabi, United Arab Emirates
Tel: 02-643-4111 Fax: 02-643-4777
E-mail: info@cityinternational.ae
Website: www.cityinternational.ae
Mr. Anthony Choueiri
Languages: English - Arabic - French
E-mail : a.choueiri@cityinternational.ae
Dr. Ali Abusedra

Specialties
    Banking/Financial
    Commercial/Business

For additional analytical, marketing, investment and business opportunities
information, please contact
Global Investment & Business Center, USA
(202) 546-2103. Fax: (202) 546-3275. E-mail: rusric@erols.com

Foreign Investments
Damages
Marketing Agreements
Copyrights
• Civil Law
Collections • Labor Relations
Commercial Law • Government Relations
Contracts
Estates
Transportation Law

Corporations

• Foreign Claims

Al Odaid Tower, 10th Floor, Airport Rd. Specialties
PO Box 126883, Abu Dhabi, United Arab Emirates • Insurance • Damages • Aeronautical / Maritime Tel: 02-414-6744 Fax: 02-414-6600 • Banking/Financial • Collections • Foreign Claims

• Commercial/Business • Commercial Law • Estates Website: www.deweyleboeuf.com • Foreign Investments • Contracts Taxes

• Marketing Agreements • Transportation Law • Government Relations

Mr. Stephen Jurgenson Languages: English • Civil Law • Corporations E-mail : sjurgenson@dl.com

Emirates International Law Firm (EILF)
Advocates & Legal Consultants Specialties Email: lawyers@emirates.net.ae • Commercial Law • Litigation Floor 3, GIBCA Tower, Khalifa Street • Arbitration

P.O. Box 469, Abu Dhabi, United Arab Emirates • Construction Tel: 02-626-5600 Fax: 02-626-5123 • Intellectual Property Website: www.eilf.com • Oil & Gas

Dr. AbdulRahman Al Shaikh
Hadef Al-Dhahiri & Associates
Specialties: Advocates and Legal Counsellors Specialties
12th Floor Blue Tower, Khalifa Street PO Box 3727, Abu Dhabi, United Arab Emirates
Tel: 02- Fax: 02-627-6556
627-6622
E-mail :   contact@hadefpartners.com
Website: www.hadefpartners.com

Mr. Roger Morris
Holland & Knight LLP - Abu Dhabi
Al Najda St, Nissan Showroom, 7th Floor, Suite 701 PO Box 112738, Abu Dhabi, United Arab Emirates
Tel: 02-676-3188
Website: www.hklaw.com
Mr. Joseph McDonough
Languages: E-mail : English joseph.mcdonough@hklaw.com

For additional analytical, marketing, investment and business opportunities information, please contact
Global Investment & Business Center, USA
(202) 546-2103. Fax: (202) 546-3275. E-mail: rusric@erols.com

Banking & Finance
- Commercial
- Corporate
- Dispute Resolution
-

Employment
- Engineering & Construction
- Financial Services
- Private Equity
- Projects, Infrastructure, & Energy

Government Regulations
- Hospitality
- Insurance
- Intellectual Property
- Jointly Owned Property (Strata) Law

Maritime, Transport, & Trade
- Mergers & Acquisitions
- Real Estate
-

Restructuring & Insolvency

Specialties

- Banking & Finance
- Commercial
- Corporations
- Collections
- Contracts
- Foreign Claims
- Foreign Investments
- Market Agreements Patents/Trademarks/

Copyrights

- Government Regulations
- Business Law
- Insurance
- Civil Law
- Damages Aeronautical / Maritime
- Transportation Law
- Labor Relations
- Immigration

Technology, Media &

Telecommunications

Languages: English - Arabic - French Email: badih.moukarzel@tll.cc Fotouh Al Khair Center Tower II - 2nd Floor - Suite 204

P.O. Box 7533, Abu Dhabi, United Arab Emirates

Tel: 02-631-4431 Website: Mr. Badih Moukarzel   Fax: 02-631-4431 www.tll.cc
Shearman & Sterling

PO Box 2948, Abu Dhabi, United Arab Emirates

Tel: 02- Fax: 02-626-8933

For additional analytical, marketing, investment and business opportunities information, please contact
Global Investment & Business Center, USA
(202) 546-2103. Fax: (202) 546-3275. E-mail: rusric@erols.com

627-4477
E-mail :   acameron@shearman.com
Website: http://www.shearman.com/abudhabi/

Specialties

- Anti-Corruption
- Antitrust / Competition
- Appellate Litigation Bankruptcy &

Reorganization

- Capital Markets
- Corporate Governance
- Criminal Law Derivatives & Structured

Products

- Executive Compensation & Employee Benefits
- Finance
- Insurance
- Intellectual Property
- International Trade

- Litigation

- Public International Law
- Pro Bono
-     Investment Funds
-     Mergers & Acquisitions
-     Private Client
-     Project Development & Finance
-     Property
      State Controlled
-     Companies / Sovereign
      Wealth Funds

Vinson & Elkins LLP
Al Bateen Complex, Tower C-2, Suite 202, Bainunah (34th) Street Specialties
Al Bateen Area • Banking & Finance • Contracts
PO Box 60935 Abu Dhabi, United Arab Emirates ˙Commercial/Business ˙Aeronautical /Maritime
Tel: 02-412-0700 Fax: 02-635-4790 • Corporatations • Foreign Investments
Website: www.velaw.com
AL AIN
Suliman Yousef PO Box 1966, Al Ain, United Arab Emirates Tel: 03-765-5350 Fax: 03-764-1750

IMPORTANT INFORMATION ON EMIRATES

ABU DHABI

For additional analytical, marketing, investment and business opportunities
information, please contact
Global Investment & Business Center, USA
(202) 546-2103. Fax: (202) 546-3275. E-mail: rusric@erols.com

Abu Dhabi is the largest of all seven emirates with an area of 67,340 square kilometers, equivalent to 86.7 per cent of the country's total area, excluding the islands. It has a coastline extending for more than 400 kilometers and is divided for administrative purposes into three major regions. The first region encompasses the city of Abu Dhabi which is both the capital of the emirate and the federal capital. Sheikh Zayed, President of the UAE resides here. The parliamentary buildings in which the federal Cabinet meets, most of the federal ministries and institutions, the foreign embassies, state broadcasting facilities, and most of the oil companies are also located in Abu Dhabi, which is also the home of Zayed University and the Higher Colleges of Technology. Major infrastructure facilities include Mina (Port) Zayed and Abu Dhabi International Airport. The city also has extensive cultural, sport and leisure facilities, together with the wonderfully engineered Abu Dhabi Corniche which offers many kilometers of risk-free walking, cycling, jogging and roller-blading along the seashore of Abu Dhabi island. Architecturally speaking the city is also a fascinating place where older buildings such as small mosques have been preserved and sit comfortably in the shade of futuristic modern skyscrapers.

Abu Dhabi's second region, known as the Eastern Region, has as its capital Al Ain city. This fertile area is rich in greenery with plenty of farms, public parks and important archaeological sites. It is also blessed by substantial groundwater resources which feed into numerous artesian wells. Points of particular interest in this region are the Ain Al Faydah Park, Jebel Hafit, the leisure park at Al Hili, Al Ain Zoo and Al Ain Museum. This is also a cultural and educational center and site of the UAE's first university, the UAE University, which includes among its many faculties a vibrant medical school. Internal transport is facilitated by a superb road network and Al Ain is connected to the outside world through Al Ain International Airport.

The Western Region, the emirate's third administrative sector, comprises 52 villages and has as its capital Bida Zayed, or Zayed City. Extensive a forestation covers at least 100,000 hectares, including more than 20 million evergreens. The country's main onshore oil fields are located here, as is the country's largest oil refiner y, at Al Ruwais. In addition to the three mainland regions of Abu Dhabi there are a number of important islands within the emirate including Das, Mubarraz, Zirku and Arzanah, near where the main offshore oil fields are located. Closer inshore are Dalma, Sir Bani Yas, Merawah, Abu al-Abyadh and Saadiyat, together with many other islands.

DUBAI

The Emirate of Dubai extends along the Arabian Gulf coast of the UAE for approximately 72 kilometers . Dubai has an area of c. 3,885 square kilometers , which is equivalent to 5 per cent of the country's total area, excluding the islands. Dubai city is built along the edge of a narrow 10-kilometre long, winding creek which divides the southern section of Bur Dubai, the city's traditional heart, from the northern area of Deira. The Ruler's office, together with many head offices of major companies, Port Rashid, the Dubai World Trade Center, customs, broadcasting stations and the postal authority are all situated in Bur Dubai. Deira is a thriving commercial center containing a huge range of retail outlets, markets, hotels and Dubai International Airport. Bur Dubai and Deira are linked by Al Maktoum and Al Garhoud bridges, as well as Al Shindagha tunnel which passes under the creek.

Jebel Ali, home of a huge man-made port, has the largest free-trade zone in Arabia housing an ever growing list of international corporations which use the zone for both manufacturing and as a redistribution point.

Jumeirah beach is a major tourism area with a number of spectacular award winning hotels and sports facilities. Inland, the mountain resort town of Hatta is an extremely attractive location. Adjacent to a lake reservoir, the Hatta Fort Hotel is set in extensive parkland and provides a perfect base for exploring the nearby wadis and mountains, which extend into Omani territory.

SHARJAH

The Emirate of Sharjah extends along approximately 16 kilometers of the UAE's Gulf coastline and for more than 80 kilometers into the interior. In addition there are three enclaves belonging to Sharjah situated on the east coast, bordering the Gulf of Oman. These are Kalba, Khor Fakkan and Dibba al-Husn. The emirate has an area of 2,590 square kilometers, which is equivalent to 3.3 percent of the country's total area, excluding the islands.

The capital city of Sharjah, which overlooks the Arabian Gulf, contains the main administrative and commercial centers together with an especially impressive array of cultural and traditional projects, including several museums. Distinctive landmarks are the two major covered souqs, reflecting Islamic design; a number of recreational areas and public parks such as Al Jazeirah Fun Park and Al Buheirah Corniche. The city is also notable for its numerous elegant mosques. Links with the outside world are provided by Sharjah International Airport and Port Khalid.

Sharjah also encompasses some important oasis areas, the most famous of which is Dhaid where a wide range of vegetables and fruits are cultivated on its rich and fertile soil. Khor Fakkan provides Sharjah with a major east coast port. Two offshore islands belong to Sharjah, Abu Musa, which has been under military occupation by Iran since 1971, and Sir Abu Nu'air.

AJMAN

Ajman, located a short distance northeast of Sharjah's capital city, has a beautiful 16-kilometre stretch of white sand beach. It is a small emirate in terms of its physical size, covering about 259 square kilometers, which is equivalent to 0.3 per cent of the country's total area, excluding the islands.

The capital city, Ajman, has an historic fort at its center. This has been recently renovated and now houses a fascinating museum. In addition to the Ruler's office, various companies, banks and commercial centers, the emirate is also blessed with a natural harbor in which the Port of Ajman is situated.

Masfut is an agricultural village located in the mountains 110 kilometers to the southeast of the city, while the Manama area lies approximately 60 kilometers to the east.

UMM AL-QAIWAIN

The Emirate of Umm al-Qaiwain, which has a coastline stretching to 24 kilometers , is located on the Arabian Gulf coast of the UAE, between Sharjah to the southwest, and Ras al-Khaimah to the northeast. Its inland border lies about 32 kilometers from the main coastline. The total area of the emirate is about 777 square kilometers, which is equivalent to 1 per cent of the country's total area, excluding the islands.

The city of Umm al-Qaiwain, capital of the emirate, is situated on a narrow peninsula which encircles a large creek 1 kilometer wide by 5 kilometers long. The Ruler's office, administrative and commercial centers, the main port and a Mari culture Research Center where prawns and fish are reared on an experimental basis, are located here. The city also has the preserved remains of an old fort, its main gate flanked by defensive cannons.

For additional analytical, marketing, investment and business opportunities
information, please contact
Global Investment & Business Center, USA
(202) 546-2103. Fax: (202) 546-3275. E-mail: rusric@erols.com

Falaj al-Mualla, an attractive natural oasis, is located 50 kilometers southeast of Umm al-Qaiwain city. Sinayah island, lying a short distance offshore has important mangrove areas together with a breeding colony of Socotra cormorants.

RAS AL-KHAIMAH

Ras al-Khaimah, the most northerly emirate on the UAE's west coast, has a coastline of about 64 kilometers on the Arabian Gulf, backed by a fertile hinterland, with a separate enclave in the heart of the Hajar mountains to the southeast. Both parts of the emirates have borders with the Sultanate of Oman. In addition to its mainland territory, Ras al-Khaimah possesses a number of islands including those of Greater and Lesser Tunb, occupied by Iran since 1971. The area of the emirate is 168 square kilometers , which is equivalent to 2.2 per cent of the country's total area, excluding islands.

The city of Ras al-Khaimah is divided into two sections by Khor Ras al-Khaimah. In the western section, known as Old Ras al-Khaimah, are Ras al-Khaimah National Museum and a number of government departments . The eastern part, known as Al Nakheel, houses the Ruler's office, several government departments and commercial companies. The two sections are connected by a large bridge built across the khor.

Khor Khuwayr is an industrial region situated approximately 25 kilometers to the north of Ras al-Khaimah city. In addition to its major cement, gravel and marble enterprises, it is also the location for Port Saqr, the main export port for the emirate and the traditional fishing district of Rams. Digdagga district, on the other hand, is a well - known agricultural area and houses the Julphar pharmaceutical factory, the largest in the Arabian Gulf.

Other important centers within the emirate include: Al-Hamraniah, an agricultural center and also the location for Ras al-Khaimah International Airport, Khatt, a tourist resort that is renowned for its thermal springs, Masafi which is well known for its orchards and natural springs and Wadi al-Qawr, an attractive valley in the southern mountains.

FUJAIRAH

With the exception of some small enclaves belonging to Sharjah, Fujairah is the only emirate situated along the Gulf of Oman. Its coast is more than 90 kilometers in length and its strategic location has played a key role in its development. The area of the emirate is 1165 square kilometers, which is equivalent to 1.5 per cent of the country's total area, excluding islands.

Fujairah city, the capital of the emirate, is a rapidly developing center which contains the Ruler's office, government departments, many commercial companies and a number of hotels, as well as an airport and the Port of Fujairah, one of the world's top oil bunkering ports.

The physical features of the emirate are characterized by the jagged Hajar mountains which border the fertile coastal plain where most of the settlement has taken place. Blessed with dramatic scenery, Fujairah is well placed to continue building upon its tourism trade.

Attractions include some excellent diving sites, the natural beauty of the mountains and coastline, cultural and historic attractions and, of course, reliable winter sunshine. The historic town of Dibba al-Fujairah, at the northern end of the emirate, is an important center for both agriculture and fishing, while the village of Bidiya has a unique four-domed mosque that is the oldest in the country.

For additional analytical, marketing, investment and business opportunities information, please contact
Global Investment & Business Center, USA
(202) 546-2103. Fax: (202) 546-3275. E-mail: rusric@erols.com

For additional analytical, marketing, investment and business opportunities
information, please contact
Global Investment & Business Center, USA
(202) 546-2103. Fax: (202) 546-3275. E-mail: rusric@erols.com

SELECTED STRATEGIC INFORMATION FOR BUSINESS ACTIVITY

GENERAL BUSINESS PROFILE

DUBAI CHAMBER OF COMMERCE

DCCI OFFICES

Main office

Address	Main Building of Dubai Chamber of Commerce, Bani Yas Road
Phone	(7914) 2280000
Fax	(7914) 2211646
E-Mail	dcciinfo@dcci.gov.ae
Services	All DCCI Services

Opening hours 7.30 AM – 2.30 PM (Sat. – Wed.)

7.30 AM – 12.30 PM (Thursday)

Jebel Ali Office

Address	**Free zone main Gate - Entrance No. 1**
Phone	**(7914) 8818333**
Fax	**(791 4) 8818330**
Services	**Certificate of Origin & Signature Verification**
E-Mail	**JabelAli@dcci.gov.ae**

Opening hours 8.00 AM – 2.00 PM (Sat. – Wed.)

8.00 AM – 12.00 PM (Thursday)

Al Hamriyah Office

Address	**AL Hamriyah Land Transportation Customs Center**
Phone	**(7914) 2685111**
Fax	**97914) 2688814**
Services	**Certificate of Origin**
E-Mail	**hamriyah@dcci.gov.ae**

Opening hours 7.30 AM – 2.30 PM (Sat. – Wed.)

7.30 AM – 12.30 PM (Thursday)

Dubai Cargo Village Office

Address	**Office No. (2033) at the Cargo Village**
Phone	**(7914) 2824224**
Fax	**(7914) 2822344**
Services	**Certificate of Origin**
E-Mail	**Gargovillage@dcci.gov.ae**

For additional analytical, marketing, investment and business opportunities information, please contact Global Investment & Business Center, USA (202) 546-2103. Fax: (202) 546-3275. E-mail: rusric@erols.com

Opening hours 7.30 AM – 2.30 PM (Sat. – Wed.)
7.30 AM – 12.30 PM (Thursday)

THE AIMS OF THE CHAMBER:

o To look after the commercial, industrial and agricultural interests as well as the relevant services and to co-operate with pertinent authorities to develop those interests. So as to attain economic and social development for the community.

o To strengthen the ties among its members, to protect their interests, providing them with the services they need to carry out their activities and commercial transactions and to assist them in solving the problems that they may face in performing their activities.

o To establish effective contacts with local authorities, other chambers and business associations and organizations that dealing with local, regional and international trade. In order to coordinate actions regarding common economic, technical and administrative matters.

o Undertaking to consolidate Dubai's economic position and to highlight its role as an international commercial and business center and organizing events and programs required to promote the Emirate's economy, and its commercial establishments both internally and externally.

EXECUTIVE COMMITTEE

The Executive committee supervises the chamber's activities and the implementation of the decisions and instructions of the Board of Directors.

It also studies the reports, suggestions and recommendations presented by the committees or the Chamber's management, and coordinates the information contained therein before presenting them to the Board.

It is equally the task of the Executive Bureau to propose the necessary statutes and internal bye-laws to the Board for adoption, besides any other functions provided for by the Executive Statute of the law on the establishment of the Chamber.

NAME	Position
Obaid Humaid Al Tayer	**President**
Abdul Rahman Saif Al Ghurair	1st Vice President
Majid Hamad Rahma Al Shamsi	2nd Vice President
Abdul Jalil Yousuf Darwish	Treasurer
Dr. Anwar Gargash	Vice Treasurer
Rashid Humaid Al Mazroei	Executive Board member
Dr. Ahmed Saif Belhasa	Executive Board member

DUBAI FOCUS COMMITTEE

For additional analytical, marketing, investment and business opportunities information, please contact
Global Investment & Business Center, USA
(202) 546-2103. Fax: (202) 546-3275. E-mail: rusric@erols.com

Dubai Focus is a group of government Departments whose objectives are:

- o To promote Dubai as a regional and international business hub.

- o To work as a direct liaison with other foreign economic organizations and agencies

- o To work as a forum where Dubai Government Departments officials can express and exchange views with other foreign organization and businessmen.

- o To conduct seminars, workshops and conferences in foreign countries with the view to shed more light on Dubai's.

- o To create a healthy investment atmosphere conducive to business.

In its drive to promote Dubai internationally Dubai Focus Committee organized its inceptions in 2007 the committee organized 11 seminars in 8 countries namely the United states, South Africa, S. Korea, Japan, Spain Portugal, Holland and Federal Republic of Germany.

JOINTS ECONOMIC COMMITTEES

The Joint Economic Committees formed by Dubai Chamber of and Industry in cooperation with Similar Organization in those countries maintaining economic and trade retations with Dubai. The prime objective of these committees is to enhance and activate trade, two way investments, manufacturing, transfer of technology, cooperating in Information Technology projects, tourism and other vital services sectors.

The Joint Economic Committees have significantly contributed to strengthening Dubai relations with other countries by recommending establishing a number joint of projects in various economic sectors. They have also made constrictive recommendations to solve the obstacles that hinder the development and flow of trade and business.

Among the prominent achievements made by the Joint Committees the recommendation of certain measures to facilitate customs and ports procedures for goods shipped from Dubai Ports to the Iranian Ports. The joint Economic Committees between Dubai and the United Kingdom has also made constrictive recommendations to the E.U in order to find suitable solution for the "Aluminum tax" levied on Dubal Aluminum products.

Recommendations to activate tourism flow between Dubai and finance was also made by the Dubai France Joint to Economic and Trade Committees.

UAE INDUSTRY INFORMATION

Economic development in general, and Industrial development in particular, necessitates all effort and resource mobilization . The U.A.E. has prepared infrastructure that enable the private sector to play the largest and distinct role in this respect. The private sector made good achievement in this field, thanks to the patronage and guidance of H.H. President Sheikh Zayed Bin Sultan Al Nahayan and H.H. Sheikh Maktoum Bin Rashid Al Maktoum Bin Rashid Al Maktoum, Deputy President, Prime Minister and Ruler of Dubai and their Highnesses Members of the Supreme Council, Rulers of the Emirates.

For additional analytical, marketing, investment and business opportunities information, please contact
Global Investment & Business Center, USA
(202) 546-2103. Fax: (202) 546-3275. E-mail: rusric@erols.com

The steady increase in local industry export products to several countries worldwide is and evidence to the quality level these products achieved and their competence in foreign trade markets.

Permanent endeavors targeted at successful national industry will continue in coherence with related industrial structure, and an industry capable of standing against the now economic international changes without any protection or help, an industry whose slogans is high quality and modern technology.

BASIC FEATURES OF THE INDUSTRIAL SECTOR IN THE UAE

Modern industry in the United Arab Emirates began with the production and export of crude oil and continued to expand as the country started to develop its productive capacity. Economic policies aimed at creating alternative sources of revenue and diversifying the economic base, were adapted by the U.A.E. to reduce its dependency on oil . The development of Industry was a strategic option taken by the U.A.E. on the basis of the availability of the factors necessary for the development of a modern industrial sector such as capital, abundant sources of energy as well as metallic and non-metallic minerals and various raw materials that can be used in building and other industries.

As a result of the huge investments directed towards the development of the industrial sectors, large number of manufacturing and processing industries were established which used hydrocarbons as raw materials such as oil refineries, gas liquefaction and fertilizer plants. In addition, a large number of consumer industries were established in order to satisfy the local consumption demand for food and other consumer products such as meat, milk and other food production industries, textile and garments , metal products and fiber glass.

EMIRATES INDUSTRIAL BANK

It is a financial and development establishment established in 1982 by the Federal Law No. (1) the year 1982 , so as to contribute to the economy of the country and diversify its productive structure by building new industries and supporting the existing ones through out the country.

The Bank fundamentally directs its efforts to private establishments and companies and mixed economy establishments and companies in the field of industry whose capital is at lest 51% owned by UAE nationals or the State.
The Bank finance the industries having convincing feasibly, technically and profitably on condition that the industrial loan does not exceed 20 % of the capital and reserve of the contributing bank; or 60% of the gross expenses of the project (including the active capital for three months) ; which is less, Financing will be made through loans or by contributing to the capital of the project owning company, This last case includes projects the Bank finds it necessary to establish and encourage, depending on their importance and influence on the development of industry in the state. had started operation and activity assigned to it in the license.

The license is to be given after registration of the project in the register in the name of the project owner. The philosophy of establishing the Bank is closely related to the long term aims and objective of the UAE economy, as the main objective of the Bank is to contribute to activate and support industry in the UAE, for the achievement of a further objective : the diversification of national income sources and creating a firm industrial sector on the long run, In this respect, before giving the loan, the Bank makes a comprehensive economic and technical feasibility study for the proposed industrial project, on the basis of which it can give the clients a specialized assessment that helps them upgrade the efficiency of their projects.

For additional analytical, marketing, investment and business opportunities information, please contact
Global Investment & Business Center, USA
(202) 546-2103. Fax: (202) 546-3275. E-mail: rusric@erols.com

This assessment includes the feasibility study, financial and engineering analysis and marketing and legal consultation research.

Since 1984, the Industrial Bank set up a special branch to study and decide the industrial sectors representing the uncovered power of the industrial investment. In January 1986 the Bank started issuing a regular pamphlet supplying industry businesses with the essential industrial information.

BANK LOAN TYPES

The Bank offers the following types of loans, as type are needed:

a) Short Term Loans : not exceeding two year duration. These loans are assigned to financing capital, acting in the existing industrial establishments.

b) Short Term Loans: not exceeding five-year duration. These loans are assigned to increase production lines or the renewal of the existing industrial establishments.

c) Long Term Loans : not exceeding eight-year duration. These loans are assigned to establishing new industrial projects.

OTHER SERVICES AND FACILITIES

1. Providing Renewed Credit Facilities for financing active capital.
2. Private Contracts Financing.
3. Credit Facility Grants for exports.
4. Transferable Loans.
5. Providing Preliminary Guarantee Statements.
6. Providing Preliminary Statements of Guaranteed performance.
7. Preparation of Assessment Studies for Industrial Projects.
8. Preparation of Marketing Studies .
9. Investigating Investment Chances in the Industrial Fields in the Country.
10. Loans Transferable to Participate in Capital.
11. Contribution to the Capital of Companies Acting within the Activity of the Bank. est. of 4% of the amount of the loan, added to a 0.5 % interest for administration fees.

    a) Industrial projects of dense capital insuring importing modern technology to the country.

    b) Industrial projects whose most needs depend on locally available primary material to produce commodities for the UAE market with the capacity of replacing imported ones and gross expenses less than those of the imported ones .

    c) Projects depending on locally available primary material which, rather than locally marketing, can be marketed in Arab and Foreign markets by multi - party by literal long term agreements.

DYBAI: BASIC INFORMATION

Lying on the calm, blue waters of the southern Gulf and flanked by majestic desert, Dubai offers year-round sunshine and five-star luxury... plus the adventure of a unique Arabian experience.

For additional analytical, marketing, investment and business opportunities information, please contact
Global Investment & Business Center, USA
(202) 546-2103. Fax: (202) 546-3275. E-mail: rusric@erols.com

One of the seven emirates that make up the United Arab Emirates, Dubai is a place of fascinating contrasts, a distinctive blend of modern city and timeless desert, of East and West, of old and new.

Known in the region as 'the city of merchants', Dubai has welcomed seafarers and traders to its shores for generations. Today, this tradition of courtesy and hospitality lives on. Dubai's streets are clean and safe, and travellers are sure to be charmed by the city's warmth and friendliness.

Dubai has something for everyone, from holidaymakers seeking a relaxing break away from clouds and crowds, to active tourists looking for a new, exciting experience. The emirate is also rapidly emerging as an international conference, exhibition and incentive destination.

Dubai has superb sports, shopping, dining and entertainment facilities. Likewise, its rapidly developing tourism sector is well equipped to cater to the diverse needs of individual travellers, families or incentive groups.

In the following pages, Destination Dubai provides comprehensive details of the emirate's tourist attractions, facilities and services.

KEY ATTRACTIONS

- A taste of Arabia with a cosmopolitan lifestyle
- Year-round sunshine
- Uncrowded, clean, sandy beaches
- Crime-free environment
- Tolerant and welcoming society

GETTING THERE

- Dubai is less than eight hours from Europe and the Far East
- Some 80 airlines provide direct links to more than 120 cities worldwide
- Efficient immigration, baggage handling and customs formalities

ACCOMMODATION

- Wide selection of luxurious, modern hotels offering superb accommodation and facilities for sports, dining and entertainment
- Choice of location — in the city, on the beach or in the mountains
- Furnished holiday apartments for longer stays

ENTERTAINMENT

- Extensive range of restaurants featuring cuisine from around the world.
- Varied nightlife — bars, cafés and nightclubs
- Family fun at theme parks, a zoo, beaches and country parks

GROUND ARRANGEMENTS

- Choice of internationally-experienced destination management companies with multilingual guides and well-qualified drivers

For additional analytical, marketing, investment and business opportunities information, please contact
Global Investment & Business Center, USA
(202) 546-2103. Fax: (202) 546-3275. E-mail: rusric@erols.com

- Modern air-conditioned coaches
- Plentiful taxis and hire cars
- Good roads, highways and wide boulevards
- First-rate cruise docking, supply and ground-handling facilities

TOURS AND EXCURSIONS

- Variety of standard or tailor-made tours available, covering the city, shopping, the desert, the East Coast, mountains, neighbouring emirates, and more
- Limousine, boat and dhow tours
- Special interest packages including golf, watersports, fishing, bird-watching, archaeology

ARABIAN EXPERIENCES

- Desert safaris, dune driving and exploring wadis (dry river beds) by four-wheel-drive vehicles
- Sand-skiing

- Moonlit Arabian desert barbecues, complete with traditional entertainment
- Camel racing, horse racing and falconry
- Cruises by traditional wooden dhow on Dubai Creek or into the Gulf
- Exploring the old city souks (markets), creekside dhow quays and traditional architecture
- Photographic opportunities galore: majestic mosques, magnificent palaces, brightly dressed children, camel and goat herds, ancient windtowers, dusty Bedouin villages, lush oases and palm groves, and dramatic sunsets

OUTDOOR ACTIVITIES AND SPORTS

- Superb watersports: sailing, fishing, windsurfing, water-skiing, jet-skiing, scuba-diving and snorkelling
- Golf on three championship-standard grass courses, with two more to open this year
- Wide range of other sports, from squash and tennis to horse riding and trekking, paragliding, cycling, ice-skating, shooting, archery, bowling and go-karting

SHOPPING

- Dubai's tax-free open market means bargains galore
- Attractive traditional Middle Eastern gifts — coffee pots, rugs, silverware, jewellery, brass, inlaid rosewood furniture and much more
- One of the world's great gold trading centres offering unbeatable value
- Wide selection of low-priced international brand name products including audio equipment, VCRs, cameras, watches, designer clothes, perfumes
- Award-winning Dubai Duty Free complex at the airport.

BUSINESS CLIMATE

Dubai presents international business with a wide range of opportunities for different activities and operations, including:

- Trade
- Transport and distribution

For additional analytical, marketing, investment and business opportunities information, please contact
Global Investment & Business Center, USA
(202) 546-2103. Fax: (202) 546-3275. E-mail: rusric@erols.com

- Manufacturing and processing
- Regional offices.

THE MARKET

As the leading regional trading hub, Dubai offers access to a market of outstanding potential for overseas companies in a wide range of sectors. Among its key characteristics are:

- A large market - more than $17 billion in domestic imports annually; gateway to a $150 billion p.a., 1.4 billion population regional import market;
- A growing market - Dubai's imports have more than doubled since 1989; regional economic growth and liberalisation is set to boost demand;
- A prosperous market - strategic location at the heart of one of the world's richest regions;
- A diversified market - wide import requirements; opportunities for suppliers of most products;
- An accessible market - served by more than 170 shipping lines and 86 airlines;
- An open market - no exchange controls, quotas or trade barriers.

Dubai offers incoming business all the advantages of a highly developed economy. Its infrastructure and services match the highest international standards, facilitating efficiency, quality and service. Among the benefits are:

- Free enterprise system
- Highly developed transport infrastructure
- State-of-the-art telecommunications
- Sophisticated financial and services sector
- Top international exhibition and conference venue
- High quality office and residential accommodation
- Reliable power, utilities etc
- First class hotels, hospitals, schools, shops etc
- Cosmopolitan lifestyle.

THE COSTS

Overseas companies setting up in Dubai can secure cost advantages not generally available internationally. Among the reasons are:

- No corporate taxes
- No income taxes
- No foreign exchange controls
- No trade barriers
- Competitive import duties (4% with many exemptions)
- Competitive labour costs
- Competitive energy costs
- Competitive real estate costs.

DOING BUSINESS

Dubai offers foreign companies a wide choice of business options, including:

For additional analytical, marketing, investment and business opportunities information, please contact
Global Investment & Business Center, USA
(202) 546-2103. Fax: (202) 546-3275. E-mail: rusric@erols.com

- Direct trade - selling directly to established dealers and distributors
- Commercial agency arrangements - appointee must be a UAE national or company; agreement to be registered with Ministry of Economy and Commerce
- Branch or representative office - 100% foreign ownership permitted; local agent (sponsor) must be appointed; Economic Development Department licence required
- Limited liability company - foreign ownership restricted to 49%; Economic Development Department licence required
- Special free zone investment incentives (see below).

SPECIAL INVESTMENT INCENTIVES

Dubai's highly successful Jebel Ali Free Zone and new Airport Free Zone provide all the advantages available elsewhere in the emirate, with the following additional benefits:

- 100% foreign ownership and control
- Renewable 15-year guarantee of no taxation
- No customs duties
- Flexible investment options
- Efficient transport and distribution facilities
- Full administrative and recruitmentsupport.

For additional analytical, marketing, investment and business opportunities
information, please contact
Global Investment & Business Center, USA
(202) 546-2103. Fax: (202) 546-3275. E-mail: rusric@erols.com

PRACTICAL INFORMATION FOR CONDUCTING BUSINESS[1]

INVESTMENT AND BUSINESS CLIMATE

DOING BUSINESS IN UNITED ARAB EMIRATES

MARKET OVERVIEW

The United States and the United Arab Emirates have a strong bilateral relationship, based on a joint commitment to the security and stability of the Gulf region. Our two governments also share many similar concerns on a host of other international issues. Exports in both directions have increased almost every year since the UAE, a federation of seven emirates on the Arabian Gulf, was founded in 1971.

The prosperity of UAE citizens is based in great part on the country's vast oil and gas reserves, most of which lie in the largest emirate and seat of the capital, Abu Dhabi. The UAE has nearly ten percent of the world's proven oil reserves and five percent of proven gas reserves. Other emirates include Dubai, Sharjah, Ras al Khaimah, Fujairah, Ajman, and Umm al Quwain. The country is an active member of the Gulf Cooperative Council (GCC), which includes Saudi Arabia, Kuwait, Oman, Qatar, and Bahrain. Per capita GDP in 2007 was estimated at over US$23,000.

The UAE, long recognized as the commercial and business hub of the Arabian Gulf, is home to the busiest man-made port in the world, Jebel Ali. This Gulf powerhouse has no corporate taxes (with the exception of banks and foreign oil companies that have concessions in UAE oilfields), no income taxes, and a relatively low import duty of five percent. The UAE is currently the largest export market for US goods in the Arab World, having recently surpassed Saudi Arabia. US goods exports to the UAE rose in 2007, to over US$11.6 billion, while imports from the UAE were just under US$1.4 billion. With a US$170 billion a year economy and excellent infrastructure, the UAE is an ideal location for US companies to conduct business. The presence of over 700 US firms here underlines this fact. To name just a very few: AM General, Citibank, Honeywell, Lockheed Martin, Boeing, General Electric, Raytheon, Northrop Grumman, General Dynamics, KBR, FedEx, Ford, Johnson & Johnson, MSD, ExxonMobil, Microsoft, Motorola, and many more. US companies see the UAE as an excellent place to establish a regional presence because of the can-do, pro-business orientation of the leadership, and the stability of the country.

The UAE, a model for digital readiness in the Middle East, has embraced the Internet age. Mobile phone and PC usage levels are among the highest in the Middle East. The Emirate of Dubai, capitalizing on its strategic trading position between Central Asia, the Middle East, and Africa, is growing dramatically. This emirate has attracted international investment, companies and visitors with landmark projects such as vast housing developments and the ambitious man-made Palm Islands, which include private residences and hotels. Abu Dhabi has also begun developing several new mega projects of its own, including Sadiyat Island, which will feature the Abu Dhabi Guggenheim Museum, designed by famed American architect Frank Gehry. Dubai's Jebel Ali Free Zone (JAFZ) has over 2,500 companies, including 150 US-owned firms. Other Dubai free zones include Media City, Knowledge Village, Internet City, and Dubai International Financial Center. Borrowing on the success of JAFZ, other emirates have also created free zones.

---

[1] This section based in part on materials of the US Department of Commerce

For additional analytical, marketing, investment and business opportunities information, please contact
Global Investment & Business Center, USA
(202) 546-2103. Fax: (202) 546-3275. E-mail: rusric@erols.com

The UAE is a member of the WTO and a signatory to the General Agreement on Tariffs and Trade (GATT), the General Agreement on Trade in Service (GATS), and the Agreement on Trade-Related Aspects of Intellectual Property (TRIPS).

MARKET CHALLENGES

The UAE, although an attractive market for a wide variety of products, can be a difficult place for American firms to do business. It is not a market for the first-time exporter. The legal system protects local entities. Foreign companies find it difficult to legally dismiss a non-performing local agent without protracted litigation, and it is difficult, if not impossible, to sell without a local agent. Payments tend to be slower than in the US and Europe. The US Embassy strongly advises companies wanting to do business in the UAE to seek competent legal counsel while exploring the market and to get to know their prospective client or business partner well prior to entering into an agreement.

MARKET OPPORTUNITIES

Although oil and gas production will remain the backbone of the UAE economy for years to come, the non-oil sector of the economy is growing at a rapid pace. Major growth areas include: aircraft & parts, security and safety equipment; IT equipment and services; medical equipment, services and supplies; architecture, construction, and engineering services; building products; air conditioning and refrigeration equipment; environmental and pollution control equipment; and sporting goods and equipment. Water and power projects continue to offer considerable opportunity due to the UAE's unquenchable thirst for water and electricity. There is no personal income tax.

US fast food and casual dining restaurants are popular in the UAE, particularly with the younger generation. Many of the ingredients are imported from the United States. Good prospects for U.S. food exports, in descending order include: Vegetable oils, beverage bases, breakfast cereals, poultry parts, fresh fruits (specifically apples and pears), honey, frozen vegetables, snack foods, cheeses, almonds, fruit and vegetable juices, and miscellaneous food products, particularly hot sauces, salad dressings, catsup, mayonnaise, vinegar, iodized salt, ice cream, frozen dough mixes, Tex-Mex foods, and coffee whiteners.

STARTING A BUSINESS

REGISTRATION REQUIREMENTS

	Procedure	Time to complete:	Cost to complete:
1	Submit the company registration application and the proposed company name to the Department of Economic Development (DED)	1 day	AED 100 fee for the initial approval
2	Notarize the company's Memorandum of Association in DED	1 day	0.25% of the capital (for 3 copies of the Memorandum of Association), AED 5 for each page of the additional copy
3	File company documents with the Department for Economic Development (DED) and obtain trade license	6 days	5 % of the value of the lease agreement + AED 1,000-3,000 waste fees + AED 600 for company registration + AED 500 fees for signboard approval

For additional analytical, marketing, investment and business opportunities information, please contact
Global Investment & Business Center, USA
(202) 546-2103. Fax: (202) 546-3275. E-mail: rusric@erols.com

4	Register with the Dubai Chamber of Commerce and Industry	2 days	AED 1,200 (application for membership certificate)
5	Make a name board	2 days	AED 1,000
6	Apply for establishment card at the Ministry of Labor	1 day	AED 2000
7	Register native workers with the Ministry of Labor	1 day	no charge
8	Register native workers with the General Authority for Pension and Social Security	1 day (simultaneous with previous procedure)	no charge

Procedure 1.

Submit the company registration application and the proposed company name to the Department of Economic Development (DED)

Time to complete:

1 day

Cost to complete:

AED 100 fee for the initial approval

Name of Agency:

Comment:

To register a company, the founder must first obtain preliminary approvals from the Licensing Section of the Dubai Department of Economic Development (DED) on the classification of the limited liability corporation's capitalization, business activities, trade name, and identity of partners.

Procedure 2.

Notarize the company's Memorandum of Association in DED

Time to complete:

1 day

Cost to complete:

0.25% of the capital (for 3 copies of the Memorandum of Association), AED 5 for each page of the additional copy

Name of Agency:

Comment:

The applicant notarizes the AOA at DED that provides a standard Memorandum of Association (AOA). Notarization takes no more than 1 day. A common practice is for the entrepreneur's lawyer to get a preliminary approval from the notary beforehand so that the client can arrive at a specified time and have the documents notarized immediately. The maximum notary fee is AED 10,000.

Procedure 3.

File company documents with the Department for Economic Development (DED) and obtain trade license

Time to complete:

6 days

Cost to complete:

5 % of the value of the lease agreement + AED 1,000-3,000 waste fees + AED 600 for company registration + AED 500 fees for signboard approval

Name of Agency:

Comment:

To obtain the Trade License and Commercial Registration Certificate, the LLC must submit the following original documents to the Commercial Registry at the DED Trade License and Commercial Registration Department.
- The prescribed application form, signed by the company manager(s) or their legal representative(s).
- The memorandum of association (an original and a copy).

For additional analytical, marketing, investment and business opportunities information, please contact
Global Investment & Business Center, USA
(202) 546-2103. Fax: (202) 546-3275. E-mail: rusric@erols.com

- A letter issued by the DED, attesting to the company name approval.
- The original letter of company approval, issued by the DED Committee of Limited Liability Companies.

If Commercial Registry officials deem the documentation to be in order, the company name will be entered into the Commercial Register. Within 3 days of the date the company is entered in the Commercial Register, the documents will be released at no charge to the company representative in a sealed envelope. afterward, the DED forwards the following documents to the Federal Ministry of Economy and Commerce to arrange for publication:
- Notarized memorandum of association (copy).
- The application for entry of the company name in the Commercial Register (copy).
- Extract of the entry of the company name in the Commercial Register.

Publication takes several months. However, this time frame is not important because the authorities will accept a copy of the Ministry's receipt of publication fee payment. After the publication, the Ministry of Economy and Commerce issues its approval letter.

Before the newly formed company can begin operations, it must apply to the DED for a trade license. After the notary public at the Commercial Registry notarizes the memorandum of association, a license application form is completed in Arabic, signed by the authorized company signatory and filed with the DED in duplicate. The DED files one copy and forwards the other to the UAE Federal Ministry of Economy and Commerce. The trade license application must be filed with the applicable fee and the following documents:
- The prescribed form for setting out the proposed company name in Arabic and English.
- The original lease for the company's office premises.
- The prescribed form for obtaining the Dubai Municipality Building Department's clearance on the suitability of the office premises.

All business activities fall into three categories of licenses: (1) commercial licenses, covering all kinds of trading activity; (2) professional licenses, covering professions, services, craftsmen, and artisans; and (3) industrial licenses, establishing industrial or manufacturing activity.

Upon the conclusion of this procedure, the DED issues the original Trade License and Commercial Registration certificates. Upon presentation of the receipts showing payment of the Ministry publication fee and the Chamber of Commerce membership fee, the DED will issue the original trade license and certificate of commercial registration for the limited liability company.

Procedure 4.
Register with the Dubai Chamber of Commerce and Industry
Time to complete:
2 days
Cost to complete:
AED 1,200 (application for membership certificate)
Name of Agency:
Comment:
Membership in the Dubai Chamber of Commerce and Industry is mandatory.
Procedure 5.
Make a name board
Time to complete:
2 days

For additional analytical, marketing, investment and business opportunities information, please contact
Global Investment & Business Center, USA
(202) 546-2103. Fax: (202) 546-3275. E-mail: rusric@erols.com

Cost to complete:
>   AED 1,000

Name of Agency:

Comment:
>   Once the company receives clearance on the use of the office premises, it must prepare
>   a name board in English and Arabic. The office premises will then be inspected by the
>   fire and civil defense authorities and by the DED Licensing Department.

Procedure 6.
>   Apply for establishment card at the Ministry of Labor

Time to complete:
>   1 day

Cost to complete:
>   AED 2000

Name of Agency:

Comment:
>   Either the owner in person or the authorized representative of the company can go in
>   person to apply for the "Establishment Card" at the Ministry of Labour. Provided the trade
>   license and the fees are paid, the "Establishment Card" can be issued the same day.

Procedure 7.
>   Register native workers with the Ministry of Labor

Time to complete:
>   1 day

Cost to complete:
>   no charge

Name of Agency:

Comment:
>   According to Ministerial decree No 1215/2005, native workers should be registered with
>   Ministry of labor.
>   The documents required to bring along at the time of this registration are:
>   - 3 copies of employment contract
>   - A copy of employers passport
>   - A copy of the trading license
>   - A paper confirming that the worker is a UAE citizen.

Procedure 8.
>   Register native workers with the General Authority for Pension and Social Security

Time to complete:
>   1 day (simultaneous with previous procedure)

Cost to complete:
>   no charge

Name of Agency:

Comment:
>   Registration requires submitting the native workers' updated salary certificates or labor
>   contracts.

PROPERTY REGISTRATION

	Procedure	Time to complete:	Cost to complete:
1	Register title at the Customer Service Department	2 days	2% transfer fee payable to the Dubai Lands Department of the purchase value (1% of the sale value paid by the purchaser; 1% of the value as local charges paid by the seller) + AED 250 (title fee)

For additional analytical, marketing, investment and business opportunities
information, please contact
Global Investment & Business Center, USA
(202) 546-2103. Fax: (202) 546-3275. E-mail: rusric@erols.com

REGISTRATION REQUIREMENT DETAILS

Procedure 1.

Register title at the Customer Service Department

Time to complete:

2 days

Cost to complete:

2% transfer fee payable to the Dubai Lands Department of the purchase value (1% of the sale value paid by the purchaser; 1% of the value as local charges paid by the seller) + AED 250 (title fee)

Name of Agency:

Land Department

Comment:

The seller and the buyer must approach the Disposal Section at the Customer Service Department together and execute and submit an application. The sale agreement is also issued at this point. All involved parties must be present at this procedure, though a lawyer is not required to be present. The transfer fee is paid directly at the Lands Department (not at a bank) and proof of payment is required to be submitted along with the other documentation mentioned.

The documentation shall include:

Original Ownership Certificate (to be provided by the seller)

ID cards of concerned parties

The trade license of both companies (to be provided by the each party)

Notarized memorandum of association of both the seller and the buyer (to be provided by each of them)

PAYING TAXES

Tax or mandatory contribution	Payments (number)	Notes on Payments	Time (hours)	Statutory tax rate	Tax base	Total tax rate (% profit)	Notes on TTR
Social security contributions	12		12	12.5%	gross salaries	14.1	
Vehicle registration fee	1		0	fixed fee (AED 750 per vehicle)		0	
Trade license fee	1		0	fixed fee (AED 550)		0	
Totals:	14		12			14.1	

Notes:

Name of taxes have been standardized. For instance income tax, profit tax, tax on company's income are all named corporate income tax in this table.

The hours for VAT include all the VAT and sales taxes applicable.

The hours for Social Security include all the hours for labor taxes and mandatory contributions in general.

**For additional analytical, marketing, investment and business opportunities information, please contact
Global Investment & Business Center, USA
(202) 546-2103. Fax: (202) 546-3275. E-mail: rusric@erols.com**

LEADING SECTORS FOR EXPORTS AND INVESTMENT

AIRCRAFT PARTS/SERVICES

Demand for aircraft parts and aviation services are driven by business and leisure air travel and the size and age of aircraft fleets. The profitability of individual companies depends on efficient operations. Large companies enjoy economies of scale in purchasing. Small companies can compete effectively in hometown markets. Companies in this industry operate airports for commercial and general aviation and provide support services such as air traffic control, aircraft fueling and maintenance, baggage and cargo handling, and rental of hangar space. Major services include aircraft maintenance and repair, fixed-base operator services and ground handling. Other services include airport administration and operation and wholesale fuel sales. Major companies include Advanced Military Maintenance, Repair and Overhaul Centre (AMROC), Abu Dhabi Aircraft Technologies (ADAT), Gulf Aircraft Maintenance Company (GAMCO), Trans-Aero, Emirates Airline Engineering, Aerostar Asset Management, Hawker Pacific Avionics, Jet Aviation and Goodrich Aero structures.

SUB-SECTOR BEST PROSPECTS

Any company that can contribute in developing a state-of-the-art sustainment center is in demand. The requirement is for the center to offer innovative maintenance solutions, performance-based reliability, all life cycle management, and affordability from one centralized location. In addition, there is a market for independent provider of maintenance, repair, and overhaul solutions for airframes, engines, and components.

OPPORTUNITIES

Designed to meet the demands of the 21st century aerospace industry by forming partnerships with aircraft OEMs and combining leading-edge technology, best practice manufacturing processes, an integrated supply chain, and a high caliber workforce, Strata delivers innovative, cost effective solutions driving growth and efficiency. Strata endeavors to become a tier-one supplier: designing, developing and manufacturing aircraft major units - such as wings and empennages - for the next generation of commercial aircrafts. Recent years have witnessed a revolution in the digitization of the commercial aircraft industry with various airlines realizing the importance of providing added features such as real-time weather details, flight operations, asset tracking, health monitoring, and airport taxi services. The future will see significant opportunities for aircraft manufacturers and OEMs to use various means of digitization as a potential source of differentiation. Today's world is increasingly adopting the digital model in all aspects of living and thus embedded sensors improve the efficiency of business processes when combined with mobility applications. The devices are expected to reduce the amount of paper required for flight operating manuals, navigation charts, reference handbooks and flight checklists. Focus is also on the new Aviation District at the Al Maktoum International Airport, with FBO operators wanting to construct their own customized solutions. The Aviation District plays a strategic role in furthering Dubai's vision to become a gateway to global markets and particularly MENASA (Middle East, North Africa and South Asia) region. MENASA is the second fastest growing market comprising 23% of the world's population – more than half of which are under 25 years old. MENASA's projected GDP is estimated to reach US$12.8 trillion by 2022-2023.

Trade shows:

For additional analytical, marketing, investment and business opportunities information, please contact
Global Investment & Business Center, USA
(202) 546-2103. Fax: (202) 546-3275. E-mail: rusric@erols.com

Dubai Air Show
Date: 8 - 12 November, 2015
Website: http://www.dubaiairshow.aero
MRO Middle East
Date: 3 - 4 February, 2016
Website: http://events.aviationweek.com/archive/2014/mme/
IDEX: International Defence Exhibition and Conference
Date: 19 - 23 February, 2016
Website: http://www.idexuae.ae/
Abu Dhabi Air Expo
Date: 8 - 10 March, 2016
Website: http://www.adairexpo.com/
Airport Show
Date: 16 - 18 May, 2016
Website: http://www.theairportshow.com
MEBA: Middle East Business Aviation Show
Date: 6 - 8 December, 2016
Website: http://www.meba.aero/

RESOURCES

Airline Update: www.airlineupdate.com
Mubadala - www.mubadala.com
Abu Dhabi Airports Company - www.adac.ae
General Civil Aviation Authority - www.gcaa.ae
Hoovers - www.hoovers.com
Dubai World Central - www.dwc.ae
http://mromiddleeast.aviationweek.com/me16/public/enter.aspx

AUTOMOTIVE

In 2014, the U.A.E.'s automotive trade value reached USD20.7 billion, up 43% from 2010. Of this value, 94% was imports. Cars represented 63% of U.A.E.'s automotive imports, followed by parts and accessories (12.6%), and trucks (12.1%). Virtually the entire U.A.E. supply of car and light vehicles is imported. Barring a couple of truck units assembling CKD components and armored vehicles factories, there is no serious automotive manufacturing activity taking place in the U.A.E.

According to media reports, the U.A.E. is the second largest automotive market (including cars, parts and accessories, trailers and semi-trailers, trucks, public transport vehicles, tractors, other) in the GCC after Saudi Arabia. The U.A.E.'s automotive retail sector grew by 6.5% y/y in H1 2014. In 2014,cars represented 63% of the U.A.E.'s total automotive imports. The U.A.E. is also one of the largest importers of used cars, making it a regional hub not only for cars but also for vehicle parts and components in the MENA region. As a result, the U.A.E. has become a strategic player in the car parts trade within the GCC region, positioning itself as a major re-exports center.

The U.A.E. market is broadly divided between passenger cars and commercial vehicles with approximately 80% being passenger cars and 20% being commercial vehicles (trucks, vans and buses). The luxury segment contributed around 12% to the U.A.E.'s total industry volume, which is growing at a rate of 17% annually. Japanese manufacturers enjoy significant market share in the U.A.E. automotive market, with Toyota maintaining its dominance in 2014.

For additional analytical, marketing, investment and business opportunities information, please contact
Global Investment & Business Center, USA
(202) 546-2103. Fax: (202) 546-3275. E-mail: rusric@erols.com

Tariffs: The tariff applied to cars is 5% customs duties on value of the vehicle plus 1% insurance plus cost of the shipment. For trucks, the customs duty is 12%.

Taxes: No VAT, luxury tax or special consumption tax exist on vehicles.

Barriers: The U.A.E.'s trade policy has been consistent with its obligations under the WTO. There are few trade barriers, viz. automotive parts should not contain asbestos, and products should not have been manufactured or transited through Israel.

Market Entry

All cars and buses entering U.A.E. have to abide by safety regulations issued by the Emirates Authority for Standardization and Metrology (ESMA). In addition, the following rules must be adhered to:

• Head restraints in all seats and air bags for the driver and the front passenger are compulsory for all passenger cars and buses with capacity up to 22 passengers.

• Safety belts and Anti Braking System (ABS) are required in all new vehicles. Extra seats in the aisles are prohibited for any motor vehicle with a riding capacity of four people or more.

• Every vehicle must have an alarm to notify when drivers exceed speed limit of 120 km in cars and 100 km on buses.

In addition, all vehicles must be exported from the country of manufacture and steering wheels must not be modified. There must be no damages on the vehicle's outer body and must be accident free.

Local Standards Requirements:

GSO Standards tests for motor vehicle spare parts:
          - Motor vehicle spare parts (draft)
GSO Standards tests for multipurpose tires:
          - Multipurpose Tires – General Requirements
          - Multipurpose vehicles tires standards
          - Multipurpose vehicles tires (testing methods)

Current Market Trends:

New Products Sector

The U.A.E. automotive industry's growth is driven by a number of factors including increasing quality awareness, high spending power, and wide offerings of automotive products across international brands. According to industry estimates, in the first half of 2013, U.A.E. companies imported most from Japan (50%), followed by U.S.A (13%) and then South Korea (6%).

During the corresponding period, vehicle re-exports grew by 13%. Oman is the top destination for cars re-exported from Dubai, accounting for 63.7%, followed by Tanzania 5.1% and Saudi Arabia 3.3%.

For additional analytical, marketing, investment and business opportunities information, please contact
Global Investment & Business Center, USA
(202) 546-2103. Fax: (202) 546-3275. E-mail: rusric@erols.com

Passenger Cars - Toyota Motors remains the dominant player with 41.9% market share. Nissan is second with a market share of 19%, followed by Mitsubishi (7.8%), Hyundai (7.1%) and Ford (5.3%). Kia is sixth with a market share of 4.8% followed by Fuso, BMW, Honda and Chevrolet.

Commercial Vehicles – With major infrastructure and housing projects being planned, this sector will experience continued growth. Truck approvals are conducted at the GCC level by the GCC Standards Organization which is based in Riyadh, KSA. The product should be first approved by GSO before the truck CAN be exported to GCC countries, including the U.A.E..

U.S. truck manufacturers or exporters can contact the office below for approval:
Conformity Assessment Department
G.C.C Standardization Organization (GSO)
Tel: +966 1 274 66 55 ext. 333; Fax: +966 1 210 53 90
E-mail: alsagr@gso.org.sa

BEST PROSPECTS

Parts and Components – The U.A.E.'s strategic positioning and economic conditions have led the country to become a regional hub for car parts and vehicle components in the entire Middle East and GCC. As a result, the U.A.E. has become a key player in the car parts trade within the Gulf region and has positioned itself as a major re-export center.

According to media reports, U.A.E.'s trade for auto parts and accessories was valued at around $12 billion, a 10 per cent growth over previous year. Imports were valued at over $ 7 billion last year, while value of exports and re-exports was around $ billion.

Three major trading partners accounted for 49 per cent of total automotive parts imports. Japan was on the top with $1.67 billion, followed by South Korea with $972 million, and China with $901 million. Imports from Germany ($860 million) and the USA ($846 million) came fourth and fifth, respectively, in terms of total auto parts trade last year.

Saudi Arabia ($645 million), Iraq ($294 million) and Afghanistan ($218 million) were the biggest export and re-export markets in 2014.

Used Car Market Sector

Passenger Cars: As a regional trade hub supporting intense international business activity, the U.A.E. presents an extremely competitive business landscape for American companies in this sector. Many successful U.S. firms already in business in the region rely on technological advantage and quality assurance in addressing current demand and facing foreign competition.

Regulations:

- All vehicles must conform to the U.A.E. standards –

- Steering wheels must not be modified

- There must be no damage on the vehicle's outer body

- The U.A.E. does not allow import of vehicles that have been subject to accidents such as submersion, fire, collision, rollover, etcetera

For additional analytical, marketing, investment and business opportunities information, please contact
Global Investment & Business Center, USA
(202) 546-2103. Fax: (202) 546-3275. E-mail: rusric@erols.com

• Vehicles previously used as taxicabs or by police are not allowed to be imported

• Vehicles may only be exported to companies (having commercial registration for business activities in vehicle sale and import) and to individuals with a valid residence authorization if the importer is not a citizen of any of the GCC States

Documents Required:

1. Proof of vehicle ownership and invoice attested by the local chamber of commerce in the U.S.

2. Export declaration of the customs administration in the U.S. (the invoice and the certificate of origin should be attached to the export declaration)

3. A document issued by Police in the U.S. indicating that the vehicle is not wanted for any criminal investigation.

Re-Manufactured/Used Auto Parts:

Importation of reconditioned/used auto parts is not allowed for sale in the U.A.E., unless reconditioned by the original manufacturer. The reseller is not allowed to claim that the part is the same as an original part. There is no difference in the treatment between remanufactured and used auto parts. This treatment applies to all motor vehicle parts.

Remanufactured/rebuilt parts are generally considered used or semi-used and are reflected in the pricing. Normally, the warranty period will not be the same as the original, if offered.

Used, not remanufactured, parts usually carry no warranty.

Local industry sources believe that there could be potential as there are a number of American cars sold within the U.A.E. and also a number of used American cars are re-exported to other neighboring countries through the U.A.E. Rebuilding of parts in the U.A.E. is limited to auto mechanics offering their clients an extra service in their maintenance of cars.

The 5% import duty for new parts also applies to remanufactured or used parts. The use of the company logo as well as the original packing design is not allowed for reconditioned/used parts. As there is a complete difference in packing from the original, advertising costs for resellers of reconditioned/used parts are higher even though the quality of the product is similar. It will not be easy to lend credibility to reconditioned/used parts in this market and a lot of effort would need to be put into the process of establishing a brand.

Local Standards Requirements:

GSO Standards tests for retreaded tires: -
http://www.esma.gov.ae/SiteCollectionDocuments/ECAS/ECAS-RT.pdf

OPPORTUNITIES

There are a number of areas within the automotive sector that provide U.S. companies increased opportunities in the U.A.E. market:

For additional analytical, marketing, investment and business opportunities information, please contact Global Investment & Business Center, USA (202) 546-2103. Fax: (202) 546-3275. E-mail: rusric@erols.com

- The Abu Dhabi Government's new initiative to develop 'The Auto City' in the Mussafah area. The cluster will cater to advanced workshops and service centers thereby attracting investment in automobile manufacturing and spare part logistics.

- Remanufactured Parts: With local government bodies showing increased commitment on greener technologies, commercial vehicles remanufactured parts should find increased acceptance.

- Luxury Vehicles: Lifestyle changes in the U.A.E. provide opportunities for U.S. manufacturers to supply luxury vehicles, RVs, specialty vehicles, etc.

- Automotive Aftermarket: With increased acceptance for U.S. manufactured parts and accessories, U.S. based OEM supplies of Japanese, European and U.S. vehicles might find opportunities to supply goods to the U.A.E. market.

In the Used Car Market Sector, U.A.E. consumers increasingly want to buy U.S. products to cater to the growing demand for used car market sector, specifically targeting:

- Classic car buyers
- Modified vehicles buyers; and
- Performance vehicle buyers

WEB RESOURCES

- http://www.rak-realestate.de/rak_pic/d03/d03i/Auto%20Survey%20report-12-1-10l.pdf
- http://www.uaeinteract.com/docs/
- http://www.zawya.com/
- http://trade.gov/static/autos_report

CONSTRUCTION

The U.A.E. lies between 22°30' and 26°10' north latitude and between 51° and 56°25' east longitude. It shares a 530-kilometer border with Saudi Arabia on the west, south, and southeast, and a 450-kilometer border with Oman on the southeast and northeast. It is in a strategic location along southern approaches to the Strait of Hormuz, a vital transit point for world crude oil.

- Area is 32,278 sq miles.

- Environmental concerns & Natural hazards: frequent sand and dust storms.

- Climate: The U.A.E. climate is generally hot and humid. The hottest months are July and August, when average maximum temperatures reach above 50.°C (About122 °F).

Construction is the third largest sector of the economy, after oil and trade. The construction sector has been a primary beneficiary of the oil boom and surge in investment. While the construction sector contributed 10.3% to the U.A.E. GDP in 2011, it was projected to contribute 11.1% in 2014.

The Emirates of Abu Dhabi and Dubai act as the country's drivers of growth. Dubai's real estate market is looking stronger and more sustainable with Abu Dhabi's market remained stable through the first and second quarters of 2014. However, a growing pipeline of projects in the

For additional analytical, marketing, investment and business opportunities
information, please contact
Global Investment & Business Center, USA
(202) 546-2103. Fax: (202) 546-3275. E-mail: rusric@erols.com

capital may increase construction spend. The activity in the Northern Emirates retains a focus on resort style hospitality projects as demand in the hospitality sector continues to grow.

The construction industry in the U.A.E. grew by 5% during 2014 to a value of $ 39 bn, and is expected to grow to $ 42.3 bn in 2015. However, during the third quarter of 2014, many projects in Abu Dhabi were slowed down, and some were put on hold, due to the drop in oil prices. For Dubai, lower oil prices pose minimal threat to this outlook, given the importance of infrastructure spending and strong growth in tourism.

The U.A.E. is leading the region in green building with the highest share of green buildings in the Middle East and North Africa. 65% of green buildings in region are found in U.A.E..

The Emirate of Abu Dhabi has a set of building codes that incorporate substantial sustainable construction requirements, particularly in water and energy consumption. Both Dubai and Abu Dhabi realize the importance of introducing sustainable architecture, design, engineering, and construction standards within their particular emirate. For example, Dubai implement provisions where all new construction projects must follow Leadership in Energy and Environmental Design (LEED) standards.

Transportation amount to 13% of the total U.A.E. construction spend, commercial amount to 62%, industrial 19%, energy and resources account for 19% and residential for 3%.

Construction projects depend on the availability of resources. The U.A.E. must compete with its two neighbors that have very strong investment plans; Qatar & Saudi Arabia. The awarding of the FIFA World Cup 2022 to Qatar will see $100 bn invested, out of which about 40% in infrastructure; meanwhile, in Saudi Arabia the construction sector is growing at about 4% per year and the country is looking to spend $500 bn on transportation, energy and education facilities.

SUB-SECTOR BEST PROSPECTS

All facets of sustainable technology are needed within the U.A.E.. There is a desire to find U.S. companies that can lead a green project from the very start of design to its ultimate completion. This includes providing the materials and leading the management of the sustainable project.

There is also a great need for companies that can modify existing buildings to become more energy efficient.

OPPORTUNITIES

In 2014, the U.A.E. construction market continued to grow by investments in infrastructure and the hospitality industry.

The Expo 2020 will focus around a planned 438-hectare site, the largest ever created for a World Expo. Located in Jebel Ali, construction at the Expo 2020 site is expected to cost between $2bn to $ 4 bn. The site will feature 180 purpose built pavilions, an underground service rail network and a photovoltaic canopy capable of producing 50% of the site's power. The master plan for the site will not receive approval until the end of 2015, with work expected to commence shortly afterwards and be completed for 2019. Given the centerpiece role of the project and full governmental backing.

For additional analytical, marketing, investment and business opportunities information, please contact
Global Investment & Business Center, USA
(202) 546-2103. Fax: (202) 546-3275. E-mail: rusric@erols.com

Away from the site itself, other major infrastructure projects are set to receive new attention and be driven towards completion thanks to the 2020 event. An estimated $1.3 bn is to be invested in transport to and from the expo event. This includes expansion to the Dubai metro network. Projects such as Nakheel's The World are reportedly being fast-tracked to be ready in time for the expo and we also expect activity at major projects such as the Mohammed bin Rashid City and residential and business districts in and around Dubai World Central Airport to pick up.

Thanks to efforts to support the diversification of the economy of the emirates, through programs such as Abu Dhabi's 2030 vision for development, there remains much opportunity in the infrastructure investment space, despite the gains already made in the U.A.E.'s market. In March 2014, Dubai Electricity and Water Authority (Dewa) announced three major power expansion projects worth $5.4 billion, including solar and clean coal. The $25 billion U.A.E. rail system, including the Blue, Gold and Purple metro lines and the Jumeirah tram in Dubai have all been approved for construction.

Al Maktoum International Airport expansion (DWC) is anticipated to be the biggest airport in the world. This is followed by a massive industrial project in Abu Dhabi for Tacaamol - Al-Gharbia Chemicals Industrial City, planned at $20 billion. There are other sectors with several billions being planned on capital projects, with the top sector for 2015 being mixed-use and residential projects amounting to $24 billion.

List of major projects include:

1. Dubai International Airport expansion $ 7.8 Bn
2. Baraka Nuclear Power Plant: Reactor 3 Power $ 4.00 Bn
3. Upper Zakum Full Field: Early Production Facility: Offshore: EPC 2 $ 3.790 Bn
4. Baraka Nuclear Power Plant: Reactor 1 Power $ 3.100 Bn
5. Abu Dhabi Airport Expansion: Midfield Terminal Complex Transport $ 2.960 Bn
6. Baraka Nuclear Power Plant: Reactor 2 Power $ 2.500 Bn
7. Ruwais Carbon Black and Delayed Coker Project Oil $ 2.470 Bn
8. Dubai Pearl: Towers Construction $ 2.400 Bn
9. North East Bab Field Development: Phase 3: Al Dabbiya Field Oil $ 2.250 Bn
10. Baraka Nuclear Power Plant: Reactor 4 Power $ 2.00 Bn
11. Abu Dhabi Alumina Refinery (Shaheen) Industrial $ 2.00 Bn

WEB RESOURCES

Abu Dhabi Urban Planning Council - http://www.upc.gov.ae
Emirates Green Building Council - http://www.emiratesgbc.org
Dubai Municipality - http://www.dm.gov.ae
Abu Dhabi Department of Municipal Affairs - http://dma.abudhabi.ae
Abu Dhabi Municipality - http://www.abudhabi.ae
The Abu Dhabi Executive Council - http://www.gsec.abudhabi.ae

CONSUMER ELECTRONICS

The U.A.E. retains its position as a leading global consumer electronics market. Thanks to its strong domestic demand that is ever growing and its strategic location as an international business hub serving the GCC and the rest of the world. Located at the crossroads of Asia, Africa and Europe, the electronics distributors of the U.A.E. serve a potential market of almost 2 billion consumers.

For additional analytical, marketing, investment and business opportunities information, please contact
Global Investment & Business Center, USA
(202) 546-2103. Fax: (202) 546-3275. E-mail: rusric@erols.com

In recent years, the domestic market in the U.A.E. has steadily become more significant in relation to re-export trade. The U.A.E. is the preferred testing ground for multinational consumer electronics companies for new product launches and marketing initiatives. The U.A.E.'s consumer electronics devices market, categorized as computing devices, mobile handsets and video, audio and gaming products, is estimated to reach a value of US$4.7bn by 2016, driven by the popularity of new electronic devices such as LED and 3G TV sets, 3G mobile handsets, smart phones, feature-rich notebooks, MP3/MP4 players and Blu-ray players. Spending on AV products will gain momentum from demand for new high-tier products such as 3D and LED TV sets. SLR cameras, high-end camera phones and smartphones are also popular products.

Unit: U.S.$ millions

Consumer Electronics (Computers, Video, Audio & Gaming, Communications)	2013	2014 (estimated)	2015 (forecast)	2016 (forecast)
Total Market Size	4291	4678	5089	5522
Total Imports	4291	4678	5089	5522
Imports from the U.S.	1419	1607	1836	2114

SUB-SECTOR BEST PROSPECTS

The U.A.E.'s consumer electronics devices market, defined as the addressable market for computing devices, mobile handsets and video, audio and gaming products, reached a value of US$4.3bn in 2014. This is expected to increase to over US$5.1bn by 2017, driven by the popularity of new electronic devices such as LED and 3G TV sets, 3G mobile handsets, smartphones, feature-rich notebooks, MP3/MP4. The rising number of devices and migration to cloud computing solutions expose organizations to a growing number of cybersecurity threats. Improving awareness of these threats combined with increased government support will underpin robust demands for cybersecurity solutions in tandem with cloud-based IT services.

OPPORTUNITIES

Investment in e-government and computers for education will lead to computer deployments in schools and government offices, while demand will also be strong in the SME and consumer segments. Telecoms operators have launched a range of managed services and corporate solutions for SMEs in the U.A.E., which we expect to drive demand for new PCs and tablets. Spending will grow at a CAGR of 9% through to 2017, led by notebooks, which account for over 60% of spending. Growth drivers will include demand for premium HD TV sets, with the roll-out of HD TV broadcasting in the U.A.E., and high-end digital cameras. An overall AV spending CAGR of 5% is projected for 2014-2017. Volume sales growth will continue to be healthy because of demand for smartphones. High government and private spending on healthcare will drive demand for IT solutions in the healthcare vertical. Investments across different consumer-centric industries, such as aviation, retail and hospitality, in the run-up to the 2020 World Trade Expo in Dubai should drive demand for IT products and services contracts. The Dubai 2020 World Trade Expo is also expected to attract investments in the wireline sector, particularly in the expansion of next-generation broadband networks.

Trade shows:

Gitex Shopper Website: http://www.gitexshopperdubai.com/

Gitex Technology Week Website: http://www.gitex.com/

Web Resources

Dubai Chamber - www.dubaichamber.com
Business Monitor International - www.businessmonitor.com
Khaleej Times - www.khaleejtimes.com
Middle East Technology News - www.itp.net

COSMETICS/PERFUME

The U.A.E.'s beauty and cosmetics market is growing fast with overall spending expected to reach US$1.3 billion (Dh 4.77 billion) by 2017. The value of imports is projected to increase primarily due to great emphasis on personal grooming and good looks. Such spending is driven not just by mere vanity, but also high consumerism, increased "discretionary" personal incomes and a strong social pressure on wellness.

Accordingly, sales of beauty products benefit from a number of factors, including high disposable income levels in the country, a strong shopping culture, travelling often and being exposed to global lifestyle and trends, and huge influx of tourists. The high demand can also be attributed to the rising trend of men beginning to use a widening range of beauty and personal care products.

Cosmetics is, therefore, one of the fastest growing preferred consumer retail categories in the U.A.E., and the booming market offers promising opportunities for quality U.S. brands. The market has seen a lot of foreign entrants to the market within the last two decades and with the organized retail in the U.A.E. getting further established, it is also creating a demand for more imported cosmetics products. France, Germany, U.K. and the United States have been the traditional suppliers with imports gradually increasing from Turkey, India, China, Thailand, and Eastern European Countries in recent years.

Market Demand

The U.A.E. cosmetics industry's growth is driven by a number of factors, including increasing beauty awareness, high spending power, and wide offerings of beauty and skin care products across international brands. According to industry estimates, in 2012, U.A.E. consumers spent the most on mass cosmetics – 43%, premium cosmetics were the second-most popular – 27%, followed by fragrances – 19% and hair care – 11%.

During that year, the skin care segment had seen a major growth, with both women and men opting to buy more anti-ageing, eye-contouring, sun protection, hair loss, and anti-cellulite products. A trend that's catching up lately is compelling companies to shift from investing in moisturizing creams with skin whitening features to see more toners and anti-ageing creams with similar features.

The organic cosmetics industry and the premium hair products also went up 30% and 25% respectively during that period. It is expected that both sectors will continue to see double-digit growth in the future. The increased preference for "Halal" cosmetics products is compelling local and international companies to adopt business strategies accordingly.

Market Characteristics

In the U.A.E., the beauty sector, comprised of cosmetics and well-being products, hair products, fragrances, etcetera, is growing due to multiple factors. Firstly, the harsh climatic conditions contribute to the demand for hair and skin care products in order to protect against dryness and

For additional analytical, marketing, investment and business opportunities information, please contact
Global Investment & Business Center, USA
(202) 546-2103. Fax: (202) 546-3275. E-mail: rusric@erols.com

damage. Secondly, change in population dynamics and growing income class has also led to disproportionate spending on luxurious beauty products. With young and largely "fashion conscious" population, there is a growing trend towards consumer urbanization and higher spending propensity. Finally, population increase coupled with rise in income has led to growth of the number of spas. The spa culture can also be attributed to increased tourism that the country has lately seen.

Apart from the above, the wide demographic spread in the U.A.E. has compelled companies to import widespread range of products from across the price spectrum. The Cosmetics and Perfumes Sector is thus one of the most competitive, innovative and dynamic sectors. This is mainly due to the current trend to increasingly accept premium beauty care products as an "affordable luxury" by both men and women in the U.A.E..

Technical Requirements

Safety and Quality Requirements:

- Products shall be completely free from substances or derivatives which are prohibited, e.g., Pork, lard, etc., and shall be safe for human health when used under normal or reasonably conditions.

- The product(s) shall comply with the requirements of U.A.E..S GSO 1943

- The product(s) should be homogenous, stable and their properties should not change during its shelf life when stored and used as per the instructions. Cosmetic products, particularly its form, odor, color, appearance, packaging, labeling, volume or size should not be confused for food products as it may result in unintended use (consumption) which may be dangerous.

- The product(s) shall be accompanied by Cosmetic Product Safety Report containing the following:

a) Qualitative and quantitative composition of the cosmetic product, including chemical identity of the substances (incl. chemical name, INCI, CAS, EINECS/ELINCS, where possible) and their intended function. In the case of perfume and aromatic compositions, description of the name and code number of the composition and the identity of the supplier.

b) The physical and chemical characteristics of the substances or mixtures, as well as the cosmetic product.

c) The microbiological specifications of the substance or mixture and the cosmetic product. Particular attention shall be paid to cosmetics used around the eyes, on mucous membranes in general, on damaged skin, on children under three years of age, on elderly people and persons showing compromised immune responses.

d) The purity of the substances and mixtures. In case of traces of prohibited substances, evidence for their technical unavoidability.

For additional analytical, marketing, investment and business opportunities information, please contact
Global Investment & Business Center, USA
(202) 546-2103. Fax: (202) 546-3275. E-mail: rusric@erols.com

e) The normal and reasonably foreseeable use of the product. The reasoning shall be justified in particular in the light of warnings and other explanations in the product labelling.

f) Exposure to the cosmetic product: Data on site(s) of application, the surface area(s) of application, the amount of product applied; the duration and frequency of use; the normal and reasonably foreseeable exposure route(s).

g) Toxicological profile of substances

h) Undesirable effects and serious undesirable effects (if any)

i) Other relevant information, such as, risk assessments carried out elsewhere.

Manufacturing Requirements

Supplying manufacturing organizations must comply with the requirements of ISO 9001 and GSO.ISO 22716.

Further information available at: https://estore.esma.gov.ae/e-store/Default/ICSStandards.aspx?ID=1277

Metrological Requirements

Cosmetics entering the U.A.E. market should comply with the metrological requirements of U.A.E..S GSO OIML R 87.

Packaging Requirements

1. The containers used for cosmetics and personal care products shall comply with article 3 of U.A.E.S/GSO ISO 22715 (packaging and labeling). In the case of glass containers they shall also meet the requirements of U.A.E.S/GSO2093.

2. Cosmetic products must be packed in appropriate containers which are clean, do not interact with the cosmetic product or vice versa, and it shall be ensured that containers are properly closed.

Labeling Requirements

For Cosmetics:

1. Information (textual and non-textual) appearing on the label shall be truthful and accurate and shall not be misleading. It should be in English or Arabic or both and must comply with the requirements of U.A.E.S GSO 1943.

2. The expiry date of the cosmetic product shall be, expressed by 'date of minimum durability' or 'period after opening', to be indicated clearly and precisely. Note: The term date of minimum durability is used in the case of expiry date is equal to or less than thirty months while the term 'period after opening' is used in the case of more than thirty months.

**For additional analytical, marketing, investment and business opportunities information, please contact
Global Investment & Business Center, USA
(202) 546-2103. Fax: (202) 546-3275. E-mail: rusric@erols.com**

3. The date of minimum durability shall be indicated by the month and year or the day, month and year, in that order. In any case it shall be preceded by either the symbol 1 of Annex 4 or by the phrase "best used before the end of". If necessary this information shall be supplemented by an indication of the conditions which must be satisfied to guarantee the stated durability.

4. The period after opening shall be indicated by month and/or years.

5. The above requirements are not applicable in the cases where the concept of the durability after opening is not relevant, that is to say for single-use products, products not at risk of deterioration or products which do not open.

6. All ingredients present in the form of nano-materials shall be clearly indicated in the list of ingredients. The names of such ingredients shall be followed by the word 'nano' in brackets.

7. The following shall not appear on the labeling:

– Pictures and illustrations those are inconsistent with prevailing U.A.E. social customs and values

– Medical claims without authentic evidence.

Further reference available at: http://www.esma.gov.ae/en-us/ESMA/Pages/Laws-and-Legislations.aspx (Refer No. 9)

For perfumes:

Apart from the above requirements, perfumes containing any allergen with concentration more than 0.001%, the presence of these allergens should be mentioned in the list of ingredients, and consumers' attention should be drawn to the presence of these ingredients. In addition, effective July 30, 2014 all perfumes traded in the U.A.E. must bear the Emirates Quality Mark or any other Mark approved by ESMA (consumers' attention should be drawn to the presence of these ingredients. In addition, effective July 30, 2014 all perfumes traded in the U.A.E. must bear the Emirates Quality Mark or any other Mark approved by ESMA (consumers' attention should be drawn to the presence of these ingredients. In addition, effective July 30, 2014 all perfumes traded in the U.A.E. must bear the Emirates Quality Mark or any other Mark approved by ESMA (

Challenges

While the current trend of eco-friendly products is likely to put cost pressures on manufacturers, stiff competition, new product innovation, wide choice of products and aggressive marketing being adopted by major companies provides obvious challenge for U.S. Companies. In addition, the need for products to comply with the U.A.E. cosmetics products regulations viz. labeling, ingredients, etc. might deter new companies from entering the U.A.E. Market. Also, with the introduction of ESMA Standards for cosmetics and perfumes in the U.A.E. and greater acceptance Halal Cosmetics, U.S. companies will do well to prepare for such changes.

SUB-SECTOR BEST PROSPECTS

For additional analytical, marketing, investment and business opportunities information, please contact
Global Investment & Business Center, USA
(202) 546-2103. Fax: (202) 546-3275. E-mail: rusric@erols.com

Perfumes, eye and facial make-up products, lip make-up, facial moisturizers, nourishing, anti-ageing products, skin whitening, etc. lead the sector, followed by hair care, oral/dental hygiene and bathing products.

OPPORTUNITIES

There are a number of areas within the Cosmetics and Personal Care Sectors where increased opportunities prevail. While perfumes, beauty, make-up and skin care products would most likely continue to rule the sector; perfumed bath products, hair preparations and room perfuming/ deodorizing products might see consistent growth in line with improved quality of life. Also, since men make up of around three quarters of the U.A.E. population, products aimed solely at men show good potential. So do products that successfully tap ethnic sensitivities and professional products e.g. halal, salon, spa products. Oral care products category also is one sector that might see high demand.

In addition, the growth of eco-consumerism has created a strong demand for green and natural products, which is expected to remain. Demand for anti-ageing products, which has witnessed increased acceptability in the last few years, is expected to continue.

Trade Events
- Beyond Beauty Arabia – Abu Dhabi & Dubai - www.beyondbeautyarabia.com
- Beauty Secrets Exhibition – Abu Dhabi - www.al-hader.com/index.php
- BeautyWorld Middle East – Dubai - www.beautyworlddubai.com

WEB RESOURCES

- Dubai Municipality: www.dm.gov.ae
- Consumer Product Laboratory Section - Dubai Central Laboratory Department - Dubai Municipality, P.O. Box 67, Dubai, U.A.E. Tel: +971 4 33 69 900; E-mail: labs@dm.gov.ae
;
- Sharjah Municipality, Lab Section, Tel: +971 6 506 8366; Web: www.shjmun.gov.ae
- GSL Product Registration

EDUCATION

Education remains a top government priority as it continues to play a major role in achieving sustainable development in the U.A.E. The U.A.E. government's vision is to continue to provide the highest level of modern education in curricula, technology and environment by creating a high quality, comprehensive education system that applies world-class standards, enhances educational opportunities and improves outcome results across the different emirates. To implement the government policy, the U.A.E. Ministry of Education (MoE) developed Education 2020, a series of an ambitious five-year plan designed to bring significant qualitative improvement in the education system, especially on how teachers deliver curriculum and how students learn. The MoE is currently introducing advanced education techniques in accordance with best practices, applying the 21st century skills in classrooms, improving innovative skills, and developing the self-learning abilities of students.

In addition, among the government main objectives is to incorporate education of information technology, eradicate computer illiteracy, preserve social values and ethics, promote traditional and leadership values among the youth. In 2014, the U.A.E. government allocated US$2.6 billion in education, accounting for 21% of its federal budget, out of which $1.6 billion is spent on

For additional analytical, marketing, investment and business opportunities information, please contact
Global Investment & Business Center, USA
(202) 546-2103. Fax: (202) 546-3275. E-mail: rusric@erols.com

improving general education and $1.03 billion on academic excellence programs in local universities.

Education System

The education system in the U.A.E. is divided into public schools, private schools and higher education. The public schools follow the Arabic curriculum whereas the private schools follow 15 different curricula. Schools following national curricula from the U.K., U.S., India and the U.A.E. MoE cater to 90% of the private school student population. Among other curricula are: International Baccalaureate (IB), Canadian, French, German, Philippines, Pakistani, Iranian and Japanese.

The MoE primary and secondary education is provided for all U.A.E. citizens and is mandatory up to the ninth grade. The existing educational structure, which was established in the early 1970s, is a four tier system covering 14 years of education as per the following:

- Kindergarten – 4 to 5 years old (1-2 years program)
- Primary – 6 to 12 years old (6 years program)
- Preparatory – 12 to 15 years old (3 years program)
- Secondary – 15 to 18 years old (3 years program)

In 2013/2014, number of private schools totaled 459, most of which are in Dubai (169) and Abu Dhabi (185), with an approximate number of 214,587 and 243,715 students in Abu Dhabi and Dubai, respectively; an increase of 9 percent from the last academic year.

PRIVATE SCHOOLS AT A GLANCE (2013/2014)

Region	No. of Private Schools	No. of Students	% of Students National	Expats
Abu Dhabi	114	145,210	22%	79%
Dubai	169	255,208	12%	88%
Sharjah	76	-	-	-
Fujairah	23	-	-	-
Western Region	12	8,993	24%	76%
Al Ain	59	60,384	31%	69%
Ras Al Khaimah	3	-	-	-
Ajman	3	-	-	-

The below figure shows students' distribution per curricula in Abu Dhabi & Dubai. Others curricula include Canadian, French, German, Iranian, Japanese, Pakistan, Philippines, and Russian (only in Dubai).

Among the key school operators in the U.A.E. are, but not limited to, Choueifat, GEMS, Mosaica, Taleem, Innoventures, Al Dar Academies, and Academia Management Solutions International.

Education Entities
The MoE oversees all U.A.E.-based education councils and authorities as per the following:
Abu Dhabi Education Council (ADEC) – Abu Dhabi www.adec.ac.ae
Knowledge and Human Development (KHDA) – Dubai www.khda.gov.ae

For additional analytical, marketing, investment and business opportunities information, please contact
Global Investment & Business Center, USA
(202) 546-2103. Fax: (202) 546-3275. E-mail: rusric@erols.com

Sharjah Educational Council (SEC) www.sec.gov.ae
The Ministry of Education (MoE)
https://www.moe.gov.ae
Ras Al Khaimah Educational Zone (RAKEZ) www.rak.ae
Ajman Educational Zone (AEZ)
Al Ain Educational Zone (ADEZ)
Fujairah Educational Zone (FEZ)
Umm Al Quwain Educational Zone (UAQEZ)

Below is a brief summary of the main educational entities:

a. Abu Dhabi Education Council (ADEC) – Established in 2005, ADEC is the regulatory body that provides licensing and accreditation to private schools in Abu Dhabi, Al Ain and the Western Emirates, sets the minimum standards that must be met in terms of educational outcomes, health, safety, building and site requirements. ADEC works closely with the MoE in formulating the Emirate education plan and focuses on developing the educational system in line with the highest standards by developing and implementing innovative approaches and initiatives.

Since September 2008, all private schools have been required by law to register with ADEC and are inspected to ensure providing a first class education and identifying strengths and weaknesses of schools' performance. The Private Schools and Quality Assurance (PSQA) Sector was established to implement ADEC's strategic plan for the rapid improvement of the school system in the Emirate of Abu Dhabi. PSQA main vision is to:

• Improve the quality of education and academic outcomes;

• Generate satisfactory outcomes for student's personal and social development besides promoting National identity and nurturing the "ideal citizen;" and

• Increase access to provide school by ensuring adequate capacity and affordable school options.

Private schools in Abu Dhabi cater for approximately 214,587 students of different nationalities including 51,925 Emirati students, representing 24% of total number of students registered in private schools. Currently, there are about 184 private schools compared to 255 public schools and 18 higher education institutes operating in 3 different regions, Abu Dhabi, Al Ain and the Western region. Private schools in Abu Dhabi offer 14 main curricula; MOE curricula account for the largest share in private schools followed by English and American curricula, respectively; accounting for 70% of total student enrolment in private schools in 2013/2014.

TOTAL NUMBER OF SCHOOLS IN ABU DHABI / AL AIN / WESTERN REGION

Region	2011/2012	2012/2013	2013/2014
Abu Dhabi	116	117	114
Al Ain	57	57	59
Western Region	10	11	12
Total	183	185	185

NUMBER OF NEWLY OPENED & PROJECTED PRIVATE SCHOOLS IN ABU DHABI

For additional analytical, marketing, investment and business opportunities information, please contact
Global Investment & Business Center, USA
(202) 546-2103. Fax: (202) 546-3275. E-mail: rusric@erols.com

Year	2012/2013	2013/2014	2014/2015	2015/2016
School	9	11	14	20
Seats	9,418	13,000	19,846	44,000

b. Knowledge and Human Development (KHDA) – Established in 2007, KHDA is responsible to inspect all private schools in Dubai to ensure proper quality of education, from early learning to higher and continuing education. Among KHDA activities are publishing education standards and reports, data collection and analysis, the provision of educational services permits, and the supervision of educational institutions on an ongoing basis. In 2014/2015, total number of private schools amounted to 169 compared to 158 schools in 2012/2013, an increase of 11 new schools. Twenty six news schools have opened in the last three years with 11,789 enrolled students. There are three main operators with the most number of schools in Dubai, namely, GEMS education (29 schools), Taaleem (11 schools) and Innoventures (4 schools and 2 nurseries).

So far, the private school sector dominates the education landscape with 89% of Dubai's students enrolled in private schools, out of which 57.4% are Emiratis. It is worth mentioning that the number of students in Dubai's private schools has doubled over the past decade. In 2014/2015 academic year, 255,208 students enrolled in private schools compared to 243,715 in 2013/2014, an increase of 11,493 from 2013/2014. This increase is attributed to the fact of increasing numbers of Emirati students preferring private schools over public schools. Also, needs and expectations of Dubai's expatriate population continue to drive the growth of private schools.

There are about 186 different nationalities attending schools in Dubai. The top ten nationalities are: India, U.A.E., Pakistan, UK, Egypt, Philippines, Jordan, Syria, U.S.A, and Iran.

Curriculum	Number of Schools by Curriculum (Dubai)
British	65
Indian	31
American	31
MOE	12
IB	7
Iranian	6
French	5
Filipino	2
Pakistani	2
SABIS	2
IAT	1
German	1
Russian	1
Japanese	1
Canadian	1
TOTAL	169

c. The Ministry of Education (MoE) – The MoE monitors the education system through secondary level at public schools in the Northern Emirates, namely Sharjah, Ajman, Ras Al Khaimah and Umm Al Quwain. The MoE develops and monitors reform activities focusing on standards and level of education.

For additional analytical, marketing, investment and business opportunities information, please contact
Global Investment & Business Center, USA
(202) 546-2103. Fax: (202) 546-3275. E-mail: rusric@erols.com

ADEC, KHDA and MoE are each tasked with education reform while continue to preserve local traditions, principles and cultural identity.

Higher Education

Higher Education has changed dramatically over the past decades in the U.A.E.. Until 1977, there was only one high education provider, namely the U.A.E. University (U.A.E.U.). However, today, there are more than 80 universities, colleges and higher institutes, admitting over 110,000 students. The U.A.E. has become an international hub for higher education, with global leading universities mainly from the U.S. and Europe. Among international universities are: New York University (NYU), Paris-Sorbonne University, American University, British University, Canadian University, Waterloo University, Wollongong University, etc. All private institutions are required to apply for licensure and accreditation from the Commission for Academic Accreditation (CAA). However, Abu Dhabi and Dubai have developed "free zones."

Higher education institutions can be divided into the following categories:

   a. Federal institutions funded by the U.A.E. government

   b. International universities that have international accreditation and quality assurance

   c. Local universities accredited by the CAA but without international accreditation or quality assurance

   d. Vocational (not awarding degrees)

According to a study conducted by the Dubai International Academic City (DIAC), the U.A.E. is seen as the fourth most attractive education destination for students seeking to pursue their studies abroad. Established in 2007, as part of TECOM Investments, DIAC is the world's only Free Zone dedicated to Higher Education, located on 18 million sq. ft. campus with state-of-the-art modern facilities. Currently, DIAC has 21 of the U.A.E.'s 37 International Branch Campuses from 11 countries with a capacity of hosting nearly 20,000 students from 137 nationalities. DIAC students also have access to over 400 Higher Education programs.

BEST PROSPECTS

- K-12 American Curriculum Schools
- Students & Teachers Leadership Programs
- Programs for Special Needs
- Vocational Training
- IT Education
- Educational Programs and Services

OPPORTUNITIES

The U.A.E. government has committed large funds toward the development of educational infrastructure, realizing the need to invest in educating their future generations to ensure growth and maintain social stability. Due to the transient nature of the expatriate population in the U.A.E., parents prefer enrolling their children within international schools. In addition to this, almost 58% of the U.A.E. nationals send their children to private rather than public schools. Hence, demand for private education has been on the rise in the U.A.E., thus leading to strong growth in the education sector. As indicated by several educational entities and private investors, the private

**For additional analytical, marketing, investment and business opportunities information, please contact
Global Investment & Business Center, USA
(202) 546-2103. Fax: (202) 546-3275. E-mail: rusric@erols.com**

education market will require an addition of 52 educational facilities across multiple curriculums, out of which 10 American schools. Several local operators are in demand to introduce K-12 American schools, especially in Abu Dhabi and Dubai. Local investors/operators are looking for establishing a medium to high American tier schools, assisting in getting accreditation from American accreditation authority, developing curriculum for American schools and recruiting skilled teachers.

One of the emerging segments that deserve attention, as well, is "Smart Learning." A new curriculum with greater emphasis on teaching technology and 21st-century skills will be rolled out to the country's public schools in the 2018-2019 academic year. Teachers and principals will be offered special training and professional development programs focused on teaching innovation in classrooms.

Another growth segment is educational and training programs for Special Needs students. Special education software and educational toys have a high potential and will make learning more interactive. In addition, teachers need to receive training on the different types of speech, language disorders, their causes, methods of diagnosis and different techniques used to assist children with these disorders.

Exhibitions/Conferences

Venue: Abu Dhabi National Exhibitions Center (ADNEC)
Official Website: www.najahonline.com
Organized by: Informa Exhibitions

The International Education Show
Date: February 10-12, 2016
Venue: Expo Centre Sharjah
Official Website: www.educationshow.ae/
Organized by: Sharjah Chamber of Commerce & Industry

Global Education Supplies and Solutions (GESS)
Date: March 1-3, 2016
Venue: Dubai World Trade Center
Official Website: www.gessdubai.com
Organized by: F&E Education

AbilitiesMe
Date: March 1-3, 2016
Venue: Abu Dhabi National Exhibitions Center (ADNEC)
Official Website: www.abilitiesme.com
Organized by: DMG World Media

Gulf Education and Training Exhibition (GETEX)
Date: April 13-15, 2016 (Dubai)
TBA (Abu Dhabi)
Venue: Dubai International Convention & Exhibition Centre
Beach Rotana Hotel (Abu Dhabi)
Official Website: www.mygetex.com
Organized by: International Conferences & Exhibitions IC&E

WEB RESOURCES
Abu Dhabi Education Council: www.adec.ac.ae

For additional analytical, marketing, investment and business opportunities
information, please contact
Global Investment & Business Center, USA
(202) 546-2103. Fax: (202) 546-3275. E-mail: rusric@erols.com

Knowledge & Human Development Authority: www.khda.gov.ae
Ministry of Education: www.moe.gov.ae
U.A.E. Embassy in Washington DC: www.U.A.E.cd.org
UNICEF: www.unicef.org

FRANCHISING

The franchise industry in the U.A.E. continues to maintain a positive momentum, driven by social and economic developments. Among the key major factors influencing the franchise industry is its economic growth, high purchasing power among consumers, growing population comprising a large percentage of expatriates, consumption patterns and the increasing penetration of international franchise brands. Franchising has developed quite extensively in the U.A.E. over a short time, especially in the fast-food sector. American, French, and British brands continue to expand and dominate the market in sectors, such as fast-food and fashion retail followed by Spain and Italy. However, the scenario has started changing and franchise opportunities are available in diverse sectors of the economy and many Asian franchisors started to enter the market.

With Dubai winning to host Expo 2020, a number of projects are being implemented to support the huge anticipated inflow of tourists, supporting to boost the infrastructure, hospitality, tourism, franchise and retail sectors in the U.A.E.. Expo 2020 will host exhibitors from 180 destinations and over 25 million visitors.

Retail outlets, fast food, casual dining franchises are mostly concentrated in the largest emirates of Abu Dhabi and Dubai. However, it is worth mentioning that the federal government plans to pursue a large scale infrastructure program in the north and to bring significant investment opportunities, particularly in Ajman, Ras Al Khaimah and Sharjah.

Though the government encourages entrepreneurs to work on franchising, until now, the U.A.E. franchise market has witnessed supremacy of few big retail conglomerates having multi-brands in their portfolio and the Master Franchisee arrangements. Among the well-known and strong franchise operators in the U.A.E. are: Majid Al Futtaim (MAF), Al Futtaim Group (AFG), Al Tayer, Landmark Group, Al Shaya and Chaloub Group, Apparel Group, and Al Ahli Group. However, the trend is for small franchisees and sub-franchising as the government and Chambers of Commerce in the U.A.E. have started to focus and promote the franchise sector to induce growth and development of small and medium size businesses.

At present, there are hundreds of international franchises in the U.A.E.; 47% are U.S. food franchises, followed by British, French, Spanish, Italian and lately Asian brands. The focus has also started to diversify from food franchises to non-food sectors, such as services in the field of cleaning, laundry, automotive, nurseries, management and education.

Though it is difficult to give an estimate of the current food franchise market size, the U.A.E. fast food market, dominated by American chains, has experienced notable expansion, and market sources expect the growth to continue with 250 stores opening across the Middle East and brands, such as Shake Shack, Red Lobster and Texas Roadhouse will continue to expand their franchises in the U.A.E..

Based in Kuwait, Americana Group is considered to be the leader in bringing Western food to the region. Americana Group is the franchise partner for a number of American food companies, such as KFC, Pizza Hut (both owned by Yum Brands) and TGI Fridays. Among new U.S. brands introduced in early 2014 include BOA Steakhouse, recently opened in Abu Dhabi, and Lemonade

For additional analytical, marketing, investment and business opportunities information, please contact
Global Investment & Business Center, USA
(202) 546-2103. Fax: (202) 546-3275. E-mail: rusric@erols.com

Restaurant in Dubai. It is worth to mention that Denny's, U.S. restaurant chain, signed a franchise agreement with U.A.E.-based Advance Investment, an affiliate of Food Quest Restaurant Management to open 30 restaurants in the Middle East over the coming 10 years, with its first opening in the U.A.E. by late 2015. In addition, 7-Eleven, the largest operator of convenience stores in the world, signed an agreement with Abu Dhabi-based Seven Emirates Investment to operate 100 stores in the U.A.E. through 2017 with the first store expected to open in late 2015.

Other well-established U.S. brands in the U.A.E. are: McDonalds, Johnny Rockets, Burger King, Wendy's, Shack Shake, Elevation Burger, Baskin Robbins, Haagen Dazs, Cinnabon, Popeye's, Chili's, Cheese Cake Factory, Hardee's, Round Table Pizza, Tony Roma's, Johnny Carino's, Dunkin Donuts, Krispy Kreme Doughnuts, among others. Among the newly introduced brands are: Five Guys (U.S.), Papa's Murphy Pizza, and Project Pie (opening soon)

Among other well-established non-U.S. brands are: Mugg & Bean, the Butcher Shop Grill and Nando's from South Africa, Kono Pizza, Pizza Express, Rossovivo, Al Forno and Santino's from Italy, the French Bakery, Paul, La Brioche, Paul from France, New York Fries from Canada, and Burger Fuel from New Zealand.

In addition to fast food and casual dining restaurants, the coffee shops' concept works very well in the U.A.E. and is on the rise, especially in Abu Dhabi and Dubai, serving as convenient places for businesses, families and friends to meet. According to the International Coffee Organization, the U.A.E. has one of the highest per capita coffee consumption in the world. Currently, Starbucks (U.S.), Costa (UK), the Coffee Bean & Tea Leaf (U.S.), Tim Horton's (Canada), Black Canyon (Asia) will continue to expand in the U.A.E..

On the other hand, non-food sector has started to gain popularity. Non-food franchises have a large market potential. Several new franchisors are actively planning to enter the U.A.E. market, and opportunities exist for additional U.S. franchise development. A number of companies in the fields of retail, hotel management, car rental, language education, health, fitness, electronics, and computer training are currently franchised in the U.A.E..

Many of the world's leading department stores are present in the U.A.E., offering the top retail brands, such as US-based Saks Fifth Ave., Bloomingdale's, the UK's Harvey Nichols, Debenhams (UK), and Marks and Spencer (UK). Macy's, one of the biggest department stores in the U.S. is planning to open at the capital's Al Maryah Island by 2018 offering a space of 205,000 square feet. The opening of a Macy's would be the first store outside the US and the department store's first entry into the region.

Among other non-food franchise brands are: Sketchley Laundry (UK), Sylvan Learning (U.S.) Nutty Scientists (U.S.), and Kidville (U.S.). Among retail franchise brands are: Virgin Megastores (UK), Hertz Car Rental (U.S.), Dial-A-Battery (New Zealand), DAISO (Japan), etc.

Local franchise brands started to expand locally and internationally. Among the famous local food and beverage brands are: "Just Falafel," "Café to Go," "X-Presse Café," "Reem Al Bawadi," and "Bateel." It's worthwhile to mention that Reem Al Bawadi Restaurant & Café, the themed family restaurant renowned for authentic Middle Eastern cuisine, has launched an international franchising model with plans to open new outlets over the next two years. Also, Bateel, famous for its gourmet products of chocolates, dates and pastries is currently operating in more than 12 countries.

For the non-food sector, Heritage for Henna has been growing rapidly since 2002 with 28 henna majalis located in stylish locations throughout the Emirates. Henna was one of the first beauty

For additional analytical, marketing, investment and business opportunities information, please contact
Global Investment & Business Center, USA
(202) 546-2103. Fax: (202) 546-3275. E-mail: rusric@erols.com

products ever developed with its rich colored dyes used in body painting across the Middle East and Asia. Established in 2008, Bedashing Beauty Lounge is a modern trendsetting beauty lounge offering the latest beauty treatments.

There is no franchise legislation or law in the U.A.E.. All franchise agreements are subject to civil and commercial laws, namely the Commercial Agencies Law, the Commercial Transactions and the Civil Transactions Law (Federal Law No. 18 of 1981 on the Organization of Commercial Agencies, amended by Federal Law No. 14 of 1988, and further amended by Federal Law No. 13 of 2006 and Federal Law No. 2 of 2010, namely the "Commercial Agencies Law"). Also, the principles of Sharia law apply to commercial transactions. Special consideration must be given to Islamic dietary laws, meat and by-meat products must be halal, and NO pork or alcohol content is permitted.

As per the U.A.E. law, only U.A.E. nationals or companies wholly owned by U.A.E. nationals or those with a U.A.E. partner or sponsor are permitted to carry out franchise operations. The Commercial Agencies Law has potential application not only to what would be strictly considered as agency agreements in many foreign jurisdictions but also to agreements regarding franchises, distributorships, commission arrangements, dealerships and other forms of sales representative or sales agency relationships. Registering the franchise agreement is more in favor of protecting the franchisee. It is worth to mention that only about 30% franchisees are registered in the U.A.E.. The Ministry of Economy recommends that franchise contracts must be registered with the U.A.E. Federal Ministry of Economy and must meet the following criteria:

- The franchisee must be a U.A.E. national or an entity that is wholly owned by U.A.E. nationals;

- The franchise agreement must grant exclusivity over all or part of the U.A.E.; and

- The franchise agreement must be registered and notarized.

It is recently notable that local retail businesses have started to franchise their business. This indicates that the franchise concept is acceptable within the region's cultural settings and shows an entrepreneurial spirit among the region's businesses.

BEST PROSPECTS

- Casual Dining and Fast Food
- Healthcare Services
- Childcare Services
- Education Services/Centers
- Entertainment Centers
- Automotive Services

OPPORTUNITIES

Benefits of Franchising in the U.A.E.:

- Considerable growth potential and investment opportunities.

- The U.A.E., especially Dubai and Abu Dhabi, is an ideal place for global luxury brands, with a long-term plan to extend investment projects in the northern emirates.

For additional analytical, marketing, investment and business opportunities information, please contact
Global Investment & Business Center, USA
(202) 546-2103. Fax: (202) 546-3275. E-mail: rusric@erols.com

• Businesses, located in the multiple free zones, enjoy tax exemption.

• The franchise sector gets ample of support from the U.A.E. government.

• The U.A.E. has a large and high-spending expatriate population.

• Investors continue to view the U.A.E. as a secured investment destination compared to other countries in the region.

Helpful Tips for New-to-Market Franchisors

• Due diligence while selecting the proper franchisee.

• Awareness of the U.A.E. Commercial Agencies Laws and other relevant laws.

• Consultation with a local legal franchise expert.

• The franchisor should carefully draft the franchise contract and operations manual for the franchisee specifying the manner in which the franchise is to be operated.

• The franchise agreement should:

o Serve as a foundation for both parties understanding the terms and operations of a franchise.

o State clearly the rights and duties of the franchisor as well as the franchisee.

o Be prepared by a legal franchise expert.

• The franchisor should also take steps to protect its intellectual property (IP) comprising its logos, trademarks, business process against potential misuse by its franchise partner.

• Awareness of the U.A.E. labor law and municipality rules.

Exhibitions/Conferences

Middle East Franchise Expo
Dates: October 20-21, 2015
Venue: Jumeirah Beach Hotel Convention Center - Dubai
Organized by: Middle East & North Africa Franchise Association (MENAFA)
www.menafa.com/expo

The 3rd International Franchise Conference & Franchise Catalogue Show
Dates: November 18-19, 2015
Venue: Abu Dhabi
Organized by: Abu Dhabi Chamber of Commerce & Industry (ADCCI)

WEB RESOURCES
Abu Dhabi Chamber: www.abudhabichamber.ae
Dubai Chamber: www.dubaichamber.com

**For additional analytical, marketing, investment and business opportunities information, please contact
Global Investment & Business Center, USA
(202) 546-2103. Fax: (202) 546-3275. E-mail: rusric@erols.com**

U.A.E. Ministry of Foreign Trade: www.moft.gov.ae
Business Monitor International: www.businessmonitor.com

HEALTHCARE SERVICES

The United Arab Emirates (U.A.E.) is among the top 40 largest medical device markets in the world and ranks fourth in the Middle East & Africa (MEA) region. Manufacturing capability is limited, therefore the market will continue to rely on imported medical devices. Population growth, a growing medical tourism industry, continuous healthcare infrastructure developments, expanding health insurance and increasing health expenditure which are all factors contributing to market growth.

Healthcare expenditure as percentage of GDP represented an estimated 3.4% in 2014, equal to USD13.8bn, and will continue at that level in the coming years. Per capita health expenditure will remain high regionally and globally, estimated US$1,465 in 2014. Although spending increased by a 2009-2014 CAGR of 8.3%, reports indicate that the U.A.E. still needs to increase health expenditure, particularly in the Northern Emirates. The U.A.E. is a zero-tax country, with excellent transportation and logistics infrastructure and is geographically well positioned to be the commercial hub in the region. These factors make it an attractive location for establishing a regional distribution center for medical devices. Healthcare is regulated at both the federal and Emirate level. Registration of medical devices is regulated by the U.A.E. Ministry of Health. The regulation of medical devices in the U.A.E. is aimed at maintaining a balance between product safety, quality and effectiveness.

Other Medical Devices Market CAGR (Compound Annual Growth Rate)

2008-2018 (%)

MARKETING PRODUCTS AND SERVICES

DISTRIBUTION AND SALES CHANNEL

The most commonly used way of selling into the UAE is by appointing a commercial agent. Other methods used, depending on the product or service, include direct sales to the end-user; sales through an informal, nonexclusive re-seller arrangement; establishment of a company presence through a joint venture; or authorization to a local firm via a licensing or franchising arrangement.

US exporters sometimes find it advantageous to appoint different commercial agents or distributors for different emirates. Multiple agencies and distributorships may also be appointed to handle diverse product lines or services. Many UAE companies handle numerous product lines, making it sometimes difficult to promote all products effectively.

DISTRIBUTION AND SALES CHANNELS – AGRICULTURE

There are numerous food importers, many of whom are also wholesalers, distributors, and retailers. Four to five companies dominate the retail food sector. Many fruit and vegetable importers also import eggs.

Dubai is a major transshipment center for a variety of food products. It is estimated that about 60% of total UAE food imports are re-exported to other destinations, primarily other Gulf countries, India, Africa and, increasingly, the NIS.

For additional analytical, marketing, investment and business opportunities information, please contact
Global Investment & Business Center, USA
(202) 546-2103. Fax: (202) 546-3275. E-mail: rusric@erols.com

USE OF AGENTS/DISTRIBUTORS: FINDING A PARTNER

The UAE legal system distinguishes between the two forms of commercial agents- the registered and the unregistered commercial agent. Local companies prefer to work as registered agents for the law favors this arrangement. On occasion, local companies will accept to go the unregistered way based on good faith, but almost always prefer exclusivity.

UAE law does not distinguish between an agent and distributor, referring to both as commercial agents. The Ministry of Economy and Commerce handles registration of commercial agents.

The provisions relating to commercial agencies are collectively set out in Federal Law No. 18 of 1981 on the Organization of Commercial Agencies as amended by Federal Law No. 14 of 1988 (the Agency Law) and applies to all registered commercial agents. Federal Law No. 18 of 1993 (Commercial) and Federal Law No. 5 of 1985 (Civil Code) govern unregistered commercial agencies. Federal law is applicable throughout the UAE.

Selection of the right agent is the most important decision. Registered agents may not be terminated, except with sufficient cause as determined by a government committee that has usually ruled in favor of the local agent. In most cases, compensation to a terminated agent is required even if the committee rules for the foreign firm. Only UAE nationals or companies wholly owned by UAE nationals can register with the Ministry of Economy and Commerce as local agents.

Agency contracts: Terms and conditions vary. Commissions and other forms of compensation typically depend on the amount of work required of the agent and sales volume. Responsibilities and performance measures should be clearly defined. Establish the geographic territory covered (UAE law awards automatic exclusivity to the agent in the geographic area covered by the agreement). An agent must have a presence and be licensed to operate in each emirate, as there is no blanket license for the whole of the UAE. In some instances agents have been appointed on a project basis, with the relationship restricted to the specified project terminating automatically upon reward or completion.

FRANCHISING

The UAE is very receptive to franchising. High per capita income, receptivity to new products, tax-free earnings and an upwardly mobile population are indicators of the future growth potential for this market. Currently, franchises are operating in fast foods; dine-in restaurants; auto leasing; apparel; soft drink bottling; beauty products; hotels; toys; photography; jewelry; vending machines; dry cleaning; furniture; hardware stores; office supplies; natural health products; publications; quick printing; garden care and florists; sporting goods; retail/convenience stores; maid and personal services. Today, the largest segment in this industry is fast food with most major US. fast food companies already established. There remains considerable potential for franchises of all kinds.

General contract and commercial law apply to franchise agreements as no special legislation for franchise arrangements are currently in place. Franchise operation rights in the UAE are usually owned 100% by a single company or individual. In other cases, the franchisee enters into a joint venture with the franchisor to operate all outlets as "company owned" stores employing local managers.

DIRECT MARKETING

The only time direct marketing can come into play is when you sell to the end user. Under local law the international company would still need to honor the commission payable to its local agent or distributor even if they had no part in the sale. Direct sale to the end-user approach is suitable

For additional analytical, marketing, investment and business opportunities information, please contact
Global Investment & Business Center, USA
(202) 546-2103. Fax: (202) 546-3275. E-mail: rusric@erols.com

only for infrequent, low volume exports as marketing in the UAE is very competitive.

Other than adverts in newspapers and magazines the only other forms of direct marketing in the UAE is by way of limited unsolicited mail, fax and catalog sales campaigns (with local pick-up or delivery arranged). Commercials via TV and satellite channels offer an effective direct marketing approach reaching conservative UAE and expatriate women in the privacy of their homes. This method of marketing will to some extent be impacted by the wide usage of the Internet in the UAE as it opens up an unlimited choice of products. Selling over the net will provide possibilities and accessibility to this market that were not available in the past.

JOINT VENTURES/LICENSING

Emphasis is given to personal relationships in the Middle East when conducting business. Maintaining a local presence offers distinct advantages. Local business and government officials prefer to deal with someone they know and trust.

In a joint venture profit and loss distribution can be prescribed even though UAE majority ownership is mandatory. It is not compulsory to license the joint venture or publish the terms of agreement. The foreign partner could deal with third parties under the name of the local venture.

Banks, insurance, and financial companies must be run as public share holding companies requiring a minimum capitalization of Dhs. 10 million (US $2.725 million). The Chairman and the majority of Directors must be UAE nationals, and a more restrictive distribution of profit is enforced as is enforced. Foreign banks, insurance and financial companies can establish a presence in the UAE by operating a branch or representative office which allows 100% foreign ownership, but, in general, limits business activities to offshore operations.

Licensing of manufacturing processes is a growing market, especially with the UAE's desire to increase the quality and diversity of local production. The total market for industrial licenses remains relatively small due to the limited manufacturing done in the UAE.

The majority of licensing in the UAE is done for the fabricating and/or marketing of trademarked items. Licensees of US. sports logos, universities, animated characters, etc., are servicing a very active market with one of the world's highest disposable incomes. License to sell US brand products (an authorized dealer), as distinct from a standard distribution arrangement, or US logos/names/ characters on a non-US product, are becoming very sought after, especially in the apparel market. Licensing effectively meets the current demand, especially among young consumers, for American styles.

ESTABLISHING AN OFFICE

Whether or not to set up an office in the UAE and what kind depends largely on the nature of the business of the US firm. To set up an office, the following procedures must be followed. First, firms must find a local sponsor, both for the firm and for its resident employees. A sponsor may be a UAE citizen or an institution, such as a free zone. The sponsor can be involved in the business, or simply a service sponsor providing, for a fee, legally required administrative functions.

Second, firms have to be licensed by the emirate of domicile before beginning business activities. In general, individual emirates will issue: trade licenses covering all kinds of trading activity, professional licenses covering professions and services, industrial licenses for industrial and manufacturing activities, and vocational licenses for craftsmen and artisans. Licenses for other categories of business require approval from federal ministries and other authorities. For example, banks and financial institutions require approval from the Central Bank of the UAE,

For additional analytical, marketing, investment and business opportunities information, please contact
Global Investment & Business Center, USA
(202) 546-2103. Fax: (202) 546-3275. E-mail: rusric@erols.com

insurance companies and related agencies from the Ministry of Economy and Commerce, manufacturing from the Ministry of Finance and Industry, and pharmaceutical and medical products from the Ministry of Health. More detailed procedures apply to businesses engaged in oil and gas production and related industries.

In addition to the required licenses, all firms must be registered with the Chamber of Commerce in each of the Emirates where the business is licensed to operate. In the UAE, Chambers are part of the government and membership is mandatory.

Percentage of US ownership depends on the business activity and the purpose of the office the US firm wishes to establish. For firms conducting regional marketing or administrative functions, a representational office, allowing 100% ownership, is a possibility. Firms conducting offshore services, a branch office, also allowing 100% ownership, is feasible. Establishing an office in any of the free trade zones available in the UAE, regardless of activity, allows 100% ownership. In a nutshell, US companies are allowed to open representative, branch, or regional offices with a 100 percent ownership, but they are restricted from conducting certain business activities. These offices are not licensed to conduct direct business or marketing operations including obtaining credit facilities, submitting offers and participating in local government tenders.

If a US firm wishes to establish an office to directly conduct business in this market, UAE law requires a joint venture with UAE nationals owning a minimum of 51% of the venture. Current exceptions to this rule include professional or artisan companies where 100% foreign ownership is permitted.

The following documents are required to establish an office in the UAE:

1. Articles of association of the company.
2. Certificate of incorporation.
3. A resolution of the board of directors of the company to set up the office and practice activities in the UAE. The resolution also gives the power of attorney to the representative to establish an office and to submit the required applications to the local government authorities.
4. The last two audited balance sheets of the foreign company together with the auditor's report, any other documents which proves the sound financial position of the company.
5. A copy of the national agent/sponsor agreement duly authenticated.
6. Photocopies of the passport of the national agent/sponsor.
7. A valid lease agreement of the company's office premises.

All the above mentioned documents should be notarized and authenticated by the concerned governmental authorities.

SELLING FACTORS/TECHNIQUES

The commercial tradition of the UAE is that of the middleman or trader acting as a conduit for goods from large manufacturers to South Asia, the Gulf, and East Africa. Today, with Dubai emerging as the hub of the Gulf, the UAE still serves those traditional markets along with those of North, South, West, and Central Africa, and the rest of the Middle East. The business style prevalent is one that puts an emphasis on personal relationships and perceptions of integrity.

Traditional approaches to business are beginning to change. There is a growing emphasis on quality, after-sales service, and maintenance requirements and costs. A new trend of impersonal businessman/consumer has changed some of the business style. However, it does not yet represent the dominant practice. Personal relationships, particularly when UAE nationals are involved, still predominate. Since these relationships take time to nurture, US firms are advised to invest time in the market with preferably a local presence or at least very frequent trips. This is

For additional analytical, marketing, investment and business opportunities information, please contact
Global Investment & Business Center, USA
(202) 546-2103. Fax: (202) 546-3275. E-mail: rusric@erols.com

not an activity that can be done long-distance. Face-to-face contact is essential. In addition, US firms should seek a local sponsor, agent, or partner with sufficient access and influence in those circles most relevant to that particular business.

In addition to personal relationships, price remains most often the dominant buying factor. For US firms selling to traders, which is the dominant business type in the UAE, there is no substitute for price. Government procurement also places heavy emphasis on selection of the low bidder, as long as the lowest price bidder is compliant with all technical specifications.

Even though the UAE is relatively less conservative than some other Gulf states and English is widely spoken, sensitivity to local traditions and Islamic beliefs is essential. The use of Arabic in packaging and advertising is both desirable and effective (and sometimes mandatory) in marketing consumer goods.

ADVERTISING AND TRADE PROMOTION

The UAE, and in particular Dubai, serves as the commercial center for the region. From late September through May, with the exception of the holy month of Ramadan (mid November – mid December 2001), the UAE hosts an almost continuous and growing series of well attended major trade exhibitions and conferences. US firms new to this region are advised to consider participation in one of these shows as an excellent method of market evaluation and initial penetration.

Advertising plays a significant role in sales promotion. The language of business is English. Only about 30% of the population are native Arabic speakers from the UAE or other Arab states. The balance of the population is a mixture of South and East Asians, Iranians, and European/North Americans. However, Arabic is the official language and is required for all governmental documentation. In addition, dual English/Arabic usage is common on signage and for many publications. English-only promotional literature is acceptable, but those that are in both English and Arabic have a decided edge. Arabic speakers in key decision making positions appreciate the extra effort and sensitivity to their culture that bilingual publications imply. Arabic labeling for consumer products, especially foodstuffs, is an important advantage in competitive marketing.

There are four major English language daily newspapers and several weekly and monthly English language magazines that are effective consumer market vehicles. There are also Arabic and third country language publications available. Radio and television broadcasts are primarily in English, Arabic, Hindi and Urdu. The UAE and other Gulf States are Islamic nations and have a different perspective on certain issues than non-Islamic states. US firms are strongly urged to consider cultural sensitivities in any promotional activity.

It is important to stress quality since US consumer goods tend to be higher priced than products from other origins. Gulf consumers recognize the high quality of US products and may be willing to pay a premium for such products. They are highly susceptible to have brand recognition.

PRICING PRODUCTS

For consumer goods, price is the primary buying factor for the middle and lower classes. These market segments are served through small stores and shops in traditional souks, or markets. Retailers in this category operate under razor-thin margins - 1% or 2% is common - and rely on volume. At the other end of the scale are the segments of the society with large purchasing power made up of the majority of the UAE nationals, 15% of the 3 million population expatriate residents, and business and tourist visitors who exceed a million each year. For this group, price is not a primary buying factor and retail margins are exceptionally high. These segments are serviced through specialty shops. US exporters must be ready to use pricing aggressively to

For additional analytical, marketing, investment and business opportunities information, please contact
Global Investment & Business Center, USA
(202) 546-2103. Fax: (202) 546-3275. E-mail: rusric@erols.com

encourage market acceptance of their products main features.

The average importer markup on food products is about 10-15%. Retail food prices are generally 20-25% above import/wholesale prices.

SALES SERVICE/CUSTOMER SUPPORT

The commercial and industrial markets are very competitive. For these markets price is also a key purchase factor, but quality, durability, and after-sales service are increasingly becoming dominant determinants for purchases by government and business. The increasing emphasis on after-sales service favors those products backed by local distributors with adequate part stocks and routine maintenance capabilities. The training of qualified maintenance and repair personnel is a critical marketing factor when catering to the more sophisticated end of the market.

SELLING TO THE GOVERNMENT

Government buyers are either federal or emirate governments. Federal purchases are administered through the respective local authority in Abu Dhabi or Dubai. For most civilian purchases, government entities will usually only deal with firms registered in the UAE, or the particular emirate, and will favor local products over imports. Only when a good or service of acceptable quality is not available locally will the procurement authority seek outside sources. It is common for bids not to go out on a public tender, but are sent to select firms that were pre-qualified with the organization in question.

For all types of government procurement and projects, US firms are encouraged to seek a presence in the UAE and get their goods/services pre-qualified for procurement tenders.

Competition in the public sector is very strong. Besides large military procurement projects, governments in the UAE invest heavily in infrastructure projects, such as roads, power generation and distribution systems, desalination facilities, sewage systems, public housing, recreational facilities, hospitals and other medical facilities and services, schools, athletic facilities, refineries and other hydrocarbon facilities, airports, and government buildings. US goods and services enjoy an outstanding reputation for quality, but, with the exception of hydrocarbon-related industries, are under- represented in this market.

PROTECTING YOUR PRODUCT FROM COPYRIGHT INFRINGEMENT

The UAE has been a major center for the production, sale, and export of pirated and counterfeit products. However, during the last five years the UAE government has passed new Intellectual Property Rights (IPR) laws and stepped up enforcement actions aimed at reducing or eliminating such practices, and bringing its IPR regime up to international standards. In April 2000, the UAE was removed from USTR's Special 301 IPR Watch List. In 2001, it was put back on due to limited pirating of US patent-protected pharmaceutical products. The UAE, however, has the best record in the Middle East when it comes to copyright protection for music software and films.

NEED FOR A LOCAL ATTORNEY

There are some general points that firms should consider before doing business in the UAE. First, the legal system of the UAE is very different from that of the US. Prior to the modern era, business was conducted according to the dictates of religious law (Sharia) and traditional custom. Codified law based on modern norms is new and is still evolving, as are practices based on the law, such as court and other legal procedures. Second, where laws appear to govern certain practices according to commonly accepted principles, terms and definitions are often at variance with usual interpretations. What the law says is one thing; how it is carried out in practice may be another. Third, the requirements of licensing, registration, sponsorship, immigration, and labor

**For additional analytical, marketing, investment and business opportunities information, please contact
Global Investment & Business Center, USA
(202) 546-2103. Fax: (202) 546-3275. E-mail: rusric@erols.com**

laws, as well as the difficulty of termination of agency agreements, partnership requirements, and preferences given to locals in dispute resolution, amongst other differences with the US system, argue strongly for US firms to consult local legal counsel. There are many law firms with experience in dealing with US clients, and some US attorneys experienced in the local market.

NEED FOR PRECAUTIONARY MEASURES

One of the most important issues to a number of US companies contemplating establishing agency relationships is their prospective ability to terminate a registered agency. It is very difficult for US firms to terminate their agreements with local companies. To date this has been done only after the US company has paid considerable amounts of money to buy their way out of an agreement. The UAE Law provides the right for local companies to maintain their agencies irrespective of any specific performance criteria which may have been agreed by the parties. In other words, establishing justified cause for termination of an agreement before the concerned authorities may be impossible, even in cases where the agent has failed to perform. The best protection is serious research and due diligence prior to embarking on an agreement. Further, an agreement should be done only after receiving competent legal advice on how to structure the document. Depending on the agreement, a few of the items that should be specified are the performance measures, the length of the contract, and some of the projects included.

TRADE REGULATIONS AND STANDARDS

TRADE BARRIERS, INCLUDING TARIFFS, NON-TARIFF BARRIERS AND IMPORT TAXES

The United Arab Emirates (UAE) maintains a free exchange and liberal trade system. The Gulf Cooperation Council (GCC), grouping the UAE, Saudi Arabia, Kuwait, Bahrain, Qatar, and Oman has been discussing a common external tariff for some years. In a step toward establishing a common external tariff, the UAE in 1994 took the decision to raise its import duties from one to four percent.

Each emirate operates its own customs authority. An agreement has been reached by the various local customs departments for the creation of UAE Customs Council. The Customs Council's main priority is to create a customs union within the UAE to unify Customs rules and regulations, procedures and documentation.

Only firms with the appropriate trade license can engage in importation. Documentation requirements follow international standards and delays in custom clearance have been infrequent. The competition for business between the port facilities of the different emirates has kept user rates to a minimum and put a premium on services. There are no duties on exports. For religious and security reasons, there are various restrictions on import of alcohol, tobacco, firearms, and pork products.

The UAE maintains non-tariff barriers to trade and investment, in the form of restrictive agency/sponsorship/distributorship requirements and restrictive shelf-life requirements for foodstuffs.

In order to do business in the UAE outside of one of the free zones (see below), a foreign business must have a UAE national sponsor, agent, or distributor. Once chosen, sponsors, agents, or distributors have exclusive rights for non-food products only. Agency law does not pertain to food products. Agents and distributors cannot be easily replaced without their agreement. Government tendering is not conducted according to generally accepted international standards. Retendering is the norm, often as many as three or four times. To bid on federal projects, a supplier or contractor must either be a UAE national or a company in which UAE nationals own at least 51% of the share capital. Federal tenders are required to be accompanied

For additional analytical, marketing, investment and business opportunities
information, please contact
Global Investment & Business Center, USA
(202) 546-2103. Fax: (202) 546-3275. E-mail: rusric@erols.com

by a bid bond in the form of an unconditional bank guarantee for five percent of the value of the bid.

The UAE has no requirement that a portion of any government tender be subcontracted to local firms. There is a ten- percent price preference, for UAE national companies, on procurement and tenders. The UAE has no requirement that a portion of any government tender be subcontracted to local firms. The UAE requires a company to be registered in order to be invited to receive government tender documents. To be registered, a company must have 51% UAE ownership. However, these rules do not apply on major project awards or defense contracts, where there is no local company able to provide the goods or services required.

The UAE has recently joined the Paris Convention for the Protection of Industrial Property, the first treaty for the protection of IPR to which the UAE has acceded. It is also a member of the World Intellectual Property Organization (WIPO).

AGRICULTURAL TRADE BARRIERS

Food products face relatively minor trade barriers. GCC-mandated shelf life requirements for close to 100 products and the stipulation that all processed products must carry both production and expiration dating constitute are the biggest impediments. In addition, all imported food products must have one half or more of their shelf life in effect at the time of import in order for import clearance to be granted.

CUSTOMS VALUATION

Customs duty is calculated on CIF value at the rate of 4%. Imports of liquor will be subjected to a 50% customs duty on their CIF value. Import duty for Tobacco Products is 90% of the CIF Value. CIF value will normally be calculated by reference to the commercial invoices covering the relative shipment, but Customs is not bound to accept the figures shown therein and may set an estimated value on the goods, which shall be final, as far as duty is concerned. Many essential items, including foodstuffs and pharmaceuticals, are allowed duty free status.

IMPORT LICENSES

Importers are allowed only to import goods which are related to the activities permitted by the Trade License which is issued by the local government authority.

All food imports including beef and poultry products require a health certificate from the country of origin and a halal slaughter certificate issued by an approved Islamic center in the country of origin.

EXPORT CONTROLS

All goods exported or re-exported from the UAE must have proper documentation issued by the Ministry of Economy and Commerce and the various Chambers of Commerce in the respective individual emirates. US firms seeking to export or re-export goods from the UAE should consult the appropriate legal authorities for specific guidelines.

IMPORT/EXPORT DOCUMENTATION

The consignee/agent should obtain a delivery order from the Shipping Agent and submit original standard trade documentation, including certificates of origin, bills of lading, commercial invoice, export declaration and various government/embassy attestations must be presented for all imports and exports. A Guide to Doing Business in the UAE which details documentation requirements is available from all US Department of Commerce District Offices, the Department of Commerce in Washington, and the US Commercial Offices in Abu Dhabi and Dubai. In addition

For additional analytical, marketing, investment and business opportunities information, please contact
Global Investment & Business Center, USA
(202) 546-2103. Fax: (202) 546-3275. E-mail: rusric@erols.com

the US Embassy's Agricultural Trade Office publishes a Food Exporters Guide for doing business in the GCC-5

TEMPORARY ENTRY

As a general rule, imports of goods into the UAE for the purpose of re-export within six months is exempted from custom duty. However, a payment of a deposit or submission of a bank guarantee in lieu of duty is required by customs. In these cases, the deposit or bank guarantee will be refunded/released by the local custom authority on proof of re-export. Goods remaining in the UAE after six months period are liable for duty.

Goods may be imported duty free and stored in any of several free zones in the UAE. Goods, which enter the UAE from these free zones, must pay the duty noted previously. There is no provision for duty free entry of parts or components, which are intended for manufacture of products which, are subsequently exported. In practice, as duties are already so low, this has not been a major impediment to manufacturing industries in the UAE.

LABELING

Food labels must contain product and brand names, production and expiry dates, country of origin, name of the manufacturer, net weight in metric units, and a list of ingredients and additives in descending order of proportion. All fats and oils used, as ingredients must be specifically identified on the label. Arabic labeling is now also officially required but not enforced.

PROHIBITED IMPORTS

All kind of illicit drugs (Hashish, Cocaine, Heroin, etc.) are prohibited in the UAE. As is forged and duplicate currency. Publications, photographs, oil painting, cards, books, magazines and sculptures that do not adhere to religion, morals or aim at causing corruption and disorder are also banned.

Irradiated food products are prohibited, while imports of alcohol and pork products are strictly regulated.

STANDARDS

The UAE's Standards and Measurements Department of the Ministry of Finance and Industry is responsible for formulating and enforcing UAE/GCC standards and in the process of establishing a separate standards organization. However, the national and emirate governments, as well as professional associations, are reviewing standards requirements. This is particularly true for the construction industry. Currently, government agencies and private firms stipulate the standards required on a project-by-project basis. This allows for a wide range of acceptable product performance, makes health and safety monitoring difficult, and permits the use of low quality products and manipulation of tender specifications. An UAE company first qualified for ISO 9000 certification in 1993. Since then, more have received the designation, and the EU is funding a standards center in the UAE to implement ISO 9000 certification.

FREE TRADE ZONES/ WARE HOUSES

The first free trade zone in the UAE was the Jebel Ali Free Trade Zone, established in 1985 in Dubai and located with the largest man-made seaport in the world. Since that time, eleven free trade zones, in varying stages of development, emerged. In most instances, these zones have been co-located with either a seaport of airport. The exceptions are the "Dubai Internet City" e-commerce free zone and the "Media City" free zone. These free trade zones offer incentives and exemptions ranging from tax holidays to assistance in recruiting labor. The biggest attraction to

For additional analytical, marketing, investment and business opportunities information, please contact
Global Investment & Business Center, USA
(202) 546-2103. Fax: (202) 546-3275. E-mail: rusric@erols.com

setting-up in a free trade zone is the right of 100% ownership; something not available elsewhere in the country. (Please see the Foreign Trade Zone / Free Port section of Chapter 7).

MEMBERSHIP IN FREE TRADE ARRANGEMENTS

The UAE is a member of the Gulf Cooperation Council (GCC). In 1981, the GCC issued the Unified Economic Agreement, a plan for complete economic integration among the six member states (Saudi Arabia, Kuwait, the UAE, Bahrain, Qatar, and Oman). In practice, the provisions of this agreement have not been implemented.

Under the agreement, all agricultural, animal, industrial, and natural resource products from member states are exempt from duties and other charges when traded among member states. To qualify as a GCC national product, the value added in a GCC member state must not be less than 40% of the final value, and produced in a factory with at least 51% local ownership and licensed by the respective Ministry of Finance and Industry. All intra-GCC shipments claiming this exemption must be accompanied by a duly authenticated certificate of origin.

TRADE AND PROJECT FINANCING

BANKING SYSTEM

There are 20 UAE-owned banks with 283 branches and 37 pay offices in the UAE and 43 branches abroad, 26 foreign banks with 109 branches, one restricted license bank, two investment banks, and 49 representative offices. The UAE Central Bank no longer issues licenses for new foreign banks to establish branches in the UAE. Citibank is the only US Bank in the UAE that offers full banking services. Bank of America and Union National Bank have representatives office in Dubai, while Bank of New York has one in Abu Dhabi.
Although the 1997 GCC summit determined that GCC banks would be able to open branches in all GCC states, so far no new GCC banks have elected to set up shop in the UAE. The largest banks in terms of assets include the National Bank of Abu Dhabi, National Bank of Dubai, Emirates Bank International, Mashreq Bank and the Abu Dhabi Commercial Bank.

Local banks are exempted from any type of taxation whereas foreign banks pay a 20% tax on their profit.

The UAE Central Bank prohibits lending an amount greater than 7% of a bank's capital base to any single customer. The Bank defines a customer as an individual, a company, or a group of companies under common ownership, and capital base as local capital. Foreign banks with branches in the UAE are not permitted to calculate loans as a percentage of their global capital (which may however be used to calculate the capital adequacy ratio). In a revision to the rule, the Bank in 1993 said it would exclude from the requirement non-funded exposures, such as letters of credit and guarantees. The Central Bank has also announced implementation of internationally recognized and accepted accounting principles, in the form of the International Accounting Standard (IAS) number 30 on disclosure.

FOREIGN EXCHANGE CONTROLS AFFECTING TRADING

Since the UAE dirham is tied to the dollar, interest rates in the UAE tend to parallel those in the US. The authorities believe that the exchange rate of 3.671 dirhams to the dollar, unchanged since 1980, promotes stability and confidence in the currency and mitigates against capital flight.

GENERAL FINANCING AVAILABILITY

For additional analytical, marketing, investment and business opportunities information, please contact
Global Investment & Business Center, USA
(202) 546-2103. Fax: (202) 546-3275. E-mail: rusric@erols.com

Local banks finance most non-oil investment in the UAE. Even so, banks lack sufficient lending opportunities for their funds and consequently place many of them abroad. Most of the manufacturing sector operates with higher levels of debt than prescribed by the 60:40 debt to equity ratio, generally the norm for this sector. Debt is almost entirely made up of bank borrowings. Some three-fourths of gross fixed capital formation in manufacturing is directly or indirectly financed by the banking system. Local banks invest in foreign stock markets to absorb excess liquidity.

The trade and building sectors receive a disproportionate share of bank loans. Banks lend to the services, trade and building sectors due to lack of major investment scope in other productive sectors. The oil sector is the province of the government and is beyond the reach of the banks. The farming sector is relatively small and is heavily subsidized.

TYPES OF AVAILABLE EXPORT FINANCING AND INSURANCE

UAE is not officially rated by any of the international credit rating agencies (S&P, Moody's) and to date, no major programs have been undertaken to finance exports into the UAE. The US Trade and Development Agency, which assists in the creation of jobs for Americans by helping US companies pursue overseas business opportunities, recently approved a US $ 425, 000 grant for a training program on behalf of GE Aircraft Engines. GE is pursuing a major engine contract with UAE's Int'l carrier, Emirates Airlines. This program will allow UAE delegates to attend bidders briefings, technical seminars, technical assistance, conferences and technology related orientation visits to the United States.

PROJECT FINANCING AVAILABLE

The development in the GCC of projects seeking financing is growing ever broader. From power to desalination complexes, through petrochemicals plants and gas development and transportation projects, the role of the private sector in large scale projects is becoming more varied and important. After a subdued 2000, GCC project finance dramatically picked-up in the second half of 2001 with about US $ 4.2 billion in project financing arranged. According to a recent survey, this number is to skyrocket beyond US $ 15 billion in the next year with UAE's share exceeding US $ 5.5 billion or 30%. Major international and local banks are behind these projects advising and arranging for the major part of financing, often exceeding 75%.

BANKS/FINANCIAL INSTITUTES OPERATING IN THE UAE:

ABN Amro Bank
ANZ Grindlays Bank PLC
Abu Dhabi Commercial Bank
Al Ahli Bank of Kuwait
*American Express Ltd.
Arab African International Bank
Arab Bank for Investment & Foreign Trade
Arab Bank PLC
Arab Emirates Investment Bank Ltd.
Banca Commerciale Italiana
Bank Melli Iran
*Bank of America (Representative Office)
Bank of Baroda
Bank Brussels Lambert
*Bank of New York (Representative Office)
Bank of Sharjah PLC
Bank of Tokyo Ltd.
Bank Saderat Iran

For additional analytical, marketing, investment and business opportunities information, please contact
Global Investment & Business Center, USA
(202) 546-2103. Fax: (202) 546-3275. E-mail: rusric@erols.com

Banque Banorabe
Banque Du Caire
Banque Indosuez
Banque Libanaise Pour Le Commerce
Banque Nationale De Paris
Banque Paribas
Barclays Bank PLC
The British Bank of the Middle East
*Citibank NA
The Commercial Bank of Dubai Ltd.
Commercial Bank Int'l PLC
Credit Lyonnais
Credit Suisse
Dubai Islamic Bank
El Nilein Bank
Emirates Bank International
Emirates Industrial Bank
First Canadian Capital Corporation
First Gulf Bank
Gulf International Bank (BSC)
Habib Bank AG Zurich
Habib Bank Limited
Investment Bank for Trade & Finance LLC
Janata Bank
Lloyds Bank PLC
Mashreq Bank
*Merrill Lynch International Co.
Middle East Bank (A subsidiary of Emirates Bank Int'l Ltd)
National Bank of Abu Dhabi
National Bank of Bahrain (BSC)
National Bank of Dubai Ltd.
National Bank of Fujairah
National Bank of Oman Ltd. (SAOG)
National Bank of Ras Al Khaimah (PSC)
National Bank of Sharjah
National Bank of Umm Al Qaiwain PSC
Oman Finance Co. Ltd.
Royal Bank of Canada
Standard Chartered Bank
Union Bank of Switzerland
*Union National Bank (Representative Office)
United Arab Bank
United Bank Ltd

DUTY FREE TRADING IN DUBAI

Dubai Duty Free retails duty free merchandise at Dubai International Airport temporary sites at sponsored events in Dubai such as golf and tennis tournaments, horse racing, offshore powerboat racing and concerts.

The company is committed to reducing the adverse impacts of its commercial and sponsored event activities on the environment, to prevent pollution and to continually improve its environmental performance.

For additional analytical, marketing, investment and business opportunities information, please contact
Global Investment & Business Center, USA
(202) 546-2103. Fax: (202) 546-3275. E-mail: rusric@erols.com

The company will consider the environmental impacts of storage, display and final packaging of merchandise during the product selection process and will comply with the requirements of CITES.

The Company will comply with relevant UAE environmental legislation and will use its purchasing influence to encourage its local suppliers to also comply.

The company will train its employees to be aware of the Company's Environmental Policy and to be involved in its implementation.

We will, where practical, seek to adopt methods of reducing the consumption of materials and energy and to indicate the re-use and recycling of materials wherever economically viable.

We will encourage our customers to either re-use or dispose of packing material in an environmentally responsible manner.

The Dubai Duty Free Environmental Management System will be used to measure the Company's environmental performance, to set and review environmental objectives and targets and to monitor the progress towards them.

This Environmental Policy is available at our Duty Free Office Reception and to anyone requesting a copy.

Dubai Duty Free got ISO 14001 certificate for Environmental Management

S.N.	ITEM	QUANTITY SOLD	UNIT OF MEASURE
1	CIGARETTES	820,838	CARTONS
2	LIQUOR	1,013,655	BOTTLES
3	GOLD	1.5	TONNES
4	WATCHES	46,465	PIECES
5	PERFUMES	357,016	BOTTLES
6	MOBILE PHONES	25,136	PIECES
7	DVD	1,738	PIECES
8	VIDEO CAMERA	5,524	PIECES
9	DISCMAN	3,545	PIECES
10	WALKMAN	3,768	PIECES
11	RADIO CASETTE RECORDER	3,261	PIECES
12	AUDIO CASSETTES	41,807	PIECES
13	VIDEO CASSETTES	7,505	PIECES

For additional analytical, marketing, investment and business opportunities information, please contact
Global Investment & Business Center, USA
(202) 546-2103. Fax: (202) 546-3275. E-mail: rusric@erols.com

14	CAMERAS	86,186	PIECES
15	TELEPHONE CARDS	143,393	PIECES
16	GOLF CLUBS	620	PIECES
17	HANDBAGS	6,611	PIECES
18	PASHMINA/SHAWL	6,310	PIECES
19	CAVIAR	2	TONNES
20	NUTS	284.6	TONNES
21	CADBURY	44	TONNES
22	TOBLERONE	39	TONNES
23	KITKAT	58	TONNES
24	MARS	16	TONNES
25	QUALITY STREET	30	TONNES
26	SMARTIES	9	TONNES
27	LINDT	25	TONNES
28	NESTLE	13.7	TONNES
29	TANG	268	TONNES
30	NIDO	197	TONNES

MILLENNIUM MILLIONAIRE

- For each Millennium Millionaire Series, 5000 tickets are sold at Dhs 1,000 (US$ 278) each and with no restrictions on the number of tickets that each passenger purchases.
- The prize for each series is US$ 1,000,000.
- Tickets are available from the following outlets:
    - DDF Finest Surprise counters at Departures, Arrivals & Terminal 2.
    - At most sales counters throughout the Dubai Duty Free shop floor.
    - The Newsagent shops in new concourse
    - Arrivals Shop.
    - Online from www.dubaidutyfree.com
- The ticket itself is in the form and size of a plastic credit card with every purchaser receiving the card as their proof of purchase after completing the ticket form. You will be required to produce this card to collect your prize (US$ 1,000,000).
- Cards are limited to 5,000 for each draw.
- Your card is valid for the series number shown on the card and is not transferable. The cash prize will be paid only to the person named on the ticket form, on production of the card and original passport for identification.

For additional analytical, marketing, investment and business opportunities information, please contact
Global Investment & Business Center, USA
(202) 546-2103. Fax: (202) 546-3275. E-mail: rusric@erols.com

- The names of the winners are announced in the local & regional press. Draw dates and names of the winners are also posted on this website. In addition, all participants in a draw are notified by mail of the winning number.
- Dubai Duty Free reserves the right to refuse sale of the cards or cancel the draw and refund all monies.
- The purchaser is required to fill in all their particulars including passport number, nationality and receives as proof of entry into the Millennium Millionaire Draw, the plastic card with coinciding number as printed on the ticket form.
- Each draw is held under the supervision of the Management of Dubai Duty Free.

Finest Surprise draw

- Every ticket holder will be kept informed about the drawn date and winning ticket number. This shall also be posted on the web.
- Dubai Duty Free will hand over the car personally to the winner upon furnishing the original ticket proof of purchase and a photocopy of the passport.
- Dubai Duty free will ship the car to the winners country of residence/nearest seaport free of charge , however all local taxes, and custom duties will be the payable by the winner.
- Ticket sales are limited to 1000 per car.
- The car will be stored in the Dubai Duty Free warehouse for a limited period (2 weeks) after the presentation.
- All Dubai Duty Free raffle cars are GCC Specifications.

CONTACTS

Customer Support
E-mail: customerservice@ddf.co.ae Tel : (971-4)2062453 FAX: (971-4)2244164 Toll Free : 8004443 (UAE) **Contact Persons** Emelita Sanchez, Ruby Ballon, Aloha Alfaro, Edna Credo, Neil Daniel, Gwen Marie Jamili, Selvyno Fernandez, Joan Suyao
Marketing Department E-mail: marketing@ddf.co.ae Fax: (971-4) 2244455
You can correspond with us at: Dubai Duty Free P.O. Box 831 Dubai United Arab Emirates Tel : (971-4) 2066444 Fax: (971-4) 2244036

For additional analytical, marketing, investment and business opportunities information, please contact
Global Investment & Business Center, USA
(202) 546-2103. Fax: (202) 546-3275. E-mail: rusric@erols.com

SELECTED ECOMOMIC SECTORS PROFILES

OIL AND GAS INDUSTRY[2]

Organizations: Abu Dhabi National Oil Company (ADNOC); Operates three main oil and gas operating companies, five Service companies, three joint ventures to fully utilize the produced gas, two maritime transport companies for crude oil, refined product and LNG and one refined product distribution company.

Major Refineries: Ruwais (132,050 bbl/d), Umm al-Nar II (80,750 bbl/d), Metro Oil (Fujairah)(75,000 bbl/d)
Major Gas Processing Plants: Bab, Bu Hasa, Das Island, Habshan (2), Jebel Ali, Ruwais
Major Oil Fields: *Abu Dhabi:* 'Asab, Bab, Bu Hasa, Al-Zakum *Dubai:* Fallah, Fateh, Southwest Fateh, Margham, Rashid *Sharjah:* Mubarak (near Abu Musa Island)
Major Associated Gas Fields: *Abu Dhabi:* Abu al-Bukhush, Bab, Bu Hasa, Umm Shaif, Zakum
Ports: *Abu Dhabi:* Das Island, Delma Island, Jebel as Dhanna, Ruwais, Abu al Bukhush, Al Mubarraz, Zirku Island, Port Zayed, Umm al Nar *Dubai:* Jebel Ali, Fateh, Port Rashid *Sharjah:* Mubarak

GENERAL BACKGROUND

The United Arab Emirates is enjoying an economic recovery as a result of the rise in oil prices which resulted from OPEC production cuts in March 2007. While the UAE has a relatively diversified economy for a Persian Gulf oil exporter, the period of low oil prices in 1998 resulted in a decline in real gross domestic product (GDP) of 5.0%. Real GDP growth for 2007 is projected at 4.5%.

POLITICAL SYSTEM

The UAE is a federation of seven emirates - Abu Dhabi, Dubai, Sharjah, Ajman, Fujairah, Ras al-Khaimah, and Umm al-Qaiwain. Political power is concentrated in Abu Dhabi, which controls the vast majority of the UAE's economic and resource wealth. The two largest emirates -- Abu Dhabi and Dubai -- provide over 80% of the UAE's income. In June 1996, the UAE's Federal National Council approved a permanent constitution for the country. This replaced a provisional document which had been renewed every five years since the country's creation in 1971. The establishment of Abu Dhabi as the UAE's permanent capital was one of the new framework's main provisions.

OTHER INDUSTRY

In recent years, the UAE has undertaken several projects to diversify its economy and to reduce its dependence on oil and gas revenues. The non-oil sectors of the UAE's economy presently contrbute more than two-thirds of the UAE's total GDP. The federal government has invested

---

[2] The United Arab Emirates (UAE) is important to world energy markets because it contains 98 billion barrels, or nearly 10%, of the world's proven oil reserves. The UAE also holds the world's fourth-largest natural gas reserves and produces significant amounts of liquefied natural gas.

For additional analytical, marketing, investment and business opportunities information, please contact
Global Investment & Business Center, USA
(202) 546-2103. Fax: (202) 546-3275. E-mail: rusric@erols.com

heavily in sectors such as aluminum production, tourism, aviation, re-export commerce, and telecommunications. As part of its strategy to further expand its tourism industry, the UAE is building new hotels, restaurants and shopping centers, and expanding airports and duty-free zones. Agriculture also makes up a significant portion of the UAE's economy. Dubai has become a central Middle East hub for trade and finance, accounting for about 70% of the Emirates' non-oil trade.

FOREIGN AFFAIRS

The UAE and Iran continue to dispute the ownership of three islands, Abu Musa and the Greater and Lesser Tunb Islands, which are strategically located in the Strait of Hormuz. All three islands were effectively occupied by Iranian troops in 1992. The Mubarak field, which is located six miles off Abu Musa, has been producing gas-rich oil since 1974. In 2007, the Iranian Foreign Ministry claimed that the islands are "an inseparable part of Iran." Iran rejected a 1996 proposal by the Gulf Cooperation Council (GCC) for the dispute to be resolved by the International Court of Justice, an option supported by the UAE. In early 1996, Iran took further moves to strengthen its hold on the disputed islands. These actions included starting up a power plant on Greater Tunb, opening an airport on Abu Musa, and announcing plans for construction of a new port on Abu Musa. In the dispute, the UAE has received strong support from the GCC, the United Nations, and the United States. Although Iran remains a continuing concern for officials in Abu Dhabi, they have chosen not to escalate the territorial dispute. Iran is one of Dubai's major trading partners, accounting for 20% to 30% of Dubai's business.

Relations between Saudi Arabia and the UAE also have shown some signs of strain in 2007, due to Saudi development of the Shaybah oilfield, with estimated reserves of 14 billion barrels of crude oil. The UAE and Saudi Arabia do not have a precisely defined border in the sparsely populated desert separating them, and the Shaybah field straddles territory claimed by both governments. Saudi Arabia began production from the Shaybah field in late 1998. The UAE has demanded an agreement to share production from Shaybah.

OIL

The UAE contains proven crude oil reserves of 97.8 billion barrels, or slightly less than 10% of the world total. Abu Dhabi holds 94% of this amount, or about 92.2 billion barrels. Dubai contains an estimated 4.0 billion barrels, followed by Sharjah and Ras al-Khaimah, with 1.5 billion and 100 million barrels of oil, respectively.

The majority of the UAE's crude oil is considered light, with gravities in the 32° to 44° API range. Abu Dhabi's Murban 39° and Dubai's Fateh 32° blends are the UAE's primary export crudes. Most of the UAE's oil fields have been producing since the 1960s or early 1970s. Proven oil reserves in Abu Dhabi have doubled in the last decade, mainly due to significant increases in rates of recovery. Abu Dhabi has continued to identify new finds, especially offshore, and to discover new oil-rich structures in existing fields.

Under the UAE's constitution, each emirate controls its own oil production and resource development. Although Abu Dhabi joined OPEC in 1967 (four years before the UAE was formed), Dubai does not consider itself part of OPEC or bound by its quotas. Consequently, if Dubai were to produce at its full capacity, Abu Dhabi would have to adjust its output in order to keep the UAE within its OPEC production quota.

In response to the period of low oil prices in 1998 and early 2007, OPEC agreed in March 2007 to reduce output in an effort to shore up the price of crude. The UAE's production quota was

For additional analytical, marketing, investment and business opportunities information, please contact
Global Investment & Business Center, USA
(202) 546-2103. Fax: (202) 546-3275. E-mail: rusric@erols.com

lowered to 2.00 million bbl/d. Actual production fell from a 2007 high of 2.25 million bbl/d in February 2007 to 2.05 million bbl/d in May 2007. In mid-2007, the UAE's maximum crude oil production capacity was estimated at 2.7-3.0 million bbl/d.

RESTRUCTURING

On October 12, 1998, the Abu Dhabi National Oil Company (ADNOC) announced a major plan to restructure its management. The plan consolidates ADNOC's operations under five new directorates: Exploration and Production, Gas Processing, Chemicals, Marketing and Refining and Shared Services (Administration).

REFINING

The UAE has two refineries operated by ADNOC. The Ruwais refinery underwent a $100-million upgrade in 2007 and is now operating at 132,000 bbl/d, producing light products mainly for export to Japan and India. Fuel oil from Ruwais is sold as bunkers by ADNOC and used for domestic power generation. A $1.2-billion second-phase Ruwais expansion will include a new 135,000-bbl/d crude distillation unit, a 130,000-bbl/d fractionation plant, and expansion of residual oil conversion facilities with a 40,000-bbl/d hydrocracker and a 36,000-bbl/d visbreaker. [Fractionation is a process of separating various hydrocarbons from natural gas or oil as produced from the ground. Visbreaking is a thermal cracking process in which heavy atmospheric or vacuum distillation bottoms are cracked at moderate temperatures to increase production of distillate products and reduce viscosity of the distillation residues]. ADNOC plans to use the fractionation unit to process increased future condensate flows from the Bab and Asab fields. When completed in 2000, Ruwais' total capacity will be around 475,000 bbl/d.

UAE has two smaller refineries. Umm al-Nar, in Abu Dhabi, is now running at 80,750 bbl/d. Since its construction in 1976, the Umm al-Nar plant has undergone debottlenecking as well as a recent expansion. The refinery primarily supplies the domestic market. Metro Oil has a 75,000-bbl/d refinery in Fujairah. Another private refinery is planned for Dubai, which is scheduled to begin operating in mid-2000 and have a capacity of 40,000 bbl/d.

A new $300-million condensate refinery built by the Emirates National Oil Company (ENOC) began operation in May 2007. The plant, located in Dubai's Jebel Ali Free Zone, produces 120,000 bbl/d of jet fuel, diesel, naphtha, and gasoline.

FOREIGN DOWNSTREAM OPERATIONS

In October 1998, the International Petroleum Investment Company (IPIC), the UAE's downstream investment outfit, agreed to purchase 50% of the Hyundai Oil Refinery Company of South Korea for $500 million. The UAE is the second-largest crude oil supplier to South Korea after Saudi Arabia, exporting 83 million barrels (15% of South Korea's total imports) in the first eight months of 1998. IPIC's overseas holdings also include a 10% stake in Spain's CEPSA and a 19.6% share of Austria's OMV. CEPSA's profits rose by 40% in 1997; OMV's profits increased by 18%.

NATURAL GAS

The UAE's natural gas reserves of roughly 212.0 trillion cubic feet (Tcf) are the world's fourth largest after Russia, Iran, and Qatar. The largest reserves of 196.1 Tcf are located in Abu Dhabi. Sharjah, Dubai, and Ras al-Khaimah contain smaller reserves of 10.7 Tcf, 4.1 Tcf, and 1.1 Tcf, respectively. In Abu Dhabi, the non-associated Khuff gas reservoirs beneath the Umm Shaif and

For additional analytical, marketing, investment and business opportunities information, please contact
Global Investment & Business Center, USA
(202) 546-2103. Fax: (202) 546-3275. E-mail: rusric@erols.com

Abu al-Bukhush oil fields rank among the world's largest. Current gas reserves are projected to last for about 150-170 years.

Reduced OPEC oil production quotas and increased domestic consumption of electricity have provided incentives for the UAE to increase its use of natural gas. Over the last decade, gas consumption in Abu Dhabi has doubled, and is projected to reach 3 billion cubic feet per day (bcf/d) by 2000 and 4 bcf/d. The development of gas fields also increases exports of condensates, which are not subject to OPEC quotas.

Projects

The past few years have seen the UAE embark on a massive multi-billion dollar program of investment in its gas sector including a shift toward gas-fired power plants and the transformation of the Taweelah commercial district into a gas-based industrial zone. An ambitious plan to interconnect the gas grids Qatar, the UAE, and Oman, the *Dolphin Project*, also is planned.

The second phase of the UAE's $1 billion onshore gas development program (OGD-2) at the Habshan natural gas complex located directly over the huge Bab oil and gas field is currently underway. This second phase includes the construction of three or four gas processing trains to process 1 bcf/d of gas, 300-500 tons per day (t/d) of natural gas liquids, 35,000-55,000 t/d of condensate and up to 2,100 t/d of sulphur. The construction contract was awarded to Italy's Snamprogetti in October 1998. Construction is scheduled to be completed in early 2001.

Another project closely linked with OGD-2 is the Asab gas development project, which was recently completed. The Asab development processes around 830 million cubic feet per day (Mmcf/d) of associated wet gas from the Thamama F and G reservoirs and produces up to 100,000 bbl/d of condensate for processing at the Ruwais refinery. The gas will also support other industries in Ruwais and be re-injected into Asab reservoirs to maintain field pressure. The $700 million project was awarded to Snamprogetti in June 1997 by UAE's Supreme Petroleum Council.

SUPPLYING DUBAI

Dubai's gas consumption is expected to grow by nearly 7% each year through 2005, due to expansion of its industrial sector, a switch to gas by its power stations, and the need for an enhanced oil recovery (EOR) system based on gas injections for its dwindling oil formations. Dubai projects future demand will average 655 Mmcf/d in 2000 and 810 Mmcf/d in 2005, with major swings between summer and winter consumption patterns. Currently, Dubai's entire gas supply comes from fellow UAE member Sharjah, which transports about 430 Mmcf/d at approximately $1.25/million Btu. Amoco operates three fields and the 800-Mmcf/d Sajaa processing facility in conjunction with the Sharjah government.

A project to pipe gas from the offshore Khuff field to Dubai and the Taweelah industrial complex was abandoned in May 2007. Instead, Dubai will be connected to the main Abu Dhabi gas receiving station by a pipeline.

In February 1998, a landmark agreement was announced for the supply of gas from Abu Dhabi to Dubai. The deal reportedly stipulates that Abu Dhabi will sell gas to Dubai for less than $1 per million Btu. The pipeline's capacity is expected to be around 800 Mmcf/d; 400-600 Mmcf/d is to be supplied to Dubai.

THE DOLPHIN PROJECT

For additional analytical, marketing, investment and business opportunities
information, please contact
Global Investment & Business Center, USA
(202) 546-2103. Fax: (202) 546-3275. E-mail: rusric@erols.com

The Dolphin Project aims to develop links between the gas infrastructures of Qatar, the UAE, and Oman, with a possible future link to Pakistan. It will allow the export of non-associated gas from Qatar's massive offshore North Dome field. A Statement of Principles for the project was signed in March 2007 between the UAE Offsets Group (UOG) and the Qatar General Petroleum Corporation (QGPC). Mobil Oil Qatar signed a memorandum of understanding covering its participation in the project's upstream component in July 2007. Estimated to cost $8 to $10 billion over the next six to seven years, the project will begin as a subsea pipeline from Ras Laffan in Qatar to a landfall in Abu Dhabi, which will then be extended to Dubai and northern Oman.

The start at 48 inches in diameter, stepping down to 30 inches by the time it reaches Oman. In its initial phase, the pipeline is to carry 3 Bcf/d of Qatari gas to the UAE and Oman, accounting for nearly 10% of total world gas supplies shipped by pipeline.

In October 2007, UOG and ADNOC issued a joint declaration dividing up gas distribution between them. Gas from the Dolphin Project will be the exclusive supply for gas-fired power plants, except in the Western Region of Abu Dhabi, and will also supply gas for ADNOC contracts with Dubai. Gas from the Dolphin Project will use the ADNOC distribution network until the project develops its own network.

The planned extension from Oman to Pakistan would be built in 2005 or later, and would carry 1.5 Bcf/d onward to Pakistan. This phase of the project is dependent on Pakistan's ability to pay for the gas, which is questionable given the current weakness of its economy, but UAE officials involved in the planning of the project have said Pakistan is being included because they take a "long term view" of Pakistan's potential for economic development, including possible UAE investments in enterprises such as independent power plants (IPP's) in Pakistan which would consume the gas.

ELECTRICITY

The UAE's soaring demand for electric power, coupled with volatile swings in peak loads, led the Emirates in 1997 to form a Privatization Committee for the Water and Electricity Sector. In early 1998, the committee called for a comprehensive restructuring, including the elimination of the state-owned Abu Dhabi Water and Electricity Department (ADWED) in favor of sweeping privatization. ADWED will be tranformed into a regulatory body, the Abu Dhabi Water and Electricity Authority (ADWEA). The government plans to take a majority holding in the new ventures with minority interests held by foreign firms. Gradually, the government will privatize its shares through initial public offerings (IPOs), allowing UAE nationals to become shareholders.

The privatization process for the Taweelah A-1 plant is entering its final stages, and ADWEA expects to announce the choice of a foreign partner which will have a 40% ownership stake by February 2000. Bids have been received from CMS Energy, Total, Marubeni, and National Power (UK).

The most significant step in the reorganization is the expansion of the Taweelah cogeneration facility. The expansion, known as Taweelah A-2, is the UAE's first independent water and power project (IWPP), and reached financial close in April 2007. It is the second independent power project in the Gulf after Oman's al-Manah facility. With a price tag of some $800 million, the expansion will add about 763 megawatts (MW) of power and 50 million gallons of desalinated water to the UAE's supplies. The first gas turbine is expected to operate by May 2000. Full-scale production is scheduled for August 2001. The Taweelah A-2 project is to be run by Emirates CMS Power, a joint venture between CMS Energy (40% ownership interest) and the newly-formed Emirates Power Company (EPC) (60%).

For additional analytical, marketing, investment and business opportunities information, please contact
Global Investment & Business Center, USA
(202) 546-2103. Fax: (202) 546-3275. E-mail: rusric@erols.com

Several other projects also have been approved:

- The al-Taweelah Power Company, which will manage the Taweelah B facility. The plant, which currently has six 122-MW steam turbines and six 13 million gallon-per-day (g/d) multi-stage flash units, is now undergoing an $360 million expansion. The addition of two new gas-turbine units will bring the plant's capacity to 1,220 MW and 103 million g/d of water.

- The al-Mirfa Power Company will operate the 246- MW, 16.2-million-g/d Mirfa cogeneration station and the 134-MW Madinat Zayed plant. Mirfa is slated for an $80 million expansion to add 130 MW of power and 25 million g/d of water.

- The Umm al-Nar Power Company will operate the plant by the same name with a 1,215-MW, 97-million-g/d facility, which will be upgraded with two new 3.5 million g/d desalination units. The new units will run on steam already available at the site. The company will also operate the 120-MW Baniyas station.

In April 1998, ABB was awarded the contract to build a $600-million cogeneration plant for ADNOC. The 500-MW, gas-fired plant will increase the available power to the Ruwais refining facility (see **Refining** section above) to 700 MW. The new plant will also supply up to 8 million g/d of water. Full operation of the plant is expected to begin in 2000.

The Abu Dhabi Water and Electricity Authority (ADWEA) currently is inspecting bids received in early December 2007 for a 1,500 MW plant at Shuweihat, west of Abu Dhabi. Plans call for a plant to be operational there by 2003.

The other emirates are also expanding their electric power generation infrastructures. Dubai plans to increase its electricity generation to 2,572 MW by 2000. To this end, the Jabel Ali "D" station will be upgraded with the installment of two new 400-MW gas turbines. In Sharjah, a new 100 MW gas turbine generator will be added to the primary Liyyah power plant, raising its production capacity to 1,065 MW.

The UAE also is taking part in a $1 billion plan to build a regional power grid throughout the countries of the Gulf Cooperation Council (GCC). The first phase of the plan would link Saudi Arabia, Kuwait, Bahrain and Qatar; the UAE and Oman would join the grid in the second phase of the plan. GCC electricity ministers signed a final agreement on the project in June 2007. The plan is based on the assumption that each country will have its own unified power grid, and the UAE is doing its part by connecting all the power stations along its western coast with the central region.

Sources for this report include: CIA World Factbook 2007; Dow Jones News Wire service; Economist Intelligence Unit ViewsWire; Oil and Gas Journal; Petroleum Economist; Petroleum Intelligence Weekly; International Market Insight Reports; U.S. Energy Information Administration; WEFA Middle East Economic Outlook.

MAJOR OIL COMPANIES

GROUP INTRODUCTION

The ADNOC Group of companies consists of three main oil and gas operating companies, five support companies providing services to the oil and gas industry, three joint ventures to fully

For additional analytical, marketing, investment and business opportunities
information, please contact
Global Investment & Business Center, USA
(202) 546-2103. Fax: (202) 546-3275. E-mail: rusric@erols.com

utilize the produced gas, two maritime transport companies for crude oil, refined product and LNG and one refined product distribution company.

In the field of Exploration and Production of Oil and Gas, Abu Dhabi Company for Onshore Oil Operations (ADCO), the largest crude oil producer in the southern Arabian Gulf, undertakes exploration, drilling, production and export activities in Abu Dhabi's onshore areas, and the shallow coastal waters.

The Company operates on behalf of ADNOC and six industry shareholders and produces oil mainly from five fields:

ASAB
BAB
BU HASA
SAHIL
SHAH

Abu Dhabi Marine Operating Company (ADMA-OPCO), operates the exploration, development and production activities of oil and gas in Abu Dhabi's offshore concession area. Many fields and reservoirs were discovered by ADMA-OPCO in its concession but oil and gas production comes only from two fields:

Umm Sheif
Zakum

The output of oil and gas from these fields is transported to the company's center of operations on Das Island for processing, storage and export via the Island's Terminal.

Zakum Development Company (ZADCO), was established in 1977 to develop and operate the Upper Zakum field, one of the largest fields in the world, on behalf of ADNOC and Japan Oil Development Company (JODCO). The development of the Upper Zakum reservoirs is considered to be one of the major technical achievements in Abu Dhabi. Besides Upper Zakum, the company currently operates Umm Al Dalkh, Satah and Arzanah fields.

In the field of Exploration and Production Services, Abu Dhabi Drilling Chemicals and Products Ltd. (ADDCAP), now a fully owned subsidiary of ADNOC, has set up a new base for its activities at Mussafah Industrial area and is now operating totally from there. The drilling chemicals are now produced at their newly constructed grinding plant at Mussafah using the latest technologies.

National Drilling Company (NDC), a leading drilling company with over 24 years of accumulated experience and one of the largest drilling contractors in the Middle East, has successfully carried out all drilling operations requirements and played an important role in the discovery of oil and gas in Abu Dhabi.

Meanwhile, the National Petroleum Construction Company (NPCC), a joint company owned by ADNOC which holds 70% interest, and the Consolidated Contractors Group (S.A.L), which holds the remaining 30%, NPCC offer complete services as a MAJOR EPC International Contractor for the offshore and onshore Oil & Gas production industry.

For additional analytical, marketing, investment and business opportunities information, please contact
Global Investment & Business Center, USA
(202) 546-2103. Fax: (202) 546-3275. E-mail: rusric@erols.com

And for the Abu Dhabi Petroleum Ports Operating Company (ADPPOC), it was incorporated in 1997 to operate in all the petroleum and industrial ports in Abu Dhabi, providing maintenance operations, safety and diving services.

On the other hand, National Marine Services (NMS) is the leading Offshore Support Service Company in Abu Dhabi. The company currently owns 25 offshore vessels of various categories including supply boats, anchor handling and rig moving tugs, safety standby, maintenance vessels and crew boats.

In the field of Natural Gas Processing, Abu Dhabi Gas Liquefaction Company Limited (ADGAS), was established in 1973 to turn gas, extracted from Abu Dhabi's offshore fields crude oil, into a new source of national income and a major source of marketable energy. The fact that gases are no longer used as fuel for oil field flares hs impacted positively on the environment.

Meanwhile, Abu Dhabi Gas Industries Limited (GASCO) is one of the largest gas processing companies in the world, and one of the biggest industrial projects in the UAE. It handles the associated gas from ADCO's onshore crude production and processes it through three NGL extraction plants at Bu Hasa, Bab and Asab.

In the field of Chemicals and Petrochemical Services, Ruwais Fertilizer (FERTIL) was established in 1980 as a joint venture between ADNOC and TOTAL for the construction and operation of a plant to produce fertilizers and market them locally and internationally.

And in the field of Refined Products Distribution, Abu Dhabi National Oil Company for Distribution (ADNOC-FOD) is specialized in marketing and distribution of petroleum products in the United Arab Emirates. ADNOC-FOD operates a vast network of filling stations covering all areas of the UAE.

Finally in the field of Maritime Transportation, National Gas Shipping Company Limited (NGSCO) provides shipping services to ADGAS and manages a fleet of carriers specially designed for LNG/LPG transportation.

Another company, Abu Dhabi National Tanker Company (ADNATCO), provides logistical support and advice on shipping to ADNOC and its Group of Companies.

Exploration & Production of Oil & Gas	ADCO ADMA-OPCO ZADCO
Exploration & Production Services	NPCC ADDCAP ADPPOC NDC NMS
Natural Gas Processing	GASCO ADGAS
Chemicals & Petrochemicals	FERTIL
Refined Products Distribution	ADNOC-FOD

For additional analytical, marketing, investment and business opportunities
information, please contact
Global Investment & Business Center, USA
(202) 546-2103. Fax: (202) 546-3275. E-mail: rusric@erols.com

Maritime Transportation	ADNATCO NGSCO

ADCO	Onshore exploration, development and production on behalf of the partners. Address: P.o. Box 2700, Abu Dhabi, UAE. Tel. 6040000, Tlx 22222 EM, Fax:669785
ADMA	Offshore exploration, development and production on behalf of the partners. Address: P.O. Box 303, Abu Dhabi, UAE. Tel. 6060000, Tlx 22284 EM, Fax720099
ZADCO	Development and production from the Upper Zakum field; also operates Umm Al-Dalkh, Satah and Arzanah fields on behalf of the partners. Address: P.O. Box 46808, Abu Dhabi, UAE Tel 6050000, Tlx 22948 EM, Fax 669448
NPCC	Construction and fabrication facilities for the oil industry. Address: P.O. Box 2058, Abu Dhabi, UAE. Tel 549000, Tlx 22638 EM, Fax 54911
ADDCAP	Production of drilling chemicals and provision of marine base and services. Address: P.O. Box 46121, Abu Dhabi, UAE Tel 6029000, Tlx 23267 EM, Fax 6029010
NDC	Provision of onshore and offshore drilling operations Address: P.O. Box 4017, Abu Dhabi, UAE Tel 316600, Tlx 22553 EM, Fax 317045
ADPPOC	Operating Ruwais, Jabel Dhanna and other oil or industrial ports. Address: P.O. box 61, Abu Dhabi, UAE Tel 777300, Tlx 22209 EM, Fax 766903
NMS	Owning and operating, chartering or leasing specialized vessels serving the oil industry. Address: P.O. Box 7202, Abu Dhabi, UAE Tel 339800, Tlx 22965 EM, Fax 211239
GASCO	Operation of onshore gas gathering and processing plants Address: P.O. Box 665, Abu Dhabi, UAE

For additional analytical, marketing, investment and business opportunities information, please contact
Global Investment & Business Center, USA
(202) 546-2103. Fax: (202) 546-3275. E-mail: rusric@erols.com

	Tel 6041111, Tlx 22365 EM, Fax 6047414
ADGAS	Operation of Das Island gas liquefaction plants Address: P.O. Box 3500, Abu Dhabi, UAE Tel 6061111, Tlx 22698 EM, Fax 6065456
FERTIL	Operation of ammonia and urea plant in Ruwais and marketing its products. Address: P.O. box 2288, Abu Dhabi, UAE Tel 6021111, Tlx 24205 EM, Fax 728084
ADNOC-FOD	Storage, transporation and domestic distribution of refined products Address: P.O. Box 4188, Abu Dhabi, UAE Tel 771300, Tlx 22358 EM, Fax 722322
ADNATCO	Transporting crude oil and refined products Address: P.O. Box 2977, Abu Dhabi, UAE Tel 331800, Tlx 22747 EM, Fax 322940

PERSIAN GULF OIL EXPORT

In 1998, the Persian Gulf countries (Bahrain, Iran, Iraq, Kuwait, Qatar, Saudi Arabia, and the United Arab Emirates produced over 27 percent of the world's oil, while holding 64 percent of the world's oil reserves. Persian Gulf net oil exports to OECD countries were up over 0.5 million barrels per day in 1998 from 1997 to more than 10.5 million barrels per day.

U.S. net oil imports from the Persian Gulf in 1998 rose to 2.14 million barrels per day from 1.76 million barrels per day in 1997. The vast majority of Persian Gulf exports to the United States came from Saudi Arabia (70 percent), with significant amounts also coming from Iraq (nearly 16 percent) and Kuwait (14 percent), with only very small amounts of oil coming from Qatar and the United Arab Emirates. Since rising from a 25-year low of 0.31 million barrels per day in 1985 to 1.97 million barrels per day in 1990, U.S. oil imports from the Persian Gulf as a percentage of oil demand declined gradually through 1996, until increasing in 1997 and 1998 (see graph). In 1998, more oil was imported to the United States from the Persian Gulf than in any year since 1977-1978. In these years, 2.45 million barrels per day and 2.22 million barrels per day of oil respectively was imported from the Persian Gulf to the United States.

Western Europe (defined as European countries belonging to the Organization for Economic Cooperation and Development, or OECD, but excluding new European OECD members Poland, Hungary, and the Czech Republic) imported nearly 4.0 million barrels per day from the Persian Gulf in 1998. This was an increase of nearly 0.5 million barrels per day from 1997. Nearly half of Persian Gulf oil exports to Western Europe came from Saudi Arabia (48 percent), with significant amounts also coming from Iran (over 25 percent) and Iraq (nearly 19 percent). After declining steadily between 1993 and 1996, Western Europe's oil imports from the Persian Gulf as a percentage of oil demand increased significantly in 1997 and 1998, rising from 22 percent in 1996 to 27 percent in 1998.

Japan imported over 4.1 million barrels per day from the Persian Gulf in 1998. Unlike the United States and Western Europe, this represented a decrease of nearly 0.2 million barrels per day from 1997. However, due to a significant decline in Japanese oil demand (0.2 million barrels per day) as a result of the Asian economic crisis, Japan's oil imports from the Persian Gulf as a percentage of demand stayed relatively flat from 1997 at 75 percent. Japan's dependence on the Persian Gulf for its oil supplies has been increasing steadily since 1988, when Persian Gulf oil imports represented only 57 percent of Japanese oil demand. In 1998, more than a third of Persian Gulf exports to Japan came from the United Arab Emirates (34 percent), with slightly less coming from Saudi Arabia (31 percent).

In 1998, Persian Gulf countries exported 17.1 million barrels per day of oil (see pie chart). This represented an increase of about 1 million barrels per day from 1997. Iraq's oil exports alone increased by 1 million barrels per day as increases in the United Nations' "oil-for-food" deal allowed Iraq to export more oil. Iran, the United Arab Emirates, Kuwait, Qatar, and even Bahrain all exported slightly more oil in 1998 than in 1997. The exception was Saudi Arabia, whose oil exports dropped from 8.1 million barrels per day to 7.9 million barrels per day. However, Saudi Arabia still accounted for about half of Persian Gulf oil exports (46 percent), with Iran, the United Arab Emirates, Kuwait, and Iraq each accounting for between 10 to 15 percent.

IMPORTS FROM THE PERSIAN GULF REGION

	As Percent of Demand			As Percent of Net Oil Imports		
	US	W. Europe	Japan	US	W. Europe	Japan
1983	2.9	27	60	10.3	41	60
1984	3.2	25	61	10.7	39	61
1985	2.0	22	58	7.3	35	59
1986	5.6	29	58	16.8	45	58
1987	6.5	27	59	18.2	43	60
1988	8.9	28	57	23.4	44	58
1989	10.7	30	64	25.8	47	63
1990	11.6	31	66	27.5	48	65
1991	11.0	27	64	27.8	43	64
1992	10.4	27	66	25.6	43	66
1993	10.3	30	69	23.4	50	68
1994	9.8	26	70	21.5	48	68
2007	8.9	24	70	19.9	47	70
1996	8.8	22	69	18.9	43	70
1997	9.4	24	75	19.2	47	74
1998	11.3	27	75	21.9	50	76

For additional analytical, marketing, investment and business opportunities information, please contact
Global Investment & Business Center, USA
(202) 546-2103. Fax: (202) 546-3275. E-mail: rusric@erols.com

AGRICULTURE AND FISHERIES

GREENING & DESERT

e UAE has made major strides in developing its agricultural sector and, due to the determination of Sheikh Zayed, the desert has undergone a remarkable transformation. Concerned authorities like Abu Dhabi Municipality and Town Planning Department and Sheikh Zayed's Private Department have played significant roles in spreading forestation and establishing farms to increase agricultural production, thereby meeting local market requirements as well as providing surplus production for export abroad.

Under instructions from Sheikh Zayed, Abu Dhabi Municipality has been extremely busy beautifying the emirate's cities. The municipality has also planted extensive green belts in order to protect these cities from the devastating effects of sandstorms. Examination of the vast areas which the municipality has cultivated under beautification projects, totaling 92,500 hectares in 1998, proves that the difficulties posed by the country's harsh climate have been successfully over come by the municipality's use of advanced technology. To date a total of 39 public parks, occupying an area of 3.7 million square meters, have been established in the emirate. Some of these leisure and entertainment parks are reserved especially for women and children, such as Al Khalidiya Park, Al Mushrif Park and the Women's Beach, all in Abu Dhabi city. The municipality has also planted approximately 2,450 hectares of greenery and flowers on the verges of internal roads and highways. Other projects include Baynunah Forest, which covers an area of 20,000 hectares. In Abu Dhabi, the municipality has also planted 2,500 hectares with palm trees, as at Ras al-Akhdar and Al Ghaf Park. Special nurseries set up by the municipality produce a total of 1.5 million tree saplings, 20 million flowers and 30,000 plants each year, supplying the raw material for the beautification process.

DISTRIBUTION OF FARMS

In accordance with Abu Dhabi's long-term urban development plan, scheduled for implementation by the year 2010, the Ruler's Representative in the Western Region and Chairman of the Abu Dhabi Municipality and Town Planning Department, Sheik h Mohammed bin Butti Al Hamed, has instructed that farms in Liwa, Ghiyathi and Bida Zayed be established for distribution to UAE nationals. Around 3,000 farms are also being created around Al Ajban where Abu Dhabi Municipality has leveled a 30-kilometre desert area to transform it into cultivable land. These farms will also be distributed to nationals.

With the completion of the project, productive farms in Abu Dhabi and adjoining areas should increase to around 15,000. Meanwhile over the past six years the number of farms has grown 12-fold from approximately 1,000 to more than 12,000. The total number of farms distributed among nationals so far totals 12,021 covering an area of 27,704 hectares.

The municipality also provides farmers with financial assistance to purchase equipment, fertilizer and seeds. As a result of the programme the country's once small-scale traditional farming has been complemented by investment that has seen more than 100,000 hectares of land being brought under the plough.

DATE PALM CULTIVATION

No. of date palm trees in 1986 was 4.6 million while in 1997 was 35 million
Date production in 1986 was 59,718 (tones) while in 1997 was 388,190 tones As the above

For additional analytical, marketing, investment and business opportunities information, please contact
Global Investment & Business Center, USA
(202) 546-2103. Fax: (202) 546-3275. E-mail: rusric@erols.com

figures indicate, Sheikh Zayed's initiatives in date palm cultivation have led to a qualitative and quantitative breakthrough,

The production of rapidly growing trees and the introduction of effective control to combat palm diseases. The UAE has become a world leader in the production of palm tissues having established a tissue culture laboratory at the Emirates University for this purpose. The Ministry of Agriculture and Fisheries plans to develop all aspects of palm cultivation and to improve productivity through the creation of experimental farms, provision of guidance services and equipment, generation of high quality varieties, studies of palm populations and establishment of date processing plants.

OFFSET TISSUE CULTURE LABORATORY

One new project which will assist in achieving the Ministry's goal is the Dh 5.75 million bio-technology joint venture, Al Wathba Marionnet LLC, which has been set up by France's Giat Industries as part of its military offset obligations. The project, the first of its kind in the UAE, will cultivate date palm seedlings using advanced tissue culture techniques. The cloning of date palms began in January 2007 in the Al Ain laboratory and the process is expected to take about three years before the high-yield trees bear quality dates. The new company, which will produce an initial 200,000 date palms annually 50 per cent of which will be exported, will assist in providing the UAE and the Arab world with disease-free, well rooted plants of selected varieties.

CHELSEA FLOWER SHOW

Sheikh Zayed's entry in the Royal Horticultural Society's Chelsea Flower Show held in London from 25 to 28 Ma y, has won a gold medal for the second consecutive year. The 2007 show, one of the world's top horticultural events, was inaugurated by Queen Elizabeth who toured the displays, stopping off to inspect Sheikh Zayed's entry. This year's garden, which was inspired by an eighteenth-century poem, featured 12 large date palms specially flown to London from the UAE. At the head of a rectangular reflective pool stood a piece of perfect white Carrera marble supporting a tablet of black granite, inlaid with an intricate design in 22-carat gold leaf. Ha n d - wired arbors placed between the palms and bedecked with black and gold cushions provided tranquil areas for peaceful meditation. The garden was designed to promote the importance of horticulture as a means of breaking down barriers between cultures. Sheikh Zayed is an Honorary Fellow of the Royal Horticultural Society.

HORTICULTURE EXPORTS

The UAE's entry in the Chelsea Flower Show highlights the increasing importance of horticulture as a UAE export. The National Horticulture Management Company, which was set up in 1997 to provide marketing and technical assistance to farm owners, has started marketing flowers produced by Franserre UAE under the brand name Shams. The company targets the local market and exports mainly to the Middle East, Europe and Asia. Last year Shams exported 70,000 flowers a month to Riyadh and Beirut. Franserre UAE, another military offset project, was set up by assault Investments, Thomson Compensation International and Al Hamed Enterprises. In the first phase of the Dh 50 million project, high-tech greenhouses we re established on 50,000 square meters of land near Sweihan in Abu Dhabi. Production is controlled by a centrally computerized system which regulates temperature, humidity, water for irrigation and the distribution of fertilizer. The project is part of the UAE's strategy to create a high, value-added agricultural sector which maximizes profits while reducing water consumption, subsidization and the foreign work force.

For additional analytical, marketing, investment and business opportunities information, please contact
Global Investment & Business Center, USA
(202) 546-2103. Fax: (202) 546-3275. E-mail: rusric@erols.com

NEW IRRIGATION TECHNIQUES

Major developments in the agricultural sector outlined above have placed huge demands on scarce water supplies, 70 per cent of which are consumed by agriculture. The need for a cost-effective source of water is therefore high. This has resulted in the implementation of a series of projects aimed at cutting expenditure on irrigation, the first of which was carried out in the 1980s when city planners decided to recycle waste water. The Mafraq sewage treatment plant which was commissioned in 1982 has an output of 18.5 million gallons of water per day. Abu Dhabi Municipality, however requires 29 million gallons of water to maintain its 45 public parks and gardens as well as its many roadside and pavement plantings.

The latest in a series of experimental water projects is under way at the Rahba farming belt in Abu Dhabi. The main objective of the experiment is to vaporize saline underground water from deep wells by using solar energy. The saline water is stored in pools 2 meters deep covered by plastic. Water with a salinity of up to 40,000 ppm is desalinated by evaporation and subsequently collected through condensation. The experiment, which will be completed in two years, is being carried out by Abu Dhabi Municipality in cooperation with the Japanese Government.

Two - thirds of the country's agricultural area is presently irrigated by modern methods. While the water-conserving drip method is most extensively used, other methods include bubbler, sprinkler and flood irrigation. Areas being irrigated by sprinklers are being supplied with desalinated water to safeguard the public from possible pathogens which may be present in the recycled waste water. The proposed new system should help ease pressure on old water treatment plants and ensure that the pathogens problem is solved.

GROUNDWATER PROJECT

The first phase of a large-scale groundwater project has been completed in the Al Khazna–Remah area between Al Ain and Abu Dhabi. The indications are that the 51 wells can produce up to 50 million gallons per day suitable for irrigation. The second phase of the project, which includes supplying farmers in the region with 50 million gallons per day free of charge to assist them in expanding cultivated areas, is under way. Plans are also in place to prospect for water in other areas. Many companies had previously prospected for underground water in the region and and had met with very little success. Sheikh Zayed insisted, however, that the exploration continue.

DAMS IN THE UAE

No. of dams 40 and Total capacity 100 million cubic meters. A number of ways of conserving precious water supplies are under discussion at federal and local level and these include building more dams in valleys to trap rainwater. Construction of the Dh 30 million Wadi al-Basirah dam between Dibba and Masafi in the Hajar mountains was finished in July 2007. The dam, which took 22 months to build, is 855 meters long and 10.7 meters in height and has a capacity of 1.7 million cubic meters of water. Three main barriers, retaining 100,000 cubic meters of water each we re built around the reservoir. Wadi al-Basirah and other dams will help to resupply under ground water reserves on both sides of the Hajar Mountains. The dam will also help reduce water salinity and protect farm produce from being destroyed during heavy rains in winter.

FISHING

In view of its lengthy coastline it is not surprising that the UAE has a successful indigenous fishing industry. In fact, it ranks fourth in the Arab world and second among AGCC states in the volume

For additional analytical, marketing, investment and business opportunities information, please contact
Global Investment & Business Center, USA
(202) 546-2103. Fax: (202) 546-3275. E-mail: rusric@erols.com

of its annual catch. Around 20 fishing ports and 25 repair workshops have been established along the coastline to provide facilities for fishermen.

New investment in the fishing industry (as opposed to fish farming) is largely confined to the field of refrigeration. Somewhere between 10 to 15 medium-sized establishments are currently engaged in refrigeration and packaging part of the local catch. With the fish catch rising, but the average catch per boat declining, the Ministry of Agriculture and Fisheries is keen to protect the fishing industry and has therefore placed legal restraints on fishing to conserve fish stocks. Fish must not be caught during the spawning season and undersized fish must be returned to the sea.

No. fishing boats	6,341
Total fish catch (tones)	114,358
Total value	Dh 617 million
Per capita consumption	33 kilos

Total fish catch (tones)	99,600	108,600	108,600	107,000	114,358
No. of fishing boats	4,303	4,303	4,464	6,341	

The ministry plans to publish a spawning timetable for each commercial fish species to encourage fishermen to suspend fishing at those times. Limits will also be set on boat registration. The fishing of shrimp in UAE waters has been banned since 1980 because of the impact of trawlers on spawning grounds. A ban ordered by HH Sheikh Hamad bin Mohammed Al Sharqi, Supreme Council Member and Ruler of Fujairah, on the use of the hayali fishing method has also been effective in preserving fishery resources. Before the ban fishermen caught quantities of both large and small fish using a 1,500-metre net. The preponderance of small fish in the catch affected the reproduction and size of the fish population. Having sold the big fish, the fishermen would dry the small ones and sell them for food or as fertilizer for palm trees.

ARTIFICIAL REEFS

Some areas in the UAE have also undertaken proactive projects to help increase stocks. For instance, Dibba Al Fujairah Municipality plans to place 300 new cone-like cement 'caves' as artificial habitats at three marine reefs about 800 meters offshore of Dibba.

Each meter long 'cave' has a 58-centimetre opening to allow small fish to enter and live within the protection of the 'cave', with eight small holes punched in the cave to facilitate water exchange. The total weight of each artificial habitat is 1.5 tones. These 300 new 'caves' are additional to the 270 installed by Dibba Al Fujairah Municipality in 2007 and 1998 at the same sites in Dibba, Al Aqqah and Al Faqit, near Dhadna. The building and placing of the artificial reefs, which it is hoped will help to promote tourism, is being carried out under the supervision of Fujairah and Dibba Al Fujairah municipalities and the Dubai International Marine Club.

FISH FARMING

Warm seawater that allows a year-round growing cycle, easy access to the coast and low labour and energy costs give the UAE, especially the Northern Emirates, a major advantage in aquaculture over other parts of the world. With regional and international fisheries shrinking, high-tech fish farming methods are used to enhance the UAE's traditional role as a seafood producer. A Dh 300 million public joint stock company, International Fish Farming Company (Asmak) was

For additional analytical, marketing, investment and business opportunities information, please contact
Global Investment & Business Center, USA
(202) 546-2103. Fax: (202) 546-3275. E-mail: rusric@erols.com

incorporated in May 2007, following an initial public offering in January 2007. The lead founders of the aquaculture venture are the UAE Offsets Group, Oasis National Food Company, a subsidiary of the Abu Dhabi Investment Company, Union Cold Stores, Dassault Investment , Athens-based Nireus Chios Aquaculture SA, Baldwin International Ltd and Gulf Investment Corporation. Asmak plans to build two hatcheries – one in Abu Dhabi and one in the Northern Emirates. The hatchery in the capital will produce 12.5 million fin-fish hatchlings annually.

The second facility will have a production capacity of 25 million fin-fish hatchlings and 360 million post-larval shrimp. Asmak also plans to build and operate three grow-out cage fish farms, two in the UAE and one in Oman, with an annual capacity of 2,000 tonnes of high-value fin fish. The company also proposes to build shrimp ponds in the Northern Emirates. Processing will take place at the company's Dubai plant. Targeted annual production will be 5,750 tonnes of full-grown marine fin-fish and 2,500 tonnes of full-grown shrimp. In July Asmak signed a 10-year management service agreement with Nireus Chios Aquaculture, one of its shareholders. Earlier in 2007 Dassault In vestissements, Nireus Chios Aquaculture SA along with Oasis National Food Company and Union Cold Stores, set up another military offset project, Ocean Fish Processing LLC, with an initial investment of US $1.5 million.

RAS AL-KHAIMAH

In July 2007 Asmak signed a fish-farming agreement with Ras al-Khaimah under which Asmak will be allocated an area of 450 hectares 8 kilometers offshore from the Al Mataf district for cage-farming. The site will be serviced from a 2,000 square metres onshore facility. Commencing in the year 2000, the project will produce 3,000 tonnes of sea bream and other marine fish estimated to be worth Dh 50 million at harvest. Production will be primarily for export to Europe and Japan.

For additional analytical, marketing, investment and business opportunities
information, please contact
Global Investment & Business Center, USA
(202) 546-2103. Fax: (202) 546-3275. E-mail: rusric@erols.com

UAE CUSTOMS REGULATIONS - NEW CUSTOMS LAW TO UNIFY RULES

The UAE's Unified Customs Law is all set to come into force in the country by the end of 2009, a senior official has said. Saeed Khalifa Al Marri, Federal Customs Authority's (FCA) Deputy Director-General, told Emirates Business that the body will soon set up a committee to start unification procedures. This will include standardising all the country's customs departments to apply the new, common law.

Al Marri said the differences in customs rules in different parts of the country are due to the operational freedom given by existing laws to the heads of all customs departments in the UAE. "Our aim in the FCA is to issue a unified executive list that is binding for the entire UAE," he said. Although the customs unification project is a huge one, steps are being taken to complete it as soon as possible, especially in Dubai, Abu Dhabi and Sharjah, which together account for 95 per cent of the UAE's customs transactions. The FCA has already completed an electronic link between the customs departments around the country. He said the FCA was currently setting up information and intelligence units in all customs departments to intensify the fight against fake goods and drugs.

Speaking about a GCC Customs Union, Al Marri said all its teething troubles should be resolved by 2009. About Saudi Arabia's concerns over smuggled and fake goods entering its market, Al Marri said: "We have discussed this with the Saudi authorities. It appears that in one of the past few years, the total value of goods that entered Saudi Arabia was SR11 billion (Dh10.7bn), including goods worth SR300 million from the UAE.

"Even if we assume that 50 per cent of UAE goods were fake – which is impossible – they will not exceed 1.5 per cent of the total commodities entering into Saudi Arabia, and this percentage is much less than the globally accepted 10 per cent."

Al Marri said the UAE was largely a transit country for global merchandise. Eighty per cent of the goods exported to the UAE are re-exported with the remaining 20 per cent distributed internally and in GCC states. He said the GCC Customs Union will hold its next meeting in Riyadh between August 24 and 27. – Emirates Business 24|7

RULES OF ORIGIN

Rules of origin are the basic significant integral part of customs formalities gaining an increasingly importance whenever the country makes new economic agreements with other countries or customs unions.

Despite the rules of origin competent authority is the Ministry of Economy, the actual application of origin since they are linked to the classification and valuation of products and for the purposes of controlling the implementation of the economic agreements provisions has become an essential part of customs procedures.

Dubai Customs has therefore created within the Tariff Department's structure a dedicated unit for origins and the economic agreements as to implement, develop, simplify and facilitate all origins-related regulations and procedures as well as delivering high quality service to the client.

This brochure outlines and identifies the most important aspects of the origins.

For additional analytical, marketing, investment and business opportunities
information, please contact
Global Investment & Business Center, USA
(202) 546-2103. Fax: (202) 546-3275. E-mail: rusric@erols.com

DEFINITION OF RULES OF ORIGIN.

The international Trade Organization defines the rules of origin as:

Laws, regulations, and administrative determinations of general application applied by members to determine the country of the origin of goods.

Definition of country of origin of goods according to Kyoto convention.

The country in which the goods have been produced or manufactured, according to the criteria laid down for the purposes of application of Customs tariff, quantitative restrictions or any other measures related to trade

Definition of rules of origin according to Kyoto convention?

"The specific provisions, developed from principles established by national legislation or international agreements applied by a country to determine the origin of goods".

Definition of origin of goods according to the Common Customs law.

Para (25) to Article (2) of the Common Customs Law defines the term origin of goods as follows: "The term origin of goods means the producing country, whether these goods are natural resources, agricultural crops or animal or industrial products.

Proof of origin of goods in accordance with the Common Customs law:

Article (25)
"Imported goods are subject of the proof of origin according to the rules of origin within the framework of the international and regional economic agreements in force".

According to this Article, any rules of origin set out in a protocol or an economic agreement with a given country shall be applicable and not the general rules of origin.

Rules of origin users:
- Customs Administrations.
- Ministry of economy.
- Ministry of Finance and Industry.
- Chamber of Industry & Commerce
- Industries
- International Organization (WCO, WTO)
- Dubai Government
- Federal Customs Authority
- GCC General Secretariat
- The Economic and Social Council of the Arab League

TYPE OF RULES OF ORIGIN

1. Preferential Rules of Origin.
Preferential rules of origin shall be defend as those laws, regulations, and administrative determinations of general application applied by a country to determine whether good qualify for preferential treatment under contractual or autonomous trade regimes leading to the granting of tariff preferences (reduced customs duty) of a specific country or countries.

For additional analytical, marketing, investment and business opportunities
information, please contact
Global Investment & Business Center, USA
(202) 546-2103. Fax: (202) 546-3275. E-mail: rusric@erols.com

2. Non-preferential rules of origin.

Non-prudential rules of origin shall be defined as laws, regulations, and administrative determinations of general application applied by a country to determine the country of origin of goods, used for the purposes of application of customs tariff, trade statistics, quantitative restrictions, anti-dumping, countervailing duties, origin marking and government procurement.

Origin determination Criteria.

1. Wholly obtained products.

Goods produced wholly in a given country shall be taken in that country for example live animal born and raised in that country, vegetable products harvested or gathered in the territorial waters of that country and mineral products extracted from the soil or sea-bed of that country.

2. Substantial transformation criterion.

- The criterion of change of tariff classification.
- Added Value percentage criterion.
- The criterion of manufacturing or processing operation.

Operations, which do not contribute to the essential characters or properties of the goods:

- Operations necessary for assuring the proper preservation of goods for the purposes of transportation or storage.

- Operations for facilitating the procedures of shipment and transportations of goods.

- Operations of packing and marketing of goods.

- Simple processes done to the goods including: ventilation, drying, varnishing, animal slaughtering.

Importance of determining the origin of a given product.

- To determine whether or not the goods may receive preferential treatment.

- For the purposes of application of trade policy tools and measures, such as anti-dumping duties and other safeguard measures.

- For the purposes of trade statistics (balance of trade).

- For the purposes of application of trademarks and labels.

- Government procurement.

Meaning of wholly obtained products.

The following goods only shall be taken to be produced wholly in a given country:

a) Mineral products extracted from its soil, from its territorial waters or from it's seabed.
b) Vegetable products harvested or gathered in that country.
c) Live animal's born and raised in that country.
d) Products obtained from animals in that country.

For additional analytical, marketing, investment and business opportunities information, please contact
Global Investment & Business Center, USA
(202) 546-2103. Fax: (202) 546-3275. E-mail: rusric@erols.com

e) Products ordained from hunting or fishing conducts in that country.
f) Products obtained by maritime fishing and other products taken from the sea by a vessel of that country.
g) Products obtained aboard a factory ship of that country solely from products of the kind covered in Para (f) above.
h) Scrap and waste from manufacturing and processing operations, and used articles, collected in that country and fit only for the recovery of raw materials.
i) Goods produced in that country solely from products referred to in paras (a) to (i).

Legal and international obligations.

Protocols and rules of origin Articles for the economic and free trade areas agreements.

Para (25) to Article (2) of the Common Customs Law.

Article (25) of the Common Customs Law.

MEMORANDUM OF UNDERSTANDING

Between

The Government of Abu Dhabi represented by the Finance Department of the Emirate of Abu Dhabi
as the Department
and as Member
relating to
The Gold Card Program

This Memorandum of Understanding ("MOU") is dated _____ and made

BETWEEN:

(1)   **The Government of Abu Dhabi Represented by the Finance Department of the Emirate of Abu Dhabi,** (the "Department"); and

(2)   [   ], (the "Member"), registered in [_____] as [_____] company and having its registered office at [_____].

Background:

(A)   The Department, through Abu Dhabi Customs, is responsible for, inter alia, facilitating trade across the Emirate of Abu Dhabi and monitoring compliance by the importers and exporters with the federal laws of the United Arab Emirates ("UAE"), the laws of Abu Dhabi and the regional and international rules and regulations to which the UAE has acceded.

(B)   The Member is regularly engaged in the business of importing and exporting goods to and from the UAE.

(C)   The Department has developed an initiative (the "Gold Card Program") that allows the Department to more efficiently and effectively conduct its business activities whilst at the

For additional analytical, marketing, investment and business opportunities
information, please contact
Global Investment & Business Center, USA
(202) 546-2103. Fax: (202) 546-3275. E-mail: rusric@erols.com

same time developing a more flexible relationship with importers and exporters and establishing a voluntary compliance regime by such parties (the "Program").

(D)   The purpose of this MOU is to set out the main terms pursuant to which the Member will operate under the Program.

THE PROGRAM

The Program adopts the World Customs Organisation ("WCO") Standards to Secure and Facilitate Global Trade and incorporates an agreed code of conduct between the Department and members of the Program who are able to establish, to the satisfaction of the Department, a history of accurate and timely provision of information and discharge of monetary and other obligations.

Under the Program, a member will be able to electronically lodge and complete the customs declaration process prior to the arrival of its goods pursuant to a pre-clearing system established for this purpose by the Department.

Instead of having to submit all necessary supporting documents to the Department, The Member will only be required to submit the information required in the Al Dhabi declaration form at the time of the relevant import or export.

MEMBERSHIP

Effective the date of this MOU, the Member shall become a member of the Program and shall, subject to the terms of this MOU, maintain such status for so long as this MOU remains in force.

MEMBER OBLIGATIONS

For the Member to maintain its status as a member of the Program, it will have to comply with the following:

maintain a data accuracy level of not less than 95% of the information supplied through Al Dhabi declaration form;

the Program's Business Rules and Standards set out in Schedule 1 hereof;

the laws, regulations and rules applicable to it, its business and the imported or exported goods whether in the UAE or abroad;

any compliance improvement plan as may be directed or agreed to by the Department;

any policies, instructions, directions or requirements made by the Department from time to time; and
not do or omit to do anything that may adversely affect the reputation of the Department.

The Member shall ensure that it has in place appropriate procedures to guarantee its compliance with the requirements of the Program and this MOU.

The Member shall nominate an authorised customs agent or an employee or officer of the Member (the "Representative") to act on its behalf in relation to transactions with the Department. For the purposes of this MOU, the Member hereby appoints [   ] as its Representative.

For additional analytical, marketing, investment and business opportunities
information, please contact
Global Investment & Business Center, USA
(202) 546-2103. Fax: (202) 546-3275. E-mail: rusric@erols.com

The Member represents and warrants to the Department that the Representative has full power and authority to act on behalf of the Member and the Department will be entitled to rely on any information, declaration or statement provided or made by the Representative as complete and accurate.

The Member shall ensure that its Representative is aware of the Member's obligations under this MOU and is at all times kept fully informed as to the business affairs of the Member.
The Representative will comply with all directions of the Department made within the scope of this MOU including, without limitation, any instruction, order, request, requirement or authorisation.

The Member will promptly notify in writing and will keep the Department fully informed at all times of all matters concerning the import and export activities of the Member to the extent they relate to customs matters and any matters which may impact on the compliance by the Member with its obligations under this MOU or may cause the Department to suffer or incur any loss, damage or expense.

The Member will obtain and maintain throughout the term of this MOU, at its own expense, all necessary permits, licences, authorisations any other permissions (whether statutory or otherwise) required to perform its business activities and obligations under and in relation to this MOU.

AUDIT AND INSPECTION

The Department or its nominated representative shall be entitled to audit and inspect the books and records of the Member at anytime to verify the compliance or otherwise by the Member with its obligations under the Program and this MOU.

The Member will and will ensure that its Representative and directors, employees, officers, professional advisors and agents will fully co-operate with the Department in relation to any audit or inspection conducted pursuant to this clause 4.

CONSEQUENCES OF NON-COMPLIANCE

Without prejudice to: (i) any other rights the Department may have; and (ii) any civil or criminal liability the Member may be responsible for, if:
following an audit by the Department, it appears that the member is not complying with any of its obligations hereunder;

either party to this MOU identifies areas that will require improvement; or

the Member fails to maintain at a data accuracy compliance standard of at least 95%;

> the Department may:

(a)   issue a notice requiring the Member to immediately rectify the relevant non-compliance in which case the Member shall comply with such notice with a maximum of 15 days from the date thereof; and/or
(b)   require the Member to adhere to a compliance improvement plan developed by the Department in consultation with the Member (broadly on the terms identified in Schedule 2 hereof) and may further instruct the Member to submit to the Department a detailed plan for the remedy of the relevant deficiencies; then
(c)   failing (a) or (b) above, terminate this MOU with immediate effect and withdraw the member status from the Member.

For additional analytical, marketing, investment and business opportunities information, please contact
Global Investment & Business Center, USA
(202) 546-2103. Fax: (202) 546-3275. E-mail: rusric@erols.com

Notwithstanding anything to the contrary in this MOU, the Department may terminate this MOU with immediate effect by notice to the Member in the event the Member is in breach of any applicable law, regulation, directive, resolution or order of a competent court of authority.

DEPARTMENT'S INTELLECTUAL PROPERTY

No Intellectual Property rights in any data, hardware, software, documentation, models, samples, tools and other materials provided or made available to the Member by the Department will transfer to the Member. The Member will return all such materials to the Department in good order and condition promptly upon request and, in any case, on termination of this MOU. The Member will not, and will procure that its Representative, directors, officers, employees and agents do not, use or copy such data, hardware, software, documentation or materials for any other purpose other than for the Member's compliance with its obligations under this MOU.

INDEMNITY

The Member will on demand fully indemnify and keep indemnified the Department from and against any and all cost, loss, expense, liability, claim or damage of whatsoever nature (including any liability for legal fees and expenses) whether direct, indirect or consequential including (without limitation), any costs reasonably incurred in preventing, avoiding or mitigating loss, liability or damage which the Department incurs or suffers as a consequence of, or would not have arisen but for any default or negligence by the Member or its Representative, directors, officers, employees or agents in the due and punctual performance of any of the Members obligations under this MOU including (without limitation) any act or omission, neglect or default of the Member or any breach of this MOU or act or omission by the Member in respect of any matter arising from the performance of the Member's import and/ or export activities.

GENERAL

No failure or delay on the part of either party to exercise any right or remedy under this MOU will be construed or will operate as a waiver of that right or remedy nor will any single or partial exercise of any right or remedy.
Nothing in this MOU will limit or exclude either party's liability in respect of death or personal injury caused by the negligence or wilful misconduct of such party or in respect of fraudulent misrepresentation by such party.

CONSULTATION OF DEPARTMENT

The mere fact of any review, inspection, check, monitoring, test, approval or recommendation in relation to any matter by the Department or any person acting on its behalf will not relieve the Member from its obligations under this MOU unless such relief is given in writing.

NO PARTNERSHIP OR AGENCY

Nothing in this MOU will constitute, or be deemed to constitute, a partnership between the Department and the Member nor will it constitute, or be deemed to constitute, the Department or the Member being the agent of the other for any purpose.
The Member shall not have any right or authority to, and will not, do any act, enter into any contract, make any representation, give any warranty, incur any liability, assume any obligation, whether express or implied, of any kind on behalf of the Department or bind the Department in any way.

NO EXCLUSIVITY

For additional analytical, marketing, investment and business opportunities information, please contact
Global Investment & Business Center, USA
(202) 546-2103. Fax: (202) 546-3275. E-mail: rusric@erols.com

- The acceptance by the Department of the Member under the Program will not preclude the Department from accepting other members under the Program.

NO GIFTS

Neither party will give or will in the future offer to give or agree to give any person employed by the other or acting on its behalf any gift, commission or consideration of any kind as an inducement or reward for doing or forbearing to do or for having done or forborne to do any act in relation to the obtaining or performance of this MOU or forbearing to show favour or disfavour to any person in relation to this MOU which would breach the Department's policy from time to time.

ASSIGNMENT

The Department may at any time assign all or any part of its rights and benefits under this MOU. The Department may disclose to a proposed assignee information in its possession relating to this MOU and the Program and concerning the Member which it is necessary to disclose for the purposes of the proposed assignment.
The Member shall not assign all or any of its rights or benefits under this MOU.

CAPACITY AND AUTHORITY

Each party warrants and represents to the other that:
it has full capacity and authority to enter into and to perform this MOU and that all necessary consents have been obtained and that this MOU is executed by its duly authorised representatives; and

it has full capacity and authority to perform its obligations under this MOU.

DISPUTE RESOLUTION AND JURISDICTION

20.1   Any dispute arising out of or in connection with this MOU, including any question regarding the existence, scope, validity, or termination of this MOU or this clause (and including any tortious or statutory claims) shall be referred to and finally resolved by arbitration in and pursuant to the rules of the Abu Dhabi Commercial Conciliation and Arbitration Centre, which rules are deemed to be incorporated by reference into this clause.

20.2   The number of arbitrators shall be three (3), one chosen by each of the parties hereof and the third appointed by agreement of the two arbitrators or, if the arbitrators cannot agree, the third arbitrator shall be appointed by the chairman of the Abu Dhabi Commercial Conciliation and Arbitration Centre.

20.3   The seat of the arbitration shall be Abu Dhabi, United Arab Emirates.

IN WITNESS WHEREOF this MOU has been duly executed the day and year first before written.

SIGNED by [   ]

for and on behalf of
Government of Abu Dhabi, represented by the Finance Department
SIGNED by [   ]

for and on behalf of
[the Member]

SCHEDULE (1):BUSINESS RULES AND STANDARDS

For additional analytical, marketing, investment and business opportunities information, please contact
Global Investment & Business Center, USA
(202) 546-2103. Fax: (202) 546-3275. E-mail: rusric@erols.com

Standard 1: Keeping Information

The Member will have available, for production to the Department on request:

An explanation of the supply chain covering international sources and trading partners that shows what business relationships exist with suppliers or sources.

A personnel list, which includes any employee or subcontractor providing facilitated trade information to the Department or who makes decisions relating to the collection and preparation of any information communicated to Department.

All information relating to the importation and/or exportation of goods capable of verification, so as to produce an auditable record. This includes capacity to store, create and recreate information made for the preparation of customs declarations;

The information held under this standard shall be held for a period of five calendar years from the date of generation unless disposal is authorized in writing by the Department.

Standard 2: Information Accuracy

The Member will comply with all statutory requirements for the declaration of goods and meet, specified accuracy standards for all importation and exportation of goods over any audit period. Until notified otherwise over any audit period, no more than 5% of the declaration entry lines can have any of the following pieces of information incorrect:

(1)   Classification;
(2)   Quantity;
(3)   Customs import or export value;
(4)   Transport and insurance, to the extent that costs of transport and insurance are not included in the customs value in (iii);

(5)   Country of origin or destination;
(6)   Port of discharge; and
(7)   Where applicable, exemptions or concessions.

For the purposes of this accreditation standard an entry line is incorrect when:

For classification of goods the entry line customs value exceeds AED [_____] and the goods classification is incorrect at the six digit HS level; or

The customs value for goods reported and the actual value differs by AED [_____] or 10% of the value of the goods, whichever is less; or

The total amount of revenues collected is under or over declared by AED [_____];

For the purposes of this accreditation standard:

Any line containing one or more of the errors set out in 2.4 is counted as a single line in error. Any line containing one or more errors other than those set out in 2.4 is not counted as a line in error.

Standard 3: Other Agencies

The Member will identify in advance if goods require a permit from a municipal or federal agency before it is either imported or exported and the relevant documentation has been obtained where possible. The relevant document number is then included on the Al Dhabi documentation.

Where goods require an approval authorization before clearance and the Member is unable to obtain the relevant authority from the agency responsible for issuing such approvals before importing or exporting the goods, the Department may issue a conditional clearance subject only to the acquisition of such an approval as required by paragraph 3.1 to become an unconditional clearance.

Once an approval authorization is obtained under paragraph 3.2 and the relevant approval number is included on the documents, customs clearance is completed.

Subsequent to the completion of the conditional clearance, the proof of existence of such an

For additional analytical, marketing, investment and business opportunities information, please contact
Global Investment & Business Center, USA
(202) 546-2103. Fax: (202) 546-3275. E-mail: rusric@erols.com

approval is to be treated as one of the documents supporting declarations under Accreditation Standard 1 ("Keeping Information") of this agreement.

To facilitate clearance and risk management the Department may allow other municipal and federal agencies access to relevant EDI documentation in electronic formats to be agreed. In each case access will be limited to the classes of transactions for which each municipal or federal agency has responsibility to issue an approval authorization.

Standard 4: Internal Systems

The applicant must have systems in place that identify and remedy systemic errors that may occur in the preparation of information for the Department.

Where information relating to import and/or export information has been sent to the Department, and is subsequently found to be incorrect because of a systemic error, the accredited company must maintain a record of:

How such errors were made; and
What action was taken to correct the error; and
What action was taken to ensure the error does not recur.

Standard 5: Internal and External Audit

The Member may conduct a self-assessment audit (see Schedule C) and demonstrate the systems and processes they have in place to mitigate identified potential risk areas in their processes for supplying information to the Department.

Provided that internal audit demonstrates how they mitigate the following identified general Customs risks, this may be considered favourably by the Department when developing its risk management and audit plans for accredited businesses.

Notwithstanding the right to access to documents and information of the Member under paragraph 5.2, the Member will allow periodic routine audits by the Department, at time periods to be mutually agreed between the parties, to verify information accuracy is maintained within the standards set out in Accreditation Standard 2: Information Accuracy.

SCHEDULE 2:COMPLIANCE IMPROVEMENT PLAN – GENERAL TERMS

If required a Compliance Improvement Plan involves the following steps:

The Member and the Department or the Member and its external auditors determine any non-compliance and its likely cause by reviewing current internal control procedures, and where breakdown has occurred.

The Member then determines corrective actions to ensure future compliance.

The Member outlines to the Department the corrective actions to be taken and timeframes for implementation and validation.

The Department will inform the Member if the plan addresses the identified deficiencies or whether additional information is necessary.

Upon full implementation, the Member should validate whether the corrective action taken was effective.

After the Compliance Improvement Plan has been fully implemented and a reasonable time has

For additional analytical, marketing, investment and business opportunities information, please contact
Global Investment & Business Center, USA
(202) 546-2103. Fax: (202) 546-3275. E-mail: rusric@erols.com

elapsed, the Department will perform a follow up review to determine whether the corrective actions taken have eliminated the compliance issues. The timing of the follow up review will be determined by the Department in consultation with the Member.

If the results show that the Member has rectified the problems, and the Member meets all other standards it will remain in the Program.

If the results show that the Member has not corrected the problem/s, then the Department will deem the Member unsuitable for the Program.

GENERAL AND SPECIFIC CUSTOMS RISKS (EXAMPLES OF RISK AREAS)

1: General Customs Risks in order of Significance

Ref	Area	Risk
1.1	National Security	Prevention of importation of goods for use in activity that will hinder national security.
1.2	Corporate Security	IT security generally: security of electronic recording systems relied on by customs.
1.3		Security of personnel: security access to recording systems relied on by customs and control of passwords.
1.4		Succession plan for loss of IT system.
1.5	Physical Security	Access of personnel to areas of Customs Control
1.6	Prohibited Imports & Exports	Import or export of prohibited goods within the business's normal transactions
1.7	Restricted Imports & Exports	Import or export of restricted in the business's normal transactions without relevant approvals.
1.8	Collusion	Agreement within the business to evade the law.
		Controls on new employees
1.9	Revenue	See Industry risks below.

2: Industry Risks for importers in order of Significance		
Ref	Area	Risk
2.1	Classification	Misclassification.
2.2	Origin & Preference	Inaccurate origin description Inappropriate usage of concessions
2.3	Exemptions	Inappropriate use of goods imported for exempt or specified usages: Defense goods. Industry development Other concessional usage
2.4	Valuation	Incorrect use of valuation principals through inaccurate recording of invoicing and payment techniques – --Price averaging, --Package deals --Overstated or ineligible deductions -- Undisclosed payments --related transactions --transfer pricing
2.5	Restricted Imports & Exports	Import or export of restricted in the business's normal transactions without relevant approvals.

For additional analytical, marketing, investment and business opportunities information, please contact
Global Investment & Business Center, USA
(202) 546-2103. Fax: (202) 546-3275. E-mail: rusric@erols.com

2.6	Surplus goods undeclared	Not invoiced or reported for adjustment.
2.7	Assists, royalties, agreements	Inappropriate usage, not included in the price,
2.8	Permits	Restrictions on usage not met.
2.9	Intellectual property & Trademarks	Inaccurate or illegal usage.
2.10	Other taxes and fees (future)	Drawbacks, refunds deferments

3: Industry Risks for service providers (agents & carriers)		
Ref	Area	Risk
3.1	Source information	Source information on supplier incorrectly provided.
3.2	Express, Couriers & Transportation	Goods imported/exported without declaration. Goods in transit not accounted for on final delivery or in transit Import linked to incorrect declaration Incorrect report of critical fields Owner Supplier, Origin Valuation Permits
3.3	Brokers	Goods imported/exported without declaration. Misclassification Misuse of exemption or free rate Incorrect interpretation of advice or binding rulings. Temporary imports not re-exported
3.4	Warehouses and Cargo Stores	Inappropriate usage Stock not accounted for.
3.5	Restricted Imports & Exports	Import or export of restricted in the business's normal transactions without relevant approvals.
3.6	Surplus goods undeclared	Not invoiced or reported for adjustment.
3.7	Assists, royalties, agreements	Inappropriate usage, not included in the price,
3.8	Permits	Restrictions on usage not met.
3.9	Intellectual property & Trademarks	Inaccurate or illegal usage.
3.10	Other taxes and fees (future)	Drawbacks, refunds deferments

CUSTOMS PROCEDURES

Mirsal is the birth of a new generation of cargo community of sea and air agents, freight forwarders, importers and free zone companies to accommodate the fast upcoming future of goods transportation and document handling for the UAE

For additional analytical, marketing, investment and business opportunities information, please contact
Global Investment & Business Center, USA
(202) 546-2103. Fax: (202) 546-3275. E-mail: rusric@erols.com

MIRSAL COMPONENTS

▉AIR AUTOMATION SYSTEM (AAS)

- Air Delivery Order
- Agents Transfer Authority
- Demand Notice

▉EXIT ENTRY CERTIFICATE (EEC)

- Free zone Export system
- Exit Entry Certificate
- Demand Notice

▉VEHICLE CLEARANCE CERTIFICATE (VCC)

- Vehicle Clearance Certificate Entry
- Cancellation of vehicle certificate

▉ACCOUNT

- Bank Guarantee Account
- Standing Guarantee Account
- Customs Duty Receipt Account
- Deposit and Refund

▉STATISTICAL INQUIRY SYSTEM (WEB-BASED)

Answer all your enquiries on Dubai statistical information on the web.

- Hscode Enquiry (import, export & re-export)
- Country of origin
- Country of shipment/destination
- Products by country and vice versa

▉MIRSAL ONLINE (WEB-BASED)

A tool to deliver a secure and fast processing of customs related documentation for just-in-time transportation environment through the use of a web based network.

- Bill of Entry processing
- Delivery Order
- Electronic Payment Gateway

▉ As part of its commitment of being one of the leading organizations in providing the best and newest services to its customers, Department of Ports & Customs intend to deploy HS Codes Directory. Every item that is imported, exported or Re-exported through Dubai should be classified according to the HS Code System. The Directory of HS Codes Application (AL

For additional analytical, marketing, investment and business opportunities information, please contact
Global Investment & Business Center, USA
(202) 546-2103. Fax: (202) 546-3275. E-mail: rusric@erols.com

MUNASSAQ) is introduced mainly to help consignees in selecting the HS Codes that best fit their good s.

OBJECTIVE OF THE APPLICATION

The benefits of this system are many, however the important ones among them are listed below:

1. Globalization and E-Commerce.
2. Dubai Customs intends to publish Online statistical information of the trade flow on the WEB. Decision-makers should be able to use this information in evaluating their business planning.

FEATURES OF ALMUNASSAQ

1. A Search engine that can search for as many keywords as required. The Domain consists of Chapters and Sections and the user can limit the search to a specific domain. The user can review search results interactively while changing the domain.
2. User can save HS Codes of frequent use in the Bookmark Tab. All search rules are applicable for bookmarked Codes in such a way that the user can find specific code from the bookmark irrespective of the number of Codes that have been bookmarked.
3. Each user can make a hard copy of HS Codes, which are displayed in the search board.
4. The application allows the User to print the Hs codes based on the Invoice as per Customs format, that can be directly processed by the Customs staff, thus releasing the importer from the task of writing documents. Before printing the document, user is prompted for the Reference number, date and document remarks
5. Every printed document is stored in the history table. History can be filtered to a specific period of time, thus the history form will display only those documents which satisfy the date filter. User can also view and manipulate the previously printed documents. All subsequent manipulations will affect only the filtered documents.
6. User can fine-tune the application tasks from the Options menu, which has a number of options that controls the behavior of the application.
7. Generate reports of mainly three types

   - List of Hs Code Entries
   - list of selected hs codes
   - list of issued documents

SYSTEM OVERVIEW

This software has been developed under Microsoft Windows 95/98 environment by Information Technology Center, Department of Ports and Customs, Dubai.
The Harmonized System Codes (HS Code) is a standard issued by the World Customs Organization (WCO) to unify the classification of the goods. These are six digit codes for identifying different products across the world. The country using these Hscodes can suffix additional digits to the existing six digits according to their needs. Dubai Customs has suffixed the Hscodes with two additional digits, thus making them an eight digit code.
HS Code system classifies goods into 21 sections based on goods categories. Every section consists of chapters, which are further divided into headings. Each heading consists of Hs codes representing similar type of goods.

From 1st January' 2000. Dubai Customs requires every Consignee to specify Hscodes instead of just goods description mentioned in the Invoice before generating a Bill of Entry. Along with each

For additional analytical, marketing, investment and business opportunities information, please contact
Global Investment & Business Center, USA
(202) 546-2103. Fax: (202) 546-3275. E-mail: rusric@erols.com

Hs code the Consignee should also give details of total weight, Quantity (if applicable), package Type, CIF Value and currency code.

SEA PORT BILLS

An importer code is a pre-requisite for importers. This is issued to traders who hold valid trade license issued by the economic or municipal departments in the U.A.E and can be obtained over the counter by submitting the application in the prescribed form together with the copy of the trade license. Importers are allowed to import only the goods in the category specified in the license.

Likewise, Clearing Agents clearing goods on behalf of importers should have a Clearing Agent code as a pre-requisite. This code is issued to Clearing and Forwarding Agents with the relevant license, on applying in the prescribed form together with the copy of the license.

The clearance for the movement of goods are given on various types of bills, the type of the bill depending on the status, destination, origin or in certain cases on the choice of the importer.

IMPORTS BILLS

The normal imports for local or any other AGCC country consumption is cleared on Import Bills.

The documents required are:

1. A delivery order from the Shipping Agent in duplicate.
2. Original Invoice
3. Original Certificate of Origin
4. Packing List
5. Bill of Lading Second original

On presenting the above documents, customs will collect customs duty, if applicable, and clear the import bill. The bill in triplicate along with the original delivery order will be returned to the client which he can present to the port section for subsequent payment of port charges and delivery of the goods. (If the importer does not possess any of the above documents other than the delivery order, customs may accept a deposit temporarily in lieu of the document).

The client can pay duty through the following methods:

• By Cash or cheque

• By Customs Duty Guarantee issued by a bank

• Through Banks authorized to collect customs in which case, the bank duty receipt should accompany the documents.

• Through Account for clients holding Customs Duty Credit facility.

Bill Registration charges apply as per relevant Customs Notices.

IMPORTS FOR RE-EXPORT

Consignees, with Customs approval, may import goods with the intention of re-exporting them within 180 days, on payment of a deposit or submission of a bank guarantee in lieu of duty. In these cases the deposit or bank guarantee is refunded/released on proof of re-export. Goods

For additional analytical, marketing, investment and business opportunities information, please contact
Global Investment & Business Center, USA
(202) 546-2103. Fax: (202) 546-3275. E-mail: rusric@erols.com

remaining in the UAE after 180 days are liable for duty payment. In such cases documentation is the same as for imports, except that:

import is declared as Import for Re-export

pay deposit or submit bank guarantee in lieu of Customs duty.

Re-exporting of such goods is subject to Customs inspection before they are re-exported.

Bill Registration charges apply as per Customs Notices.

NOTE:For both Import and import for re-export of restricted goods, written approval from the concerned government department or ministry must be provided.

TEMPORARY ADMISSION

In both the cases documentation is the same as for Import for Re-export except declared as for "Temporary Admission".

Goods imported for exhibitions must be re-exported within 90 days of import. Permits to such exhibitions which are issued by the concerned authorities must be presented at the time of import. The goods must be inspected prior to packing them for re-export. On request Customs will arrange sealing consignments, after they have been stuffed in container at the exhibition site, pending re-export.

Equipment imported for temporary use in construction, scientific research, development projects, for repair or maintenance are given sufficient time to re-export considering the period of contract or other documentary evidence to justify the period required.

In both the cases documentation is the same as for Import for Re-export except that the import should be declared as for "Temporary Admission".

Bill Registration charges apply as per Customs Notices.

TRANSIT

Consignments received on a through bill of lading and consigned to destination outside the UAE, and dispatched overland are cleared on a "Transit Bill". The agent should submit to Customs the following:

• Delivery Order by the Shipping Agent.

• Copy of Bill of Lading or Manifest.

• Evidence of value (if available or else Customs will estimate.)

• Deposit or Guarantee amounting to the potential duty liability shall be required which will be refunded or released on production of proof of exit of the goods out of the UAE within 30 days of the Transit Bill date.

Bill Registration charges apply as per Customs Notices.

TRANSSHIPMENT

For additional analytical, marketing, investment and business opportunities
information, please contact
Global Investment & Business Center, USA
(202) 546-2103. Fax: (202) 546-3275. E-mail: rusric@erols.com

Consignments received on a through Bill of lading and consigned to a destination outside the UAE and dispatched by sea direct from the port (SHIP-SHORE-SHIP or SHIP-TO-SHIP) are cleared on Transshipment Bill. The ship's Agent should submit to Customs a Delivery Order.

Bill Registration charges apply as per Customs Notices.

RE-EXPORT PROCEDURE FOR GOODS OF FOREIGN ORIGIN

Documents required:
• Original Invoice
• Re-export Declaration duly completed
• Copy of the import bill for re-export.
• In the case of vehicle re-export, export permit from the Traffic Department required.
• Goods imported for re-export are subject to Customs inspection before they are re-exported in order to get the deposit refunded or guarantee released.

The re-export is cleared on an Export Bill. While re-exporting goods on which the importer intends to claim the deposit paid on importation, the following documentation should be completed:
Re-Export by Road:

- An Exit/Entry Certificate duly certified by the customs inspector evidencing the stuffing or packing etc. and by the customs authorities at the point of exit..
- Road Manifest.

By sea:

- An Exit/Entry Certificate duly certified by the customs inspector evidencing the stuffing or packing etc. and by the customs authorities at the point of exit..
- Clear the export Bill.

By Air:

- An Exit/Entry Certificate duly certified by the customs inspector evidencing the stuffing or packing etc. and by the customs authorities at the point of exit..
- Airway bill
- Export Bill.

Exports by launches or other country crafts:

- An Exit/Entry Certificate duly certified by the customs inspector evidencing the stuffing or packing etc. and by the customs authorities at the point of exit..
- Export Manifest.
- Bill Registration charges apply as per Customs Notices.

EXPORT PROCEDURE FOR GOODS OF UAE ORIGIN.

There is no duty on exports, but shippers are required to provide Customs with the following information:

• Original Invoice

• Export Declaration duly completed

For additional analytical, marketing, investment and business opportunities
information, please contact
Global Investment & Business Center, USA
(202) 546-2103. Fax: (202) 546-3275. E-mail: rusric@erols.com

• In the case of vehicle export, export permit from the Police Department required. Export Declaration must NOT be raised for export covered by Free Zone, DFSA, Transit Bills. Breaches of this rule shall result in the imposition of fines in accordance with Customs Notice No. 110/84.

The export is cleared on an Export Bill.

Bill Registration charges apply as per Customs Notices.

CUSTOMER SERVICE DESKS

CUSTOMER HOTLINE NUMBER: 8004410

CENTER NAME	OPERATOR	EXTENSION	DIRECT	FAX
PORT RASHID CUSTOMS	3455555	737 / 787	3023737	3453458
JEBEL ALI CUSTOMS	8816375	218	8055218	3453458
CARGO VILLAGE CUSTOMS	2828888	236	7051236	3453458
AIRPORT FREE ZONE CUSTOMS	2994444	------	----------	3453458
DUCAMZ CUSTOMS	3335000	204	----------	3453458
HAMRIYAH CUSTOMS	2660066	------	----------	3453458
COSTAL CUSTOMS	2241222	230	----------	3453458
LAND CUSTOMS	2652018	-------	----------	3453458
POST OFFICE CUSTOMS	3374546	-------	----------	3453458
AWEER CUSTOMS	3378473	-------	3378473	3453458

E-MAIL : customersservicedirectorate@dxbcustoms.gov.ae

CUSTOMS FAQS

Question:
I WANT TO KNOW THE CUSTOMS PROCEDURE AND CUSTOMS TARIFFS.

Solution:
the customs Tariff has been divided to the unified GCC Tariff as following :-

1. List of exempted commodities according to the unified GCC Tariff.
2. Tobacco to be collected as 100 % of value of per kg. Of gross weight, whichever is higher.
3. Alcohol to be collected as 50 % of CIF value.
4. All other items to be collected as 50% of CIF value.

Bill/Document Delivery Order Invoice Certificate of Origin Bill of Lading Packing List
Import ü ü ü ü ü
Import for re-export ü ü ü ü ü
Overland Transit ü copy ü
Transshipment ü ü
Vehicle import for personal use (copy of Passport) ü ü

1. Issue delivery order from shipping company.

For additional analytical, marketing, investment and business opportunities information, please contact
Global Investment & Business Center, USA
(202) 546-2103. Fax: (202) 546-3275. E-mail: rusric@erols.com

2. Affix Israel boycott stamp.
3. Bill clearing by operations staff & payment of duties.
4. Payment of ports fees.
5. Goods inspection, if necessary.
6. Collection of goods from Port.

Question:

I am a manufacturer of gold jewellery in South Africa.
I have plans to come to Dubai to market my product and want to carry about 100kg of readymade gold chains in 18k. My inquiry is what are the custom duty and how is it processed. I was told by my friends in Dubai that if you are bringing in bulk there is a special duty on KGs. I don't know how far that is true but please inform me on the same as soon as possiable.
Your early attention to this request is highly appreciated.
Thanking you in advance.
Yours
mayers seagal

Solution:

You are welcome to Dubai with your 18k gold chains with the following condition :-

Any gold Trader in dubai must sponsor you .
Invoice for the gold shipment.
Duty or deposit amount will be 5% on CIF value , and no special duty on KGs .

We hope you to requires this details to serve you purpose and assure of our best cooperation and service always .

Question:

I am planning to visit Dubai for a short period of 15 days and interested to bring my personal car, which is Audi TT 1.8 300bhp Model 2001. You are kindly requested provide the following information

1) What will be the any Custom Duty on import of personal used car for a short period as this car in not for sale and am shippign back to UK.

3) What documents are required to clear the car from Customs and and what are the UAE car import standard.
Your immediate guidance will be highly appreciated.
Yours faithfully
Mr J Govind

Solution:

Dear Govind,

Thank you for your enquiry dated 17th September 2003,pertaining to the subject matter.

We are sorry for delaying and pleased to inform you that the vehicle will be cleared after inspection for GCC specification, if the vehicle is not coming under GCC specification, you have to approach min of Finance & Ind for a GCC standardization from .

Since the car is intended for Re-export back to UK within six months, you have to keep a deposit equivalent to 5% of the assessed value which will be refunded after re-exportation.

Delivery order from the Shipping Co., Ownership documents of the vehicle .

For additional analytical, marketing, investment and business opportunities information, please contact
Global Investment & Business Center, USA
(202) 546-2103. Fax: (202) 546-3275. E-mail: rusric@erols.com

We hope the above will serve you purpose and assure of our best cooperation and service always .

Question:
what is Hs Code?

Solution:
Dear Subash,

Thank you for your enquiry dated 9th September 2003, pertaining to the subject matter.

The Harmonized System (HS) is a multipurpose tariff nomenclature classifying over 5225 type of commodities crossing international borders. Under is 1243 classified headings , commodity groups, there describe the basis of classification, chapter 97 is left for future use whilst chapter 98 and 99 are left for special purpose used by any member state.
The items in chapters 98 and 99 are classified based upon the HS but only each individual country knows the contents.
Moreover , supplementary publication such as HS Explanatory Notes, HS Commodity Database, and compendium of classification Opinions are published by WCO to ensure uniform application of classification rules worldwide.
According to WCO, currently over 179 countries and customs unions use the HS as a basis for their customs tariff and more than 98 percent of the commodities of the international trade are classified under the HS.

Question:
Our Managing Director is relocating from United States of America to Dubai, and he is interested to bring his personal car, which is BMW X5 3.0L Model 2001. You are kindly requested provide the following information

1) What will be the Custom Duty on import of personal used car
2) How you evaluate the value of the car
3) What documents are required to clear the car from Customs

Your immediate guidance will be highly appreciated.

Regards

Naeem Elahi
Office Administrator
Overseas Equipment Services, FZE
Mob. 050-5710599
[UPDATED ON: 9/9/03]
Thank you very much for your reply, But it seems that you have replied anyone else"s question. As my question is still unanswered, please see where is the mistake. As my question is regarding import of car.

Thanks and regards

Naeem
[UPDATED ON: 9/9/03]
Thank you very much for your reply, But it seems that you have replied anyone else"s question. As my question is still unanswered, please see where is the mistake. As my question is regarding import of car.

**For additional analytical, marketing, investment and business opportunities
information, please contact
Global Investment & Business Center, USA
(202) 546-2103. Fax: (202) 546-3275. E-mail: rusric@erols.com**

Thanks and regards

Naeem

Solution:
Dear Sheikh Naeem,

Thank you for your Updated enquiry dated 7th September 2003,pertaining to the subject matter.

Please be informed that this email has send to you by mistake so ignore the last email, and we re sorry for delaying .

1- Duty or deposit amount will be 5%on CIF value.
2- Assessing the value based model vehicle make and condition by our vehicle inspection section.
3- Registration paper from the exporting country or proof of ownership .

Question:
I like know what is the Custom Duty Fee for any Item brought from Outside.

As I recent brought a used PDA Cellphone from USA which a price of US $ 96.00
I end up paying Customer Duty .When a person visit Dubai he brings any item from outside he does not pay any Custom Duty.The Item I brought is for person use only .Why do I have to Pay Customer Duty fee..

My Next question is ,Is the Customer duty fee for other emirates is different from Dubai.Please kindly let me know what persentage do you calculate the Customer Duty.

Please kindly reply me as soon as possible by email or by calling me.

Thank you.
Ahad
0504948884

Solution:
Dear Ahad,

Thank you for your inquiry dated 4th October 2003, pertaining to the subject matter.

We are sorry for the delay and pleased to inform you that there is no duty on personal effects and the duty is same in all port of entries of UAE.

Question:
We are a steel fabrication unit presently engaged in the expansion works for Cargo Villiage, Dubai Airport.
For this project we have to import certain machinary items from Germany.
Kindly let us know the procedure to be adopted for exemption of Customs Duty.
Best regards
M G Thadani
Yerevan Steel Construction Co

Solution:

For additional analytical, marketing, investment and business opportunities information, please contact
Global Investment & Business Center, USA
(202) 546-2103. Fax: (202) 546-3275. E-mail: rusric@erols.com

Dear Thadani,

Thank you for your enquiry dated 20th September 2003,pertaining to the subject matter.

We are pleased to inform you that there is no exemption of customs duty, except the industrial license basis or according to unified G.C.C rules and regulation of customs H.S.code Tariff .

Question:
Dear sir,

As I know Dubai means Business The Opportunities, The Market, The Business Environment presents international business with a wide range of opportunities...

Since I am expatriate, Indian and having residence visa to work here in Adnoc, Abudhabi and my brother-in-law living India, he is doing export & import business and supplying handicraft items to European & American continents.
He is quite interested to cater the world market through Dubai too with innovative and environmental friendly handicraft items. Since individual, we would like to import handicraft items & gold jewellery for the local buyers in UAE.

I wish to know all details what are the terms & conditions (rules & regulation) for the custom clearance and to allow us as a individual to import such items in Dubai for local buyers.

Therefore, I look your support & extended f! avour for proper guidlines to put our products in Dubai market.

Anticipate your reply.

Thanks & best regards,

Suvesh

E-mail:sunnykumar_2@hotmail.com
Mobile +971 50 5469356

Solution:
Dear Suvesh,

Thank you for your inquiry dated 10th November 2003, pertaining to the subject matter.

We are pleased to inform you that as Dubai rules & Regulation first of all you must apply for handicraft & Gold Jewellery licenses as per Dubai Economic Department & Chamber of Commerce then you can import & clear handicraft & gold Jewellery Products with proper invoices and packing list provided having company import & export code and representative card with the payment of 5% customs duty on CIF value.

For additional analytical, marketing, investment and business opportunities information, please contact
Global Investment & Business Center, USA
(202) 546-2103. Fax: (202) 546-3275. E-mail: rusric@erols.com

STATES ECONOMIC PERFORMANCE AND OPPORTUNITIES

World oil prices fluctuations in1997havehad a significantimpact on the GCC economies.Prices sharp drop of 6.0per cent below 1996 levelwas a direct stimulus to the GDP reduction in the GCCStates from 5.9 per cent in 1996 to about 3.0per cent in 1997. The GCCstates GDP'sgrowth rate is projected to drop in 1998 compared with 1997.This could basically beattributed to the fact that these countries rely heavily on oil.

As it was projected that average oil price per barrel is to swing between 12.0 to 15.5 US dollars.In 1997, it was further assumed that the GCCstates oil revenues would drop below 1997 levels, and such drop would be sharp in certain GCC states.Accordingly oil sector'sgrowth is anticipated to decline in 1998 , as these sectors contribute the highest GDP share in theGCC states.Governments would be forced at the same time to adopt austerity economic measures to slash spending, due to fall in oil revenues which would have a negative economic impact on these countries.

 With respect to structural adjustments and economic major reformProgrammes been braced to improve internal and outside imbalances, certain GCCstates in 1997 have dropped the policyaiming to diversify and broaden tax revenues base, and reduce services and commodities subsidiesoffered by Governments.Gradual implementation of this policy should be maintained by GCC states to avoid sharp and sudden slumps in their revenues whenever there is a major decline in their oil revenues.

Inflation rates inmost GCC states in 1997 were less than most advanced and developing countries worldwide.Inflation rate recorded in most GCC states was less than3.0 per cent.As all GCC states currencies are tied to the US dollar, inflation has increased with the rise in the value of the Dollar against the Yen and most European and South EasternCurrencies.GCC commodity import Prices were reduced as a result of this, which helped to contain inflation rates at a low level.

Estimates indicate that GCC total exports were reduced by 4.8 percent in 1997 as a result of oil prices decline by 8.0per cent.It is projected that total exports would drop by 14.4 per cent in 1998 less than 1997 level.GCC imports have increased in 1997 by 3.5 per cent, and it is estimated to make a slight increase of 1.3 per cent in 1998 compared with 1997.

Estimates also indicate that the trade balance which has recorded US 49.8 billion surplus in 1996and increased by 34.2 per cent over its 2007 level, has shown a surplus too in 1997, despite its 16.9 per cent decline.It is estimated that in 1998 trade balance surplus would drop by 46.4 per cent- due to projected decline in oil exports revenues.

It is worth to refer to the staunch efforts exerted by GCC states regarding custom tariffs unification issue, which was recommended by member states.This issue was the basis of all inter-trade negotiations carried out in between GCC states in 1997.In addition to this, the European Union has decided to revive an old trade agreement with GCC states, whereas the only condition stipulated for signing this new trade agreement is to unify custom tariffs.

DUBAI PORT AUTHORITY

Dubai Ports Authority (DPA) is firmly committed to providing Quality Service to its customers. This is underlined by the ISO 9002 certification that we have achieved in our container terminal and general cargo operations. Our focus on continuous improvement has enabled us to maintain our position as the best port in the Middle East and a leading port in the world.

Dubai has become a major international center of trade in an evolving region. Dubai's infrastructure development plan spells out the government's commitment to trade and industry.

Always the entrepot, Dubai is the preferred regional headquarters for numerous multinational organizations, and home to a thriving commercial community. Some 50% of container cargo passing through Port Rashid and Jebel Ali terminals is now destined for Dubai whilst the rest is transshipped regionally. While we work to maintain our hub position, we will also increase our focus on the home market for which valuable import and export cargo can be generated. Our quality orientated, competitive service will continue to foster the import, export and transshipment possibilities through DPA, and in so doing, enhance Dubai's position as the center of trade in the region.

While striving to anticipate our customers' requirements we continue to invest in state-of-the-art cargo handling technology and information management systems, together with skilled personnel to run them. By continuing to develop in advance of need, we will be able to maintain our hub position and the distinction of being the most modern and technologically advanced port in the region.

Sultan Ahmed bin Sulayem
Chairman of Jebel Ali Free Zone Authority &
Managing Director of Dubai Ports Authority

ADVANTAGES

The emirate of Dubai is renowned for its pro-business culture and relative absence of red tape. The buoyant local economy offers increasing business opportunities.

Dubai's strategic location at the crossroads between East and West has made it the leading hub between Europe and the Far East . The city is the acknowledged gateway to a market of an estimated 1.5 billion people in the Gulf countries, Arab world, and surrounding region.

Due to Dubai's traditional trade links with its neighbours, shippers are keen to capitalize on Dubai's proven distribution capabilities.

GROWING LOCAL MARKET

Exports and re-exports are on the rise from Dubai, and the Jebel Ali Free Zone in particular. DPA has frequently demonstrated its ability to adapt quickly to changing trade patterns by picking up considerable business such as in the re-export of cotton and base metals from CIS countries and the sub-continent.

PORT PERFORMANCE

DPA is one of the leading transshipment centers in the world, serving more than 125 shipping lines. It is ranked 10th among the container ports of the world. In 1997, it handled 2.6 million TEU's, an increase of sixteen per cent on the previous year's achievement. The two terminals of Jebel Ali and port Rashid handled 10,243 vessels including 4,600 container vessels increasing seven per cent over 1996. The total tonnage handled rose to 36.0 million tonnes, up 18 percent over 1996.

ONE STEP AHEAD

Dubai Ports Authority takes pride in remaining one step ahead of its competition and in step with its customers. Strategic planners in all departments maintain close watch on developments within

For additional analytical, marketing, investment and business opportunities information, please contact
Global Investment & Business Center, USA
(202) 546-2103. Fax: (202) 546-3275. E-mail: rusric@erols.com

the industry, and are quick to forecast trends. For this reason, the port has invested in the most technically advanced cranes in the world. As ship builders re-think design, DPA plans for the possibility of handling the larger vessels required to cope with ever- increasing international container traffic. Equipment available with DPA**EFFICIENCIES OF EDI**

The advantages of Electronic Data Interchange (EDI) are recognized globally and DPA has pioneered an electronic manifest system. Working with the shipping community and related government departments, DPA has developed its own system as part of an ambitious plan for paperless cargo clearance in the near future.

AN AWARD WINNING PLAYER

For container customers, the key consideration is turn-around time and efficiency. DPA leads the region in these respects and was named best seaport in the Middle East for the fourth consecutive year in 1997, and best container terminal operator in the region.
DPA pursues quality in all of its operating areas. It is one of the few ports in the world, with ISO 9002 accreditation for its container and general cargo business. Achieving ISO standards commits the organization to a continual program of improvement in its processes. In June 1998, the Jebel Ali Free Zone Authority, which works in synergy with DPA, achieved ISO 9002 certification.

The service benefit: DPA's customer-driven service is second to none in the Middle East, and the port prides itself in finding creative solutions to the unique requirements of its business partners. DPA Sales and Customer Services departments maintain a close link with all customers to ensure that individual requirements are known and responded to.

DPA maintains an open door policy that encourages feedback and consultation. A business-like attitude permeates the organization from the chief executive to the rank and file. DPA is different, and the difference is service.

SERVICES

Customer-driven service ensures that Dubai Ports Authority (DPA) consistently listens to its customers' needs and responds by providing superior handling and storage capabilities. These range from cold and cool store facilities in Jebel Ali to a purpose-built berth for import of bulk aluminum oxide and expanded tanker jetties to handle the requirement for petroleum and petrochemical products. A built-in over capacity in container handling equipment gives DPA the flexibility to respond quickly to customers' requests, and to generate additional business

A sophisticated control system for the cargo-handling equipment is also planned. This will increase efficiency of movement about the port, by allocating ample units as required on any given assignment.

Additionally, DPA's efficient commercial trucking department provides cost-effective, reliable transportation anywhere within the United Arab Emirates. This value-added service is available to customers upon request.

Storage
The Container Freight Station (CFS) at Port Rashid terminal provides covered space in seven warehouses with a combined capacity of 52,000 square meters and a total 66,000 square meters of uncovered area. In addition, the CFS offers a 24-hour service to receive and deliver both import & export cargo as per customer requirements. Jebel Ali terminal's CFS has two warehouses and one Dutch barn with a combined capacity of 27,140 square meters of covered space and a total of 50,000 square meters of uncovered area dedicated to this cargo type.

For additional analytical, marketing, investment and business opportunities information, please contact
Global Investment & Business Center, USA
(202) 546-2103. Fax: (202) 546-3275. E-mail: rusric@erols.com

These facilities, together with DPA'S advanced cargo handling equipment, provide an efficient service to LCL consolidators. Unstuffing and cross-stuffing for onward carriage is an attractive, and growing, value-added service to consignees and shippers.

Container Repair

Each terminal has a well-equipped container repair yard where maintenance is carried out by Emirates Container Repair and Middle East Container Repair Company to IICL standards and approved by Bureau Veritas and the American bureau of Shipping. Both yards can take all types of containers in their paint and blast shop facilities for hot and cold works. Steam cleaning and chemical washing are also available. Combined, the yards have a storage capacity for more than 2,000 units and all container owners and operators have access to the facilities.

Tanker Facilities

Four tanker berth are available at Jebel Ali which can accommodate ships up to 120,000 tons deadweight, with overall length of 275m and draft of 15m. Privately-operated storage tanks are also available for rent by companies who wish to hold stocks of oil for delivery elsewhere in the world.

Within Port Rashid terminal, a jetty operated by Shell can handle tankers of up to 40,000 tonnes, as well as bunker barges. It is protected by the latest safety equipment including plastic-faced fenders. remote-control fire monitors and high-tech telescopic access ladders.

Bunkering is provided through private vendors at both terminals.

Dedicated Aluminum Berth

One of the world's largest aluminum smelters is operated at Jebel Ali by Dubai Aluminum (Dubal). The company imports raw material via its own dedicated berth at the Jebel Ali terminal and exports high-quality ingots to major markets around the world. A US$500 - million expansion which doubled the plant's capacity was inaugurated in early 1997 and further expansion shall take effect in 2007.

ACTIVITIES AND SERVICES

TEUs				
2000	Inbound	Outbound	Transhipment	Total
Jan	66,903	54,625	106,783	228,311
Feb	67,636	55,867	116,437	239,940
Mar	70,636	56,066	118,951	245,653
Apr	70,380	59,169	113,904	243,453
Total	275,555	225,727	456,075	957,357

Container, General Cargo, Petroleum Tonnage								
2000	Container Tonnage	General Cargo Tonnage			Petroleum Tonnage			Total Tonnage
		Bulk Cargo	General Cargo	Cold Storage	Oil	Gas	Other Products	
Jan	1,806,633	292,043	272,317	1,567	1,015,082	10,465	13,308	3,411,415
Feb	1,895,549	364,466	277,613	251	1,078,710	9,037	11,113	3,636,739
Mar	2,020,152	426,592	223,411	708	1,137,993	23,991	9,390	3,842,237

For additional analytical, marketing, investment and business opportunities information, please contact
Global Investment & Business Center, USA
(202) 546-2103. Fax: (202) 546-3275. E-mail: rusric@erols.com

Apr	1,944,368	395,080	250,349	801	1,059,761	27,410	11,003	3,688,772
Total	7,666,702	1,478,181	1,023,690	3,327	4,291,546	70,903	44,814	14,579,163

Vessel Calls

2000	Container Vessels	Ro - Ro Vessels	Gen. Cargo Vessels	Tankers	Supply Vessels	Others	Total Vessels
Jan	390	26	70	68	124	174	852
Feb	400	23	71	66	164	169	893
Mar	414	34	66	73	152	185	924
Apr	405	28	70	66	124	183	876
Total	1,609	111	277	273	564	711	3,545

FUJAIRAH

....Emirate of Fujairah, one of the seven emirates forming the United Arab

Emirates, witnessed a rapid rate of economic and social development and tourism activities under the wise guidance of **H.H.Sheikh Hamad Bin Mohammad Al Sharqi**, Supreme Council member and ruler of Fujairah.

....After the emirate had completed its infrastructure, it set out to implement its ambitious development plan to achieve the ideal exploitation of its resources and to extend the base of industrial, commercial, and agricultural production.

....The historical importance of Fujairah goes back to the period that preceded birth of the christ (peace be upon him), it was known in the old ages as land of the sea giants, and was the first home for immigrants who came from the southeast of Arabian Peninsula and who were later known as the Phoenicians. Some of those immigrants came from Yemen after the collapse of Ma'areb Dam, and of whom the Sharqis tribes descend.
....Emirate of Fujairah lies on the eastern part of the arabian peninsula, bordered from the east by Omani coast, from the west by emirates of Ras Al Khaimah and Sharjah, from the south Kalba and it faces Omani coast. Fujairah extends 70 km. on the Gulf of Oman from Ousla village to Dibba to the north.

..Total aria of Fujairah is 1450 sq.km., made of varying heights mountains and hills, plains, cast, oasis and desert areas.

....The climate in Fujairah is semi tropical with varying temperature, rare rain, high level of evaporation and varying degree of humidity.

For additional analytical, marketing, investment and business opportunities information, please contact
Global Investment & Business Center, USA
(202) 546-2103. Fax: (202) 546-3275. E-mail: rusric@erols.com

....Last census showed that total population of Fujairah was 100,000. Main cities are Al Fujairah, Dibba, Mirbeh, Al Bidiah and Masafi.

MAJOR CITIES

Dibba

Dibba Al Fujairah, considered of the ancient historical civilization areas in the UAE, lies in the far northern frontiers of Fujairah where the coastal plains are rich and fresh water is plenty. Dibba is known of its many ancient castles, fortresses and remains. History of Dibba goes back to the eras of ancient civilizations whenit was an important commercial centre during the phoenician era.

Al bidya

Al Bidya city considered as an important human residence and settlement area all through the old history. Located 38 km north of Fujairah City and 25 km of Dibba City.
Al Bidya mosque is one of the most important archeological sites in Fujairah is surrounded by Al Bidya castle.

Masafi

Masafi is located in the Hajar mountains on the crossroads of the highways to Fujairah and Dibba. It is well known for its freshwater springs, which provide water for extensive orchards.

An extensive 'Friday market' has developed near Masafi, with articles as diverse as vegetables, fruits and garden plants, woolen carpets, candy floss and roasted corn-on-the-cob, toys and items of pottery. Most of the fruit is imported, but some of the vegetables are grown locally. The pottery is based on local designs

Qidfa

Eighteen kilometres north of Fujairah, along the coast road, lies the village of Qidfa. This is where an Iron Age (500 BC) horseshoe-shaped communal tomb was found during bulldozing work. It was excavated in 1986-1987 and yielded an important hoard of bronze weapons and bowls, jewellery, pottery and soapstone boxes and bowls. The collection is on display in Fujairah museum.

For additional analytical, marketing, investment and business opportunities information, please contact
Global Investment & Business Center, USA
(202) 546-2103. Fax: (202) 546-3275. E-mail: rusric@erols.com

Al Bithna

Driving from Fujairah into the mountains at the back of the city, the first village on the right set on the plain above Wadi Ham is Bithna. It is the site of a megalithic T-shaped tomb from the second millennium BC, Wadi Suq period, which was reused in the late first millennium BC; and of an impressive Late Islamic fort, commanding a strategic passage to the Wadi Ham, one of the main routes from east to west to the UAE's Hajar mountains.

HISTORY

...For the historian, Fujairah is a hidden treasure waiting to be discovered The old fort in Fujairah's historic town which is approximately 300 years old and the many small wind towers still standing in neighbouring villages as proud reminders of the town's recent past. However, archaeological ations have shown that man's presence in the region actually dates back to the Iron Age. In fact, some of -the most important archaeological finds in the Arabian Gulf have been made in the area.

Fujairah Fort

Situated just two km away from the main town. It is a strategically located mud brick structure. A huge castle built in 1670 A.D. which consists of 3 major parts and several halls and towers surrounded by the old Fujairah. The fort was fully renovated in year 2000.

Al Bidya Mosque
Dates back 400 years and displays a unique feat of engineering for the time. All four domes are supported by one central pillar and internal decoration combines stone carvings with special shelves to house the Holy Quran.
Al Bidya Mosque is located close to Al Bidya village about 30 km North of Fujairah.

Al Heil Castle

At Al Heil village, 8km south-west of Fujairah city.
One of the most famous castles in the Emirate of Fujairah, it used to be headquarters for the ruler and had been used for patrolling, surveillanc and to defend neibouring area.

AL Bithnah Forte

Built in 1735 near Al Bithnah Village 13 km west of Fujairah city, it has guarded the strategic route across the Hajar mountains throught Wadi Ham since the 18th Century, and was considered among the most important forts and castles in eastern part of UAE.

Archeological Sites

Some of the most important archeological finds in the Arabian Gulf have made in the area, and archeological excavations have shown that man's presence in the region actually dates back to the Iron Age.

Fujairah's unspoiled natural beauty and have all nice faces of rich and beautiful nature: mountains, waterfalls, oases and long beaches and more than 30 large valleys in addition to several smaller ones. It is also the land of water springs, cold and warm.

For additional analytical, marketing, investment and business opportunities information, please contact
Global Investment & Business Center, USA
(202) 546-2103. Fax: (202) 546-3275. E-mail: rusric@erols.com

...**Ain Madhab Park:** A 50 hectare park and resort for families, is a popular park in Fujairah, looks like a green carpet with the grass and many kinds of trees and flowers planted.

IMPORTANT INFORMATION AND CONTACTS

Fujairah International Airport
Established in 1987, and since it's operation the airposrt played vital role to link Fujairah worldwide and to develop tourism, the airport designed to take it into the next century.

Road and Transportation
Fujairah has established modern new highway network which link the Emirate with other sister's Emirates plus excellent internal roads inside the city of Fujairah.

Communication
National and International network as well as phone, Fax and other telecommunication services are available. Direct dialling and international calls are possible throught ground satellite station. Mobile phone and fast Internet connection are easily available.

Banks
Fujairah has national and international banks offering professional banking services of all kinds.

Driving License
Visitors can easily obtain a one-month temporary license by presenting their valid foreign license, International driving license also acceptable for visitors.

Visas
Citizens of GCC and Europe nationals can enter UAE and Fujairah without visas. Other nationalities can get a 14 days transit visa or visit visa throught a hotel, tour operators, travel agencies and Emirates & Gulf Airlines

Working Hours
From 8.00 to 2.30, Saturday to Wednesday for the public sector, and Saturday to Thursday for the private sector.
Local Time GMT +4 hours

GOVERNMENT DEPARTMENTS

Fujairah Museum Phone: +971 9 2229085 Fax....: +971 9 2229539 P.O.Box: 1, Fujairah, UAE.	Fujairah International Airport Phone: +971 9 2226222 Fax....: +971 9 2224205 P.Box: 977, Fujairah, UAE. Email: fiadgm@emirates.net.ae Web Site:fujairah-airport.com
Port of Fujairah Phone: +971 9 2228800 Fax....: +971 9 2228811 P.Box: 787, Fujairah, UAE. Email:fujport1@emirates.net.ae	Fujairah Free Zone Phone: +971 9 2228000 Fax....: +971 9 2228888 P.Box: 283, Fujairah, UAE. Email: freezone@emirates.net.ae

For additional analytical, marketing, investment and business opportunities information, please contact
Global Investment & Business Center, USA
(202) 546-2103. Fax: (202) 546-3275. E-mail: rusric@erols.com

	Web Site: www.fujairahfree.com
Fujairah Exhibition Centre Phone: +971 9 2231212 Fax....: +971 9 2231616 P.Box: 1550, Fujairah, UAE. Email: fujcci@emirates.net.ae	Fujairah Trade Centre Phone: +971 9 2222661 Fax....: +971 9 2226212 P.Box: 1433, Fujairah, UAE. Email:ftcfuj@emirates.net.ae Web Site:
Fujairah Municipality Phone: +971 9 2227000 Fax....: +971 9 2222231 P.Box: 7, Fujairah, UAE.	Dibba Municipality Phone: +971 9 2444233 Fax....: +971 9 2444727 P.Box: 11462, Dibba, Fujairah, UAE.
General Post Office Phone: +971 9 2222235 Fax....: +971 9 2229011 P.Box: 760, Fujairah, UAE.	Fujairah Police Phone: +971 9 2224411 Fax....: +971 9 2222213 P.Box: 5, Fujairah, UAE.
Naturalisation & Immigration Administration Phone: +971 9 2222727 Fax....: +971 9 2226606 P.Box: 6, Fujairah, UAE.	Fujairah Hospital Phone: +971 9 2242999 Fax....: +971 9 2229077 P.Box: 10, Fujairah, UAE.

HOTELS AND RESIDENCE

Fujairah Hilton Phone: +971 9 2222411 Fax....: +971 9 2226541 P.O.Box: 231, Fujairah, UAE.	Al Diar Siji Hotel Phone: +971 92 2232000 Fax....: +971 9 22232111 P.Box: 1199, Fujairah, UAE.
Ritz Plaza Hotel Phone: +971 9 2222202 Fax....: +971 9 2222203 P.Box: 1919, Fujairah, UAE.	Fujairah Beach Motel Phone: +971 9 2228111 Fax....: +971 9 2228054 P.Box: 283, Fujairah, UAE.
Sandy Beach Motel Phone: +971 9 2445555 Fax....: +971 9 2445200 P.Box: 659, Fujairah, UAE.	Holiday Beach Motel Phone: +971 9 2445540 Fax....: +971 9 2445580 P.Box: 1433, Fujairah, UAE.
Summerland Residents P.O.Box 818, Fujairah, UAE. Tel: +971 9 2232922 Fax: + 971 9 2231272	Oasis Residents P.O.Box 1325, Fujairah, UAE. Tel: +971 9 2232823 Fax: + 971 9 2232813

TRAVEL AGENCIES

For additional analytical, marketing, investment and business opportunities information, please contact
Global Investment & Business Center, USA
(202) 546-2103. Fax: (202) 546-3275. E-mail: rusric@erols.com

Fujairah Aviation Services Phone: +971 9 2226969 Fax....: +971 9 2226949 P.O.Box: 989, Fujairah, UAE. Email: fastb@emirates.net.ae	Fujairah Aviation Services International Phone: +971 9 2222596 Fax....: +971 9 2222598 P.Box: 2100, Fujairah, UAE.
Travel Link Phone: +971 9 2226116 Fax....: +971 9 2226118 P.Box: 1618, Fujairah, UAE. Email:trvllink@emirates.net.ae	DNATA Phone: +971 9 2222985 Fax....: +971 9 2222986 P.Box: 445, Fujairah, UAE.
Fujairah National Air Travel Agency Phone: +971 9 2222524 Fax....: +971 9 2222555 P.Box: 96, Fujairah, UAE. Email: aliali7@emirates.net.ae	Arabian Travel Agency Phone: +971 9 2221561 Fax....: +971 9 2221461 P.Box: 638, Fujairah, UAE.

BANKS

UAE Central Bank
Phone: +971 9 2224040
Fax...: +971 9 2226805
P.O.Box: 768, Fujairah, UAE.

Fujairah National Bank
Phone: +971 9 2224513
Fax....: +971 9 2227992
P.Box: 887, Fujairah, UAE.
Email: fuj@emirates.net.ae
Web Site: www.fujairah.com

AL Mashreq Bank
Phone: +971 9 2226018
Fax....: +971 9 2226509
P.Box: 270, Fujairah, UAE.

Dubai Islamic Bank
Phone: +971 9 2221550
Fax....: +971 9 2229249
P.Box: 1007, Fujairah, UAE.

Abu Dhabi Commercial Bank
Phone: +971 9 2223900
Fax....: +971 9 2224900
P.Box: 770, Fujairah, UAE.

Abu Dhabi National Bank
Phone: +971 9 2222633
Fax....: +971 9 2227241
P.Box: 79, Fujairah, UAE.

Middle East British Bank
Phone: +971 9 2222221
Fax....: +971 9 2221750
P.Box: 21, Fujairah, UAE.
Email:
Web Site: www.britishbank.com

Al Arabic Bank
Phone: +971 9 2222050
Fax....: +971 9 2224024
P.Box: 300, Fujairah, UAE.

Umm Al Quwain Bank

Union National Bank

For additional analytical, marketing, investment and business opportunities
information, please contact
Global Investment & Business Center, USA
(202) 546-2103. Fax: (202) 546-3275. E-mail: rusric@erols.com

Phone: +971 9 2232100
Fax....: +971 9 2232220
P.Box: 1444, Fujairah, UAE.

Phone: +971 9 2222747
Fax....: +971 9 2224851
P.Box: 268, Fujairah, UAE.
Email:
Web Site: www.unb.com.ae

Middle East Bank
Phone: +971 9 2223423
Fax....: +971 9 2223433
P.Box: 1472, Fujairah, UAE.
Email: sandrad@emirates.net.ae
Web Site: www.emiratesbank.com

CAR RENTALS

Future Rent A Car Phone: +971 9 2224481 P.O.Box: 201, Fujairah, UAE.	Classic Rent A Car Phone: +971 9 2222222 Fax....: +971 9 2222089 P.Box: 481, Fujairah, UAE.
Avis Rent A Car Phone: +971 9 2225384 Fax....: +971 9 2225778 P.Box: 6891, Fujairah, UAE.	Autobahn Rent A Car Phone: +971 9 2232226 Fax....: +971 9 2232148 P.Box: 1254, Fujairah, UAE.
Al Massa Rent A Car Phone: +971 9 2229982 Fax....: +971 9 2241320 P.Box: 481, Fujairah, UAE. Email: aliali7@emirates.net.ae	Dubai Rent A Car Phone: +971 9 2221318 Fax....: +971 9 2221325 P.Box: 684, Fujairah, UAE.

SHARJAH

Sharjah is the third largest of the seven states which form the United Arab Emirates.

Sharjah is the only Emirate to have land on both the Arabian Sea and the Indian Ocean.

The Emirate covers approximately 2,600 square kilometers.

In addition to Sharjah City which is located on the three mile deep subkhat (salt) strip along the coast, the Emirate has three provinces on the Batinah (the East Coast), Hisn Dibba, Khor Fakkan and Kalba, plus the Islands of Abu Mousa and Sir Abu Nu'air.

The Batinah consists of the spectacular, rugged Hajar mountains rising in places to 2,500 feet, intersected by sheer sided wadis, with gravel beds and rich soil.

For additional analytical, marketing, investment and business opportunities
information, please contact
Global Investment & Business Center, USA
(202) 546-2103. Fax: (202) 546-3275. E-mail: rusric@erols.com

Beautiful sandy beaches and the clear blue Indian Ocean have made this coast a haven for diving, fishing and relaxing.

The towns of Dibba and Khor Fakkan have grown steadily with modernization gently nudging out the traditional ways, fortunately not completely.

Khor Kalba, the southern most tip of the UAE's Indian Ocean coastline ends in an extensive mangrove marsh which has recently been designated as a Nature Reserve for several endangered species.

The hinterland is a red sand desert with impressive dunes, becoming a gravel plain along the eastern border which runs along the line of the foothills. This fertile, well watered area, rich in gardens and natural shrub is interspersed by innumerable wadis (steep sided dry valleys) running East to West. There are many small villages in this area where people still live in the traditional manner.

An excellent area for 'wadi bashing' but beware of flash floods in times of heavy rainfall!

Al Dhaid, the peaceful falaj based palm oasis in the center of the Emirate is the third largest town and producer of the renowned Al Dhaid strawberries, in addition to many other fruits and vegetables.

HISTORY

The earliest settlements found in the Emirates date back 7000 years. Research indicates that Sharjah was probably a mangrove swamp and the settlers were fishermen.

The most important archaeological finds so far have been the tombs and settlements of *Meliha* and *Tell Abraq*.

In 1970, an Iraqi team made the first find at *Meliha,* located on the plain close to *Al Dhaid* and *Jebel Fayha*. The civilization, sophisticated for its time, dates back 2000 years. The 12 kilometers of land excavated reveals a palace and a small town with a fair sized tomb cemetery. One tomb has an inscription of old Yemeni writing and is the oldest of its kind to be found in the Emirates.

This once fertile plain lay on the caravan route from the East to West coast and was perhaps the gateway for trade and travel with Oman.

Tell Abraq (dating back approximately 4000 years) is on the border of Sharjah and Umm Al Quwain.

This site is by far the largest settlement to be discovered in the region and the only one to have been inhabited continuously for 2000 years. The settlement contained a circular fort of 40 meters in diameter with its walls still preserved reaching a height of 8 meters, plus nearby a collective tomb built of stone.

An 11 cm long bone comb, surprisingly well preserved, with intricate carvings is a very unusual discovery.

For additional analytical, marketing, investment and business opportunities information, please contact
Global Investment & Business Center, USA
(202) 546-2103. Fax: (202) 546-3275. E-mail: rusric@erols.com

The treasures found here help to piece together the lifestyles of these obviously wealthy and aristocratic people.

The exciting discoveries from these sites include amphorae from Greece, iron weapons, glass jars and coins dating back to Alexander the Great.

These and many other fascinating finds are on display in the Archaeological Museum, in Halwan.

The Islamic Museum, also exhibits magnificent archaeological discoveries found in Sharjah Emirate, dating from the Islamic period

The settlement of Sharjah dates back some 6,000 years when it is believed to have been called **Sarcoa**. The population was small and people relied on trade and sea faring in addition to, farming, hunting, fishing and pearling. Many of the early settlements were based around the 'falaj', a man-made underground water course.

From the 16th century onwards, times were turbulent. In 1507, the Portuguese savagely took command of the East Coast in order to establish control of the spice trade. They built forts at **Khor Fakkan**, **Kalba** and **Dibba** and their reign lasted a century till the Dutch gained supremacy for the same reason.

By the 17th century the British arrived and began trading with the **Qawassim**, the forefathers of today's ruling family. The Europeans favored the Gulf and the Red Sea as principal routes of communication between the Mediterranean and India.

In the 18th century, the ruling Qawassim tribe became the mighty seafarers who created an important maritime power in the southern Gulf. Their strongholds were based in Ras Al Khaimah and Sharjah. **Sheikh Sultan bin Saqr bin Rashid Al Qassimi**, the patriarch of today's rulers became the Sheikh of Sharjah in 1804 and governed for over 50 years.

By the turn of the century relationships between the **Qawassim** and the British deteriorated. As documented in '**The Myth of Arab Piracy in the Gulf**', **H.H. Dr. Sheikh Sultan bin Mohammed Al Qassimi,** member of the Supreme Council and Ruler of Sharjah, has shown, that whilst the British blamed all the attacks on their ships on the Qawassim, the latter were often blamed for the other's misconduct.

In 1809, the British mounted their initial land based attack on the **Qawassim** in Ras Al Khaimah. By 1820, the first of several Treaties of Peace was signed guaranteeing peace at sea and protection of the British against attack for 150 years. The coast became known as the **Trucial Oman** and the Sheikhdoms as the **Trucial States**. These names remained from 1853 up until the formation of the **United Arab Emirates** in 1971.

Whilst the Emirate prospered from trade and pearling, Sharjah had many 'firsts' to its credit during these years of development.

Between 1823 and 1954, Sharjah was the base for Britain's only political representative on the Trucial Coast.

In 1932, a staging post was established by the British Government in Sharjah, for the **Imperial Airways** flights en route from England to India. This was the first airport in the Emirates and is still in use today, as a main road, not a runway!

For additional analytical, marketing, investment and business opportunities information, please contact
Global Investment & Business Center, USA
(202) 546-2103. Fax: (202) 546-3275. E-mail: rusric@erols.com

At the time of its establishment, the airport was located two miles across the desert from the town. All provisions for the air traveler were brought by donkey including the *in-flight catering* and water from wells. Traders traveled from the town by camel to do business with the foreigners.

The **Sheikh's Fort (Al Hisn)** was located where Sharjah's modern banking center (**Al Boorj Avenue**) now stands and **Al Arouba Street** was used for horse racing.

The importance of the airport helped cushion the collapse of the pearl trade in the 1930's. Sharjah suffered another set back thirty years later when the sea trade also declined due to the silting up of the Creek.

Sharjah remained the regional base for the **British RAF** and **Trucial Oman Scouts** until British presence officially ended in 1971 with independence.

In 1953, the first properly organized school in the UAE was established in Sharjah attracting students throughout the country.

Sharjah joined the United Arab Emirates as a founder member on 2nd December, 1971.

In 1972, **His Highness Sheikh Sultan bin Mohammed Al Qassimi** succeeded as the ruler of Sharjah.

The same year, oil was struck in the **Mubarak** field, 80 kms offshore, close to the island of **Abu Mousa**. Two years later production began and at its peak 35,000 barrels were produced per day. A few years later gas condensate was discovered and drilling started in 1990.

This natural wealth combined with the foresight of **His Highness Dr. Sheikh Sultan bin Mohammed Al Qassimi** has allowed Sharjah to enjoy prosperity and vitality whilst retaining the charms and traditional values of an Islamic city.

CULTURE AND TRADITIONS

The official religion of the United Arab Emirates is **Islam** and the call to prayer sounds five times a day on almost every street corner. People adhere closely to the tenets of **Islam** in all aspects of their lives.

Family ties are very strong and nearly sacred. National dress for men is the **kandora (dishdasha)**, the long white robe and headdress. Women wear the traditional **abbaya** or black cloak.

The most popular national sports include camel racing, falconry and football.

The **Sharia' Court** enforces the law of the land which constitutes a mixture of written and verbal laws passed down from generation to generation.

The laws of the government are passed by **His Highness Dr. Sheikh Sultan bin Mohammed Al Qassimi,** through the **Emiri Diwan,** to the various ministries and to the Municipality (Baladia) for implementation.

For additional analytical, marketing, investment and business opportunities
information, please contact
Global Investment & Business Center, USA
(202) 546-2103. Fax: (202) 546-3275. E-mail: rusric@erols.com

You must understand and respect the traditions of the UAE society in order to settle and to do business here. The cultural traditions go back to the days of the desert tribes and the influence brought upon them by migration.

Whilst the UAE is now a modern thriving entity, 50 years ago the towns were small with few facilities - electricity was powered by generator and water supplied by well. The leap into the developed world has taken place over a very short span of time.

An enormous amount of adjustment and flexibility by the national people, have been key factors sustaining this change. All expatriates are welcome but care must be taken to respect and honor the local traditions which are still very much part of life here.

We can only touch on the fascinating culture and customs of the Arab world but it is worth spending time to discover the hospitality and generosity of the Arab people.

Islam

Some of the basic values of *Islam* include honesty, courtesy and hospitality which help govern the society. One fifth of the world's population are *Muslims*, the followers of *Islam* and 19% of these live in the Arab world.

The Qur'an, God's words revealed to *The Prophet Mohammed (PBUH)* by the Angel Gabriel in the 7th century AD, recounts the written law, forms of worship and morality.

The Prophet Mohammed (PBUH) was born in *Makkah* around 570 AD (571 AD to 632 AD) and grew up appalled by the corruption around him. At the age of forty he received his first revelation from the God and he set out to spread the words of Islam. By 630 AD he returned to Makkah having gained the submission of most of the Arabian Peninsula's people to Islam.

There are *FIVE PILLARS OF ISLAM* on which religious duty rests.

The first is the profession of *Iman* or *Faith*. "There is none worthy of worship, except God and Mohammed (PBUH) is the messenger of God." This simple declaration of faith is called the Shahadah, a simple formula that all the faithful pronounce. The significance of this declaration is the belief that the only purpose of life is to serve and obey God, and this is achieved through the teachings and practices of the Last Prophet, Mohammed (PBUH).

Prayer is the second pillar of faith. *Salah* is the name of the obligatory prayers that are performed five times a day, and are a direct link between the worshipper and God. There is no hierarchical authority in Islam and there are no priests. Prayers are led by a learned person who knows the Qur'an and is generally chosen by the congregation.

The five daily calls to prayer are, *Fajr* (dawn), *Dhuhr* (midday), *Asr* (mid-afternoon), *Maghreb* (early evening) and *Isha* (late evening). Prayer times vary according to sunrise and sunset and are listed in the daily newspapers.

An important principle of Islam is that everything belongs to God and that wealth is therefore held by human beings in trust. The work *Zakat* means both *purification* and *growth*. Our possessions are purified by setting aside a proportion for those in need and for the society in general. Like the pruning of plants, this cutting back balances and encourages new growth.

For additional analytical, marketing, investment and business opportunities information, please contact
Global Investment & Business Center, USA
(202) 546-2103. Fax: (202) 546-3275. E-mail: rusric@erols.com

Each Muslim calculates his or her own *Zakat* individually. This involves the annual payment of a fortieth of one's capital, excluding such items as primary residence, car and professional tools.

The fourth pillar is *Fasting* or *Sawm.* Every year, in the month of Ramadan, all Muslims fast from dawn until sundown -- abstaining from food and drink. Non-Muslim expatriates and visitors must also respect the fast by not eating, drinking and smoking in public. Working hours throughout the country are reduced during the Holy Month. The end of Ramadan is marked by the sighting of the new moon and the start of the *Eid Al Fitr* festival.

The last pillar of Islam is the Pilgrimage, *Haj*. The pilgrimage to *Mekkah* (the *Haj*) is an obligation only for those who are physically and financially able to do so. Nevertheless over two million people go to Makkah each year from overy corner of the globe providing a unique opportunity for those of different nations to meet one another.

The close of the *Haj* is marked by a festival, the *Id Al Adha*, which is celebrated with prayers and the exchange of gifts in Muslim communities everywhere. This and the *Id Al Fitr*, a festive day celebrating the end of Ramadan, are the two holidays of the Islamic calendar.

PEOPLE

The population of the Emirate has risen dramatically during the past 10 years from 159,595 in 1981, to an estimated 450,000 in 2007.

The majority of people living in *Sharjah* are based in the city, with an estimated population of 350,000 in 2007, followed by the towns of *Al Dhaid* (24,716) and *Khor Fakkan* (10,888).

The population of the UAE in 2007 was estimated at 2.5 million.

The national population descends from 4 main tribes:

Qawassim
The ruling family are descendants of the *Qawassim's*. Relatively small in numbers yet very powerful and highly regarded.

Al-Ali, Shewaihain and some mixed tribes
These comprise much of the remaining national population of Sharjah town. These tribes were the settled fishermen of former times.

Bani Qitab
These people are the principal tribe of the Sharjah sand desert. Originally semi nomadic, they are mainly based in *Al Dhaid.* The *Tunaij* are a smaller tribe existing in the same area.

Naqbiyin
The principal tribe of many found in the mountainous areas, the *Naqbiyin* are also the settled fishermen and gardeners of *Khor Fakkan*, *Kalba* and *Hisn Dibba*.

DESERT LAW
Honor is everything to the strong and courageous bedu tribes who live in the desert. Children learn in the majlis (meeting place) the 'wrongs and rights' of life. The law sets the rules between the man and the family and between the tribes. The strength of the law deters crime, many say more effectively than modern civil law.

For additional analytical, marketing, investment and business opportunities information, please contact
Global Investment & Business Center, USA
(202) 546-2103. Fax: (202) 546-3275. E-mail: rusric@erols.com

TRAVEL

Sharjah has been a major Middle East tourist Destination since 1932!

Tourists intending to visit Sharjah do not have to go far to get what they are interested in. That's why Sharjah was the first emirate to attract tourist groups in 1980. Since then, tourism has developed in leaps and bounds.

The number of tourists entering Sharjah and the UAE in general in 1981 was about 4,000. However Sharjah has developed and so have its tourist attractions. Today the number of tourists visiting the emirate has reached 250,000.

Since 1997 Sharjah and Tourism Development Authority has been working to develop and promote tourism in Sharjah. This has been possible following the mobilization of all available facilities and services, be it airlines, travel agents and other authorities concerned.

In addition, Sharjah paid special attention to its recreational facilities like hotels, bazaars, parks, restaurants and the attractions of the Emirate are being spread between the two gulfs in the east and west.

The civility of the people of Sharjah and the high standard of its tourist facilities makes it highly attractive to tourists who appreciate the safety and security of the emirate and its free economy.

CLIMATE

Sharjah's climate is idyllic from November to April with warm sunny days, cool evenings and low humidity. Daytime temperatures range from 18 to 30 degrees C.

You can expect some rainfall and tropical storms during January, February and March. After heavy rains you will need a good pair of rubber boots to negotiate the streets ! (Rainwear can be purchased in Rolla Square)

From May to September the climate is hot with midday temperatures in July and August reaching in excess of 45 degrees C. Even the nights are warm averaging 25 degrees C.

Humidity is often at 100% so all in all, it's stifling! Most people head to cooler climates during the summer.

PORTS

Khorfakkan Container Terminal (KCT) in recent years has undergone a continuous rolling program of improvements. The multi-million dollar developments have reinforced its acknowledgment position as the logical container transshipment port for the United Arab Emirates, Upper Arabian Gulf States and the Indian Sub Continent.

The most recent project, completed in May 2007, was its 350 meter quay extension. The ultra modern container terminal now has 1,060 meters of berths, dredged to a depth of 15 meters alongside at MLW. The enlarged turning circle and seaward approaches have also been dredged to 15 meters.

For additional analytical, marketing, investment and business opportunities
information, please contact
Global Investment & Business Center, USA
(202) 546-2103. Fax: (202) 546-3275. E-mail: rusric@erols.com

Managers and operator of KCT, Gulftainer Co Ltd, have matched the quay construction program with the introduction of sophisticated container handling equipment. The terminal now boasts eight ship-to-shore gantries including four Panamax, two Post Panamax, two Super Post Panamax cranes. The most recent acquisitions are the largest in the region and capable of handling vessels stowed 18 containers across. Additional Super Post Panamax gantry cranes are now under consideration.

On the landward slide, container stacks in KCT's 300,000sq meters plus storage areas can now accommodate 18,000 TEUs. The fourth original rail mounted yard gantries plus six recently introduces rubber tyred gantries (RTGs) serve them. The new RTGs can handle containers one over five high and seven across plus a roadway. Four more enhanced specification Liebherr RTGs will arrive in the port by the end of the year (2007) and the number of reefer points has been increased to 214.

The only natural deepwater port in the Middle East, KCT is located on the east coast of the Emirate of Sharjah, close to the main east-west shipping routes and outside the sensitive Straits of Hormuz. Via a modern dual carriage-way Khorfakkan Container Terminal (KCT) - which now has a potential throughput of over 1.5 million TEUs annually - is just three hours form the dynamic commercial and industrial markets on the UAEs Gulf Coast.

KHORFAKKAN CONTAINER TERMINAL
PO Box 10326, Sharjah, United Arab Emirates
Tel : +971 (9) 2385604/5 Fax : +971 (9) 2387212
E-Mail : gtlkct@emirates.net.ae

Port Khalid

The first major port of call within the Arabian Gulf is Port Khalid, on the West Coast of Sharjah, one of the most advanced ports in the region. Here the majority of Sharjah's general cargo traffic is being handled, using the latest in-cargo handling machinery. Its 13-berth deep water harbor is capable of managing vessels of varying draughts.

Many UAE-based importers favor Port Khalid to ship their cargo because of its modern storage facilities - amongst which two berthed cold stores that can handle up to 5,000 tons at any given time. It is also popular because of its proximity to the city, the customer-oriented service, the minimum turnaround time and the absence of customs duties on import and export. Over 40 percent of the UAE's manufacturing is in the Emirate of Sharjah and much of it is less than an hour by truck from SCT. Port Khalid also boasts the only passenger terminal facility in UAE.

Situated on Sharjah's Gulf coast and managed and operated by Gulftainer Co Ltd., it is fully equipped to offer immediate berthing, expert merchandised handling of dry and refrigerated containers, documentary back-up, bonded warehousing and groupage facilities. Gulftainer's NCR 3430 Pentium based computer management system provides complete terminal control, statistical reports, ship planning and EIR functions.

The terminal's 586 meter quay has a minimum depth alongside of 11.5 meters at MLW and can accommodate two third generation container ships simultaneously or two roll-on roll-off vessels. Covering over 150,000 sq. meters the terminal provides storage for 8,000 TEUs and there is a 9,300 sq. meter dedicated transit shed and storage area and a 100 tons capacity weighbridge.

For additional analytical, marketing, investment and business opportunities
information, please contact
Global Investment & Business Center, USA
(202) 546-2103. Fax: (202) 546-3275. E-mail: rusric@erols.com

Ship work is handled 24 hours a day, seven days a week by two Liebherr T115, 35 tons capacity gantry cranes. The yard handling equipment inventory includes 30 tons capacity Transtainers, 40 tons SWL top loading forklifts plus a full range of smaller forklifts, flatbeds, skeletal trailers, tractors and other ancillary equipment.

In addition to being one of the most efficient and flexible ports in the region, SCT is cost effective. Gulftainer Co Ltd operates to a keenly competitive scale of charges exercising tight cost control and high productivity.

SHARJAH CONTAINER TERMINAL

PO Box 225, Sharjah, United Arab Emirates
Tel : +971 (6) 5284205 Fax : +971 (6) 5284513
E-Mail : gtlsct@emirates.net.ae

GULFTAINER CO. LTD

PO Box 225, Sharjah, United Arab Emirates
Tel : +971 (6) 5274201 Fax : +971 (6) 5724711
E-Mail : gtluae@emirates.net.ae

INTERNATIONAL AIRPORT

Sharjah International Airport, its design reflecting traditional Islamic architecture, is one of the most modern in the region, offering state-of-the art facilities. Situated approximately 10 km from Sharjah town, it is linked by a four lane highway with Port Khalid and Port Khorfakkan, as well as the other Emirates.

The airport boasts modern passenger handling facilities and has an annual capacity of over 2.5 million passengers. The terminal is designed for ultimate comfort and convenience and is comparable to the best in the world.

The Airport's main features include jet ways to the aircraft, full passenger services, including air-conditioned waiting lounges, well-equipped duty-free areas, banks, rent-a-car companies, hotel reservations, restaurants, a well-appointed Airport Hotel and excellent transit facilities with a minimum turnaround time. Apart from these, the Airport boasts modernized first class and business class lounges have been modernized, well coordinated ground services and a high standard of aircraft line maintenance.

Cargo handling facilities include four warehouses, each with a 7,400 sq. meters storage space, separate cargo apron for up to 6 aircraft, 24-hour customs clearance, free zone facilities and speedy and efficient document procedures.The airport handles the largest amount of air cargo in the Middle East and is the main air cargo handling center for Lufthansa Cargo in the region.

Warehouses offer the customer security for his shipment and protect it against cargo handling irregularity, including theft. The warehousing facilities may be utilized as a distribution center for the Gulf. For those operating from Sharjah, goods can be stored at the airport without incurring any liability for duties, unless the goods are for internal distribution, Foreign goods may be stored safely for re-export. Furthermore a repair and spare parts service is offered on a worldwide scale.

The airports facilities have recently been upgraded. The runway has been extended of by 300 meters, making the complete distance available for take off of an aircraft 4060 meters and a 3 site runaway visual range system has been installed. There are individual packages available, tailored

For additional analytical, marketing, investment and business opportunities information, please contact
Global Investment & Business Center, USA
(202) 546-2103. Fax: (202) 546-3275. E-mail: rusric@erols.com

to meet the needs of different companies by offering flexible facilities, the airport promises the best possible assistance to companies.

SHARJAH INTERNATIONAL AIRPORT
PO Box 8, Sharjah, United Arab Emirates
Tel : +971 (6) 5581111 Fax : +971 (6) 5581167
E-Mail : mktg@shj-airport.gov.ae
http://www.shj-airport.gov.ae

EXCHIBITION CENTER

The Expo Center Sharjah, the exhibition organization of the Sharjah Chamber of Commerce and Industry, has the distinction of having pioneered the exhibition medium in the Gulf. As a consequence it is not only widely respected in the Gulf region, but also has a pioneer's experience in organizing shows that are well attended and successful.

Set up in 1977, the Center has been a conduit not only for the success of thousands of companies in the Middle East and all over the world, but also for many successful products and services. It has been hosting exhibitions that reflect the most opportune lines of business activity at any given time. As a result, the Expo Center's exhibition mix consists of some of the most prestigious trade fairs in the region. The profiles of each exhibition are fine-tuned to optimize its specialist status and exhibitor-trade visitor interaction.

Expo's track record for introducing some of the region's truly-international, specialist fairs is impressive. Leather Expo, for instance, has the distinction of being the Middle East's only professional exhibition to enjoy the prestigious ICHSLTA's (International Council of Hides, Skins and Leather Traders' Associations) sponsorship, as well as the support of the Arab Union of Leather Industries. In addition, its Watch & Jewelry Fair enjoys the sponsorship of the World Gold Council, its International Food Fair has the support of the Arab Federation for Food Industries and UAE's Ministry of Agriculture & Fisheries, and TEXPO (the International Fair for Textiles and Accessories), Image Expo, and Kid Expo, to name a few, are the only events of their kind in the region.

Expo Center's strong points and specialized services include:

- A databank which is one of the strongest in the region.
- Fixing of appointments with pre-registered trade buyers.
- Mailing of trade invitations to active world buyers.
- Extensive promotional coverage in international trade publications of the industry.
- Coverage in the regional bilingual media and coverage in Expo Center newsletters published during the exhibitions.

Spread over a sprawling 88,000 sq. meters, Expo Center Sharjah is one of the few exhibition venues anywhere to provide such a complete range of facilities under one roof. The exhibition grounds include both 8000 sq. meters of covered exhibition space and an uncovered area stretching over 10000 sq. meters; ideal for static or moving open-air displays.

The centrally air-conditioned covered area incorporates three high-domed pillar-free exhibition halls whose modular structures allow enormous flexibility in terms of layout and exhibition design. High-vaulted artificial ceilings, and a sophisticated user-friendly lighting and sound system complete the effect.

For additional analytical, marketing, investment and business opportunities information, please contact
Global Investment & Business Center, USA
(202) 546-2103. Fax: (202) 546-3275. E-mail: rusric@erols.com

The state-of-the-art Expo auditorium, the setting for numerous up-market shows and designer fashion presentations in the past, can be purpose-adapted to a wide variety of functions.

Conferencing

Instead of having one all-purpose exhibition hall, conference facilities at Expo are divided into distinct need-based units.

The tastefully furnished main conference hall can seat up to 450 people and is equipped with ultra- modem sound and lighting and state-of-the-art audiovisual facilities. The main hall has been the venue for some major conferences and seminars held in the region in the past, and houses a full-fledged interpreter's cabin capable of simultaneous interpretation in three languages.

For large-scale international conferences, the Sharjah Business Club's user-friendly facilities enable anything from personalized across-the-table discussions to larger gatherings. In addition to seminars and conferences that habitually accompany trade exhibitions, the Expo Center also leases out its conference facilities to independent groups of companies, particularly those organizing financial or management seminars.

Expo Direct Mail & Advertising Services

Expo Center's trump card is Expo Direct, a fully-equipped Direct Marketing Division geared to off exhibitors and trade visitors a complete range of market-support facilities.

The cornerstone of Expo Direct is one of the region's most comprehensive data banks which, additional support, interfaces with the Sharjah Chamber of Commerce and Industry's database. Moreover, networking tie-ups with international agencies provide powerful global connections. The data bank enables the Listings Department to do a first-rate job with correct audience target in enabling it to arrange exhibitor meetings with firms that fall in the category of activity and line of product the exhibitor is interested in.

The Tele Sales Department works in concert with the Listings Department. An outbound tele-sales unit handles research, data base development and follow-up to direct mail, while an inbound tele-sale team is responsible for response handling.

In addition to servicing Expo Center's in-house requirements, Expo Direct can provide exhibitors and trade visitors an entire range of services, ranging from data base rental and sourcing to direct response advertising and mailing.

A special Product Promotion Cell can handle everything from supermarket promotions and sampling surveys to product launches and fashion or road shows. Expo Center also has a full-fledged Advertising & Promotions Division that performs a complete rang of advertising services both for the Center as well as outside clients.

A full range of back-up services

Every trade exhibition at Expo Center Sharjah is backed by a full complement of professional support services. The Center is equipped with the latest communication facilities, offering instant access to any part of the world in a matter of seconds by telephone, fax or electronic mail. The modem administrator building houses a smart reception, sophisticated secretarial services and an impressive Research & Development department. A dedicated team of young professionals is always on the alert to attend to a client's every requirement. They do pre-and post exhibition market surveys, follow up on business leads and provide exhibitors and trade visitors with a comprehensive picture of the regional market.

Expo Center has also introduced a catering service capable of handling large-scale banqueting assignments. The Center's Technical Services Department can provide customized stands for exhibitors at a nominal cost.

Expo Center even has its own design department to plan entire exhibitions. Other services include clearing and forwarding and packing, and a huge parking facility that can accommodate up to 1600 cars. Expo Center also helps business visitors with hotel reservations and sightseeing at special group rates. The Center thus serves as a one-stop exhibition venue, with services extending from market surveys, product promotion and trade tie-ups to in-house catering and conferences. Moreover, since the Center's primary objective is to boost trade and investment, it offers these benefits at a fraction of what it would cost at similar exhibition venues.

The exhibitions calendar runs from September to May each year, with an impressive coverage of specialized shows which support and promote trade and industry in the UAE. The exhibition schedule directly from the Expo Centre web site may be viewed

For more information, contact the Expo Centre.

EXPO CENTRE SHARJAH
PO Box 3222, Sharjah, United Arab Emirates
Tel : +971 (6) 5551888 Fax : +971 (6) 5552888
Telex : 68306 EXPO EM
Sharjah, United Arab Emirates
E-Mail : expocs@emirates.net.ae
http://www.expo-centre.co.ae/

WORLD TRADE CENTER

Sharjah is constructing a world trade center at a cost that exceeds a US$ 100 million. The building rises to 304 meters and consists of 52 floors.

Once complete, it will be visible with its tilting shape and beams made of stainless steel and huge columns of concrete and natural stone from miles away.

The main block will house the Sharjah Chamber of Commerce and Industry, Expo Center, conference halls and other commercial representative offices.

The Expo included in the center would have a capacity to host 7,860 people with exhibition area of up to 20,000 sq. m.

The Trade Center would include also a mosque, a sailing club and parking spaces for 2,500 cars.

The Sharjah World Trade Center is to be built in Al-Khan area. In line with the comprehensive development of the region, H.H. Dr. Sheikh Sultan bin Mohammed Al Qassimi has approved the final stages of the Sharjah World Trade Center.

HOTELS

The following hotels are located in Sharjah. Please click on the hotel name for more information.

**For additional analytical, marketing, investment and business opportunities information, please contact
Global Investment & Business Center, USA
(202) 546-2103. Fax: (202) 546-3275. E-mail: rusric@erols.com**

HOTELS IN SHARJAH	FURNISHED APARTMENTS IN SHARJAH
AL BUSTAN HOTEL	SPARK RESIDENCE
AL HARMOODI PALACE	AL BUHEIRA RESIDENCE
AL SHARQ HOTEL	BASMA RESIDENCE
BEACH HOTEL	CROWN SUITES
CITY HOTEL	DIPLOMAT RESIDENCE
CORAL BEACH HOTEL	INTERHOME
FEDERAL HOTEL	JAWHARAT AL GHUWAIR
GOLDEN BEACH HOTEL	KUWAIT TOWER
GULF BEACH HOTEL	MINA HOUSE
HOLIDAY INN RESORT, SHARJAH	THE SUITES
HOLIDAY INTERNATIONAL HOTEL	
KHALEEJ TOURIST HOTEL	
LOU' LOUA BEACH HOTEL	
MARBELLA RESORT	t
BREEZE MOTEL	HOTELS IN KHOR FAKKAN
MONACO HOTEL	t
NOVA PARK HOTEL	OCEANIC HOTEL
ROYAL CROWN HOTEL	
SHARJAH AIRPORT HOTEL	
SHARJAH CARLTON HOTEL	
SHARJAH GRAND HOTEL	
SHARJAH ROTANA HOTEL	
PRIME TOWER	

TRAVEL AGENCIES	CONTACT INFORMATION
AL FAISAL TRAVEL AND TOURISM AGENCY Mr. Yassin Diab, General Manager	Harbour Street, Kithab and Alami Building POB 2275, Sharjah, United Arab Emirates Tel : +971 (6) 5527111 Fax : +971 (6) 5527666
ARABIAN TRAVEL AGENCY LIMITED Mr. RGK Nair, General Manager	POB 1477, Sharjah, United Arab Emirates Tel : +971 (6) 5610000 Fax : +971 (6) 5610202 Telex : 68959 ATA EM E-Mail : attravel@emirates.net.ae
ARABIAN LINK TOURS	Airport Road, POB 821, Sharjah, United Arab

For additional analytical, marketing, investment and business opportunities
information, please contact
Global Investment & Business Center, USA
(202) 546-2103. Fax: (202) 546-3275. E-mail: rusric@erols.com

Mr. Jerome Gomes, Manager	Emirates Tel : +971 (6) 5726666 Fax : +971 (6) 5721440 E-Mail : arablink@emirates.net.ae http://www.arabianlink.com
AEROFLOT RUSSIAN INTERNATIONAL AIRLINES	POB 22748, Sharjah, United Arab Emirates Tel : +971 (6) 5721991 Fax : +971 (6) 5721993
AL KHALIDIAH TOURISM AND CARGO	POB 12666, Sharjah, United Arab Emirates Tel : +971 (6) 5610557 Fax : +971 (6) 393082
AL WAHADA TRAVEL AND CARGO AGENCY Mr. Hassan Abbas, Senior Sales Officer	POB 6825, Sharjah, United Arab Emirates Tel : +971 (6) 330477 Fax : +971 (6) 337041
AL ZORA TRAVEL AND CARGO AGENCY Mr. A M Beic, General Manager	POB 328, Sharjah, United Arab Emirates Tel : +971 (6) 5725977 Fax : +971 (6) 5723511
BUHAIRA TRAVEL AGENCY	POB 4841, Sharjah, United Arab Emirates Tel : +971 (6) 5614593 Fax : +971 (6) 5623855
CHINA SOUTHERN AIRLINES	POB 6577, Sharjah, United Arab Emirates Tel : +971 (6) 5371029 Fax : +971 (6) 5366339 Telex : 68767 CSN 650 EM
CORDIAL TOURS AND CARGO	POB 4614, Sharjah, United Arab Emirates Tel : +971 (6) 5725142 Fax : +971 (6) 5724921 Telex : 68898 CORDIA EM E-Mail : cordial@emirates.net.ae
DNATA Mr. Jose Cyriac, Sales Executive	POB 4033, Sharjah, United Arab Emirates Tel : +971 (6) 5723131Fax : +971 (6) 5723498 SITA : SHJAWTG
EMIRATES WORLD TRAVEL, TOURISM AND CARGO Mr. Ali Mohammed Sukker, General Manager	POB 1975, Sharjah, United Arab Emirates Tel : +971 (6) 5735666 Fax : +971 (6) 5733371
EMIRATES TRAVEL AND FREIGHT AGENCY	POB 20, Sharjah, United Arab Emirates Tel : +971 (6) 5361000 Fax : +971 (6) 5364595
FLYING STAR LTD. TRAVEL TOURISM & CARGO	POB 20223, Sharjah, United Arab Emirates Tel : +971 (6) 5736677 Fax : +971 (6) 5736868
INDIAN AIRLINES LIMITED	POB 1477, Sharjah, United Arab Emirates Tel : +971 (6) 5616635 Fax : +971 (6) 5372789
INTERCONTINENTAL TRAVEL AND TOURISM	POB 21220, Sharjah, United Arab Emirates Tel : +971 (6) 5363553 Fax : +971 (6) 5371441
ISIS TRAVEL	POB 4152, Sharjah, United Arab Emirates Tel : +971 (6) 5359555 Fax : +971 (6) 5722214

JARNAS CARGO TOURS Mr. Abdul Kareem Doweedar, Director General	POB 12822, Sharjah, United Arab Emirates Tel : +971 (6) 5725212 Fax : +971 (6) 5725943 E-Mail : jarnctrz@emirates.net.ae
KANOO TRAVEL Mr. Varghese Daniel, Assistant Travel Manager	POB 153, Sharjah, United Arab Emirates Tel : +971 (6) 5616058 Fax : +971 (6) 5618655
KHALID TRAVEL AND TOURISM AGENCY Mr. Amir Singh, General Manager	POB 21766, Sharjah, United Arab Emirates Tel : +971 (6) 5620166 Fax : +971 (6) 5620788 E-Mail : emirus@emirates.net.ae
KUWAIT AIRWAYS	POB 17, Sharjah, United Arab Emirates Tel : +971 (6) 5378126 Fax : +971 (6) 5366877
MARHABA TOURISM AND TRAVELS	POB 5394, Sharjah, United Arab Emirates Tel : +971 (6)5355320 Fax : +971 (6) 5355300
MIDDLE EAST EXPRESS LIMITED	POB 622, Sharjah, United Arab Emirates Tel : +971 (6) 5726327 Fax : +971 (6) 5723832
NAPOLI TRAVELING, TOURS AND CARGO AGENCY	POB 6699, Sharjah, United Arab Emirates Tel : +971 (6) 5357545 Fax : +971 (6) 5351257
NATA TRAVEL AND TOURISM	POB 20757, Sharjah, United Arab Emirates Tel : +971 (6) 5723434 Fax : +971 (6) 5723003
ORIENT TOURS	POB 26820, Sharjah, United Arab Emirates Tel : +971 (6) 549333 Fax : +971 (6) 5525077 E-Mail : otshj@emirates.net.ae
ORIENT TRAVEL, HOLIDAYS AND CARGO Mr. Asim Arshad, General Manager	POB 772, Sharjah, United Arab Emirates Tel : +971 (6) 5549333 Fax : +971 (6) 5725012
PLANET TRAVELS AND TOURISM	POB 8, Sharjah, United Arab Emirates Tel : +971 (6) 5581401 Fax : +971 (6) 5581341
REDLINE TOURIST SERVICES AND EXHIBITIONS	POB 27111, Sharjah, United Arab Emirates Tel : +971 (6) 5740740 Fax : +971 (6) 5740400
SPEED TRAVELS AND TOURS	POB 855, Sharjah, United Arab Emirates Tel : +971 (6) 333222 Fax : +971 (6) 336026 E-Mail : speed1@emirates.net.ae
STALCO TRAVEL SHARJAH	POB 5283, Sharjah, United Arab Emirates Tel : +971 (6) 5351150 Fax : +971 (6) 5358950
SUNSHINE EMIRATES	POB 23528, Sharjah, United Arab Emirates Tel : +971 (6) 324939 Fax : +971 (6) 324936 Telex : 68358 E-Mail : sunshine@sharjah-welcome.com
SWIFT INTERNATIONAL TOURISM	POB 144. Sharjah. United Arab Emirates

For additional analytical, marketing, investment and business opportunities
information, please contact
Global Investment & Business Center, USA
(202) 546-2103. Fax: (202) 546-3275. E-mail: rusric@erols.com

	Tel : +971 (6) 5539966 Fax : +971 (6) 5539988
SNTTA	POB 17, Sharjah, United Arab Emirates Tel : +971 (6) 5351411 Fax : +971 (6) 5374968 Telex : 68021 SNTTA EM E-Mail : sntta@emirates.net.ae http://www.sntta.com
SKYLINE TRAVEL AND TOURIST	POB 40085, Sharjah, United Arab Emirates Tel : +971 (6) 5355923 Fax : +971 (6) 5367968 Telex : 68812
TRANSAVIA TRAVEL AGENCY	POB 9362, Sharjah, United Arab Emirates Tel : +971 (6) 5522833 Fax : 971 (6) 556600
TRANSWORLD AIR TRAVEL	POB 852, Sharjah, United Arab Emirates Tel : +971 (6) 5725088 Fax : +971 (6) 721781
TOP TOURISM	POB 6722, Sharjah, United Arab Emirates Tel : +971 (6) 5544022 Fax : +971 (6) 5548191
TOP TOURS	POB 6722, Sharjah, United Arab Emirates Tel : +971 (6) 5724022 Fax : +971 (6) 5725191 Telex : 68746 TOP TRS EM
UZBEKISTAN AIRWAYS	POB 23088, Sharjah, United Arab Emirates Tel : +971 (6) 5543732 Fax : +971 (6) 5548322
VICTORIA TRAVELS	POB 58, Sharjah, United Arab Emirates Tel : +971 (6) 5617444 Fax : +971 (6) 5617722

RESTAURANTS

As in any city Sharjah has restaurants and cafes of many nationalities and specialties.

Sharjah is a place for takeaways, any dish can be delivered to your door hot and fresh at almost any time of the day or night. Choosing a favorite restaurant may be the problem.

The following selection of restaurants and cafes offers a cross section of the food available.

Where to go?

Sharjah's restaurants are dotted throughout the city but the following areas have shops to browse in, and here, the most popular restaurants can be found.

- *Al Wahda Street* for fast food, International restaurants, coffee shops and shawarma stands.
- *Jammal Abdul Nasser Street,* parallel to Al Wahda Street has many restaurants ranging from shawarma stands and coffee shops to medium sized Arabic and International restaurants.

For additional analytical, marketing, investment and business opportunities information, please contact
Global Investment & Business Center, USA
(202) 546-2103. Fax: (202) 546-3275. E-mail: rusric@erols.com

- *Al Wahda and King Faisal Street junction* finds the most popular Arabic restaurants of Al Fawar, Al Nomade and Al Jerash. Other coffee shops and restaurants can be found along both these streets.
- *Al Qassimia Street and roundabout* have most of the Chinese, Filipino and some Arabic restaurants.
- *Rolla Square* and the surrounds have the Indian and Pakistani restaurants.
- *Corniche Road* has a number of juice bars and cafes serving roast chicken on a spit and shawarmas.

PUBLIC SERVIES

A wide range of services is being provided by Sharjah Municipality, especially in the infrastructure of the public facilities to keep pace with construction and urban development.

The Municipality is active in road construction, the creation of parks and other public facilities.

The municipality also provides a wide range of public health services and issues trading, professional and industrial licenses. More information on health and hospitals can be found here.

Sharjah Municipality

Sharjah Municipality includes numerous departments, centers and branches. These include :

- The Engineering Department
- Public Works Department
- Quality Control and Building Research Laboratory
- Solid Refuse Section
- Health Section
- Public Health Clinic
- The Central Laboratory for Food Control and Consultations
- Agriculture Section
- Fertilizer Factory
- Legal Affairs Section
- Information Technology Section
- Garage Section
- Sharjah Driving Institute

The **Department of Planning and Survey** has four sections:

- Planning Section
- Land Registration Section
- Real Estate Registration Section
- Survey Section

THE SHARJAH MUNICIPALITY

PO Box 22, Sharjah, United Arab Emirates
Tel : +971 (6) 5623333 or 378392
Fax : +971 (6) 5626455
E-Mail : munitc@emirates.net.ae

For additional analytical, marketing, investment and business opportunities information, please contact
Global Investment & Business Center, USA
(202) 546-2103. Fax: (202) 546-3275. E-mail: rusric@erols.com

Location : Municipality Round About, Down town, Sharjah

Working Hours
Saturday to Wednesday (7:30 am to 2:30 pm)
Thursday and Friday holidays

HOSPITALS

Health is an important issue for anyone. In the UAE, there are no specific risks although the climate can be harsh during the summer months. No special immunizations are required.

The quality of health care and facilities in Sharjah is generally good. You have a choice of public and private hospitals, clinics, and individual practitioners to choose from.

Health Card

It is a requirement for expatriates to have a health card in order to live and work in the UAE. These cards are available to all residents of the UAE for a fee. The medical is usually done at the Public Health Clinic, however some of the private hospitals also offer this service.

Listed below is the necessary paperwork required to apply for a health card:
1. Passport photocopy
2. Covering letter from sponsor
3. Visa application or photocopy
4. 2 passport size photographs
5. Ministry of Health form duly filled
6. Dhs 300 for the health card
7. Dhs 200 for the medical examination

For a renewal:
1. Last health card
2. Passport copy with visa stamp
3. Same as above from Nos. 4 to 7

You will find typists, a photocopier and people to explain and help you through the procedure.

It can be quite hectic and time consuming, so try and go as early in the morning as possible.

A health card will give you access to the government hospitals listed below. If you do not have a health card, the government hospitals are open in case of emergency only and for up to 24 hours stay. If you have health insurance, you can also choose to use the private hospitals and clinics. Without insurance private medical care is costly.

Government Hospitals

HOSPITAL NAME	TELEPHONE
Kuwaiti Hospital Kuwait Road Open 24 hours for emergency and health card holders.	+971 (6) 5242111

For additional analytical, marketing, investment and business opportunities
information, please contact
Global Investment & Business Center, USA
(202) 546-2103. Fax: (202) 546-3275. E-mail: rusric@erols.com

New Al Qassimi Hospital Wasit Road Reserved for national patients. Open 24 hours for emergency and health card holders.	+971 (6) 386444
Al Dhaid Hospital	+971 (6) 8822221
Dibba Hospital	+971 (9) 2446666
Kalba Hospital	+971 (9) 2777011
Khor Fakkan	+971 (9) 2370222

Private Hospitals

HOSPITAL NAME	TELEPHONE
Al Zahra Private Hospital	+971 (6) 5620079
Zulekha Hospital	+971 (6) 5378866
Click on the hospital name for more information.	

Clinics

NAME	TELEPHONE
Al Buhairah Medical Center	+971 (6) 5599699
Bhatia Clinic	+971 (6) 5522936
Al Mueed Clinic	+971 (6) 5522429
Al Salam Clinic	+971 (6) 5614262
Chinese Clinic	+971 (6) 5616446
Click on the name for more information.	
Emirates PVT. Poly Clinic	+971 (6) 5551666
Al Siddique Clinic (Dhaid)	+971 (6) 8822046

Emergency Services	Number
Fire	997
Ambulance	998 or 999
Police	999
Anjad (Police Emergency)	5512222
UAE Coastguard	5281667
Electricity	5322511
Water	5541414
Ministry of Health	7429333

For additional analytical, marketing, investment and business opportunities information, please contact
Global Investment & Business Center, USA
(202) 546-2103. Fax: (202) 546-3275. E-mail: rusric@erols.com

Kuwaiti Hospital	5242111
New Al Qassimi Hospital	5386444
Kalba Hospital	09-2777011
Khor Fakkan Hospital	09-2370222

For Public Health Clinic at Al Nasseriya, Sheikh Sultan bin Saqr Al Qassimi Road, between Mohammad Abu Khater R/A and Fire Station R/A, dial +971 (6) 5522301 or 5523316.

GOVERNMENT CONTACTS

ORGANIZATION	CONTACT INFORMATION	TELEPHONE	FAX
Federal Government Ministries			
General Postal Authority	POB 4444, Sharjah	+971 (6) 5722219	+971 (6) 5722953
Ministry of Agriculture	POB 926, Sharjah	+971 (6) 5522968	+971 (6) 5526363
Ministry of Communications	POB 3522, Sharjah	+971 (6) 5281234	+971 (6) 5281764
Ministry of Economy & Commerce	POB 3803, Sharjah	+971 (6) 5745000	+971 (6) 5745450
Ministry of Education and Youth	POB 452, Sharjah	+971 (6) 5723082	+971 (6) 5725866
Ministry of Electricity & Water	POB 1672, Dubai	+971 (6) 5341111	+971 (6) 5341548
Ministry of Foreign Affairs	POB 155, Sharjah	+971 (6) 5722623	+971 (6) 5726347
Ministry of Health	POB 2072, Sharjah	+971 (6) 5541117	+971 (6) 5355473
Ministry of Information & Culture	POB 5051, Sharjah	+971 (6) 5723011	+971 (6) 5725877
Ministry of Interior (Police HQ)	POB 29, Sharjah	+971 (6) 5541111	+971 (6) 5541595
Ministry of Islamic Affairs & Endowments	POB 501, Sharjah	+971 (6) 5722328	+971 (6) 5736573
Ministry of Justice	POB 377, Sharjah	+971 (6) 5541821	+971 (6) 5351398
Ministry of Labor & Social Affairs	POB 301, Sharjah	+971 (6) 5515777	+971 (6) 5357369
Ministry of Planning	POB 1134, Sharjah	+971 (6) 5722704	+971 (6) 5723852

For additional analytical, marketing, investment and business opportunities information, please contact
Global Investment & Business Center, USA
(202) 546-2103. Fax: (202) 546-3275. E-mail: rusric@erols.com

Ministry of Public Works & Housing	POB 1515, Sharjah	+971 (6) 5745577	+971 (6) 5745588
UAE Armed Forces	POB 162, Sharjah	+971 (6) 5582111	+971 (6) 5584418
UAE Central Bank	POB 645, Sharjah	+971 (6) 5592592	+971 (6) 5593977
Government Departments			
Al Diwan Al Emiri	POB 101, Sharjah	+971 (6) 5725222	+971 (6) 5723366
Administration Control Dept.	POB 201, Sharjah	+971 (6) 5542007	+971 (6) 5518886
Department of Civil Aviation	POB 8, Sharjah	+971 (6) 5581158	+971 (6) 5580880
Committee of Admin. & Technical Development	POB 4693, Sharjah	+971 (6) 5545917	+971 (6) 5543448
Department of Culture & Information	POB 5119, Sharjah	+971 (6) 5541116	+971 (6) 5362126
Department of Customs & Ports	POB 510, Sharjah	+971 (6) 5281666	+971 (6) 5281425
Economic Dept.	POB 829, Sharjah	+971 (6) 5734222	+971 (6) 5734111
Finance Dept.	POB 201 , Sharjah	+971 (6) 5542007	+971 (6) 5518886
Financial Control	POB 201, Sharjah	+971 (6) 5546411	+971 (6) 5362141
Department of Islamic Affairs & Endowments	POB 501, Sharjah	+971 (6) 5727722	+971 (6) 5736573
Islamic Center	POB 1087, Sharjah	+971 (6) 5723999	+971 (6) 5724000
Sharjah Municipality	POB 22, Sharjah E-Mail : munitc@emirates.net.ae	+971 (6) 5623333	+971 (6) 5626455
Petroleum & Mineral Affairs	POB 188, Sharjah	+971 (6) 5541888	+971 (6) 5378647
Real Estate Registration	POB 22, Sharjah	+971 (6) 5623333	+971 (6) 5546455
Sharjah Airport Authority	POB 8, Sharjah	+971 (6) 5581111	+971 (6) 5581051
Sharjah Chamber of Commerce & Industry	POB 580, Sharjah E-mail : scci@sharjah.gov..ae Website: http://www.sharjah.gov.ae	+971 (6) 5541444	+971 (6) 5541119

For additional analytical, marketing, investment and business opportunities information, please contact Global Investment & Business Center, USA (202) 546-2103. Fax: (202) 546-3275. E-mail: rusric@erols.com

Sharjah Electricity & Water Authority	POB 135, Sharjah E-mail : sewa@emirates.net.ae	+971 (6) 5541414	+971 (6) 5366515
Sharjah Television	POB 111, Sharjah	+971 (6) 5361111	+971 (6) 5541755
Social Services Dept.	POB 4424, Sharjah	+971 (6) 5725333	+971 (6) 5722066

AMERICAN UNIVERSITY

The American University of Sharjah (AUS) is a non-profit, coeducational American style institution of higher education formed on the American model. It was established and is funded by His Highness, Sheikh Dr. Sultan bin Mohammed Al Qassimi, Member of the Supreme Council, Ruler of Sharjah and Supreme President of the University.

Architecturally distinguished facilities will accommodate 4,000 undergraduate students.

The language of instruction is English.

Bachelor's degrees are offered in 18 majors by the Faculties of four Colleges: Arts and Sciences, Architecture and Design, Business and Management, and Engineering.

The **Continuing Education Center (CEC)** provides businesses and individuals access to the educational resources of AUS and offers quality educational programs to meet the ongoing professional and personal needs of the Northern Emirates' adult community at large.

For additional analytical, marketing, investment and business opportunities information, please contact
Global Investment & Business Center, USA
(202) 546-2103. Fax: (202) 546-3275. E-mail: rusric@erols.com

FREE ECONOMIC ZONES

AJMAN FREE ZONE

ADVANTAGES

- Cheap energy
- The most economical wage structure and easy access to vast work force
- Total exemption from all import and export duties
- Total elimination of all service charges and hidden fees
- Exceptionally low handling charges
- 20 years contract renewable to another 20 years guaranteeing 40 years tax and customs free operations
- Low lease prices
- World class infrastructure
- Lowest tariffs in the region

CORPORATE BENEFITS
100% foreign ownership
100% repatriation of capital and profits
No personal income tax
No corporate tax

CUSTOM DUTY EXEMPTION IN GCC COUNTRIES
Goods produced by companies having a National Industrial License in the Ajman Free Zone with 51% share holding with GCC nationals are eligible for a "UAE Certificate of Origin" from the Ministry of Economy and Commerce, UAE, qualifying them for customs duty exemption in member states of GCC, provided the value addition in Ajman Free Zone has been at least 40% of the total final value of the relevant product.

QUESTIONS AND ANSWERS

Q. Does Ajman Free Zone finance projects?
A. No, Ajman Free Zone doesn't provide financing services to the projects.
Q. Could I transfer my money outside UAE?
A. Yes, there is no any restriction in this regard.
Q. Is there any Income tax applied on companies or individuals?
A. There is neither any personal income tax nor any corporate tax.
Q. Could my Company compete freely with similar companies?
A. Yes, Ajman Free Zone follows opened and free business policy without any restrictions against competition.
Q. Do banks and financial institutes provide services to the Companies that are registered in Ajman Free Zone?
A. Yes, but they should obtain the required permission.
Q. Is it possible for more than one company to participate in the rent?

For additional analytical, marketing, investment and business opportunities information, please contact
Global Investment & Business Center, USA
(202) 546-2103. Fax: (202) 546-3275. E-mail: rusric@erols.com

A. No, this is not permitted.
Q. Is it possible for me to be a partner in more than one project inside the free zone?
A. Yes, there is no any restriction regarding number of projects that the investor can participate in.
Q. Do I need a local partner to invest in Ajman Free Zone?
A. No, there are no any restrictions on the Foreigner's exclusive proprietorship.
Q. Is it possible for me to sell my merchandise and services in UAE?
A. Yes, as per the valid-laws.
Q. Is it possible for me to obtain a certificate of origin for the goods that the goods that are manufactured in the Free Zone?
A. Yes, if 40% of production cycle is completed in the Free Zone.
Q. Is it possible for me to freely move from and to Ajman Free Zone?
A. Yes.
Q. Is it possible to change the activities covered in the license?
A. Yes, but after obtaining the approval for such application and pay the necessary fees for change.
Q. What is the validity period of the Ajman Free Zone License?
A. It is valid for one year, renewed annually if the investor is having a valid tenancy contract and paid all the dues.
Q. Could I open a branch for my existing company?
A. Yes, you may open a branch or a representation setup to your existing company.
Q. What are the types of activities permitted to be practiced in Ajman Free Zone?
A. All good types of activities shall be reviewed.
Q. Is it possible for me to import and export goods?
A. Yes, as per the license granted to you.
Q. What is the validity period for my residence visa?
A. Three years.
Q. Is it possible for my family to stay with me in the U.A.E.?
A. Yes, but you have to follow the official immigration procedures.
Q. Will my family members be allowed to work?
A. Yes, after obtaining residence visas.
Q. Is there any restriction to transport between the Emirates?
A. No you may freely transport.
Q. Is there any restriction regarding my departure?
A. As soon as you obtain a valid visa, you may enter and leave the country without any restriction.

For additional analytical, marketing, investment and business opportunities information, please contact
Global Investment & Business Center, USA
(202) 546-2103. Fax: (202) 546-3275. E-mail: rusric@erols.com

Q. Do I have to recruit UAE staff?
A. No, companies may recruit staff from nationalities of their choice.
Q. Is my staff allowed to reside in my factory or store?
A. No, they shall be accommodated in residential complexes inside the free zone.
Q. What are the communication services available in the free zone?
A. International and local telephone line services, fax, and e-mail and Internet services through telephone.
Q. Is the hired unit ready for connection?
A. Yes all units for offices, store and land are ready for connection.
Q. Is there any maximum limit for number of service lines that I may obtain?
A. No, there is no maximum limit.
Q. What are the available international communication lines?
A. To all countries around the world.
Q. Are the communication rates competitive to rates of other countries in the region?
A. Yes, prices are competitive to you and available in the investor's directory.

JEBEL ALI FREE ZONE

The Jebel Ali Free Zone offers a unique opportunity to do business in the Middle East. It is the ideal industrial, warehousing & distribution hub for a market of some 1.5 billion people, combining the services of the best port in the Middle East with an efficient, dynamic infrastructure.

Stable regulations, well-developed communications and transportation systems and the pro-business environment of Dubai make this Free Zone one of the best in the world. It is already the base of more than 1600 companies from more than 85 countries, including many global brand leaders - companies such as Sony, Black & Decker, Daewoo, Estee Lauder, Grundig, Colgate Palmolive, Nokia, IBM and Samsung.

so, if you are considering expanding your business, wanting to re-locate your business to a vibrant, stable, safe and prospective location, there can always be a place for you in the 100 sq. km. Jebel Ali Free Zone in Dubai.

For more details about JAFZ, the incentives it offers for prospective investors, please browse through the rest of this site. If you have any comments and/or questions, please feel free to e-mail/fax or call.

ADVANTAGES

MAIN ADVANTAGES
No major markets in the Middle East are more than 24 hours drive
No major port in the region is more than 48 hours steaming
Europe is 14 days, Japan 20 days and South East Asia 9 days away

For additional analytical, marketing, investment and business opportunities
information, please contact
Global Investment & Business Center, USA
(202) 546-2103. Fax: (202) 546-3275. E-mail: rusric@erols.com

Over 125 of the world's major container shipping lines call into Dubai, including feeder vessels to Iran, Africa and the Indian sub-continent
Dubai International airport, just 30 minutes by road from JAFZ is serviced by more than 80 airlines to and from over 130 destinations
Over 175 countries can be reached through direct dialling

The Jebel Ali Free Zone Authority was created by a Government of Dubai decree on 9th February 1985.

As a Government body, JAFZA is charged with the supervision of the Jebel Ali Free Zone. Its responsibilities include providing companies wishing to operate within the Free Zone: -

Appropriate licences to operate.

Lease facilities such as Office Units, Light Industrial Units, Land Sites and Storage Facilities. Administration, Engineering and Utility services.
An interface with the Dubai Ports Authority for its services.
A continually improving service by investing in upgrading and updating its equipment, infrastructure, and facilities.

Every Free Zone client can enjoy the combined benefits of the services and facilities offered by the Jebel Ali Free Zone Authority(JAFZA) and Dubai Ports Authority.

COMPANIES

J ebel is a business base for over 1450 companies from 85 countries. While their businesses span a whole range of activities, they can be broadly classified into three distinct groups, namely Trading, Industrial and Service companies. About 74% of the companies hold trading licences, 22% industrial and the rest 4%, service licences.

Among the countries, the top ten are UAE, India, UK, USA, Iran, Japan, Pakistan, France, Germany and Saudi Arabia.

Several of Free Zone's clients are either Fortune 500 companies, Multinationals or are market leaders in their own fields.

COMPANIES IN JEBEL ALI FREE ZONE - REGION & COUNTRY-WISE STATISTICS

REGION	COUNTRY	Total Number of Companies	Industrial Licences	Trading Licences	Service Licences	Sub Total	Total Licences
AUNZ	Australia	10	1	10	0	11	
	New Zealand	1	1	0	0	1	12
CIS	Armenia	4	1	3	0	4	
	Azerbaijan	1	0	1	0	1	

For additional analytical, marketing, investment and business opportunities information, please contact
Global Investment & Business Center, USA
(202) 546-2103. Fax: (202) 546-3275. E-mail: rusric@erols.com

	Russia	5	0	5	0	5	
	Ukraine	3	0	3	0	3	
	Uzbekistan	1	0	1	0	1	14
					-		
EURO	Austria	4	1	3	0	4	
	Belgium	4	0	4	0	4	
	Bulgaria	2	1	1	0	2	
	Channel Island	1	0	1	0	1	
	Cyprus	8	1	7	0	8	
	Czechoslovakia	1	0	1	0	1	
	Denmark	7	3	5	0	8	
	Finland	8	0	8	0	8	
	France	35	8	33	1	42	
	Germany	46	10	41	1	52	
	Greece	1	0	1	0	1	
	Ireland, Republic	1	0	1	0	1	
	Italy	14	5	11	0	16	
	Liechtenstein	3	0	3	0	3	
	Luxembourg	1	0	1	0	1	
	Malta	2	0	2	0	2	
	Netherlands	17	2	17	0	19	
	Norway	5	1	5	0	6	
	Poland	1	0	1	0	1	
	Portugal	4	3	1	0	4	
	Spain, Canary.Is	4	0	4	0	4	
	Sweden	4	0	4	0	4	
	Switzerland	19	1	19	0	20	
	United Kingdom	181	33	165	1	199	411
FARE	China	12	2	11	0	13	
	Hongkong	17	2	16	0	18	
	Indonesia	2	0	2	0	2	
	Japan	59	2	58	0	60	
	Malaysia	2	0	2	0	2	
	North Korea	1	1	0	0	1	
	Philippines	1	0	1	0	1	

For additional analytical, marketing, investment and business opportunities
information, please contact
Global Investment & Business Center, USA
(202) 546-2103. Fax: (202) 546-3275. E-mail: rusric@erols.com

	Singapore	18	1	18	0	19	
	South Korea	10	3	8	0	11	
	Taiwan, Province	10	4	10	0	14	
	Thailand	4	2	2	0	4	145
FEIN	Afghanistan	4	1	3	0	4	
	India	158	59	129	1	189	
	Mauritius	3	0	3	0	3	
	Pakistan	30	16	22	0	38	
	Sri Lanka	5	2	4	0	6	240
GCCE	Bahrain	6	2	4	0	6	
	Kuwait	12	3	9	1	13	
	Oman	6	1	5	0	6	
	Qatar	4	1	4	0	5	
	Saudi Arabia	34	10	25	0	35	
	U.A.E.	279	66	163	58	287	352
GCME	Egypt	10	1	9	0	10	
	Iran	86	12	78	0	90	
	Iraq	5	2	4	0	6	
	Jordan	25	6	22	1	29	
	Lebanon	17	4	15	0	19	
	Palestine	1	0	1	0	1	
	Syrian Arab Rep	6	2	4	0	6	
	Turkey	8	1	8	0	9	
	Yemen Arab Repu	5	2	3	0	5	175
IACI	Algeria	6	0	6	0	6	
	Djibouti	1	0	1	0	1	
	Kenya	4	1	4	0	5	
	Latvia	1	0	1	0	1	
	Libyan Arab Jam	3	0	3	0	3	
	Morocco	1	0	1	0	1	
	Nigeria	1	0	1	0	1	

	Sierra Leone	1	0	1	0	1	
	South Africa	4	2	3	0	5	
	Sudan	10	1	10	0	11	
	Tanzania, United	5	4	4	0	8	
	Tunisia	3	0	3	0	3	
	Uganda	1	0	1	0	1	47
USCA	Bahamas	8	2	8	0	10	
	Bermuda	5	0	5	0	5	
	British West In	2	0	2	0	2	
	Canada	23	4	23	0	27	
	Cayman Islands	2	0	2	0	2	
	Chile	1	0	1	0	1	
	Panama	9	0	9	0	9	
	Saint Vincent A	1	0	1	0	1	
	TAHITI	1	0	1	0	1	
	U.S.A.	114	14	107	1	122	180
ZZZZ	Lithuania	1	0	1	0	1	1
86 COUNTRIES		1446	308	1204	65	1577	1577

THE HAMRIYAH FEE ZONE SHARJAH

The Hamriyah Fee Zone Sharjah, was established by an Emiri Decree issued on November 12, 2007. Since the decree was issued no effort has been spared in fast-tracking the development of the Free Zone to serve as a cornerstone in Sharjah and the United Arab Emirates (UAE) industrial development strategy. The Hamriyah free Zone Authority (HFZA) manages the Free Zone area, which comprises approximately 10 million square meters of industrial and commercial land. Included in the Free Zone area is a 14m-deep water port, which is designed to incorporate dedicated petrochemical bulk handling and general cargo berths.

GENEROUS INCENTIVE FRAMEWORK

As a Next Generation Free Zone, the Hamriyah Free Zone's mission is to provide incentives which exceed that of its competitors and which meet the needs of firms competing for market penetration in the new millennium. Taking up this challenge, Hamriyah Free Zone has sought to both match the standard terms offered by competitor Free Zones and to exceed it.

INVESTMENT INCENTIVES

- 100% Foreign company ownership
- 100% import & export tax exemption

For additional analytical, marketing, investment and business opportunities information, please contact
Global Investment & Business Center, USA
(202) 546-2103. Fax: (202) 546-3275. E-mail: rusric@erols.com

- 100% exemption from all commercial levies
- 100% repatriation of capital and profits
- Leases for 15 years renewable for a further 15 years

FACILITIES

- **Land for Lease for investor development:** Land is available for lease within the Free Zone in plots of 5,000 square meters and above and can be developed by investors to suit their exact requirements.

- **Pre-built warehouse/factory/office units:** Warehouse, factory and office units have been constructed on the site and are available in two convenient sizes, 416 and 614 square meters.
- **Executive Suite Offices:** The International Business Center provides space for 100 executive suite offices with state-of-the-art conferencing and Internet facilities.

SPECIAL ADVANTAGES

- Strategic, friendly location
- Access to 3 seaports on the Arabian Gulf & Indian ocean
- Access to Sharjah International Airport, the largest sea-air transit cargo hub in the Middle East
- Rents fixed for 5 years
- Quick and simple procedure for approval of License Applications
- Recruitment and sponsorship of personnel and procurement of visas
- Access to inexpensive workforce
- Access to Internet, secretarial services, vehicle registration services and driving licenses.
- An established abundant and inexpensive energy.

INDUSTRIES AND ACTIVITIES

Typical activities, which will benefit from being in the Free Zone, include manufacturing, assembling, processing, storage, distribution, general trading, packaging and consolidating. Hamriyah Free Zone has already signed several contracts over the last 12 months with capital commitments of approximately US$ 350 million. These projects include: oil refining, bulk grain storage, oil blending, Soya bean crushing facility, flour mill, printing ink blending, furniture assembling, furniture restoration, electronics and computer components, clothing recycling, satellite TV systems assembling and distribution, trading and many more.

Click here to go to the official Hamriyah Free Zone web site.

HAMRIYAH FREE ZONE
PO Box 1377, Sharjah, United Arab Emirates
Tel : +971 (6) 5263333 Fax : +971 (6) 5263444
E-Mail : hfz@emirates.net.ae
http://www.hamriyahfz.com/

SAIF ZONE

An Ideal Business Hub

For additional analytical, marketing, investment and business opportunities information, please contact
Global Investment & Business Center, USA
(202) 546-2103. Fax: (202) 546-3275. E-mail: rusric@erols.com

With the distinction of being the world's first ISO 9001 certified Airport Free Zone, SAIF-Zone has a highly developed infrastructure, providing state of the art services. It is ideally located in the vicinity of Sharjah City, adjacent to Sharjah International Airport. Its close proximity to major UAE Airports and Seaports on the East Coast (Arabian Gulf) and 120 kms to the West Coast (Indian Ocean) of the UAE is a vital strategic advantage especially for export, import and industrial establishments. Located adjacent to the best Airport in cargo operations in the Middle East and North Africa, it is also the Middle East cargo hub for Lufthansa and the Airport International Counsel (ACI) ranks it to be one of the best ranked (ranked 29th) airports in the world in cargo operations.

These integral links give investing companies direct access to a potential market covering over 1.6 billion consumers from the Middle East, Iran, Asian subcontinent, East Africa and the emerging markets of the CIS countries. Companies based in SAIF - Zone have direct access to both the East and West coasts and sea-air transfers can be made in 6 to 8 hours. Speed, safety, reliability and cost-effectiveness are Sharjah's unique selling points as a cargo hub. The UAE accounts for the highest volume of sea-air cargo handled in Asia with Sharjah International Airport accounting for the highest volume of sea-air tonnage movement.

SAIF- Zone Advantages

- 100% foreign ownership and repatriation of funds with no currency restrictions
- No personal income or corporate tax
- Sponsorship/visas for all staff with no restriction to a 100% expatriate workforce along with an economical wage structure
- Low cost accommodation for on-site work force
- Administration and Management services
- Highly qualified bilingual staff
- 24 hour hotline for hire of equipment and cargo movement
- Abundant and inexpensive energy
- Modern telecommunication infrastructure
- Land for unrestricted development, pre-built warehouses in different sizes with office space, furnished office suites with reception and temporary auxiliary warehouses available on lease.

Our Growth Path

Number of companies registered with SAIF Zone rose from 55 in 2007 to 382 in 2007 representing companies from 50 countries.

SAIF ZONE
PO Box 8000, Sharjah, United Arab Emirates
Tel : +971 (6) 5570000 Fax : +971 (6) 5571010
E-Mail : saifzone@emirates.net.ae
http://www.saif-zone.com/

For additional analytical, marketing, investment and business opportunities
information, please contact
Global Investment & Business Center, USA
(202) 546-2103. Fax: (202) 546-3275. E-mail: rusric@erols.com

UNITED ARAB EMIRATES TODAY[3]

ECONOMY

FAHIM BIN SULTAN AL QASIMI UAE MINISTER OF ECONOMY AND COMMERCE

Our nation has made remarkable progress in the span of three decades. The UAE of today bears little resemblance to the UAE of December 1971, when we achieved our independence. In the Arab world, we say that it takes two hands to clap. This is manifested in the partnership between the United Arab Emirates and the United States of America. The U.S.A. was among the very first nations to recognize the UAE¼s independence in 1971. And the ties between our two nations have grown progressively stronger ever since. At the heart of this relationship lies our mutual commitment to tolerance, cultural diversity, respect for religion, the principles of a free economy, the defense of our shared interests, and the vital role played by federation.

The UAE has been blessed with peace, prosperity and leadership. Let me elaborate, first on peace. Because of expansionist designs on the part of some states in the region, the Middle East has traditionally been regarded as a region of instability and turmoil. In this environment, it is all the more remarkable that the UAE has steered clear of most hostilities, called for a peaceful resolution of conflicts, and helped to mediate some of the Middle East¼s most intractable disputes.

The UAE has been able to keep the peace because it maintains good relations and open communications with all of its neighbors. We believe that conflict strains our economic resources and undermines political stability, the very foundation of UAE society.

Second, prosperity. By investing and reinvesting the nation¼s wealth in productive enterprises, the UAE has been transformed into a nation with one of the highest per capita incomes in the world and, arguably, the best quality of life in the Middle East. The gross domestic product is now $50 billion. Health care is free, and the infant mortality rate is among the lowest in the world. Schooling is also free. And the UAE has one of the highest literacy rates in the developing world. Between 1971 and the late 1990s, the UAE¼s population increased more than 15-fold. Life expectancy jumped from 60 years to 75.

U.S. exports to the UAE, not including defense, have grown nearly 50-fold to some $3 billion per year. The UAE added nearly 7,000 kilometers of paved highways. The number of ports in the UAE grew from three to 19. And two small airstrips evolved into six world-class international airports. Hotels have surged from fewer than 10 in 1971 to nearly 350 today, and hotel rooms in the UAE recently rose past the 25,000 mark. The International Defense Exhibition (IDEX) in Abu Dhabi and the Dubai Air Show are considered among the best in the world. The UAE has become a major player in media and communications and will launch its own satellite later this year.

Fortunately for us and for our neighbors, we have developed without undermining the social, cultural and political fabric of our society. This has been due in large part to leadership. Sheikh Zayed has served as president of the UAE since its inception in 1971. And his leadership is based on consensus among the seven emirates. In keeping with Islamic tradition, he is seen as

---

[3] Following are excerpts from an April 20, 1999, conference convened by the Middle East Policy Council. The papers these presentations are drawn from will be published as a book, forthcoming in 1999

For additional analytical, marketing, investment and business opportunities information, please contact
Global Investment & Business Center, USA
(202) 546-2103. Fax: (202) 546-3275. E-mail: rusric@erols.com

first among equals, continuing to serve as president because he commands the respect of the nation¼s other leaders and the reverence of the people.

Our system, like the American, is based on a living constitution. Our system combines the best of the old with the best of the new. We have retained democratic Islamic traditions, foremost among which is the majlis, the open council in which national and local leaders meet regularly with citizens to discuss issues of concern. Another pillar of our constitutional system is the national assembly, our parliament, which serves as a forum for debating government policies and legislation.

It is our good fortune to have an abundance of oil and gas, but our most important asset remains our human resources, the men and women of the UAE, who are dedicated to professionalism and excellence.

In conclusion, I am pleased to quote His Highness Sheikh Zayed, who shared these observations on the UAE in his jubilee address in 1996, on the twenty-fifth anniversary of the founding of the state:

> We believe that wealth in itself is of no value unless it is dedicated to the prosperity and welfare of the people. States cannot be built upon wishes, nor can hopes be achieved by dreams. Our federation has stood firm in the face of crisis. It has prospered through hard work, perseverance and sacrifice and by placing the interests of the nation above any other. In this way only can we attain our goals, strengthen the foundation of our state, preserve its stability and serve God.

"GENERAL ASPECTS AND DETERMINANTS OF GROWTH"

Fatima S. Al-Shamsi
Assistant Professor of Economics, University of the UAE, Al-Ain

The general characteristics of the UAE economy are as follows: It is dependent on a single depletable resource, hydrocarbons. There are two levels of authority , federal and local , and no strategic plan that covers the country as a whole. There is a lack of human resources, both skilled and unskilled.

Oil revenue has permitted sharp expansionary growth. But the fear of oil depletion has necessitated a search for other sources of income and the promotion of economic diversification. As a result, investment has been channeled to productive sectors like agriculture and manufacturing. There are generous subsidies to attract private investment. Manufacturing has expanded, as has the service sector. As regards human resources, UAE nationals represent a small percentage of the work force; the economy depends on expatriates.

In the hydrocarbon sector there is variation in the degree of government control and organization and policy related to production, marketing, etc. The government of Abu Dhabi has been generous in supporting agricultural products. However, the potential for this sector to grow is not great, given the environmental constraint, and problems such as water shortage and absentee landlords. The manufacturing sector has been expected to play a major role promoting diversification and propelling economic growth. The government has given this sector priority and encouraged private participation. The banking and financial sector has also played a major role in the economy, but I will leave this sector to Professor Richards.

For additional analytical, marketing, investment and business opportunities information, please contact
Global Investment & Business Center, USA
(202) 546-2103. Fax: (202) 546-3275. E-mail: rusric@erols.com

Trade has been a very important factor in development, but since oil is the major export commodity, the fluctuation in oil revenue has a certain effect on the balance of payments. Recently, however, the composition of exports has changed, due to the expansion of non-oil-based industries. Re-export plays a major role as well. The economy is dependent on imports, both for consumption and investment, and oil proceeds are used to finance them.

As to development policy, the UAE has opted for a free-exchange-rate system and liberal trade with an outward-oriented strategy. The main objective is to build a diversified economy and create domestic productive capacity. Both federal and local governments have started to encourage private participation, first by building a modern infrastructure base, and then trying to start a joint stock company with the private sector. The local government also recognizes the importance of the free zone in encouraging foreign and local investment.

The government role has been very important, first in building the infrastructure base, both social and economic. A great percentage of fixed-capital formation went into this. The share of private-sector infrastructure formation has also been substantial. However, the type of investment the private sector prefers is in the field of commerce and services. I tried to examine the determinants of growth and found, as expected, that government expenditures and exports play the major role. Private capital has no effect on GDP growth.

Great emphasis has been put into encouraging the non-oil sector, and that share of GDP has increased. However, such development has some shortcomings: institutional constraints, the absence of efficient mechanisms for channeling funds to productive projects, a prevalence of high income and consumption sustained without recourse to local production, the existence of high levels of conspicuous investment, and the prevalence of easy government employment and productive jobs relegated to expatriates.

Here are some needs for the future: enhancement of the private-sector role in the economy, decentralization of public administration, rationalization of the legal environment, upgrading of national education and training, and improvement of the information system. To be successful, a privatization program should be part of overall development reform aimed at increasing organizational efficiency, performance and innovation through efficient organization, management and technology.

"THE ECONOMICS OF NATIONAL AUTONOMY"

Mary Ann Tétreault
Professor of Political Science, Iowa State University

The UAE is what many economic writers call a competition state, a state that provides a lot of space for entrepreneurial activity and one that pursues supply-side policies. A competition state is one that supplies resources: capital, infrastructure, social services for the domestic population and for the economy. A competition state also supplies extranational partnerships or the opportunities to make such partnerships. The state works to attract foreign states and firms to engage in long-term, mutually beneficial relations with domestic counterparts. Finally, a competition state provides effective regimes: legal regimes, regulatory regimes and allocative systems, so that the system works for the domestic population and for outsiders coming in to invest.

Recall that among these late developers that were helped by state intervention were the United States, Germany and Japan.

For additional analytical, marketing, investment and business opportunities information, please contact
Global Investment & Business Center, USA
(202) 546-2103. Fax: (202) 546-3275. E-mail: rusric@erols.com

Where is the UAE on this trajectory? The UAE is a "later developer." It comes to the process of development 500 years after this process began in Western Europe. And late developers in general have always required an active government to intervene to help them along. Relying solely on entrepreneurial efforts has not been a good strategy. Recall that among these late developers that were helped by state intervention were the United States, Germany and Japan. This is a very old, established pattern.

Second, the UAE is a grantor state. It is the owner of territorially generated wealth that should be widely distributed among the population for maximum long-run adaptability and growth. If the state keeps it all, not much is going to happen. To get this growth and adaptability takes diversity and risk spreading, which are characteristic of the UAE economy.

Finally, the United Arab Emirates is a federation; decentralization and political accommodation are embedded in the structure and ethic of the state. This leads to competition, both political and economic. This generates innovation in policy generally and in social investment.

What should the United Arab Emirates be investing in? There are a number of contrasting models, and I will just outline briefly some of the issues in hydrocarbon and non-hydrocarbon development.

The UAE controls about 10 percent of the world¼s total hydrocarbon reserve. Should it undertake capacity expansion? It has to measure the effect of increasing average costs of production against the market power it would have if it were to undertake a massive capacity-expansion program.

It also needs to look at the effects of these decisions on its private-sector partners. Abu Dhabi has all of its oil and gas produced by joint ventures with mostly foreign firms. There is the very large question of who gets what in the case of production restraints. The outcome isn¼t particularly clear, though there are a number of interesting models, including the pattern in the original Kuwait Oil Company concession between Gulf Oil and BP many years ago.

Finally, there is the issue of preemptive investment. All of the oil and gas producers in the Gulf are facing the possibility of a flood of oil and a cloud of gas coming from the Central Asian republics. A lot of this has been held off because of transportation difficulties, but when these are resolved, there¼s going to be downward pressure on prices. A lot of investment that we are seeing in capacity expansion in the Gulf could be described as preemptive investment for that reason.

There also is a question of oil versus gas. In the UAE, gas is far more plentiful and has fewer negative environmental consequences, so you can be a clean producer and a good guy by selling more gas. However, as Tom Stauffer has shown in some of his work, you have a very low or even negative amount of rent coming from gas exports. And gas exports by OPEC countries also compete directly against OPEC oil. Stauffer estimates that OPEC exporters lose $9 billion a year from their own self-competition for the lower amount that they get for the gas that replaces the oil that they could have sold had they not sold that gas.

A third issue is processing. Should the UAE or any oil-exporting country be selling crude or selling products? Stauffer again argues for crude sales, but I disagree very strongly. Crude sales provide more rents, but processing provides more control over your market and it adds a great deal more to your overall economic capacity in the future.

For additional analytical, marketing, investment and business opportunities information, please contact
Global Investment & Business Center, USA
(202) 546-2103. Fax: (202) 546-3275. E-mail: rusric@erols.com

If, indeed, you are going to do processing, what are you going to process, fuels or petrochemicals? I am not a great fan of investment in petrochemicals. I¼m looking forward to seeing how this works out in the UAE, because it is the only Gulf country that has the possibility of utilizing a great deal of its production in locally based industry. There you might really have an advantage. Otherwise, petrochemical markets are very volatile and the losses extensive. I¼ve studied the Kuwait experience before the new joint venture with Union Carbide, and the Kuwaitis have had horrible problems making money in petrochemicals. Let me note that Union Carbide has also had trouble making money in petrochemicals. So I would lean toward fuels rather than petrochemicals unless you¼re going to use them locally.

This is where non-oil investment becomes very important. The UAE has been criticized very heavily in the industry and politically for duplicating manufacturing and industrial investment. When I first started studying this industry, I did my dissertation on the Organization of Arab Petroleum Exporting Countries, and everyone was mad at Dubai for having built a shipyard moments after OAPEC decided that it would be building a shipyard in Bahrain. However, multiple ventures add to flexibility over time because they promote diversity and competition in the region. This forces firms to develop new techniques and get a whole lot better at things. Over time, you make more money and become much more innovative.

There is also the call for coordination through the GCC. But the GCC countries have incompatible financial and regulatory regimes. The GCC has to do a lot of political and economic infrastructural work before it can approach something like this. A more serious problem in terms of maintaining flexibility is that central planning through the GCC or any other kind of institution adds to rigidity and is biased against private-sector entrepreneurship. So, as messy as it is, the way things are going now is probably the better way, considering the alternatives.

A second focus for non-oil investment is portfolio investment overseas. Since the Gulf War and the spending down of the Kuwaiti portfolio, the UAE now has the highest amount of such investments among oil exporters today. This diversifies income sources and provides a non-hydrocarbon-dependent income stream. Again, to allude to Tom Stauffer¼s work, by 1983 Kuwait was actually making more money on its overseas investment than it was on crude sales. So we are looking at a source of income for a developing country that adds a great deal to economic security.

Finally, the other important aspect of portfolio investment is that it is a path to generational equity. Oil will run out eventually. Hopefully, the stock market won¼t crash or stay down forever, and there will still be money coming in over time from these investments.

In addition, I also recommend direct foreign investment, again looking at the Kuwaiti model. One of the things that was extremely helpful politically and economically to Kuwait was having direct foreign investment overseas that provided it with political and economic support during the crisis with Iraq.

To conclude, here is a short list of things that I think need some serious attention. One is legal regimes. Legal regimes are crucial, and none of the Gulf countries has a particularly well-established or independent one. If you¼re going to guarantee contracts and make investors feel safe and be able to make long-term plans, your courts have to be in place, and they have to be sophisticated.

Equity markets also need development. There has been a lot of expansion in equity markets in the Gulf region, and it is likely going to continue. It will develop more local investment and be able to channel that investment and make these markets much more liquid than they are today.

**For additional analytical, marketing, investment and business opportunities information, please contact
Global Investment & Business Center, USA
(202) 546-2103. Fax: (202) 546-3275. E-mail: rusric@erols.com**

As Dr. Al-Shamsi noted, one of the things that the UAE needs to do is to consider a labor policy. The UAE has the highest proportion of foreigners in its labor force of any Gulf country, around 82 percent. This distorts demand for labor, and sends distorted signals to people in school. I interviewed a former planning minister in Kuwait who said, people think they can major in Arabic literature and then go get a job anywhere. But if you don¼t have labor-market signals, how can you expect a young person to know?

Finally, I would look also at population policy. The last figures I saw showed that 40 percent of the population of the UAE was under 10 years old. This is not only a burden on services for children, but there is a lot of social stress from having an extremely young population. In the United States the children of the baby boomers have passed through their teenage years and into their twenties. This is a restless population that needs things to do. If you have a great many adolescents and young people, there is a lot more opportunity for political instability. A rapidly growing population is an asset that brings with it liabilities.

In closing, for the United Arab Emirates, oil has been far more a blessing than a curse. Indeed, the UAE has tried policies that my chemistry professor used to say aren¼t "trial and error. It¼s trial and success."

"GOLDEN SHOW IN A STORM: THE FINANCIAL AND BANKING SYSTEM"

Alan Richards
Professor of Economics, University of California-Santa Cruz

Banking and finance are crucial to facilitating and supporting the economy, though Louis XIV was once said to have remarked that "credit supports the populace as the rope supports the hanged man." We see this in the Asian crisis.

It is essential to put my remarks about the regulatory structure in the UAE in the context of the theme of this particular conference, a century in 30 years. Most economists would say that the UAE¼s problems are inherent in any financial and banking system. Finance inevitably involves the problems of allocating resources over time. None of us is God. None of us knows the future. Imperfect information is part and parcel of the whole system. Consequently, mistakes can be made. Different agents have, alas, incentives to shade the truth. Therefore, it is essential that public authorities set out rules of the game that induce these agents to act in a way that is truthful. However, when they do this, these very rules of the game themselves create new kinds of incentives.

This is exactly the kind of discussion that has been raging in Washington ever since the onset of the crisis with the Thai baht and the debacle in East Asia, which then spread to Russia, to Brazil, but so far, mercifully, has not spread too much to the Gulf. But we are talking about exactly the same problems that we might, very appropriately here in the Ronald Reagan Building, be talking about regarding the savings and loan debacle in the United States.

The UAE has had a very sensible development policy. It has taken very large amounts of oil rents and transformed them into a more diversified economy, focusing specifically on the development of human skills and human capital. The usual indicator that economists use to gauge the size of the banking and financial system relative to the economy is the ratio of money and quasi-money to GDP. That stands at about 54 percent in the UAE. That¼s comparable to 59 percent in the United States and 51 percent in Ireland. So we are dealing, at this very simple macroindicator level, with a developed financial system.

For additional analytical, marketing, investment and business opportunities information, please contact
Global Investment & Business Center, USA
(202) 546-2103. Fax: (202) 546-3275. E-mail: rusric@erols.com

Now, what can we say about the structure of the financial industry? We economists have a whole kit bag of models for any and all occasions, no matter how profound the depths of our ignorance. In this case the perfect model would be "an oligopoly with a competitive fringe." The financial system, in that sense, looks very much like the oil business.

There are some 46 banks in the UAE, but five major banks account for about half of assets and more than 75 percent of all deposits. In trying to determine the quality of these banks and their positions, the issues are universal. The most recent issue of *The Economist* contains a special survey of international banking, "On a Wing and a Prayer," which shows a prayerful banker sitting atop a jerry-rigged contraption flying through the air. So the issues that arise are hardly limited to the UAE.

Standard & Poors, in a recent report gives the UAE a "double B PI" rating. A PI is a special category that Standard & Poors has created to talk about publicly available information that they¼re developing for emerging markets. There¼s one bank which gets an A PI rating. So generally, we are talking about respectable kinds of banks.

More to the point, as we stand on the edge of the millennium, what do we see down the road? In particular, if we look at the kinds of crises that emerged in the Asian markets, are there any parallels in the current situation in the UAE? What can we learn by looking at that particular situation?

Every economist will have his or her own favorite take on the Asian financial crisis. There are various ways to look at it. There was pressure from the United States and international agencies. Countries like Thailand and Korea permitted local banks to borrow dollars. Unfortunately, the central-bank authorities were relatively poorly informed. Large amounts of foreign capital came in, and there was a boom. Risky investments were made, some would argue, because of a problem called moral hazard. This is a "heads, I win; tails, you lose" proposition: if you are insured and make an investment that succeeds, you make money; if you make an investment that loses, the government or some public regulatory agency will bail you out so you don¼t lose either. This is often thought to lead to various difficulties.

There are four major issues worth thinking about in the general context of the UAE. First, the consistency of their macroeconomic policy; second, the transparency of information; third, the regulatory oversight by the central monetary authority; and fourth, the problem of moral hazard.

The UAE has done quite well with respect to macroeconomic policy consistency; and rather less well with respect to transparency of information. There is a mixed but generally respectable picture with respect to regulatory oversight by a central monetary authority. Finally, with respect to moral hazard, the difficulty is that the problem does not formally exist in the UAE because the government does not formally guarantee deposits. But there are implicit guarantees. This is very similar to the situation that many believe prevailed in Thailand and Indonesia , the absence of formal moral hazard, but potential risk of informal moral hazard.

The key threat in financial stability for macroeconomic policy is rather simple. If a government makes non-credible commitments such as "we¼re going to maintain a band around our exchange rate" at a time of deficits, when the government is unlikely to have the reserves to sustain that pre-announced goal, speculators are not dumb. They gamble against the currency. Because of the vast amounts of money circulating, the government will inevitably lose that particular gamble. So if the fundamentals aren¼t right, staking everything on keeping one fixed band around the currency is very dangerous.

For additional analytical, marketing, investment and business opportunities information, please contact
Global Investment & Business Center, USA
(202) 546-2103. Fax: (202) 546-3275. E-mail: rusric@erols.com

The UAE does have a relatively narrow band around the dirham. It is, in effect, a fixed currency. Is this a sensible policy? Is it sustainable? So far, yes, for three simple reasons: first, although the governmental structure of the UAE makes assessment somewhat complicated, in general, fiscal deficits have either been nonexistent or relatively modest. Second, current-account surpluses continue to prevail. The country remains a net capital exporter. Finally, the government has very large foreign-exchange reserves. So announcing a relatively narrow band around the currency remains credible.

Of course, if oil prices were to go back down and stay down for a long time, things could change. After all, there was a time when the Saudis had very large financial reserves as well. It¼s relatively easy to lose those in an all-too-brief amount of time. But, very helpfully, unlike the situation in many of the East Asian countries, the fiscal-monetary policy mix, the macroeconomic policy consistency seems reasonably good.

If capital markets are to function efficiently though, investors need to be well-informed about the quality of a financial institution¼s assets. Any bank anywhere in the world always has an incentive to overstate the quality of its assets because that will lead people to think it is a better credit risk and hence loan it money at lower rates. This is why there are so many very clear, specific rules about disclosure of information. It enables others, who have different incentives, to assess the quality of those assets.

In general, it¼s widely believed that the UAE banking system suffers from a relatively low level of disclosure. Let me quote what Standard & Poors recently asserts: "The disclosure falls short of international best practice and even compares unfavorably with some regional peers like Saudi Arabia. Any analysis of the UAE banking system must thus take into account a rather high information risk." That is to say, given these kinds of rules of the game, macroeconomic policy consistency is good. That¼s very desirable. But there are some deficiencies with respect to the transparency of the system.

What about the third issue, regulatory oversight by the central monetary authority? There are three or four kinds of inevitable crises that occur in banking and finance. It is useful to look at these as a learning process for the monetary authority. For example, in 1977, there was exactly the kind of exchange-rate crisis that is relatively unlikely now. Perhaps the reason is that in 1977 there were fiscal imbalances, a fixed exchange rate and inadequate reserves. And the currency was hammered. I think that lesson has been well learned, and some institutional changes have been put in place to try to cope with it.

In the early 1990s, of course, there were two additional crises, one brought about by the Iraqi invasion of Kuwait. Then there was the BCCI (Bank of Credit and Commerce International) scandal. In regard to the latter, one of the difficulties in any banking and financial system is that it doesn¼t really matter what actually happens. What matters is what other people think happens.

One can plausibly argue that some of the worst victims of the BCCI scandal were citizens of the UAE. They were the ones who really got burned by the particular corruption involved in that bank. The difficulty is that other people in other parts of the world thought: Here we have a system with relatively low transparency, and we get this scandal; this seems risky to me; I¼m going to demand higher premiums; maybe I¼ll stay out of that place.

The impact of this episode has waned considerably during the current decade. The government intervened quite successfully to prevent what Charles Kendelberger (*Manias, Panics and Crashes*) calls "the emergence of swindles," which sends a signal to investors and depositors to rush for the window to try to take out their money. Then we have a run on the bank, requiring

For additional analytical, marketing, investment and business opportunities information, please contact
Global Investment & Business Center, USA
(202) 546-2103. Fax: (202) 546-3275. E-mail: rusric@erols.com

strong intervention by the central monetary authority. The central monetary authority in the UAE was, indeed, able to guarantee that adequate credit for legitimate businesses remained flowing at a time when one would expect economic agents to start pulling their money out. That was managed fairly well.

> **There is no formal moral hazard problem in the UAE, [but] if there¼s a history of non-failure, then some investors may believe that they are, in fact, insured from downside risk.**

Finally, we come to moral hazard. As I said, there is no formal moral hazard problem in the UAE, specifically because the government recognizes its dangers. However, the absence of formal guarantees doesn¼t eliminate the potential problem. If important elements of the ruling family or other members of the political elite are closely associated with banks, and if there¼s a history of non-failure , banks don¼t really fail but are restructured in various ways , then some investors may believe that they are, in fact, insured from downside risk.

In the UAE there are close linkages between the banks and the government or key members of the ruling families, and there is a record of past crises that suggests that banks will not be allowed to fail. Let me stress, though, that neither of these considerations necessarily implies that a serious moral-hazard problem exists. The ruling families are closely tied to the banks, but that also means these same powerful actors have very good reasons to ensure that the banks with which they are closely allied remain financially sound. It¼s not in their own private interest, not to mention the public interest, to have these banks make unsound loans. The difficulty is that these people are very busy. How much time do they have to monitor exactly what is going on? That would be a question mark for me.

To summarize, I would give the UAE an A-minus or an A on macroeconomic policy consistency. On transparency, a C, I¼m afraid. On regulatory oversight by the central monetary authorities, a B-plus/A-minus. This is particularly good when you consider their lack of experience when they were hit by these kinds of crises in the 1970s. As to moral hazard, analysts will have differences of opinion on how serious they think that is. It is also a kind of problem that will shift with different configurations of the internal economy.

The theme of this conference , a century in 30 years , applies very much to the banking system of the UAE. From a small, quite rudimentary financial system, the UAE now enjoys a banking system similar to those in many emerging markets. As so often in human affairs, though, the system¼s strengths are also its weaknesses. Close ties to government actors reassure depositors and business partners and provide important incentives for prudent management, offering the prospect of backing by vast accumulations of financial reserves. These are important strengths. But the weaknesses are equally clear: potential moral hazard and a low level of disclosure, which makes assessing asset quality difficult.

One can only hope that in the next 30 years the UAE will continue to modernize its banking system by simultaneously deregulating , privatizing certain key banks , and also re-regulating , making them conform to international standards of information disclosure. If they do this, I suspect that in 2030 the UAE banking system will be a fully developed component of the global financial system.

Robert L. Mallett
Deputy Secretary of Commerce, U.S. Department of Commerce

For additional analytical, marketing, investment and business opportunities
information, please contact
Global Investment & Business Center, USA
(202) 546-2103. Fax: (202) 546-3275. E-mail: rusric@erols.com

To your minister of commerce and economy, Minister Fahim al-Qasimi, and to Ambassador al-Shaali and other distinguished Gulf ambassadors, I offer a very warm welcome to this conference, and I would like to pay a special tribute to His Excellency Sheikh Zayed and his son, Deputy Prime Minister Sheikh Sultan, who are not here today but who have done so much to ensure the success of the UAE.

It really doesn't seem like so long ago actually. The Dow Jones was at 950 points, Intel Corporation had just introduced a device they called the "microprocessor," and a federation of seven states won independence from Great Britain. And they did it a lot more easily than the United States had done some 200 years before.

I'd just like to take this opportunity to applaud the development of the United Arab Emirates over the last three decades. There is much to applaud, including the wise leadership that UAE founder Sheikh Zayed has shown in the years since independence. You don't have to take my word for it, if you read the article recently published in *The Wall Street Journal* that showed that the UAE was growing and diversifying through petrochemicals, metals and natural-gas projects, while much of the rest of the Gulf is still suffering from depressed oil prices.

There are those who say that the success of the UAE is largely a matter of luck. They point out that the UAE has a population about the size of Washington, D.C. , a little less than 600,000 people , and yet it has 10 percent of the world's oil reserves. Clearly it is due to luck that this small state has done as well as it¼s done. But as I reviewed the record, it occurred to me that the progress of United Arab Emirates has not been solely a matter of luck. Having an abundant supply of oil is not a guarantee of continuous or permanent prosperity. Just look at some of its neighbors.

The success of the UAE has been the result of sensible decisions and statesmanship. And if we look at what some of those decisions were and what they have meant for the UAE¼s relationship with the United States, and the things that we need to do together to keep our relationship strong, we will soon see that the success of the UAE has not, in fact, been a matter of luck.

In a way, these decades of progress result from decisions that seem in hindsight to have been naturally ordained and years in the planning. Who would have done anything else looking back on it now? It didn¼t seem so clear three decades ago. Hindsight, as you know, is always 20-20; and so many others would have made these decisions. But lots of people made different choices some 30 years ago.

In point of fact, through the seventies and eighties, countries around the world were still enamored of very strong state control, of protectionist policies that discouraged foreign investment, of an over-reliance on a single industry or a single crop. By today the evidence is in. Countries that lower their trade barriers, countries that encourage investors from outside their own borders, countries that seek to diversify are the ones with the best chance for success in the current global market. And the UAE's positive approach to encouraging trade has shown itself many times over, and those decisions 30 years ago have redounded to its benefit.

We see it in its willingness to award an independent power and desalinization project to a company from Dearborn, Michigan. We see it in efforts to form a customs union with other Gulf states to reduce tariffs significantly. We see it in the easing of the rules-of-origin requirements for products from joint ventures with the United States and other countries in the Gulf region. And we see it in the progress that the UAE has made in eliminating motion-picture, sound-recording and computer software piracy. All nations have to be vigilant and united when it comes to protecting intellectual property.

For additional analytical, marketing, investment and business opportunities information, please contact
Global Investment & Business Center, USA
(202) 546-2103. Fax: (202) 546-3275. E-mail: rusric@erols.com

We also see the benefits of the UAE¼s decisions three decades ago in another way. We see it in its respect for diversity and a commitment to a pluralistic society. Now at this very moment, we see in Kosovo the fruits of a policy that suppresses diversity, one that strives for ethnic and ideological purity at the point of a gun.

But since the UAE¼s independence, it has preserved diversity among its people. It is a devout Islamic state tolerant of differences. In fact, the UAE has been able to balance the twin demands of diversity and unity to forge a federal structure uniting seven independent emirates. That¼s not an easy task. Would that all countries would follow this example. These are not just policies that have worked in the past. They are policies that are, in fact, working now.

Still there is much work to be done to persuade others that your model is the right one. Because the idea of open markets and global trade can be threatening to the uninitiated, some people have grown comfortable with the low rate of international investment in the Middle East. They do not aspire for the Middle East's non-energy exports to grow significantly. And some of that same thinking would have energy prices repeatedly and indefinitely bailing out the single-industry countries.

But as we all know, that is unlikely. Even if it were to come to pass, it would be short-lived because the world is changing, and it¼s changing fast. The advent of new technology and new reserves, and the adverse impact of statist policies on the Asian economies make it more important than ever that countries of the Middle East follow the lead of the UAE.

The UAE is diversifying. It is creating a financial center. It has rescued Gulf Air. UAE investors even own part of the Manchester United soccer team. What incredible diversity. And as you know, in the United States, we value diversity and we value our relationship with the UAE enormously. The easiest way to demonstrate that is to quote numbers and figures to you, but just one figure today: We enjoy a $3-billion two-way trade with the UAE, and, of course, that number will increase. We look forward to finalizing our F-16 deal.

But of course, in any relationship between equals, between mature commercial partners, between nations which share a fundamental admiration and respect for one another, there are bound to be differences , different points of emphasis , and a different pace to the promise of our full potential. So I think it is helpful to be candid with one another about all of the points in our bilateral relationship.

Are there areas where we could be moving more quickly? There certainly are. We believe the UAE has the potential to become a role model for the rest of the Middle East. We think that the UAE can set new standards for good business practices, including more privatization, increased transparency and more respect for intellectual-property rights , including the enactment of copyright and patent laws consistent with World Trade Organization practices.

We hear from American firms that they are eager to participate in additional privatization projects. They are eager to invest in the pharmaceutical domain, for instance, if their rights are fully respected and protected. American companies would like greater flexibility regarding commercial agents, majority ownership and more vigorous contract-dispute resolution methodologies.

Frankly, there is no reason whatsoever why the UAE cannot be a model for the rest of the Middle East. It has the entrepreneurial tradition, it has a solid financial base, and the tested leadership to not only bring prosperity to its own people , which it has already done , but to serve as an example of free-market reforms. In that way, it can better compete, not just within the Middle East, but worldwide.

For additional analytical, marketing, investment and business opportunities information, please contact
Global Investment & Business Center, USA
(202) 546-2103. Fax: (202) 546-3275. E-mail: rusric@erols.com

Ever since the invention of the steam engine people have written about how the planet is shrinking. It¼s getting smaller. It¼s getting easier. It¼s getting closer. But only within our time has it shrunk to the point where we can connect to any place on the globe at the speed of light. You can call Abu Dhabi as easily as calling upstairs or across the street. The microchips that make such communication possible are small, but the implications for the partnership that we share are large indeed.

This means the obstacles to trade traditionally posed by distance will simply disappear. It means investors who might have shrunk from investing far beyond their own borders can now embrace investment because it makes it easier to do. And it is a great opportunity. And we should certainly make the most of it.

Since 1971, the UAE has created an oasis of prosperity in the Middle East. It is especially poised to take advantage of this changing world. John Kennedy used to like to tell the story about a man talking to a gardener about planting a tree. And the gardener would say to the man who owned the yard , he said, "You know, that tree won't flower for 100 years." The man who owned the yard said, "Well, then, plant it today, plant it this afternoon."

The tree planted in the UAE¼s year of independence has already borne fruit in just 30 years. And there's a lot more work that we can do together and a lot more work that you¼re planning to do , a lot more trees to plant, if you will. And it's through sessions like these that we plant the seeds. I look forward to seeing the trees grow.

SOCIO-POLITICAL ISSUES

"DIVERSITY IN UNITY: POLITICAL INSTITUTIONS AND CIVIL SOCIETY"

Fatma Al-Sayegh
Associate Professor of History, University of the UAE, Al-Ain

I am going to concentrate on political institutions and civil society in the United Arab Emirates. In the last three decades, the UAE, despite its small size and population, has become more well-known worldwide due, in large part, to its abundant oil reserves but also to its role as a force for peace in the war-torn Middle East.

Prior to December 2, 1971, the situation was vastly different. Not only did the UAE not exist as a country on any world map, but its history, culture and people were unknown to all but a select few. Under the federation, the seven sheikhdoms retained local government, but a federal government oversaw national affairs. The transition from tribal loyalties to loyalty to the new country took a lot of effort, but eventually it was achieved.

The period from February 1968 to July 1971 witnessed an intensive and extensive series of negotiations between the rulers of the seven Trucial sheikhdoms, along with Bahrain and Qatar, to form a federation. The outcome was the establishment of a federation comprising only the six sheikhdoms. It was not until February 10, 1972, that the seventh sheikhdom, Ras al-Khaimah, joined the union.

To better explain the political process of UAE development, I have divided the study into three stages. The first stage, 1971-76, I have called "stabilizing the federation." This era started with the birth of the UAE. Sheikh Zayed of Abu Dhabi, the president of the UAE, and Sheikh Rashid, the vice president, were the most important rulers in the former Trucial sheikhdoms. Yet, they

For additional analytical, marketing, investment and business opportunities information, please contact
Global Investment & Business Center, USA
(202) 546-2103. Fax: (202) 546-3275. E-mail: rusric@erols.com

held different views of the federation. Zayed saw federalism as the only way to build a modern state, whereas Rashid wanted the local governments to have greater power. The rulers of the other emirates also wanted to protect their autonomy.

Building a proposal to which all the rulers could agree proved challenging. Sheikh Zayed and the rulers of other emirates worked closely together to form a unique federal government that united and, at the same time, protected the autonomy of each individual emirate. The new federal government also had to be restructured to better meet the needs of the fledgling federation, while local governments had barely established their own system before the whole exercise began once more.

In the early days, the main obstacle to development was the lack of human resources. In fact, until very recently, the UAE had to cope with a shortage of trained and educated local people. The country lacked the skills required to make the newly federated state successful. The need was acute for highly skilled and informed nationals to take on jobs as ministers, ambassadors and high-ranking officials representing not only their own local governments, but also the newly created federal government.

There was also a need to establish additional ministries, departments and affiliated sections to coordinate and implement all the work that needed to be done. Considering the enormity of the task and the tools available at that time, the federation succeeded quite admirably.

There are four political bodies at the federal level: the Supreme Federal Council, the president and vice president, the Federal Council of Ministers, and the Federal National Council. The Supreme Federal Council consists of the rulers of the seven emirates, according to the constitution. The Supreme Federal Council elects the UAE president and vice president from among the seven rulers. In 1971, it elected Sheikh Zayed as the federation¼s first president and Sheikh Rashid as its first vice president and established Abu Dhabi as its temporary capital. The Supreme Federal Council also represents the highest political authority. It charts the general policy of the federation, elects the president and vice president, and ratifies a federal budget.

The second is the president, the head of the government. The president¼s executive powers are both exclusive and shared. In his own right, he performs numerous ceremonial and procedural functions, such as convening the Supreme Federal Council and presiding over its meetings. He represents the UAE in its foreign relations and functions.

The third is the Federal Council of Ministers, the seat of legislative authority. It is a federal cabinet, made up of the prime minister, a deputy prime minister, a number of ministers who are the heads of federal departments, and a minister of state.

The fourth element is the Federal National Council, an advisory body whose members are appointed by the rulers. It consists of 40 members drawn from the seven emirates, each according to its size and contribution to the federal budget. The FNC resembles a parliament or legislature. Its members are supposed to be representatives of the people of the UAE. They are chosen from the seven emirates according to a weighted formula reflecting the population and influence of each. Thus, Abu Dhabi and Dubai are each allocated eight seats; Sharjah and Ras al-Khaimah, six each; and the remaining emirates of Ajman, Fujairah and Umm al-Qaiwain, four each. Members serve two-year terms, renewable without limit. The FNC meets in annual sessions of not less than six months beginning in November.

The second stage, "accepting the federation," started in 1979 and ended in 1986. Until 1976, Abu Dhabi was the only contributor to the federal budget. But the demand on financial resources was

For additional analytical, marketing, investment and business opportunities information, please contact
Global Investment & Business Center, USA
(202) 546-2103. Fax: (202) 546-3275. E-mail: rusric@erols.com

greater than its vast oil wells could sustain. According to the constitution, each emirate should contribute to the federal budget in accordance with its national resources. After a heated debate in the National Federal Council, the national interest prevailed. It is believed that since 1979, Dubai has been contributing 2-3 billion dirhams annually to the federal budget. Sharjah also promised to contribute 50 percent of its oil income to the 1986 federal budget, as did Ras al-Khaimah. The move towards total unification ensued, as steps were taken to unify the armed forces and create a central bank.

The most serious issue to threaten the stability of the federation occurred in 1979. Abu Dhabi was pressing for centralization, but Dubai preferred a loose federation with economic autonomy for each individual emirate. The crisis was soon solved, and a memorandum to strengthen the federation was submitted. Meanwhile, external events, such as Iranian revolution, the outbreak of the Iraq-Iran War in 1980 and its aftermath, persuaded the emirates to show greater unity to preserve its federal system.

The third stage, 1986-99, I call the "maturity of the federation." During this stage, the federation moved toward a period of greater unity, understanding and acceptance of union as the only form of government. Since 1986, all of the emirates have been contributing to the federal budget, each according to its national income. Regular meetings of the National Federal Council meant that issues of general interest would be discussed regularly. Issues relating to internal boundary disputes were also discussed.

This period also witnessed the rise of civil society, brought about by oil wealth and its social impact as well as a new political way of thinking. Civil society started before independence; in 1967, the first female society was established in Ras al-Khaimah. Arab communities also were established before independence, and in 1978, there were 17 of them. During the 1980s, many other civil societies appeared, all of which are dependent on government support. Political parties, however, were seen not only as unwanted institutions, but also as a threat to national solidarity and political unity. But the weakness of civil society in the UAE does not mean it is absent. It is connected to a great extent to the new middle class, although its development has been dependent largely on the development of the legal and executive bodies of the society itself.

"SOCIO-POLITICAL ORIGINS OF EMIRATI LEADERS"

Joseph A. Kechichian
Kechichian & Associates, LLC

Sheikh Zayed Bin Sultan Al Nahyan is indeed a unique leader. Any objective assessment of his accomplishments during the past five decades indicates that, while many people spoke, Zayed acted. He had vision, but he was and is a man who is very much in a hurry. Still, as His Excellency Sheikh Fahim stated in his opening remarks, the UAE leadership has been healthy in more ways than one. What was accomplished was done against immense odds, and Sheikh Zayed and his fellow rulers solidified, as well as earned, their legitimacy.

The seven emirates of the UAE boast rich historical backgrounds, although little of their past glories have survived into the first half of the twentieth century. The destruction of the Qawasim by British forces in 1819, for example, and the forced sedentarization of the remaining tribes after that date essentially meant that the entire coast would be subjugated until the early 1960s. Remarkably, however, throughout this period of British rule, no single emirati leader conceded his authority, perceived or otherwise, to successive British political residents, even if reality required them to cooperate with London.

For additional analytical, marketing, investment and business opportunities information, please contact
Global Investment & Business Center, USA
(202) 546-2103. Fax: (202) 546-3275. E-mail: rusric@erols.com

The 1971 experiment jelled well for a variety of reasons, including, as I¼ve said, Sheikh Zayed¼s unique attributes ranging from foresight to generosity. And as is frankly acknowledged by senior UAE officials, unification was not easy. Few anticipated the UAE would last, much less celebrate a silver jubilee.

Sheikh Zayed was fortunate to deal with fellow rulers who were legitimate in their own right. An entire generation of men, led by six very talented and politically savvy rulers, accepted Zayed¼s mantle. In turn, these seven men operated within very specific tribal confines that defined the sociopolitical life of the UAE.

Long before they joined the UAE as a state, the seven federation members were under the influence of three major foreign powers: the Portuguese, the Ottomans and the British. In the Gulf region, the Portuguese, who ruled over vast expanses of Asia ranging from Macao to Goa, settled on the island of Hormuz, today in Iran, as well as in Bahrain and the Omani Coast. In fact, the two main forts in Muscat today are still referred to as the Portuguese forts. With the waning of their influence, however, Lisbon ceded its power to London around the beginning of the nineteenth century, as Britain ventured into the area to protect its interests, primarily in India.

Britain entered the Gulf because the seafaring inhabitants of the coastal communities, especially the Qawasim, represented a credible challenge to British might on the high seas. Indeed, the fearsome reputation of the peoples of the lower Gulf was so well known that London quickly labeled the area the Pirate Coast even if, objectively speaking, the British were the intruders. The East India Company organized several major naval expeditions against the Qawasim and, having deployed overwhelming military power, subjugated the entire coast through a series of treaties and agreements starting in the early 1800s.

After that time, East India Company ships became safe. In exchange, London recognized the legitimacy of several tribal leaders to rule in specific areas as well as the need to defend the lower Gulf from both seaborne and land attacks. It was only after the 1820 agreements that the British began referring to the area as the Trucial Coast, a name that was still in use in 1971. Of course, the actual treaty that defined Britain¼s obligations towards the Arab Gulf sheikhdoms that became the UAE was the 1853 Maritime Treaty.

Senior British political figures and historians have recognized that the center of British political authority and influence was, until 1946, at the Persian port of Busheir, which was also the seat of the British consulate general for southwestern Persia. In other words, the lower Gulf region did not rise high enough on the empire¼s political pecking order to warrant direct contact but, as necessary, enjoyed a privileged relationship to the East India Company. Ostensibly, such an arrangement allowed tribal leaders in the lower Gulf to conduct their internal affairs freely while dealing with the paramount power, Britain, and through it the rest of the world via the political resident.

After the Qawasim defeat, tribal leaders on the Trucial Coast were bound to these accords with the British, but they were also cognizant of the undeniable fact that the Ottoman Empire had extended its influence all the way down to Basra in Iraq, as well as the Hijaz on the western side of the Arabian Peninsula down into Aden. The leaders of the lower Gulf were very much interested in maintaining their friendly relationship with Britain as time went on because they were equally afraid of the Ottoman Empire's intentions.

Let me now turn to the various pre-federation socioeconomic developments that led to the formation of the state and the role that the leadership played in it. First and foremost, all seven of these states share the same tribal environment. Second, all of them were led by legitimate ruling

For additional analytical, marketing, investment and business opportunities information, please contact
Global Investment & Business Center, USA
(202) 546-2103. Fax: (202) 546-3275. E-mail: rusric@erols.com

families. Third, the governmental apparatus of each of the emirates was already there, even if primitive. Fourth, the impact of oil discoveries accelerated the process of integration. By 1971, it was a foregone conclusion that united they would rise; otherwise, they would pay the consequences.

The tribalism referred to frequently in discussions of the UAE was really never a serious obstacle to federation. It did not prevent the leaders from taking matters into their own hands and forging ahead with a federation. The power and the role of the ruling families in the seven emirates were of far greater importance than tribal differences and rivalries. Indeed, the attitudes and the structure of the ruling families provide us a great many clues about the federation.

The problem of forming a federation rested mainly with the leaders of the six ruling families: the Al Nahyans in Abu Dhabi, the Al Maktums of Dubai, the al-Qasimis of Sharjah and Ras al-Khaimah, the al-Nayims of Ajman, the al-Muallas of Umm al-Qaiwain, and the Sharqis of Fujairah. The Al Nahyans and Maktums , both of the Benias tribe , have been in power, respectively, since 1855 and 1886. Likewise, the al- Qasimis have been ruling since 1883 (Sharjah) and 1915 (Ras al-Khaimah). The ruling families of the three smaller emirates have been in power for a long period as well.

At the time of the formation of the UAE, the general attitude of the rulers was political conservatism shaped by the proclivities of Islam. The traditionalist mentality and common historical experiences of colonialism, especially with the British, favored some form of political integration.

Finally, the loyalty of the populations of the seven emirates to their respective leadership was really never questioned. As a consequence, the hostile physical environment and the colonial pressures did not prevent the coming together of the federation because loyalty was present on both sides.

In the UAE today there is a new generation of leaders coming up who are well-qualified to continue the work started by their fathers. In Abu Dhabi, the crown prince, Sheikh Khalifah is well-known to all those who have dealt with him. Sheikh Zayed's other sons are equally qualified. In Dubai, Sheikh Muhammad bin Rashid is the leading candidate of the next generation to succeed Sheikh Maktoum. In Sharjah, as I have said, Sultan al-Qasimi is one of the original founders, and his cousin will take over from him. The same is true for Ras al-Khaimah, Fujairah and Umm al-Qaiwain. Qualified men are ready to continue the vision and action of their forefathers.

What remains to be determined is whether the circumstances that existed 30 years ago will be duplicated in the future. Today's challenges are very different. They're primarily social, economic and political and relate to the entire neighborhood. Yet if the past is an indication of the future, the UAE is well equipped to assume the mantle of leadership in the next generation as well.

FOREIGN RELATIONS AND DEFENSE

"UAE POLICY TOWARD THE SUB-REGIONAL POWERS"

Hassan H. Al-Alkim
Professor of International Relations, University of the UAE, Al-Ain

The UAE is a mini-state: 82,880 square kilometers with a population of around 2.4 million, no more than 12.5 percent of whom are nationals. Its geographical location imposes a heavy burden

For additional analytical, marketing, investment and business opportunities
information, please contact
Global Investment & Business Center, USA
(202) 546-2103. Fax: (202) 546-3275. E-mail: rusric@erols.com

on its foreign-policy undertakings. In addition, the nature of the UAE political system , a federal state, not yet solidly unified , has enabled Saudi Arabia, Iran and Iraq to influence its foreign policy on different issues. Intersecting regional pressures are reflected in the paradoxes inherent in UAE relationships with all three of these subregional powers.

The pervasive influence of Saudi Arabia can be detected in almost every aspect of UAE foreign policy. However, the differences between the two countries are an indication that the UAE is able to follow its own course when circumstances require it.

Relations with Tehran also have an edge of paradox. On the one hand, the Iranian government under the shah occupied the three islands of Abu Musa and the Tunbs. On the other, cooperation has been sought between the two countries on economic, cultural, health and defense issues. Relations also were strengthened through intergovernmental contacts. With the success of the revolution in Iran, the new regime showed itself eager to strengthen its ties with the UAE but so far has failed to settle the islands dispute.

Paradox has also characterized UAE relations with Iraq. At the beginning, the Iraqi people saw the British withdrawal announcement and the declaration of the proposed federation as a new British conspiracy, intended to divide the Arab nation. Later on, however, all three countries supported the establishment of the United Arab Emirates.

To give some historical perspective, British intervention increased the isolation of the Omani Coast emirates by imposing treaties and curbing seafaring activities, restricting the main channel of communication with the outside world. The British also controlled trade and the trade routes, as well as mineral resources through an agreement signed in 1922. The British colonial rule not only left the emirates without experience in the conduct of foreign policy, but also had the effect of aligning the emirates with the West, thereby preventing them from acting freely in their relations with the outside world.

A further outcome was the British complication of the islands question. The British orchestrated a memorandum of understanding with the shah over Abu Musa, but failed to do so on the Tunbs. The ruler of Ras al-Khaimah revealed that Sir William Luce proposed to Ras al-Khaimah that it cede sovereignty over the two Tunbs in return for annual payment of 2.7 million pounds by Iran and a 49-percent share of the income from any oil exploration in their off-shore waters.

The root of the current border dispute among the GCC states and between them and Iran and Iraq goes back to the British role in redrawing the boundaries. The British role in the Abu Dhabi-Saudi Arabia border dispute exacerbated the situation and caused the Saudis to withhold recognition of the emirates for three years, until August 22, 1974. Iraq saw the formation of the UAE as a new form of British divide-and-rule policy designed to weaken the Arab nation and maintain Western hegemony.

From 1820 to 1971, when the Omani Coast emirates were under the British protectorate, the regional powers were deterred from pressing their territorial claims against the sheikhdoms. The independence of the UAE opened the door to regional pressure. Being a small country, the UAE recognizes that it cannot obtain security primarily by use of its own capabilities but must rely in large part on other states and institutions.

Saudi Arabia considers itself a power with direct responsibility for as well as interests in the Gulf. Therefore, after the British withdrawal, the Saudis began to think in terms of how to extend their own power and influence.

For additional analytical, marketing, investment and business opportunities information, please contact
Global Investment & Business Center, USA
(202) 546-2103. Fax: (202) 546-3275. E-mail: rusric@erols.com

Iran, on the other hand, determined to play its self-appointed role of Gulf policeman, was ready to sacrifice its claim to Bahrain in the interest of stability and good relations with its Arab neighbors. However, having climbed down once, it would have been very difficult for the shah's government also to renounce its claim over Abu Musa and the Tunbs. The British plan to withdraw compelled Iran first to safeguard the shah's regime; second, to ensure uninterrupted passage through the Strait of Hormuz; and third, to protect Iranian resources and facilities.

At the same time, competition among the subregional powers for hegemony caused Saudi Arabia and the small Gulf states to exploit the differences between Iran and the Arabs. Being encircled by the two regional powers, they have tried to work one against the other, aligning themselves with the shah until the success of the Iranian revolution, then aligning themselves with Saddam Hussein , until he turned against Kuwait. Now they are apparently going back to Iran.

Competition between the regional powers weakens the UAE position because its federal structure of seven not-yet-solidly connected entities makes it a target for external influences. The regional powers have always been capable of taking advantage of this to influence UAE foreign policy.

During the colonial period, the problems between the Omani sheikhdoms and Saudi Arabia were solved through the British. Ibn Saud, in his quest for security and support against his rivals, signed a treaty with the British in 1915 by which he undertook to refrain from any hostile action or interference in the affairs of the Arab sheikhdoms. In a 1927 treaty, he promised to maintain good ties with the Omani Coast emirates, but made no commitment in regard to the frontier question. Although the British decision to withdraw from East of Suez was welcomed publicly by the Saudi royal family, in private they tried to persuade the British not to pull out.

According to Harold Wilson (May 19, 1967), "Faisal gravely urged us not only to leave military units in the area, but also to accept a binding military commitment to use them to defend the new Saudi Arabian state against attacks from infiltration from UAR-inspired Arab nationalism." However, official Saudi reaction was revealed by King Faisal: "There need be no vacuum in the area when the British leave, as long as the federal states receive the support of the United States and its neighbors. We support the federation unconditionally."

Some analysts argue that the switch in the Saudi position came as a result of the Saudi-Iranian dialogue. Others argue that the British withdrawal provided an opportunity for Saudi Arabia to push some long-dormant territorial claims against the sheikhdoms. Anthony Cordesman points out that Iraq's support for various radical movements in the Gulf from 1972 to 78 led Saudi Arabia and Iran to cooperate in supporting the growth and stability of the UAE.

Relations between Saudi Arabia and the UAE have gone through three main stages. During the early period, 1971-74, Saudi Arabia pursued an unsympathetic attitude toward the federation, opting for bilateral relations with Ras al-Khaimah and Dubai. Cooperation was limited to economic, cultural and social interactions, though there was no formal agreement between the parties. Trade relations were developed as a result.

The territorial agreement of 1974 marked a turning point in UAE-Saudi relations. However, Saudi Arabia continued to pursue a dual policy, maintaining its bilateral relations with individual states while dealing with the federal government. Cordesman argues that Saudi Arabia became a source of aid rather than a threat, able to extend as well as legitimize its hegemonic role over the UAE. Since the UAE.-Saudi rapprochement, it is difficult to find a UAE stand on regional issues that contradicts the Saudi position.

For additional analytical, marketing, investment and business opportunities
information, please contact
Global Investment & Business Center, USA
(202) 546-2103. Fax: (202) 546-3275. E-mail: rusric@erols.com

The events of 1979 , the success of the Iranian revolution, the seizure of the Grand Mosque, the Soviet invasion of Afghanistan , and later the inception of the Iraq-Iran War forced Saudi Arabia to conclude that maintaining a strong UAE would contribute to Gulf security and stability. Growing apprehension over internal and external threats led Saudi Arabia and the states of the lower Gulf to a new form of cooperation, the GCC.

The second Gulf crisis forced the UAE closer to Saudi Arabia. The historical, social and religious ties between the emirates and Saudi Arabia and the similarity of their sociopolitical and economic systems, as well as regional and international developments, did not prevent serious difficulties from arising between them.

The territorial dispute has not yet been finally settled; the UAE has no official map. The UAE disagrees with Saudi Arabia on various oil issues and is a bit suspicious about the recent Saudi-Iranian rapprochement. The UAE, therefore, pursues an independent policy from that of Saudi Arabia and other GCC states whenever its national interests are threatened. The UAE has also been able to take advantage of bilateral ties and the consensus of the Arab states expressed through the Arab League.

On UAE-Iran relations, the British decision to withdraw from east of Suez was welcomed by Iran. In search of regional security, the shah sought to coordinate policy with Saudi Arabia. As a result, he relinquished his claim to Bahrain, but at the same time laid claim to the three islands. Diplomatic relations were not established between the UAE and Iran until December 23, 1972. The UAE attitude toward the revolution in 1978 was cautious. The UAE was quick to respond positively to the victory of the Iranian revolution, however, not waiting to see whether the CIA, as had occurred in 1953, might reinstall the shah. The UAE ambassador to Iran returned to Tehran on March 4, 1979. The development of trade indicated the strength of relations between the UAE and Iran. And the new Gulf policy adopted by the Iranian regime even led to speculation that the islands question might be solved.

Revolutionary Iran confronted the Arab Gulf states with three problems. First, it changed Iran from a strategic shield to a potential threat. Second, it placed these states between two mutually hostile regimes, Iraq and Iran. Third, it constituted an immediate threat to freedom of navigation. Hence, the regional threat shifted, causing a change of alliance from an Iranian-Saudi axis to an Iraqi-Saudi axis.

The Saudi-Iraqi rapprochement was manifested in the Saudi support for Iraq in the war with Iran, 1980-88. The two nations concluded a border agreement in 1985 that was sealed during King Fahd¼s state visit to Baghdad March 23-26, 1989. It was short-lived.

Iran could claim sovereignty over the oil fields and oil reserves lying within the 12-mile zones of the territorial waters of Abu Musa and the Tunbs.

Iran's foreign policy continues to be a casus belli. It is reactive and opportunistic as well as ambiguous, revealing a desire to deny extremism while exploiting it. There are ongoing programs to develop a conventional military arsenal and acquire weapons of mass destruction. Iran sponsors extremist groups and covert operations around the world. At least before Khatami, Iran actively attempted to destabilize Arab Gulf states. Iran is attempting to dominate the Gulf by intimidating the GCC countries in order to achieve economic objectives. For example, Iran could claim sovereignty over the oil fields and oil reserves lying within the 12-mile zones of the territorial waters of Abu Musa and the Tunbs.

For additional analytical, marketing, investment and business opportunities
information, please contact
Global Investment & Business Center, USA
(202) 546-2103. Fax: (202) 546-3275. E-mail: rusric@erols.com

There is the possibility of a peaceful settlement of the islands dispute now that winds of change are sweeping over Iran: Khatami's election, the indirect American-Iranian dialogue, and the Saudi-Iranian rapprochement. An American-Iranian rapprochement would remove one of the main obstacles confronting a settlement. The Iranians would no longer see U.S.-GCC relations and the American presence in the Gulf area as directed against them. Also, the success of the moderates could inspire a new pragmatic Iranian approach. In addition, the rapprochement between Iran and Saudi Arabia encourages the latter to use its good offices to mediate between Iran and the UAE to reach an acceptable settlement on the islands.

UAE-Iraq relations have gone through several phases. At the beginning Iraq laid down conditions for recognition: the UAE should reject the Sharjah-Iran agreement over Abu Musa and refrain from establishing diplomatic relations with Iran, pending the Iranian return of Abu Musa and the Tunbs to Sharjah and Ras al-Khaimah, respectively. The UAE was unable to fulfill these conditions, though the president did criticize the agreement. Nevertheless, in the second phase, 1975-80, relations between the UAE and Iraq progressed steadily, with both countries participating in Gulf conferences and projects.

The outbreak of the Iran-Iraq War in the fall of 1980 marks the beginning of a new period characterized by gradual UAE alignment with Iraq. The Gulf States, led by Saudi Arabia, were divided between fear of Ayatollah Khomeni's militant Islamic Revolution and continuing distrust of the socialist Iraqi government.

Iraq brought the issue of the three islands into the center of conflict, calling for an immediate Iranian withdrawal. However, the UAE was keen not to be seen as taking sides in the war, and refrained from public support for Iraq while quietly siding with it. As a member of the Gulf community, the UAE could neither pursue an independent policy nor risk offending Iran.

The alliance between the GCC states and Iraq was short-lived. The unsettled border dispute between Iraq and Kuwait and the increased oil production by both Kuwait and the UAE prompted the Iraqi government to adopt a hostile posture toward these states. Saddam, on July 17, 1990, blasted Kuwait and the UAE as stooges of America for keeping oil prices low. The Iraqi invasion on August 2 forced the GCC to change its foreign-policy orientation to an alliance against Iraq. After Kuwait was liberated, however, and in light of Iraq¼s uncertain future, the UAE is now for the reintegration of Iraq, to reactivate the equilibrium of power.

Sheikh Zayed has been very critical of U.S. Gulf policy. He was the first Arab leader to call for an Arab reconciliation summit and to speak about Iraq's reintegration. Though UAE policy since the second Gulf crisis has undergone a significant shift, increasing the closeness of its security relationship with the United States, it is reluctant to engage in a binding alliance with the Western powers. The UAE has refused to permit American use of its military base and facilities in air strikes launched against Iraq and has negotiated a treaty with Iraq to allow a passenger ferry to travel between Dubai and Basra.

The UAE cannot stand alone in the face of Saudi Arabia's hegemonic role in the area. On the other hand, the UAE is able to follow its own course when circumstances require and does not identify totally with the views of the Saudis. The absence of a stable regional balance of power since the second Gulf crisis and the continued perception of an Iranian threat necessitates the reintegration of Iraq. A shift in the balance of power in favor of Iraq and its reintegration into the international community are likely to result in a stronger UAE-Iraqi alliance.

"THE UAE AND THE BROADER MIDDLE EAST: THE CASE OF PALESTINE"

For additional analytical, marketing, investment and business opportunities information, please contact
Global Investment & Business Center, USA
(202) 546-2103. Fax: (202) 546-3275. E-mail: rusric@erols.com

Khalil E. Jahshan
President, National Association of Arab Americans

UAE policy toward the Palestine question remains a useful example of how this relatively new and small country managed to maximize its four basic assets , strategic location, economic weight, credible leadership and political stability , to enhance its influence and reputation throughout the region and the world.

The general direction and broad parameters of UAE foreign policy emerged quite early in the history of the federation. In a speech before the Federal National Council on February 14, 1972, His Highness Sheikh Zayed set the tone for the international relations of the emerging nation by stating, "The foreign policy of the United Arab Emirates aims at supporting Arab and Islamic causes and interests and strengthening the bonds of friendship and cooperation with all nations and peoples on the basis of the United Nations Charter and international principles."

This quote reflects Sheikh Zayed's belief in the need for Arab harmony and unity, his genuine concern for the welfare of mankind, and his strategic depth in fully understanding the vulnerability of his small country and the need to protect its interests from external intrusions in a turbulent region. Consequently, UAE foreign policy became anchored in this deep national commitment to cooperation and commonality of interests among Arab and Islamic nations. Over the past three decades, Sheikh Zayed has maintained his cherished role as the premier advocate of Arab coordination, reconciliation and tolerance.

Second, UAE leadership has displayed a keen understanding of power politics in the region. They have created a role for themselves as a significant player in global economics and politics by using their strategic location and oil wealth to enhance their international stature.

Third, the UAE has taken seriously the responsibility that comes with economic power by embarking on a very deliberate and generous foreign-aid program aimed at sharing part of its wealth with developing countries. Since 1971, billions of dollars, exceeding in certain years 15 percent of the country's gross income, were disbursed in the form of loans, grants and technical aid to assist developing countries in modernizing their infrastructures and carrying out numerous developmental projects.

In a region where moderation has become synonymous with defeatism or readiness to compromise principles and abdicate national rights and to collude with the enemy, real or perceived, the UAE has managed to follow a credible and moderate line while adhering to its long-held principles.

Three cases illustrate this trend. On the islands issue the UAE has never wavered in its claim of sovereignty. Yet, in spite of provocations by Iran year after year, it has remained committed to its long-held principle of the peaceful resolution of conflict and recently suggested referring the matter for arbitration to the International Court of Justice at The Hague if no progress is achieved. This makes the issue one of the few border disputes in the Middle East that has not escalated into a military confrontation.

In 1990-91, the Emirates joined ranks with its GCC partners in confronting Iraqi aggression against Kuwait and condemning its subsequent threats against its neighbors. Abu Dhabi has also been very vocal and consistent about the need for Iraq to abide fully by all relevant U.N. Security Council resolutions. However, the UAE has been clearly and vocally uncomfortable with the continued military escalation in the Gulf and U.S. double standards.

For additional analytical, marketing, investment and business opportunities information, please contact
Global Investment & Business Center, USA
(202) 546-2103. Fax: (202) 546-3275. E-mail: rusric@erols.com

Furthermore, the Emirates has clearly been more forthcoming than most of its neighbors in expressing concern for the suffering of the Iraqi civilian population brought about by the economic sanctions regime imposed on Iraq after the Gulf War. Moreover, the UAE was among the first Arab countries, particularly in the Gulf, to call for lifting the sanctions, preserving the sovereignty and territorial integrity of Iraq, and eventually reconciling with Baghdad.

Third, the widespread respect and credibility enjoyed by Sheikh Zayed and the UAE have often positioned the emirates to play a unique role in mediating conflicts in the region. Such diplomatic efforts were made over the past three decades in Yemen and Lebanon, between Algeria and Morocco, and more recently between Bahrain and Qatar, just to mention a few.

Based on this strong commitment to Arab rights, the UAE has been unwavering in its support for the Palestinian cause. Since its establishment it has consistently called for the realization of the inalienable rights of the Palestinian people to self-determination and independent statehood. Furthermore, the UAE has always maintained special relations with the Palestinian leadership, the PLO, which it recognized as the sole legitimate representative of the Palestinian people. Sheikh Zayed has often stated that "the primary cause for the Arabs is the Palestine issue." He always emphasized that the Arab-Israeli conflict will not be resolved without a comprehensive and just solution to the Palestine problem.

Historically, the UAE has stood by the Palestinians through thick and thin, including some very trying times when some in the Arab world chose to keep their distance , during the civil-war years, for example, in Lebanon, particularly during the Israeli invasion, which, in addition to destroying the infrastructure of Lebanon, destroyed the PLO infrastructure.

The UAE was equally supportive during the difficult years of the *intifada,* as the Palestinians paid a heavy human toll for challenging continued Israeli occupation. The Emirates was always a dependable and understanding friend, even when it harbored some justified reservations about Palestinian policies and practices, as it does today.

Furthermore, the UAE leadership has always given the Palestinian cause its unqualified support, even at the expense of its own vital relations with the West. A case in point was 1973, when the Emirates became the first Arab oil-producing country to advocate using the oil weapon in support of Arab rights. During that crisis, Sheikh Zayed, coined the phrase, "Arab oil is not more precious than Arab blood."

This solid support was further strengthened by the emirati leadership's belief in the indivisibility of regional security and stability. Thus, they tended to perceive Gulf security and stability as directly and organically linked to the situation in Palestine, and to the prospects of resolving the Arab-Israeli conflict. Therefore, the UAE has been supportive of the Middle East peace process since its inception at Madrid in 1991. It has, however, been critical of the lack of progress, particularly after the election of Benjamin Netanyahu as Israel's prime minister in 1996.

Today, the UAE remains committed to a comprehensive, just and lasting peace in the region, based on U.N. Security Council Resolutions 242 and 338 and the principle of exchanging land for peace. Yet the UAE does not endorse Arab-Israeli peace at any price. It has insisted on the following guidelines:

1. Respect for the rights and aspirations of both sides. Sheikh Zayed stated on August 24, 1981, "Peace without justice is a meaningless and deceptive concept."

For additional analytical, marketing, investment and business opportunities information, please contact
Global Investment & Business Center, USA
(202) 546-2103. Fax: (202) 546-3275. E-mail: rusric@erols.com

2. Total withdrawal of Israeli forces from the territories occupied in 1967, including Jerusalem.
3. Recognition of the inalienable rights of the Palestinian people to return to their homeland, determine their own future, and establish an independent state.
4. The right of the Palestinians to choose their own negotiators. No party, Arab or otherwise, is entitled to speak or negotiate on their behalf.
5. No normalization before a political agreement. In spite of strong and public pressure by Washington, Abu Dhabi refused to attend the October 1997 MENA economic summit held in Doha, for lack of progress on the Palestinian-Israeli track.
6. American evenhandedness. While acknowledging the historical role of the United States as mediator in the Arab-Israeli conflict, the government of the UAE nevertheless has been quite critical of the lack of U.S. management of the peace process. In a rare interview with *The New York Times* on May 31, 1998, Sheikh Zayed was brutally frank: "As close friends of the United States, . . . it would have sincerely been our wish to see American policies that are far more strict on the side of justice." The UAE president accused the United States of having failed to act as an evenhanded mediator because "whatever the Palestinians say and accept is discarded. Whatever the Israelis want is imposed."

"BETWEEN PAX BRITANNICA AND PAX AMERICANA"

F. Gregory Gause III
Associate Professor of Political Science, University of Vermont

It has been almost 30 years since the independence of the UAE and the end of Pax Britannica. The big change from the British peace to the putative Pax Americana has been the shift from a foreign policy based on accepting the hegemony of an outside power and allowing it to run your foreign affairs to the foreign policy of an independent country based on balance and conciliation.

When the British left in 1971, they weren't being pushed out by the leaders of what became the United Arab Emirates. Most of those leaders would have been very comfortable had the British stayed or had another power been willing to assume the role that Britain was playing. They would have accepted that kind of tutelage in exchange for protection. Today the UAE would not be willing to accept the kind of status that they accepted 30 years ago under British protection. That's the real change between Pax Britannica and Pax Americana.

I want to emphasize three elements of this independent UAE foreign policy developed under the leadership of Sheikh Zayed. The first, which was more than adequately covered by Professor Al-Alkim, is a foreign policy based on maintaining some kind of balance of power in the Gulf, so that no one state can dominate that local region. Upon independence, the UAE was presented with an immediate territorial dispute with Iran. Yet because of regional balance considerations , the fact that Iraq had expressed hostility to the new state and Saudi Arabia had not diplomatically recognized it , the UAE engaged in a policy of regular relations with Iran despite their dispute over the islands.

Yet when the shah began to assert himself in the late seventies and tried to put together some kind of regional security program in the Gulf under his own aegis, the UAE refused to join. Why? Saudi Arabia and Iraq had greatly improved their relationship with the UAE, and balancing considerations led the UAE to decide it didn't have to accept Iranian leadership in that case.

During the Iran-Iraq War, the UAE attempted to maintain channels to both sides while strengthening the third leg of balance in the Gulf, by joining the GCC. We shouldn't underestimate

For additional analytical, marketing, investment and business opportunities information, please contact
Global Investment & Business Center, USA
(202) 546-2103. Fax: (202) 546-3275. E-mail: rusric@erols.com

the obstacles to putting the GCC together, the various rivalries among the peninsular states. Yet the UAE, in search of that regional balance, was willing to put those concerns aside and accept what was inevitably Saudi leadership for the sake of regional balance.

While the UAE opposed the Iraqi invasion of Kuwait and Iraqi attempts to assert its own hegemony over the Gulf, now that Iraq¼s military power has been greatly reduced, it is Iranian power that worries Abu Dhabi. And while Sheikh Zayed¼s humanitarian concerns regarding the fate of the Iraqi people are no doubt sincere, balancing has more to do with the UAE's call for Iraq, if it accepts the U.N. resolutions, to be rehabilitated.

This interest in balance is also reflected at the international level. Obviously, during the Cold War the UAE sided with the West against the East. As a country with a political system based upon hereditary rule, free markets and Islam, it wasn't a very attractive partner for the communist side in the Cold War. But even within its own side, the UAE was very careful to maintain a balance among friends, avoiding overt reliance upon any one great-power friend to help assure its security. It had made that mistake and was left holding the bag when the British, for their own reasons, decided to leave at the end of the 1960s. Thus, unlike some of its other Gulf neighbors, the UAE was very careful to cultivate strong security relations with Western powers besides the United States, most notably France, but also Britain.

The ability to keep the Americans over the horizon is much reduced in the 1990s, as a result of the Iraqi invasion of Kuwait. But even now, the UAE, uniquely among the GCC states, has been careful to try to maintain multiple lines of security relations with friendly outside powers in order to avoid too much dependence upon one single power. This is clear from the defense agreements that the entire federation has signed not just with the United States, but also with Great Britain and from the talk about the expansion of the security and arms relationship even with Russia.

The second characteristic of UAE foreign policy has been conciliation. UAE foreign policy under Sheikh Zayed has exhibited a desire for conciliation with regional neighbors when this will contribute to regional stability. The UAE has been more than forthcoming on a whole range of disputes in an effort to remove potential causes of conflict from the regional agenda.

This was clear in the formation of the UAE itself. Abu Dhabi expressed absolutely no criticism publicly of the decision by Bahrain and Qatar to leave the negotiations of the nine and become independent themselves. At the same time, Abu Dhabi didn't try to follow their path, even though economically it had as strong a claim to independence and to the ability to maintain itself as an independent country. But in the interest of regional stability, Abu Dhabi took the lead in putting together a federation of the seven and paid a price in terms of enticing the other members of that federation into joining it.

In its border issues with Oman and Saudi Arabia, the UAE has been willing to compromise to remove troublesome issues from the agenda and to contribute to regional stability. It has been willing to go more than halfway in addressing its neighbors as long as that conciliation served the larger purpose of maintaining regional stability.

As Mr. Jahshan pointed out, in its use of aid through the Abu Dhabi Fund for Arab Economic Development and other funds, and more directly in state-to-state aid, the UAE has attempted to spread its wealth locally and regionally to conciliate neighbors and promote an atmosphere of cooperation. I note particularly Abu Dhabi's aid to Oman before oil revenues began to come into Oman and to Yemen. Sharing the wealth contributes to regional stability.

For additional analytical, marketing, investment and business opportunities information, please contact
Global Investment & Business Center, USA
(202) 546-2103. Fax: (202) 546-3275. E-mail: rusric@erols.com

Finally, in its oil policy the UAE has also exhibited a willingness to conciliate neighbors. The UAE has nearly 10 percent of the world's oil reserves yet provides less than 4 percent of world production. They have made a conscious decision not to push production up to the level their reserves would justify. That would be taking market share away from its neighbors.

The one place where you don't see this conciliation practiced is over the issue of Abu Musa and the Tunbs, although the UAE is willing to settle this issue through negotiation and international judicial processes. It should be noted that it wasn't until 1992, when the Iranians started making the moves, that this issue came to the top of the UAE foreign-policy agenda. In this case, given the changed power relationship in the Gulf, with the destruction of Iraq and the rise of Iran, conciliation of Iranian aggressiveness on the islands could only have been read as weakness. It would have encouraged thoughts of Iranian hegemony rather than contributing to regional stability.

Q & A

Panel Moderator, Amb. Richard Murphy (Council on Foreign Relations): What will be the U.S. legacy ten years from now?

Dr. Al-Alkim: I believe the American presence in the region is causing tension within the Gulf states and probably preventing the strengthening of ties between Iraq and the GCC, Iran and the GCC or the UAE, in particular. The issue of security is exaggerated; military spending is draining the budgets of the Gulf States in favor of the American military industries. This is another issue that will shake the legitimacy of the Gulf States in the future, when they don't have the cash to spend on education, health care and infrastructure. Unfortunately, the Americans are trying to protect the regimes instead of pushing for more democratization, more liberalization, more accountability. The regimes feel secure, and don't want to give more concessions to their people.

Mr. Jahshan: The legacy of the United States may be judged very harshly in the next 10 to 15 years. Our credibility in the region is dwindling. The criticism we are hearing now from the top leadership of these countries, the closest allies of the United States, leaves you with some very serious food for thought. It centers on the double standards on which U.S. policy is based, whether with regard to counterterrorism, weapons of mass destruction, or the acquisition of territory by force. Our insistence on viewing the region through an Israeli prism, refusing to look at our interests on their own merits, based on national interests, is causing a lot of problems for us.

Dr. Gause: I think 10 years from now, people will say that the United States presence helped maintain the territorial status quo in the Gulf, but I worry that the longer the American military presence remains in the Gulf, the more likely it will become a domestic issue, as we've seen in Saudi Arabia.

Amb. Chas. W. Freeman, Jr. (President, Middle East Policy Council): All three of you posited some form of reintegration of Iraq into the region as necessary and desirable from the point of view of the UAE and most of its GCC partners. What form would such reintegration take? Does it depend on the United Nations or are countries in the Gulf prepared, as the United States apparently is in Kosovo, to act outside the U.N. process? What sorts of commitments would have to be made by an Iraq still headed by Saddam Hussein? Would it make a difference whether Iraq has new leadership?

Dr. Gause: This is one of the issues that's going to tear at GCC unity. People in the lower Gulf see Iraq as a balance-of-power counterweight. But the Saudis and Kuwaitis can't accept any kind of reintegration of Iraq as long as Saddam Hussein is in power.

For additional analytical, marketing, investment and business opportunities information, please contact
Global Investment & Business Center, USA
(202) 546-2103. Fax: (202) 546-3275. E-mail: rusric@erols.com

Mr. Jahshan: I share that pessimism with regard to reintegration of Iraq as long as Saddam is in power. But Saddam could last for another 20 years. The question is, can the region survive the current status quo, particularly the continued military conflict that is eroding the security of the region and the economies of these countries.

Dr. Al-Alkim: How long do we let the Iraqi people suffer? There is the feeling in the Gulf that the Americans want to keep Saddam there as a puppet so that they can exploit the GCC states. But with the militants in Iran pushing hard against the UAE, I think another way will have to be found, whether Kuwait likes it or not. We believe that without Iraq we cannot bring Iran to the negotiating table. For the Americans the question is this: Is Saddam the only dictator in the Middle East? For the United Nations, is Iraq the only country that is not abiding by U.N. resolutions? What about Israel? I think it's in the interest of the region that the United States take its hands off the Gulf area.

Q: Is any thought being given in the Gulf or the UAE to a transition to a new regime, multilateral or otherwise? How do you assure the security you want without Pax Americana?

Dr. Al-alkim: I'm convinced that there should be a new formula, "six plus three," integrating Iraq, Iran and Yemen into the security regime for that part of the world.

Q: Has there been, since the new government in Iran came in, any indication whatsoever that Iran's position on the future discussion, if not more, of the three islands is to be anything more than simply a bilateral issue in which sovereignty does not arise?

Dr. Al-alkim: We cannot go to the International Court of Justice if Iran does not agree beforehand. So we are in a vicious circle. Insiders have said that the islands are not a matter of life and death, but this is not the right time to discuss it. Iran is still divided between the militants and the moderates. I think the American-Iranian dialogue will buy time for the moderates so that they could negotiate.

Mr. Jahshan: Sheikh Zayed has said that since the change of government in Tehran, we are hearing a softer tone but no progress on this issue and that actions speak louder than words.

Amb. Murphy: Balance of power in the Gulf has become a dirty word in the American vocabulary. The critics of those in the administration or outside who even suggest some change in American policy say balance is discredited. They say, you tried to grow close to Iran, then Iraq, and failed both times; why do you come to us suggesting any such thing again?

Dr. Al-Alkim: It's less expensive. How much are we paying for this arms race within the Gulf? How much are we paying for the American presence in the area? If the governments in the GCC states and Iraq and Iran are accountable to their people, they will get there. As long as the Americans are providing protection to these regimes, we will never get there.

Amb. Murphy: I would not exaggerate the idea that Americans are protecting regimes. Americans cannot protect regimes; they can protect against external aggression.

Dr. Gause: We weren't too successful in protecting the shah. I'm not as optimistic as Hassan is that you can get local powers to come up with an understanding among themselves on a common definition of non-resort to the use of force and other basic rules of engagement with one another. At least some of the local powers will continue to want the United States there. It's a question of how much it's perceived by people in the region as being a burden in their security

For additional analytical, marketing, investment and business opportunities
information, please contact
Global Investment & Business Center, USA
(202) 546-2103. Fax: (202) 546-3275. E-mail: rusric@erols.com

agendas. Dual containment will continue to be a problem for American policy because it relies upon a strong U.S. military presence and, in effect, basing in the GCC states.

"PAST, PRESENT AND FUTURE LEADERSHIP"

William A. Rugh
President, America-Mideast Educational and Training Services Incorporated (AMIDEAST)

Who are the leaders in the UAE? What are the characteristics of leadership there, and how should it be evaluated? The Supreme Federal Council, the highest authority in the UAE, consists of seven members , the rulers of the emirates that make up the federal state. But one man stands out as the primus inter pares, the most respected leader, the person who has done the most to bring the UAE together and make it prosperous: Sheikh Zayed Al Nahyan.

Prior to the establishment of the UAE, 1968-71, after the British announced their plans to depart, there were a number of meetings between the rulers of not seven but nine emirates, including Qatar and Bahrain. That federation didn't materialize; it became a federation of first six and then seven. But all of the rulers of those seven Trucial States plus Qatar and Bahrain, elected Sheikh Zayed as their president in 1969, recognizing his skill and statesmanship. He was elected president of the UAE at the beginning in 1971 and has been re-elected five times. Many people thought the office would rotate, but it did not.

Anyone who has lived in the UAE knows of the enormous respect that Sheikh Zayed enjoys among the people, not just in Abu Dhabi but in Dubai and Sharjah and throughout the emirates. This intangible factor is evidence of his extraordinary leadership. And he has the respect of the Arab world as well.

But how do you evaluate leadership objectively? One good way is to look at how leaders like Sheikh Zayed deal with opportunities and challenges. The enormous wealth of Abu Dhabi and the UAE is not enough to guarantee success economically or stability politically. We've heard today many examples of achievement in the UAE, and I would argue that much of that is due to Sheikh Zayed's leadership. Secretary Mallett said it was not luck but statesmanship. I would say it's not only wealth, but leadership.

I would like to identify some characteristics of leadership that have been exhibited by Sheikh Zayed. First of all, his creativity. Sheikh Zayed had an extraordinary ability to construct a nation composed of three major elements: the bureaucratic structure of a modern state, diverse tribal elements, and a federal system. This is a hybrid. As Sheikh Zayed said when the state was founded in 1971, there are no examples of a federal state in the Arab world to follow. There still aren't, and federal states in other parts of the world have failed. Why has the UAE succeeded?

It is partly because of this unique combination of tribalism, modern state and federalism. The tribal system works if you have a small community with direct access to the rulers. In a federal system, you have smaller units that allow the continuation of that face-to-face tribal system. The legitimacy of the rulers, who descended in a straight line from ancestors who ruled their territories, also contributed. Finally, there is enough bureaucracy in the central government to carry out the functions of national defense, foreign policy, and health, education and welfare.

Second, Sheikh Zayed exhibited enormous patience, flexibility and vision. He didn't jump to hasty conclusions or make decisions quickly. In 1968-70 he was interested in a union of nine and even considered trying to bring in Oman. He settled for seven. Later he was a major force in bringing

For additional analytical, marketing, investment and business opportunities
information, please contact
Global Investment & Business Center, USA
(202) 546-2103. Fax: (202) 546-3275. E-mail: rusric@erols.com

the GCC together, which helped to expand the unity of the Gulf. He always had a broad vision of the maximum reasonable number of states in this union, yet he didn't expand it too fast or too far. When the Iraqis presented the idea of a pact including Iraq along with the GCC, he politely declined, showing foresight. Iraq was not the kind of state that would be compatible with the others in that group.

Sheikh Zayed was patient. It was 25 years before the UAE had a permanent constitution, 25 years before Abu Dhabi was named the capital. In the issue with Iran over Abu Musa and the Tunbs, he did not confront the Iranians. He gained recognition from Iran and bided his time. Since 1992, he has made a major issue of it, without provoking a military conflict, which would so damage the UAE.

His choice of 1992 to make an issue out of Abu Musa was dictated more by the circumstances in the region than by Iranian actions. The Iranians had been militarizing the island throughout the eighties, during the Iran-Iraq War, and he didn't make an issue out of it. He didn't even make an issue out of it during the Kuwait crisis of '90-'91. He waited until all of that was over, and in 1992, when he had the support of the international community, he made an issue of Abu Musa and the Tunbs. He didn't give up his demand for sovereignty over these islands, which he inherited, but he was patient.

Another example of his patience and far-sightedness is in the petroleum sector. When other countries of the region were nationalizing ownership, taking it away from the foreign oil companies in the 1973-75 period, Sheikh Zayed took over 60 percent, but not 100 percent. He wanted to retain a connection with the international oil companies to maintain access to technology. And now we see his neighbors talking about reversing their 100-percent nationalization and perhaps inviting the international oil companies to come back in. Sheikh Zayed doesn't have to reverse anything. He went to 60 percent and stopped there. Very prudent.

A third characteristic is generosity. He started out by paying all of the bills of the federal government. He helped the poor emirates, and he has given a great deal of assistance abroad. In addition, he is personally modest, even austere. Ibn Khaldoun says, "Royal authority claims all glory for itself and goes in for luxury." Not Sheikh Zayed. He contributes to the atmosphere of the country , its balance, tolerance and generosity , by his personal behavior.

Sheikh Zayed has helped the poor emirates, and he has given a great deal of assistance abroad. In addition, he is personally modest, even austere.

A fourth and related characteristic: he believes the wealth of the country should be used to benefit the people. He has created a welfare state and enhanced the environment and quality of life to an extraordinary degree. He has planted more date palms than Iraq ever had, and Iraq is famous for date palms. The gardens and parks and clean streets of Abu Dhabi make the quality of life extraordinary. Some of my American friends have left the Foreign Service in order to stay in Dubai to enjoy the quality of life there.

Sheikh Zayed has, of course, pushed rapid economic development as fast as possible in order to create an environment that is felicitous for his countrymen. In making the decision, along with the other rulers, to bring economic advancement by spending oil revenues, he can be contrasted with his predecessor, Sheikh Shakbut, the previous ruler of Abu Dhabi, who didn't want to spend the money to bring development to the country.

The consequences of this decision for the demography of the UAE were very important. In order to press economic development as rapidly as they did, they had to bring in very large numbers of

For additional analytical, marketing, investment and business opportunities
information, please contact
Global Investment & Business Center, USA
(202) 546-2103. Fax: (202) 546-3275. E-mail: rusric@erols.com

foreign workers, four for every UAE national, perhaps the highest ratio anywhere in the world. These foreign workers come from different political cultures, speak different languages. Theoretically, this is importing trouble; in fact, there has been no serious social unrest or political conflict.

The reason, in my view, is that Sheikh Zayed and the rulers have taken deliberate measures to deal with that potential set of problems. They haven't made the UAE a melting pot, and they don't intend to. They don't give citizenship easily to anybody. But they've provided generous salaries and benefits, and the quality of life and educational advancement and the other advantages of the nationals are also shared by the foreign workers.

He has created an extraordinary live-and-let-live environment. If you go to the UAE, you will appreciate the tolerance of the people, starting at the top with Sheikh Zayed. In addition, he promotes traditional culture and tries to avoid the problem of the large number of foreigners undermining it.

My sixth and last characteristic of leadership of Sheikh Zayed and his fellow rulers involves foreign affairs. He has a policy of peaceful settlement of disputes and good neighborly relations, but he is decisive when necessary. This is clear from his dealings with Iraq and Iran. When it comes to an essential national interest, he has drawn the line. Abu Musa since 1992 is a good example.

The Palestinian question is another good example. He was very critical of the United States throughout the eighties, and he continues to be critical of the United States on Palestine and Israel, although he did support the Madrid and Oslo peace processes. He didn't go so far as to support "track two" or the Doha-MENA conference. He has pressure from the Arab community. He has pressure from his American friends, and he's found a felicitous middle ground.

In terms of the relationship with the United States, for most of this period he refused to have any military cooperation or close political cooperation with the United States. Since Desert Storm, he has supported a much closer U.S.-UAE military cooperation, although he does not permit bases in his country and he has recently not allowed the launching of American fighter aircraft from his territory into Iraq.

Nobody can predict the future. Anybody who looks at the last three decades of the UAE and tries to predict the next three is very ambitious. But leadership can be judged by how it deals with tests and opportunities. Here are some of the tests that may come up in the next three decades: First, the demographic challenge, the overwhelming numbers of foreign workers who will, under current economic circumstances, continue to live there indefinitely. There have been occasional discussions of reducing their numbers, but not enough to make a difference.

Will the youth of the UAE stop learning Arabic because they have Filipina nannies? Will they become so international that they lose their own culture? A more important question is the educational challenge. Will they learn the skills that they will need if there is a downturn and the foreign workers leave? Will they take over positions in the private sector? Is the educational system dealing sufficiently with preparations for the expected growth of privatization?

Third, there is the political challenge. Will the tribal system continue to work as the population grows? Maybe the face-to-face requirements of tribal rule will no longer work as the size of the population makes direct access less feasible. Will the federal system endure? I'm inclined to believe that it will, but we've seen examples of failure in other parts of the world.

For additional analytical, marketing, investment and business opportunities information, please contact
Global Investment & Business Center, USA
(202) 546-2103. Fax: (202) 546-3275. E-mail: rusric@erols.com

Will the quality of life be maintained? Will the successor generations put as much investment and concern into those parks and gardens and clean streets and clean water as Sheikh Zayed has?

Finally, will the dangerous neighborhood get out of hand? Sheikh Zayed has managed to cope with the potential and real foreign threats. Will future generations be so wise? I hope the answer to these questions is yes. But it depends primarily on the quality of the leadership. Because Sheikh Zayed and the other rulers have laid such a solid foundation, I am personally very optimistic about the future of the UAE.

For additional analytical, marketing, investment and business opportunities information, please contact
Global Investment & Business Center, USA
(202) 546-2103. Fax: (202) 546-3275. E-mail: rusric@erols.com

SELECTED INVESTMENT AND BUSINESS OPPORTUNITIES

I.T. SECURITY SYSTEMS – SOFTWARE

Successful economic diversity into non-oil sectors, coupled with an open and liberal pro-business environment and a world-class telecommunication infrastructure has undoubtedly turned the United Arab Emirates into the regional business hub for the Middle East. Acceptance of information technology as a way to move forward was quickened by the guidance of farsighted individuals who are key to the success of this country. From focusing on education to setting up of special designated free-zones where Information Communication and Technology (ICT) companies such as Dubai Internet City could operate from to adopting e-government services– the UAE has managed to get this all up and running in an extremely short span of time.

The government takes legal issues associated with technology related offenses (cyber crime, copyright infringement, piracy, etc) very seriously. Being a young country, the UAE, as many other countries often times have to grapple with new legal questions that arise due to the information age. Increasing adoption and reliance on ICT is growing the awareness among organizations of the threat to the security of their networks, computer systems and databases that have on occasion come under threat. It is well known that migration to open systems, more specifically to the Internet, has made information assets increasingly vulnerable to intrusion, theft and destruction. It is estimated that the losses suffered by public and privates companies from security breaches in the GCC crossed the $200 million mark in 2004.

The level of security awareness among top-level management, IT professionals and end-users has significantly grown compared to five years previously. GCC (Gulf Co-operative Countries viz., Bahrain, Kuwait, Oman, Qatar, Saudi Arabia and the UAE) generated attacks have reportedly increased 300 percent in 2004. Symantec analyzed in 2003 that 60 percent of the attacks came from within Saudi Arabia itself. This indicates the growing number of sophisticated hackers operating within the region as well as the vulnerability of unprotected computer networks and personal computers (PCs) operating within this region. Avoidance of coming under attack leads to adoption of measures to ensure security of systems and integrity of networks from external factors.

Symantec's study uncovered that unsolicited e-mail or spam is the most common form of security threat being experienced rated at an average of 8.5 in terms of frequency or probability of occurrence, with a risk level of 7.1 medium. Spyware came second scoring 8.3 points in terms of frequency or probability of occurrence and 6.6 in terms of risk level medium. It was the virus, which is no surprise that scored the highest risk factor for GCC users at 8.9 points, but was less common problems when compared to spam and spyware.

Computer and network security products for the U.A.E. are imported. There is no local production for security-related software except for customization of software to fit local requirements. Encryption features are also customized, if required.

MARKET DEMAND

The Yankee Group valued the overall GCC IT security market covering software applications, firewall appliances and managed security services at $105 million in 2004, a mere 0.8 percent of the estimated global spending of $13 billion in 2004. The forecast for the entire market was for

For additional analytical, marketing, investment and business opportunities information, please contact
Global Investment & Business Center, USA
(202) 546-2103. Fax: (202) 546-3275. E-mail: rusric@erols.com

growth of approximately 23% in 2005 to reach $129 million, with maximum growth for Intrusion Prevention/Detection and Vulnerability Assessment segments. Security Content Management will still remain the leading area of investment.

IT SECURITY MARKET GROWTH (2004 2005)

IT Security Segment	2004 (in Million US$)	2005 (in Million US$)*	Growth Rate (%)
Secure Content Management	40.0	49.0	22
Intrusion prevention/detection and vulnerability assessment	13.0	17.0	30
Identity Management	12.0	15.0	25
Threat Management (Firewall, VPN Software & Appliances)	25.0	30.0	18
Managed Security Services	15.0	19.0	25
Total	105.0	130.0	23

The GCC IT market is valued at approximately $6.6 billion as of end 2004 and the IT security market represents 1.59% of this total. It is expected that total IT security spending in the GCC will grow at an average of 22% annually within a five year period starting 2005, culminating in a market value approaching $350 million by 2010. It is anticipated that the UAE and Saudi Arabia will contribute towards 75% of this growth.

MARKET DATA

The United Arab Emirates has little computer hardware assembly operations and minimal software development of any type. Yet the country attracts the major players to set up regional offices to manage their channel and distribution partners for the region. Chart 2 illustrates the main market drivers to the IT security market within the GCC region in general. The biggest driver for adoption of security solutions is first hand security breaches. It also shows promise for future growth for the industry.

The need to safeguard an organization's corporate image will be a high factor in the growth of this sub-sector. Events like the recent Etisalat Middle East IT Security (MEITSEC) conference will contribute in growing awareness for IT security.

Chart 3 identifies factors that could have a negative impact on spending for IT security.

The growth rate in security spending in the UAE is estimated to increase by 24 percent in 2005 as illustrated in chart numbers 4 and 5.

Chart 4 -*Madar Research Journal*

BEST PROSPECTS

Secure Content Management Intrusion prevention/detection and vulnerability assessment Identity Management Threat Management (Firewall, VPN Software & Appliances) Managed Security Services

For additional analytical, marketing, investment and business opportunities information, please contact
Global Investment & Business Center, USA
(202) 546-2103. Fax: (202) 546-3275. E-mail: rusric@erols.com

KEY SUPPLIERS

Most of the major international companies are present in the UAE through their locally appointed agent/distributor. A list of key contacts for this sub-sector of the computer industry is available upon request for a nominal fee.

PROSPECTIVE BUYERS

The UAE will change from a monopolistic telecom infrastructure to a duopolistic offering. It is anticipated that services by the duopoly would be expanded services resulting in the need to have sophisticated networks to maximize capabilities offered.

Buyers could be broken into three categories – individual end user and the public and private sectors. The smallest segment is the end-user who buy products at the low end sufficient to meet the needs of basic computing systems.

The push towards turning government interaction with their customer base towards offering e-system solutions will increase the need for secured systems offering uninterrupted service by the public sector.

In the private sector -the financial sector was the leader in terms of IT security spend, accounting for 24 percent of the market in 2004. GCC banking in general and UAE banking in particular are basically the second biggest industry next to hydrocarbon. Charts 6 illustrates break up of market share by industry for 2004.

Saudi Arabia and the UAE together account for approximately 73% of the total GCC IT security market. Individual market share for the UAE (28%) and Saudi Arabia (45%) reflects the utilization and development of the two countries.

MARKET ENTRY

The United Arab Emirates offers an open import market in which American products are highly regarded and well accepted. Co-operation with U.A.E. companies familiar with the techniques of preparing and presenting applications to local government agencies is extremely important.

In order to enter the U.A.E. market, service firms must appoint a sponsor or a commercial agent. Local representation is a legal condition for doing business in the U.A.E. Great care is advised in the selection of the commercial agent. The law favors local businesses and the cancellation of agency agreements is difficult and costly, regardless of contract terms. Local firms generally prefer exclusive distribution rights for all of the

U.A.E. They then supply direct from their base, appoint representatives in other emirates, or have a network of offices throughout the U.A.E.

U.S. firms who do not have a direct presence in the U.A.E. usually operate through a two-tier distribution channel that would have locally appointed partners and several value added resellers (VARs). These are well established throughout the country, offer good pre-sales assistance and after-sales technical service, have experience in the different market sectors and maintain person-to-person contact with customers. American companies interested in entering the U.A.E. market should consider cooperative/licensing arrangements or joint ventures with carefully selected U.A.E. partners.

For additional analytical, marketing, investment and business opportunities information, please contact
Global Investment & Business Center, USA
(202) 546-2103. Fax: (202) 546-3275. E-mail: rusric@erols.com

Appointed agents have the right to appoint sub-agents or distributors to sell into this market. Companies using the distributor or VAR sales channel benefit from the expertise of their local representative's knowledge of this market, cultural and technological differences, existing customer base or dealer network, local marketing and sales experience and support services.

Foreign companies can set up a branch or representative office in the U.A.E., with prior approval from the Department of Economic Development and the Ministry of Economy and Commerce. Representative offices and branches of foreign companies are legally barred from conducting business operations or marketing directly within the U.A.E. Their legally stipulated role is to promote their products and to facilitate contacts between the company and its U.A.E. clients/agents.

Companies who prefer to have 100% ownership right tend to set up their office in one of the eleven free trade zones that are located in the U.A.E. all of whom offer many incentives and exemptions.

Customs regulations are relatively straightforward and include the following documentation: commercial invoice and certificate of origin. Import duty is a flat rate of 5% for computer IT security products and can be exempted on goods sold directly to government agencies. There are no exchange controls or restrictions on repatriation of capital or profits.

Though the U.A.E. dirham is linked to the dollar, exchange rate fluctuations of the dollar against other major international currencies can affect prices and profit margins.

MARKET ISSUES & OBSTACLES

In 1992, copyright protection for software was incorporated into U.A.E. law. Enforcement of this law began in earnest in 1994. In recent press articles the local chapter of the Business Software Alliance has stated that the appropriate sections of the U.A.E. government has been very active in ensuring that counterfeiting of software is being stamped slowly out of existence. The country still has a way to go but progress in relation to the surrounding countries has been excellent.

Shipments to the U.A.E. are usually under letters of credit (L/C) and sight drafts, depending on the exporter's preference and the extent of past dealing with the purchaser. For payment of L/Cs, the normal period is 90 days after acceptance of the draft. The extension of credit terms and other marketing assistance are key factors in a successful business relationship. A certain degree of flexibility is considered normal in the establishment of terms and conditions. Suppliers to the U.A.E. government usually receive payment six months after delivery.

RESOURCES

Emirates Telecommunication Corporation (Etisalat) – http://etisalat.ae (The organization that pre-approves hardware/software that is used in-country for all telecommunication service.)

Comtrust – http://www.comtrust.ae (Comtrust, the Digital certificate provider, which is part of eCompany, a fully owned subsidiary of Etisalat)

The Institute of Electrical & Electronics Engineers – http://www.emirates.org/ieee/ (Computer Society, UAE Chapter)

**For additional analytical, marketing, investment and business opportunities information, please contact
Global Investment & Business Center, USA
(202) 546-2103. Fax: (202) 546-3275. E-mail: rusric@erols.com**

USE EDUCATION MARKET

Sheikh Mohammed bin Rashid Al Maktoum, Vice President and Prime Minister of the U.A.E. and Ruler of Dubai informed the World Economic Forum in Dalian, China earlier this year that "educational development is vital to economic success". A natural follow through is the federal budget of Dhs.7.11 billion (approximately $1.9 billion) allocated to the Ministry of Education towards education programs, accounting for 33% of the total budget allocations.

Today the U.A.E. offers a comprehensive education to all male and female students from K1 through university with education for the country's citizens being provided free at all levels. The emiratisation of teaching staff in government schools is scheduled to reach 90% by 2020, in order to ensure that the Islamic principles and traditions of the U.A.E. are maintained.

The existing school educational structure, established in the 1970, is a four-tier system over 14 years: 4 to 5 year olds-attend kindergarten, 6 to 11 year-olds attend primary schools, the preparatory stage caters for children aged between 12-14 years and 15 to 17 year-old attend secondary schools. A school leaving certificate or diploma is awarded on successful completion of the board exam that the school is affiliated to. Technical Secondary School is a six-year program between the ages of 12-18. A Technical Secondary Diploma is awarded on completion of a board exam that the school is affiliated to.

There are two categories of schools in the U.A.E. – public and private. Primary and secondary education is compulsory up to ninth grade for U.A.E. citizens and is offered at no cost in the public school system. U.A.E. population by nationality and educational status as reported for 2005 was:

Expatriate children attend registered private schools, some of which offer foreign language education geared towards expatriate communities following the curriculum of the home country that the institution is affiliated with. Through ongoing school activities and programs, children enrolled in private schools get the opportunity to learn some of their heritage and culture.

Nationals can attend government tertiary-level institutions free of charge, and a wide and rapidly increasing range of private institutions, many with international accreditation, supplement the private sector. A Cabinet decision issued in 2001 excluding expatriate students from government schools, was rescinded in mid-2006. Commencing in the academic year 2006/07, admission for expatriate students will be based on merit and fees will be levied.

With the emphasis on education, it is reported that approximately 95% of all female and 80% of all male students enrolled in the final year of secondary school apply for admission to a higher education institution. This could be in country or overseas.

The United Arab Emirates University (UAEU) based in Al Ain continues to be the country's flagship national institution of higher education, whilst newer institutions such as Zayed University (ZU) have been established to educate national women to prepare them to be active participants in the development of this country. The Higher Colleges of Technology (HCT), on the other hand offer a more technically oriented education in well-equipped colleges across the U.A.E. HCT, in conjunction with its commercial arm, the Centre of Excellence for Applied Research and Training (CERT), prides itself on responding quickly and effectively to current needs in the regional and international workplace.

**For additional analytical, marketing, investment and business opportunities
information, please contact
Global Investment & Business Center, USA
(202) 546-2103. Fax: (202) 546-3275. E-mail: rusric@erols.com**

Notable private institutions include the American Universities of Sharjah and Dubai, Sharjah University, University of Wollongong in Dubai, Ajman University of Science and Technology, Abu Dhabi University, Al Hosn University in Abu Dhabi and an Abu Dhabi chapter of the Sorbonne.

The U.A.E. Ministry of Education has produced a policy document outlining a strategy for further educational development in the U.A.E. up to the year 2020, based on several five-year plans to ensure that U.A.E. nationals are well equipped to enter the work force and assist in the country's development.

A regional center, located on the University of Sharjah campus, for educational planning has been opened in the U.A.E. under UNESCO. The centre, the second in the world, will respond to the pressing need to improve educational planning in the Gulf.

The scholarship program offered to emirati students requires or requests students to study in the US. In 2002-2003 there were 1792 emirati students studying in the U.S. Female illiteracy rate in the U.A.E. in 2005 was 7.6% compared to 10% for men. 2.1% of U.A.E. national women dropped out of educational institutions in the 2005-06 academic year.

Most postgraduate course providers in the U.A.E. tend to focus on MBA programs with limited options for undergraduate degree programs.

In the U.A.E. the U.S. continues to be perceived as offering quality education by students, employers, school administrators, scholarship-granting institutions and U.A.E. government officials including the Minister of Education, Sheikh Nahyan Bin Mubarak Al Nahyan.

Local media reports that Dubai is considering offering scholarships for the first time to wards of long-time expatriate residents to pursue higher education in the emirate or abroad in an effort to develop an educated workforce.

Local media reported that the U.A.E. Minister of Education, Dr. Hanif Hassan, said that the U.A.E. is eager to benefit from international educational organizations, and their expertise and experience, to improve the quality of education in the country. UAE federal strategy can be summed up by its pursuit to become a knowledge based world class government.

The U.A.E. offers an educational system for boys and girls from primary level through to university. Education for the country's citizens is provided at no cost through government schools, colleges and universities. An extensive private education system exists that is primarily used by children of expatriate workers.

Grades K-12 are offered in the public school system, supervised by the U.A.E. Ministry of Education. All courses are taught in Arabic with English introduced in grade one and taught for one period per day. Primarily set up for the citizens of the U.A.E., in the past year admission to expatriate children has been introduced for a nominal school fee. Enrollment of expatriate children in the public school system is based on a number of criteria and subject to a number of seats not to exceed a pre-determined set number.

A private school system exists that caters to an expatriate population from across the globe. Varied country community schools exist (American Community School, Iranian School, Japanese School, Indian School etc.) using the same standards as applied in the home country. These school systems need to be accredited by the U.A.E. Ministry of Education. Graduates from these

For additional analytical, marketing, investment and business opportunities information, please contact
Global Investment & Business Center, USA
(202) 546-2103. Fax: (202) 546-3275. E-mail: rusric@erols.com

schools must score 500 on the TOEFL and 400 on the math portion of the SAT I to prove their diploma's equivalency to the U.S. diploma.

In 2004 the U.A.E. Ministry of Education, Department of Educational and Institutional Research, reported that there were 452 schools offering private education in the U.A.E. providing 14,052 classes for a student population of 315,797 by 23,000 teachers and administrators. In 2007, the Ministry of Education has a total of 1465 schools on record comprising 763 public schools and 702 private schools.

Tuition fees range from free to minimal in the local public university system. Currently only U.A.E. citizens are allowed to apply for enrollment to the public university system. The norm in education in the U.A.E. is to have separate campuses for the two sexes. The U.A.E. University is the only public university that offers a medical program.

Higher education in the numerous private universities currently available in the U.A.E. caters mainly for the expatriate student population. Tuition cost is extremely high. Institutes offering a western curriculum tend to have staff who have studied from the US, UK and Canada on board.

Statistics indicate a sustained increase in the total number of students at the Higher Colleges of Technology, Zayed University and U.A.E. University (all public universities) with a noticeable increase in the number of female students. In 1999/2000 academic year, the total enrollment in three federal institutions was 27,696. By 2005/2005, this number increased to 34,207 students. Correspondingly, the number of graduates also increased from 4834 in 1999/2000 to 6632 in 2003/2004. The institutions have taken on a combined total of 9,825 new U.A.E. national students. Subjects that proved popular this year were engineering, business studies and IT.

International universities that have been accredited by the U.A.E. Ministry of Education to be found across the U.A.E. are listed at www.caa.ae . Some institutions with a presence in the U.A.E. offering a curriculum from the home country as well as with U.A.E. accreditation are:

France: Paris Sorbonne University

USA: New York Institute of Technology, Michigan State University

India: Birla Institute of Technology & Science Pilani

UK: British University in Dubai; University of Strathclyde Business School

Canada: Canadian University of Dubai

Australia: University of Wollongong in Dubai

Instruction at the post-secondary level is in English. The public university system offers up to two-one year Foundation Programs for those students that are determined to require additional attention.

The U.A.E. has a very young population with 71% between the ages of 15-64 years of which 60% are male with a median age of 35.2 years. The balance 40%, which are female, has a median age of 22.9 years. Languages spoken are Arabic, Farsi, English, Hindi and Urdu. 96% of the population is muslim.

For additional analytical, marketing, investment and business opportunities
information, please contact
Global Investment & Business Center, USA
(202) 546-2103. Fax: (202) 546-3275. E-mail: rusric@erols.com

Factors affecting fewer students from the U.A.E. to the US post 9/11 are:

It is important for US higher education institutions interested in attracting students from the U.A.E. to participate at local education trade fairs or focussed US education programs arranged by companies such as Linden Tours, ISN, Top MBA Tours among others.

An avenue that US institutions may wish to explore in getting their institution known to students in the U.A.E. is through the "Web Exposure Program" that is offered by the U.S. Commercial Service-U.A.E. web site (www.buyusa.gov/uae).

The Abu Dhabi Education Council (ADEC), an independent, Abu Dhabi based corporate body was established by H.H. General Sheikh Mohammed bin Zayed Al Nahayan, Crown Price of Abu Dhabi and Deputy Supreme Commander of the U.A.E. Armed Forces in 2005. ADEC has been entrusted with the task of developing education and educational institutions in the emirate. The council will work closely with the Ministry of Education in formulating the emirate's education plan within the framework of the U.A.E.'s general education policy.

ADEC is in the early stages of implementing their project entitled 'Public-Private Partnership for Public School Management' that enables leading local and regional private education providers to manage selected public schools in the Emirate of Abu Dhabi in conjunction with ADEC. Launched as a three-year pilot program commencing September 2006, selected Abu Dhabi schools, including kindergarten and primary schools for boys and girls in the three educational zones of Abu Dhabi, Al Ain and the Western Region, are involved in the project. It is hoped that the participating schools and their students would enjoy a richer educational environment, including better school facilities, efficient and less bureaucratic school administration systems, modern teaching and assessment methods, up-to-date curricula, more intensive use of information technology and additional extra-curricular activities. Principals and teachers, including national staff, will experience improved working conditions and professional development opportunities.

ADEC issued a decree in 2006 abolishing fees at model schools in Abu dhabi. ADEC will be responsible for all costs at the model schools, which will be directly involved in the development and evaluation of the educational process. ADEC and the Model Schools Committee are setting new standards for admission of students.

Third world countries that have become keen competitors to U.S. education are:
Australia:
- Image of political neutrality and safety
- More education recruiters in Gulf region
- Increased recruitment efforts post 9/11
- Increase in tourism from Gulf region
- Lower tuition and fees rates (approximately 1/3 of cost of US higher education).

- **United Kingdom:**
- More educational recruiters in Gulf region
- Closer geographic location that U.S.
- Historical ties to the region and better cultural understanding of local customs

- **Canada:**
- Perceived as similar educational institutions to the U.S. without the political implications

- **Other Arab Countries:**

For additional analytical, marketing, investment and business opportunities
information, please contact
Global Investment & Business Center, USA
(202) 546-2103. Fax: (202) 546-3275. E-mail: rusric@erols.com

- Closer geographic location
- Familiar culture
- Less expensive than Western education

ADEC has also entered into an agreement in which Zayed University will assist in developing the English language skills of elementary level students at four model schools. Thirty faculty members from ZU will work with the first and fourth grade students at these schools, observing and evaluating English language teaching methods, and designing modern academic programs. This initiative will be extended to all schools at a later stage.

Law No. 30 for 2006 by H.H. Sheikh Mohammad bin Rashid Al Maktoum, Vice-President and Prime Minister of the UAE and Ruler of Dubai established The Knowledge and Human Development Authority (KHDA) to be responsible for licensing of all educational, human development and training institutes and service providers in Dubai.

The Vice President and Prime Minister of the U.A.E. and Ruler of Dubai, Sheikh Mohammed bin Rashid Al Maktoum, unveiled the modern Arab "House of Wisdom". The Knowledge Complex is a $10bn education initiative of the Mohammad bin Rashid Al Maktoum Foundation. It will include scholarships for young Arab professionals, online programs for women who have family, and a loan program for refugees to start small businesses.

Forsa Centre for Excellence, recently launched in Dubai, will provide young executive women in the region with a one-year executive management program in collaboration with Insead, the world business school. The program targets women who are serious about becoming CEOs.

With the emphasis on quality education and the interest in turning the U.A.E. into a regional learning center, the timing to bring educational programs to the U.A.E. could not be better. The list below briefly describes institutions that have either set up a presence or are in the process of setting up a presence in the U.A.E.

Educational programs that would be of interest in the U.A.E. could vary from a graduate/post graduate program to specialized occupational training programs that could be brought over to the U.A.E. Courses of study at reputable educational institutions will continue to be of interest in this market.

Interest in U.S. educational programs would be varied in this market. Prospective buyers could include direct end users such as students. Some public and private institutions offer scholarship programs that predetermine the place and/or program of study. Institutions as well as private investors are normally interested in learning about opportunities that could be of possible interest to them particularly if unavailable in the U.A.E.

Programs have to be approved by the U.A.E. Commission for Academic Accreditation (CAA) of the Ministry of Higher Education and Scientific Research. Accredited programs available in the U.A.E. are listed at www.caa.ae .

Universities in the U.A.E. are open to working with an overseas educational institution to offer a course of study in this market. Preference is always given to popular programs from well renowned institutions that would broaden the scope on offer to those students whose preference is to remain in the U.A.E. to study. This market also caters to students from outside the U.A.E. who prefer to live within the region, close to home.

For additional analytical, marketing, investment and business opportunities information, please contact
Global Investment & Business Center, USA
(202) 546-2103. Fax: (202) 546-3275. E-mail: rusric@erols.com

Getting included as a preferred institution with organizations that award scholarship programs is definitely helpful in gaining a student population from the U.A.E.

Market Demand With the emphasis on quality education and the interest in turning the U.A.E. into a regional learning center, the timing to bring educational programs to the U.A.E. could not be better. The list below briefly describes institutions that have either set up a presence or are in the process of setting up a presence in the U.A.E

Cornell University and the Queen's University of Canada will create a joint research team to assist Dubai Municipality in the continued development of its e-government program. The team will assess current DM e-government initiatives in the context of DM's strategic plan and overall Dubai e-government initiatives.

Abu Dhabi officials and New York University have formally reached agreement to establish an Abu Dhabi campus of NYU, which will be paid for by the local government. Set to receive students by 2010, the tie up will be the first comprehensive liberal arts campus established abroad by a major US research university. Lecturers will be hired externally and the campus should cater to around 2000 students.

The Canadian University of Dubai (CUD) has signed a collaboration agreement with France's Universite Lumiere Lyon 2 to initiate exchange programs and to promote academic and research partnerships. The Canadian University of Dubai, a subsidiary of the Emirates Investment and Development Company, already has a number of tie-ups with other European and North American universities.

CUD has signed a MOU with University of New Brunswick, the first English Speaking University in Canada. The schools will develop joint programs at undergraduate and graduate levels and promotes collaborative research. CUD students will also be able to transfer credits to UNB.

Michigan State University (MSU) in a joint venture with Tecom Investments is to set up a non profit-making regional branch campus at Dubai International Academic City (DIAC). Expected to begin accepting students from August 2008, MSU is planning to offer around nine courses for undergraduate/postgraduate degree programs spread across various subjects including media, communications, public relations, computer engineering, construction management, family studies and business cognates. Until the campus opens, MSU will maintain an office in Dubai Knowledge Village.

Alpha Aviation Group and Air Arabia have signed a joint venture agreement to establish a multi-million dollar aviation-training academy in Sharjah. Once approval has been received from the U.A.E. General Civil Aviation Authority, operations are due to commence in early 2008. The new facility will be based on Alpha Aviation's existing academy, Clark Aviation, in the Philippines

DAE University, Dubai Aerospace Enterprise's new aerospace educational institution is offering two Bachelor degree programs in flight and aviation management and aviation business administration starting classes on September 16, 2007.

Located at the Dubai International Financial Centre (DIFC), Dubai, the London Business School started operations in December 2007 by offering an Executive MBA and has announced six more programs aimed at top companies and executives. Students will receive a London Business School MBA degree.

For additional analytical, marketing, investment and business opportunities information, please contact
Global Investment & Business Center, USA
(202) 546-2103. Fax: (202) 546-3275. E-mail: rusric@erols.com

London-based Cass Business School will offer Executive MBA programs, including a course specializing in Islamic Finance, in association with DIFC. Courses will also be offered in energy and general management and finance. The program started in September 2007 to be taught over 24 months.

The Dubai International Financial Exchange Academy and the Ecole Superieure des Affaires have teamed up to collaborate on the running of joint courses. The first course was scheduled for November 2007

Dubai Education, a subsidiary of Emirates Investment and Development, has announced its second academic institute in Dubai, L'Université Francaise de Dubai, a part of Lyon Lumiére of France. Expected to open its doors to students in the forthcoming academic year, the new university campus will be located centrally in Dubai.

The Abu Dhabi Vocational Education and Training Institute (ADVETI) under the auspices of New South Wales Technical and Further Education (Australia) will offer Emirati students locally and internationally recognized qualifications at the Diploma and Certificate levels. The program will involve academia as well as on-the-job training.

George Mason University- Ras Al Khaimah (GMU-RAK) started its first academic year in Fall 2006. American standards with regard to curricula and faculty will be maintained allowing GMU-RAK to award degrees that would be the same as those obtained at GMU-USA. In line with GMU-USA staffing requirements, senior faculty appointments such as Provost (Academic President) and Academic Deans of the various departments will come from the USA, as the quality of faculty and curricula in the U.A.E. will remain consistent to that of the US.

The Dubai Health Authority (DHA) has signed an agreement with the Harvard Medical Faculty Physicians (HMFP) to help strengthen clinical and scientific standards. The DHA and the HMFP will explore joint opportunities in education, training, research and clinical care.

Dubai Maritime City has commenced negotiations with the International Association of Maritime Universities regarding setting up a Maritime Education University. Subjects to be offered would include maritime law, maritime engineering management and IT in maritime. The 270,000 sq. ft university would also be affiliated to a research and development institute to assist students undertaking doctorates.

Dubai Real Estate Institute (DREI), the region's first specialized academic institute for real estate studies has signed an agreement with the National University of Singapore to offer customized graduate degrees and executive training programs in real estate.

DREI has signed an agreement with the Centre for Real Estate Studies at the New York Law School (NYLS). The tie-up will enable the two institutions to develop a law graduate program and to offer educational courses on the different legal aspects of the real estate business. The two institutes will also work together to develop collaborative research initiatives and a student exchange program.

Dubai Industrial City has teamed up with UK based Technical Training Centre to establish the Dubai Industrial Academy (DIA), which will serve as a dedicated vocational training centre. Emphasis on areas such as quality, health, safety and the environment will be among the 199 specialized industrial training courses.

The Dubai Professional Trading Group (DubaiPTG) has launched a hands-on training course for those wanting to start a career in trading on regional and global financial markets. The program, beginning January 2008 will be taught in English over a period of six months with a total of ten trainees per course. Dubai PTG offers a high-tech trading room, risk management systems and dedicated leased line connections.

Abu Dhabi University (ADU) is to launch new initiatitves at its English Language Institute from next spring. ADU will offer a course in English for Special Purposes, a summer camp for high-school students as well as multimedia computer assisted language learning (CALL). The university's CALL labs offer flat-screen TVs, WiFi Internet connections and a range of language software.

The Young Arab Leaders (YAL) and Singapore's Keppel Corporation have launched an Arab Asian internship program. The three month long program, running from June-August 2008, will take 10 students from the Arab world to 10 Asian countries in which Keppel operates to experience employment in an Asian environment and culture. The interns will learn about sectors such as marketing, sales, finance and controlling and IT.

The e-TQM College signed a partnership agreement with the Wisconsin University in the US as part of a series of agreements with international academic institutions and establishments.

The Ministry of Presidential Affairs along with the UAE Academy have partnered with a number of leading education institutions namely: University of Washington, Montana State University, Texas International Education Consortium to offer the IBDAA program to young emirates. This program provides participants with training leading to internationally recognized certificates that will open private sector job opportunities for them in many fields.

The Emirates Group, in partnership with Western Australia's Edith Cowan University, announced the opening of the Centre for Security & Aviation Excellence. The center, run by Transguard Education Academy, will offer programs for security professionals, including those working in the aviation industry, plus other aviation related training programs.

Emaar Education, a subsidiary of Emaar Properties, has unveiled a new program to promote arts education n the MENA region and the subcontinent. The University of the Arts headquartered in Dubai, will create a network of campuses, each distinct and with its own identity but linked as an international networked university. The new university is part of Emaar Education's plans to open more than 100 educational institutions in locations close to and within its master planned communities.

Aldar Properties has set up a dedicated division, Aldar Academies, to build and operate up to 20 new schools, the first that opened in September 2007. The schools will form part of the company's future residential projects.

A low-cost market entry program to get information to students, parents and institutions on programs of study available in the U.S. is by getting the institution listed of the CS-UAE website (www.buyusa.gov/uae) under the 'Web Exposure Program'. Subscription to this service for a minimal fee, allows U.S. educational institutes to get information on their school/programs on-line. This also includes a hyperlink to a preferred email address and URL that the institute would like included for direct communication. Subscription is in multiples of a year at a time.

**For additional analytical, marketing, investment and business opportunities
information, please contact
Global Investment & Business Center, USA
(202) 546-2103. Fax: (202) 546-3275. E-mail: rusric@erols.com**

Trade magazines provide an excellent means of 'testing the market'. Overseas education is mainly promoted through exhibitions, road shows and open days. Road shows aim at attracting and giving advice to students about education programs in the US, in addition to details of tuition methods, living costs, accommodation options and extra curricular activities. Advertising in local printed media is used to promote these events.

Discussions indicate U.A.E. companies generally feel they have a good knowledge of the U.S. market and its products. Participation by U.S. institutions in U.A.E. events is an excellent means of recruiting potential students from the U.A.E.

Advertising in professional trade journals is a well-accepted method of product promotion. The following English language paper has a special educational feature called Notes, that is circulated weekly on Sunday Notes enjoys wide distribution in the U.A.E. Notes is published through the year other than the summer months.

Gulf News
P.O. Box 6519
Dubai
Tel: 971-4- 344 7100
Fax: 971-4- 349 2190
Email: education@gulfnews.com
www.gulfnews.com/notes

The body responsible for Education in the UAE is the Ministry of Education. Contact details to their offices in Abu Dhabi and Dubai are listed below:

Ministry of Education
P.O. Box 295
Abu Dhabi
Tel: 971-2- 621 3800
Fax: 971-2- 635 1164
Email: moe@moe.gov.ae
www.moe.gov.ae

Ministry of Education
P.O. Box 3962
Dubai
Tel: 971-4- 263 3333 / 217 6899
Fax: 971-4- 263 8194
Email: moe@moe.gov.ae
www.moe.gov.ae

The following bodies are responsible for licensing of educational institutes in their respective emirates.

Abu Dhabi Education Council (ADEC)
P.O. Box 36005
Abu Dhabi
Tel: 971-2- 696 4100
Fax: 971-2- 642 1808
Email: info@adec.ac.ae
www.adec.ac.ae

For additional analytical, marketing, investment and business opportunities information, please contact
Global Investment & Business Center, USA
(202) 546-2103. Fax: (202) 546-3275. E-mail: rusric@erols.com

Knowledge and Human Development Authority
P.O. Box 500008
Dubai
Tel: 971-4- 364 0000
Fax: 971-4- 364 0001
Email: info@khda.gov.ae
www.khda.gov.ae

**For additional analytical, marketing, investment and business opportunities
information, please contact
Global Investment & Business Center, USA
(202) 546-2103. Fax: (202) 546-3275. E-mail: rusric@erols.com**

TRAVEL TO UAE

US STATE DEPARTMENT SUGGESTIONS

COUNTRY DESCRIPTION: The United Arab Emirates (UAE) is a federation of seven independent emirates, each with its own ruler. The federal government exists as a constitutional republic, headed by a president and council of ministers. Islamic ideals and beliefs provide the conservative foundation of the country's customs, laws and practices. The UAE is a modern, developed country, and tourist facilities are widely available. The capital is Abu Dhabi.

ENTRY REQUIREMENTS: A passport and visa are required. In addition, an AIDS test is required for work or residence permits; testing must be performed after arrival. A U.S. AIDS test is not accepted. For further information, travelers can contact the Embassy of the United Arab Emirates, Suite 700, 1255 22nd Street, N.W., Washington, D.C. 20037, telephone (202) 955-7999.

DUAL NATIONALITY: The UAE Government does not recognize dual nationality. Children of UAE fathers automatically acquire UAE citizenship at birth and must enter the UAE on UAE passports. UAE authorities have in the past confiscated U.S. passports of dual (UAE/U.S.) nationals. This does not constitute loss of U.S. citizenship, but should be reported to the U.S. Embassy in Abu Dhabi or the U.S. Consulate General in Dubai. Dual nationals may be subject to UAE laws that impose special obligations. For additional information, please see the Bureau of Consular Affairs home page on the Internet at http://travel.state.gov for our flyer on dual nationality.

SAFETY/SECURITY: Taking photographs of anything that could be perceived as being of military or security interest may result in problems with authorities.

CRIME INFORMATION: Crime is generally not a problem for travelers in the UAE. The loss or theft of a U.S. passport should be reported immediately to local police and the nearest U.S. embassy or consulate. Useful information on safeguarding valuables, protecting personal security, and other matters while traveling abroad is provided in the Department of State pamphlets, *A Safe Trip Abroad* and *Tips for Travelers to the Middle East and North Africa*. They are available from the Superintendent of Documents, U.S. Government Printing Office, Washington, D.C. 20402, via the Internet at http://www.access.gpo.gov/su_docs, or via the Consular Affairs home page at http://travel.state.gov.

MEDICAL FACILITIES: Basic modern medical care and medicines are available in the principal cities of the UAE, but not necessarily in outlying areas. Serious medical problems requiring hospitalization and/or medical evacuation to the United States can cost thousands of dollars or more. Doctors and hospitals often expect immediate cash payment for health services, and U.S. medical insurance is not always valid outside the United States. U.S. Medicare and Medicaid programs do not provide payment for medical services outside the United States.

MEDICAL INSURANCE: Uninsured travelers who require medical care overseas may face extreme difficulties. Please check with your own insurance company to confirm whether your policy applies overseas, including provision for medical evacuation. Please ascertain whether payment will be made to the overseas hospital or doctor or whether you will be reimbursed later for expenses that you incur. Some insurance policies also include coverage for psychiatric treatment and for disposition of remains in the event of death. Useful information on medical emergencies abroad, including overseas insurance programs, is provided in the Department of

For additional analytical, marketing, investment and business opportunities information, please contact
Global Investment & Business Center, USA
(202) 546-2103. Fax: (202) 546-3275. E-mail: rusric@erols.com

State's Bureau of Consular Affairs brochure, *Medical Information for Americans Traveling Abroad*, available via the Bureau of Consular Affairs home page or autofax: (202) 647-3000.

OTHER HEALTH INFORMATION: Information on vaccinations and other health precautions may be obtained from the Centers for Disease Control and Prevention's hotline for international travelers at telephone 1-877-FYI-TRIP (1-877-394-8747); fax 1-888-CDC-FAXX (1-888-232-3299) or via the CDC's Internet home page at http://www.cdc.gov.

TRAFFIC SAFETY AND ROAD CONDITIONS: While in a foreign country, U.S. citizens may encounter road conditions that differ significantly from those in the United States. The information below concerning the UAE is provided for general reference only and may not be totally accurate in a particular location or circumstance.

Safety of Public Transportation: Good
Urban Road Conditions/Maintenance: Excellent
Rural Road Conditions/Maintenance: Good
Availability of Roadside Assistance: Good

Passers-by are in general very willing to assist in road accidents, but they can be very unprofessional in medical emergencies requiring first-aid treatment. Mobile phones are widely used throughout the UAE, so passers-by usually request emergency police and medical services quickly. Response time by emergency services is adequate. However, medical personnel emphasize transport of the injured to the hospital rather than treatment on site. Traffic accidents are a leading cause of death in the UAE. Unsafe driving practices are common, especially on inter-city highways. On highways, wandering camels, unmarked speed bumps and drifting sand create additional hazards.

Country-wide traffic laws impose stringent penalties for certain violations, particularly driving under the influence of alcohol. Penalties may include hefty jail sentences and fines, and, for Muslims, lashings. Persons involved in an accident in which another party is injured automatically go to jail until the injured person is released from the hospital. Should a person die in a traffic accident, the driver of the other car is liable for payment of compensation for the death (known as "dhiyya"), usually the equivalent of $41,000 (US). Even relatively minor accidents may result in lengthy proceedings, during which both drivers may be prohibited from leaving the country.

In order to drive, UAE residents must obtain a UAE driver's license. Foreign driver's licenses are not recognized, and temporary UAE licenses are no longer issued. However, a non-resident visitor to the UAE can drive if he/she obtains a valid international driver's license issued by the motor vehicle authority of the country whose passport the traveler holds. The UAE recognizes driver's licenses issued by other Gulf Cooperative Council (GCC) states only if the bearer is driving a vehicle registered to the same GCC state. Under no circumstances should anyone drive without a valid license. Non-GCC citizens departing the UAE via land are required to pay a departure fee of UAE dirhams 20 (equivalent to $5.45 US). This fee is payable only in the local UAE dirham currency.

AVIATION SAFETY OVERSIGHT: As there is no direct commercial air service by local carriers between the United States and the UAE, the U.S. Federal Aviation Administration (FAA) has not assessed the UAE's Civil Aviation Authority for compliance with international aviation safety standards for oversight of the UAE's air carrier operations. For further information, travelers may contact the Department of Transportation within the U.S. at tel. 1-800-322-7873, or visit the FAA Internet web site at http://www.faa.gov/avr/iasa/.

For additional analytical, marketing, investment and business opportunities information, please contact
Global Investment & Business Center, USA
(202) 546-2103. Fax: (202) 546-3275. E-mail: rusric@erols.com

The U.S. Department of Defense (DOD) separately assesses some foreign air carriers for suitability as official providers of air services. As a result of the August 23, 2000 crash of a Gulf Air flight in the Persian Gulf, DOD has recommended that military commands use air carriers other than Gulf Air for DOD official travel, at least until investigation of the crash is complete. For information regarding the DOD policy on specific carriers, travelers may contact the DOD at tel. (618) 229-4801.

CUSTOMS REGULATIONS: UAE customs authorities enforce strict regulations concerning temporary importation into or export from UAE of items such as firearms, including fireworks, pornographic materials, medications, religious materials and communication equipment. It is advisable to contact the Embassy of UAE in Washington for specific information regarding customs requirements. UAE customs authorities also impose additional requirements for the importation of pets into the country. Prior permission in the form of a permit from the UAE Ministry of Agriculture and Fisheries must be secured before the pet's travel. To obtain the permit, the following items will need to be submitted to the UAE Ministry of Agriculture and Fisheries at the following address: P.O. Box 213, Abu Dhabi, UAE, telephone 971-2-662-781 or 971-2-485-438. A) The pet's travel itinerary; B) Copies of veterinary health certificates, showing that the animal is free of disease and indicating all shots which have been given to the pet; C) The sex and color of the pet; and D) A completed import permit application form (available from the Ministry).

CRIMINAL PENALTIES: While in a foreign country, U.S. citizens are subject to that country's laws and regulations, which sometimes differ significantly from those in the United States and may not afford the protections available to the individual under U.S. law. Penalties for breaking the law can be more severe than in the United States for similar offenses. Persons violating the UAE laws, even unknowingly, may be expelled, arrested, or imprisoned. The penalties for possession, use, or trafficking in illegal substances are strict in the UAE, and convicted offenders can expect jail sentences and heavy fines. Legislation enacted in January 1996 imposes the death sentence for convicted drug traffickers. A variety of drugs normally taken under a doctor's supervision in the United States are classified as narcotics in the UAE. A doctor's prescription should be carried along with any medication that is brought into the country.

In addition, the UAE's tough anti-narcotics program also includes poppy seeds, widely used in other cultures, including the U.S., for culinary purposes, on its list of controlled substances. The importation and possession of poppy seeds in any and all forms is strictly prohibited. Persons found to possess even very small quantities of the controlled substances listed by the UAE are subject to prosecution by the authorities and may be given lengthy prison terms of up to 15 years. Travelers with questions regarding the items on the list of controlled substances should contact the U.S. Embassy in Abu Dhabi or the U.S. Consulate General in Dubai.

If suspected of being under the influence of drugs, individuals may be required to submit to blood and/or urine tests so that local authorities may make a determination as to usage. UAE authorities have been known to arrest travelers upon their arrival into the UAE and, based on recent prior drug use, to prosecute these travelers.

Crimes of fraud, including passing bad checks and non-payment of bills (including hotel bills), are regarded seriously in the UAE and can result in imprisonment, as well as fines. Penalties are generally assessed according to religious law. If imprisoned, bail is generally not available to non-residents of the UAE.

Drinking or possession of alcohol without a Ministry of Interior liquor permit is illegal and could result in arrest and/or fines and imprisonment. Alcohol is served at bars in most major hotels. However, this alcoholic beverage service is for those persons who are staying at the hotel.

For additional analytical, marketing, investment and business opportunities information, please contact
Global Investment & Business Center, USA
(202) 546-2103. Fax: (202) 546-3275. E-mail: rusric@erols.com

Persons not staying at the hotel who come in to use the facility's bar technically are required to have their own personal liquor license. Liquor licenses are obtainable only by non-Muslim persons who possess UAE residency permits. Drinking and driving is considered a serious offense.

SPECIAL CIRCUMSTANCES: American citizens may become involved in disputes of a commercial nature involving the withholding of the American citizen's passport by the local firm or courts. Travel bans may also be enforced on American citizens involved in financial disputes with a local sponsor or firm. These bans, which are rigidly enforced, prevent the individual from leaving the UAE for any reason until the matter is resolved. Although it is customary for a local sponsor to hold an employee's passport, it is not required under UAE law. Most contractual/labor disputes can be avoided by clearly establishing all terms and conditions of employment or sponsorship in the labor contract at the beginning of any employment. Should a dispute still arise, the UAE Ministry of Labor has established a special department to review and arbitrate labor claims. A list of local attorneys capable of representing Americans in such matters is available from the Consular and Commercial sections of the U.S. Embassy in Abu Dhabi and the U.S. Consulate General in Dubai.

Travelers intending to reside and work in the UAE should have their academic and occupational certificates duly authenticated by the Department of State's Office of Authentication in Washington, D.C. before traveling to the UAE. UAE labor law requires local sponsors to produce employees' academic and/or professional certificates duly authenticated by the Foreign Ministry of the individual's country before a work permit can be issued. Travelers intending to bring their families to reside with them in the UAE will also need to have their marriage certificates, and children's birth certificates duly authenticated by the State Department in Washington, D.C.

CHILDREN'S ISSUES: Children of UAE fathers automatically acquire UAE citizenship at birth and must enter the UAE on UAE passports. Child custody decisions are based on Islamic law. It is difficult for an American woman, even a Muslim, to obtain custody of her dual national (UAE/U.S.) children through the UAE courts. Custody cases are complex and involve the court's consideration of parents' religion, place of permanent residence, income, and the mother's subsequent marital status. Children involved in custody disputes in local courts are generally subject to travel bans regardless of their nationality. For information on international adoption of children, international parental child abduction, and international child support enforcement issues, please refer to our Internet site at http://travel.state.gov/children's_issues.html or telephone (202) 736-7000.

REGISTRATION / EMBASSY AND CONSULATE LOCATION: Americans living in or visiting the UAE are encouraged to register with the Consular Section of the U.S. Embassy in Abu Dhabi or the Consulate General in Dubai where they can obtain updated information on travel and security within the UAE. The U.S. Embassy in Abu Dhabi is located on 11th St., also known as Al-Sudan St., P.O. Box 4009. The telephone number is (971) (2) 443-6691 and the Consular Section fax number is (971) (2) 443-5786. The after hours telephone is (971) (2) 443-4457. The Embassy Internet web site is http://www.usembabu.gov.ae. The U.S. Consulate General in Dubai is located on the 21st floor of the Dubai World Trade Center, P.O. Box 9343. The telephone number is (971) (4) 331-3115 and the Consular Section fax number is (971) (4) 331-6935. The workweek for both the Embassy in Abu Dhabi and Consulate in Dubai is Saturday through Wednesday.

IMPORTANT INFORMATION

Population: With a 1998 estimate of 2.8 million, the population of the United Arab Emirates has been growing about 3.0% annually. Major ethnic groups include Arab, Pakistani, Indian, Iranian,

For additional analytical, marketing, investment and business opportunities
information, please contact
Global Investment & Business Center, USA
(202) 546-2103. Fax: (202) 546-3275. E-mail: rusric@erols.com

Afghan, Bangladeshi and Filipino, while exact data is not available. Less than 20 percent of the population are believed
to be nationals of the United Arab Emirates.

Religion (s): The official religion is Islam, 90 percent of the total population (including expatriates) are Muslims. The authorities permit worship of other religions. There are Christian churches and Hindu temples in Abu Dhabi, Dubai and Sharjah.

Government Systems: The government is a federation of the seven Emirates headed by a president and a vice president (since its respectively). The rules of each of the Emirates belong to the supreme council, which is the U.A.E.'s highest legal authority and promulgates federal laws. The Federal National Council,
consisting of 40 nationals appointed by the rules, acts as an advisory legislative body. The Council of Ministers, appointed by the supreme council, manages the day to day affairs of the federation.

Each Emirates has its own local government involved with
municipal affairs, and in some cases major public utilities like power and water.

Language (s): The official language is Arabic, but English is widely used in business. Hindi, Urdu, and Farsi (Persian) are
also spoken.

Work Week: The regular work week is from Saturday to midday Thursday. Most private business offices are also open on Thursday afternoon. Working hours vary. Government offices and banks close for the day at 1:00 pm, but commercial outlets re-open in the afternoon from about 4:30 pm - 8:00pm.
Note: The oil sector in Abu Dhabi works 07:00 a.m. - 15:00 p.m.,
Saturday through Wednesday. The oil sector in Dubai works 8:00
a.m. - 5:00 p.m., Sunday through Thursday. Many other Dubai
companies are trending this way.

Drugs and Crime Penalties: Travelers are subject to the laws and legal practices of the country in which they travel. Penalties for possession, illegal substances are strict in the United Arab Emirates. A variety of drugs normally taken under a doctor's supervision in the United States are classified as narcotics in
the U.A.E.. Doctor's prescriptions should be carried along with any medication that is brought into the country.

U.A.E. authorities have been known to arrest travelers upon their arrival here and based on recent prior drug use, to prosecute these travelers.

Crimes of fraud, including passing bad checks and non-payment of bills (including hotel bills), are regarded seriously in the U.A.E. and can result in imprisonment, as well as fines. Penalties are generally assessed according to religious law. If imprisoned, bail is generally not available to non-residents of
the U.A.E..

Drinking alcohol without a ministry of interior liquor permit is illegal and could result in arrest or fines and imprisonment. Alcohol is served at bars in most major hotels. However, this alcoholic beverage services is for those persons who are residing at the hotel. Persons not residing at the hotel who come in to

For additional analytical, marketing, investment and business opportunities information, please contact
Global Investment & Business Center, USA
(202) 546-2103. Fax: (202) 546-3275. E-mail: rusric@erols.com

use the facility's bar technically are required to have their own personal liquor license. Liquor licenses are obtainable only by persons who possess U.A.E. residency permits. Drinking and driving is considered a serious offense.

Driver's license: In order to drive, U.A.E. residents must obtain a U.A.E. driver's license. Foreign driver's licenses are not recognized and temporary U.A.E. licenses are no longer issued. However, a non-resident visitor to the U.A.E. can drive if he/she obtains a valid international driver's license issued by the
motor vehicle authorities of the country whose passport the travelers holds. Under no circumstances should anyone drive without a valid license.

Visas are required by all visitors to the UAE, except GCC nationals and UK citizens. Visas may be obtained from the Department of Naturalization and Residence through hotels. Passports must be valid for at least six months from the time of application.

Many people think that because the United Arab Emirates looks very modern and familiar, they should dress as they would in any other hot climate or Western resort destination.

But the United Arab Emirates is an Islamic country and, as a visitor, please respect that different codes of dress and behavior apply.

Muslim men and women are generally conservative in their dress and behavior and find it offensive to see too much exposed flesh - which is against their moral beliefs, daily habits and traditional dress codes going back to the beginning of history.

While foreigners are not expected to be fully covered - there are a few simple rules that we would like to ask you to observe in order to get the best out of your visit:

1. Do not wear beach clothes, sleeveless or low cut tops and shorts in public - only at the beach or private clubs.
2. Embracing in public is not acceptable behavior.
3. Women should not first offer their hand for a handshake, but if offered, should shake hands gently.
4. Never take photographs of local citizens, especially women, without asking permission.
5. During the Holy Month of Ramadan, absolutely no eating, drinking or smoking are allowed in public during daylight hours. Meals will be served in the hotel areas or your hotel room.

Following these simple rules will make you an even more welcome guest in one of the world's safest, most secure and friendly vacation destinations.

VISAS

Citizens of the Arab Gulf Cooperation Council (GCC) countries and British nationals, with the right of abode in the UK, do not need visas to enter the UAE.
Britons can stay for one month, renewable for a further two months. Generally, all other visitors must obtain a visa from a sponsor, which can be a company, individual or hotel.

For additional analytical, marketing, investment and business opportunities
information, please contact
Global Investment & Business Center, USA
(202) 546-2103. Fax: (202) 546-3275. E-mail: rusric@erols.com

For an individual to sponsor a visit visa, you must earn over Dhs 3,000 per month and hold a valid residence visa.

US and German citizens can obtain tourist or business visas through any UAE embassy. It can however, be quicker if you apply in your home country.
A business visitor may enter the UAE on either a transit or visit visa. Visa holders may enter and exit the UAE through any port of entry. Airlines may require evidence that the incoming visitor has a sponsor who holds a valid visa.
Transit and visit visas must be deposited at the airport immigration one hour before the arrival of a flight.

Visit Visa

A visit visa is valid for 60 days, renewable once up to a total of 90 days. To obtain a visa from a UAE embassy you require the following:

- Passport with at least 6 months validity remaining
- 2 photographs
- Duplicate application form
- Letter or fax from the sponsor in the UAE to the embassy concerned
- A letter from the applicant's company plus photocopy

All nationalities resident in GCC countries, holding a valid resident visa and of a managerial status, can obtain a 30 day visit visa on arrival in the UAE.
You can expect it to take one week to 10 days for a visit visa to be issued. An express service exists.

Department for Naturalization and Residence - Sharjah
PO Box 858
King Abdul Aziz Road/Al Istiqlal Road,
Al Qassimia, Sharjah
Tel: +971 (6) 5726777
Fax: +971 (6) 5723572
Open: 7:30 am - 2:30 noon (Saturday through Wednesday. Thursday and Friday holidays)

Transit Visa

These are issued for 15 days only and cannot be extended or renewed. You must have a UAE company who sponsors your visit. Larger hotels can sponsor transit visas for tourists and business visits.

Residence Visa

Formalities are normally handled by the company of employment. Dependents (spouse and family) are sponsored usually by the husband, once he has his company sponsorship. A medical, including blood test and chest x-ray, is required for adults before the visa process starts. These are taken at the Public Health Clinic in Nasseriya. Anyone who works in the Emirates must have a valid labor card issued by their employer. It is usual for the employer to hold an employee's passport or labor card. On leaving the Emirates permanently, your residence visa should be canceled and proof of this in writing, is given to the sponsor.

For additional analytical, marketing, investment and business opportunities information, please contact
Global Investment & Business Center, USA
(202) 546-2103. Fax: (202) 546-3275. E-mail: rusric@erols.com

MONEY

The history and development of the currency from the Maria Teresa Dollar in the 18th century , to the Dirham of today, can be explored in the Trade Room of Al Hisn Fort in Sharjah City. Today's currency took over from the rupee when the UAE was formed in 1971.

The UAE Dirham is divided into 100 fils. Coins include Dhs.1, 50 fils, 25 fils, 10 fils and 5 fils. The latter two are rarely used. Notes are of Dhs. 5, 10, 20, 50, 100, 200, 500 and 1000 denominations.

Currency Exchange

The Dirham is freely convertible, making exchange of travelers checks and currency easy. The local currency is index linked to the US Dollar.

1 US Dollar = Dirhams 3.68 (buying and selling)

Costs

The UAE is not a low budget country and the cost of living for an expatriate could be on par with New York, depending on life style. Having said that, you can find a meal for less than Dhs 10. Getting around is also cheap, either by purchasing or renting a car or by taxi.

Banks

Both locally incorporated and International banks are represented in Sharjah. A number of banks are located in Al Boorj Avenue (also called Bank Street). As Sharjah has expanded, some banks have moved to other areas, mainly King Faisal Street, Khalid Lagoon and Old Airport Road.

Banking Hours

Banks are open to public from Saturday to Wednesday between 8 am and 1 pm and from 8 am to 12 noon on Thursday. Mashreq and Standard Chartered banks are also open from 4.30 pm to 6.30 pm. Banks are closed on Fridays and public holidays.

Lost Credit Cards

AMERICAN EXPRESS	800 0004
BRITISH BANK	800 6111
CITIBANK	800 4000
EMIRATES BANK INTERNATIONAL	800 4080
MASHREQ BANK	800 4010
STANDARD CHARTERED	800 4884
VISA	800 4420

Money Changers

The best rate of exchange is usually found in the privately owned bureaux de change. These are open later than the banks which can be very convenient. Working hours are generally 8.30 am to 1 pm and 4.30 pm to 8.30 pm on weekdays (Saturday to Thursday). Most are open on Friday afternoons. The UAE Exchange Center on Al Arouba Street is open on Friday mornings from 8.30 am to 11 am. Closed on public holidays.

In addition to the banks and hotels, money changers are common (Blue Souk, Al Arouba Street and Rolla Square) and it is worth shopping around for the best cash deal. You will find most currencies available. Some accept certain travelers checks, but not all. It is also advisable to check the bank rates before making any transactions with the money changers. The business section of the daily newspapers displays the closing Dirham and dollar exchange rates.

Thomas Cook Al Rostamani	+971 (6) 5614656
UAE Exchange Center	+971 (6) 5547725
Wall Street Exchange Center	+971 (6) 5522831
Al Ansari Exchange EST	+971 (6) 5544113
Al Fardan Exchange	+971 (6) 5350371
Habib Exchange CO	+971 (6) 5351885
Western Union Money Transfer Box	+971 (6) 5614028

DRIVING

A vehicle is a necessity as cities tend to be spread out with residential areas set away from schools and shops. Apart from taxis there is no public transport system. Driving is on the right hand side of the road. It can be erratic at times. Try to avoid the rush to Dubai in the mornings, from 7 am - 8.30 am and back, between 6 pm - 8 PM Look out for camels, particularly on highways at night.

Third party insurance is compulsory. The penalty for drinking and driving is severe.

Ladies should always use the Ladies Section at the police station, which tends to speed up the procedure and affords you comfort and privacy. All payments for licenses, fines etc. must be made in cash.

Whenever you drive, you must carry your license and registration document. GCC nationals may drive on their respective licenses within the UAE. Other nationalities see below. Forms must be completed in Arabic. There are typist shops located within the compound walls of the various traffic departments. Typing costs are around Dhs 5 - 10 per form.

Licenses (full and temporary) are issued at the Traffic Police Headquarters (Murrur) in Abu Tina, (Tel : +971 (6) 5541111). You can only obtain a full driving license, valid for 5 years, if you have a valid Sharjah residence visa. If you are a visitor on a visit visa you can obtain a temporary driving license provided you hold a valid license from a recognized country (see below). This is valid for one month and is renewable for a further two months.

For additional analytical, marketing, investment and business opportunities information, please contact
Global Investment & Business Center, USA
(202) 546-2103. Fax: (202) 546-3275. E-mail: rusric@erols.com

It is not necessary to take a driving test to obtain a license if you hold a valid license from one of the following countries:
EC, USA, Japan, Korea, Ireland, Turkey, Iran, Norway or Czech Republic.

Documents for a full licence

1. A no objection letter from your sponsor in Arabic.
2. A photocopy of your passport including the visa page.
3. A photocopy of your sponsor's passport.
4. 2 photographs.
Eye and blood tests, necessary for the license, are carried out at the Police Station. Cost: Dhs 140 plus Dhs 50 for the blood test.

Documents for a temporary licence

Available for visitors from the countries mentioned above only. Other nationalities - refer to International Driving Permits below.
1. A no objection letter from your sponsor in Arabic.
2. Your passport.
3. A photocopy of the visa page.
4. Two photographs
Cost: Dhs 30 per month.

Procedure

Take all the necessary documents and cash to the Traffic Police.
International Driving Permit.
Valid for one year and issued by the Automobile & Touring Club for the United Arab Emirates (Tel : +971 (6) 5523183). The office is located in Al Arouba Street, 1st floor of the Bank of Cairo Building.
You need 2 photographs and a copy of your driving license plus Dhs 100. The whole procedure takes 5 minutes. Visitors other than European, Scandinavian, American, Canadian and Japanese can drive a rented vehicle, provided they hold an International Driving License, issued by their home country. Residents must hold a valid UAE license to rent a vehicle.

Car Registration

For registration of a new vehicle go to the Traffic Police Headquarters in Abu Tina. For a renewal, go to the Traffic Department in Wasit. You must hold a valid residence visa for Sharjah and a valid UAE driving License. Every vehicle must have a fire extinguisher with a validity paper. After registration, you receive a laminated document which must be kept in the vehicle at all times.

Documents for a new vehicle

1. Letter in Arabic from the dealer to traffic department with all of the car particulars and the name of the buyer.
2. Car registration application form, available at the traffic police, to be typed in Arabic.
3. Passport copy.
4. Driving License copy.
5. One photograph.

For additional analytical, marketing, investment and business opportunities information, please contact
Global Investment & Business Center, USA
(202) 546-2103. Fax: (202) 546-3275. E-mail: rusric@erols.com

6. Insurance valid for one year.
7. No objection letter from your sponsor.

Procedure for a new vehicle

Take the application form and documents to the registration counter in the main building. Fee is to be paid to the cashier. Back to the Counter where you are given a slip to obtain the number plates. Collect number plates from another building in the main compound. Return in half an hour to collect the laminated registration book from the main building.

Cost : Variable, depending on the model and make of vehicle.

Car Registration Renewal

Registration renewal to be done at the Traffic Department by Wasit Roundabout Any police tickets (speeding and other traffic violations) have to be paid before the renewal process starts. The police will advise you there and then.

Documents for renewal

1. Car Insurance certificate valid for a full year.
2. Copy of passport.
3. Registration document.
As you proceed you will collect the following documents:
1. Renewal form typed in Arabic
2. Inspection certificate.
3. Renewal of fire extinguisher, valid for a full year.

Procedure

The car is first inspected at the testing center. Any faults must be rectified before proceeding. All documents are taken to the counter. The fee is paid and the registration issued for one year.

Cost : Up to Dhs 305 plus traffic fines! The cost is related to the size of the vehicle.

Ownership transferral and sale of vehicle

Traffic Police Headquarters, Abu Tina.

Documents

1. Application form completed in Arabic to be signed by the person selling the car.
2. Insurance paper.
3. Driving License or ID.
4. Number plates.
5. Registration Document.
6. Inspection certificate (not necessary if the transfer is within the UAE).
7. 'Malkiya'- ownership document.

Procedure

For additional analytical, marketing, investment and business opportunities
information, please contact
Global Investment & Business Center, USA
(202) 546-2103. Fax: (202) 546-3275. E-mail: rusric@erols.com

Forms and documents to the transfer counter. Fee paid to cashier. If buying, the procedure is as per a new registration.

Driving test

Traffic Department, Wasit Roundabout. You need to open a file here with :
1. A no objection letter from your sponsor.
2. A copy of your passport (and take along the original).
3. Blood group and eye test certificates.
A date for the test is given and a paper which must be taken to Nasseriya Driving School. Here you pay a fee of Dhs 250 to attend lectures in English or Arabic. An oral test is given, and once you pass, you then apply for driving lessons. These can be taken through the private schools or the Government's Driving Institute. Once completed you wait for your test date.

Speed Limits

The speed limit in and around built up areas is 60 kph. On highways, cars may drive up to 100 kph, heavy vehicles up to 80 kph. Many areas are controlled by stationary and mobile radar. The fine in Sharjah Emirate is Dhs 200 each time you are caught speeding.

Accidents and breakdowns

In the event of either of the above you can contact the Anjad (The Special Branch of the Traffic Police) on +971 (6) 5512222. The Anjad patrol the streets to assist the public in all traffic related and security matters. Do not move any vehicles involved in an accident until a report has been made and permission is given by the police. All accidents, no matter how small, must be reported to the police. No repairs can be made without a police report. It is customary to obtain two quotations for repairs. If your car has broken down and obstructs the free flow of the traffic, do your best to move the vehicle to the side of the road, out of the way.

CUSTOMS REGULATIONS

The twin ports of Khorfakkan (on the east coast of the UAE); and Port Khalid (the main Sharjah seaport, on the Arabian Gulf) are controlled by common customs laws and management. Goods can be cleared from either port after documentation has been filed and completed from the main Customs Office in Port Khalid.

Airlines using Sharjah International Airport as their hub get special services from the Customs Department. A separate customs office can be made available for these airlines. Thus regular importers with the airline can benefit from the newly introduced accounts system for Customs duty payments. Attractive facilities are granted to L.C.L. operators and users by transporting goods to their warehouse FREE OF CHARGE. The Commercial section of the Sharjah Customs Department deals with the problems of consignees and meets with consignees regularly to develop a strong consignee Customs Department relationship.

HOLIDAYS

Holidays for	Actual Dates of Holidays	Day
New Year's Day(observed)	December 31, 2015	Thursday
Birthday of Martin Luther King, Jr.	January 17, 2016	Sunday

For additional analytical, marketing, investment and business opportunities information, please contact
Global Investment & Business Center, USA
(202) 546-2103. Fax: (202) 546-3275. E-mail: rusric@erols.com

Washington's Birthday**	February 14, 2016	Sunday
The Prophet's Ascension Day*	May 5, 2016	Thursday
Memorial Day	May 29, 2016	Sunday
Independence Day (observed)	July 4, 2016	Sunday
Eid Al Fitr*	July 7-9, 2016	Thurs-Sat
Labor Day	September 4, 2016	Sunday
Arafat(Haj) Day*	September 12, 2016	Monday
Eid Al Adha*	Sept. 13-15, 2016	Tue-Thurs
Columbus Day	October 9, 2016	Sunday
Veterans Day	November 10, 2016	Thursday
Thanksgiving Day	November 24, 2016	Thursday
Martyr's Day	November 30, 2016	Wednesday
National Day	December 2, 2016	Friday
The Prophet's Birthday	December 12, 2016	Monday
Christmas Day	December 25, 2016	Sunday

* Denotes UAE religious holidays. Dates for religious holidays are dependent upon the sighting of the moon and are likely to vary from the above estimated dates. Please note that only the U.S. Embassy and Consulate are closed in the U.A.E. for the U.S. holidays.

For additional analytical, marketing, investment and business opportunities information, please contact
Global Investment & Business Center, USA
(202) 546-2103. Fax: (202) 546-3275. E-mail: rusric@erols.com

SUPPLEMENTS

NEW LIST OF EXEMPTED COMMODITIES UNDER UNIFIED G.C.C.

Tariff as per1 st of January2003

Rates of Duty	Commodity Description	H.S. Code	Heading
	Pure-bred breeding animals :		
Duty Free	Arabic origin horses.	10 01 01 10	
Duty Free	Other	10 01 01 20	
	Other :		
Duty Free	Sport horses	90 01 01 10	
Duty Free	Pony	20 90 01 01	
Duty Free	Asses	30 90 01 01	
Duty Free	Mules	40 90 01 01	
Duty Free	Hinnies	50 90 01 01	
Duty Free	Other	90 90 01 01	
Duty Free	Pure-bred breeding animals	02 01 00 10	
Duty Free	Other	02 01 00 90	
	Live sheep and goats	00 00 04 01	01.04
	Sheep :		
Duty Free	Pure – bred breeding animals	01 10 04 10	
Duty Free	Other	90 0410 01	
	Goats :		
Duty Free	Pure – bred breeding animals	10 0420 01	
Duty Free	Other	90 0420 01	
	Weighing not more than 185 g :		
Duty Free	Fowls of the species Gallus domesticus	11 05 01 00	
Duty Free	Turkeys	05 01 12 00	
Duty Free	Other	01 19 05 00	
	Other :		
	Fowls of species Gallus domesticus weighing not more than 2000 g :		
Duty Free	Chickens for laying eggs	05 01 9210	

For additional analytical, marketing, investment and business opportunities information, please contact
Global Investment & Business Center, USA
(202) 546-2103. Fax: (202) 546-3275. E-mail: rusric@erols.com

Duty Free	Chickens for meat	05 01 9220	
Duty Free	Chickens mothers	05 01 9230	
Duty Free	Other	05 01 9290	
	Fowls of species Gallus domesticus weighing more than 2000 g :		
Duty Free	Chickens for laying eggs	05 01 9310	
Duty Free	Chickens for meat	05 01 9320	
Duty Free	Chickens mothers	05 01 9330	
Duty Free	Other	05 01 90 93	
	Other :		
Duty Free	Ducks, geese	05 01 9910	
Duty Free	Turkeys	05 01 9920	
Duty Free	Other	05 01 9990	
	Other live animals.		01.06
	Mammals :		
Duty Free	Primates	11 06 01 00	
Duty Free	Whales, dolphins and porpoises (mammals of the order Cetacea); manatees and dugongs (mammals of the order Sirenia)	12 06 01 00	
Duty Free	Camel	10 19 06 01	
Duty Free	Live rabbits & hares.	20 19 06 01	
Duty Free	Dears & Chamois	30 19 06 01	
Duty Free	Dogs	40 19 06 01	
Duty Free	Live foxes, minks & other fur animals.	50 19 06 01	
Duty Free	Live animals for zoos, scientific & research labs.	60 19 06 01	
Duty Free	Other	90 19 06 01	
Duty Free	Reptiles (including snakes and turtles)	20 06 01 00	
	Birds :		
Duty Free	Birds of prey	31 06 01 00	
Duty Free	Psittaciformes (including parrots, parakeets, macaws and cockatoos)	32 06 01 00	
Duty Free	Wild pigeons, partridges, pheasants, quail, woodcocks, snipe, ortolah, wild ducks.	10 39 06 01	
Duty Free	Ornamental birds	20 39 06 01	
	Other	90 39 06 01	

For additional analytical, marketing, investment and business opportunities information, please contact
Global Investment & Business Center, USA
(202) 546-2103. Fax: (202) 546-3275. E-mail: rusric@erols.com

Duty Free	Other :		
Duty Free	Live bees (whether or not in traveling boxes or hives) & other insects.	90 06 01 10	
Duty Free	Other	90 06 01 90	
Duty Free	Carcasses and half carcasses	00 10 02 01	
Duty Free	Other cuts with bone in	00 20 02 01	
Duty Free	Boneless	00 30 02 01	
Duty Free	Carcasses and half-carcasses of lamp, fresh or chilled	04 02 00 10	
	Other meat of sheep, fresh or chilled :		
Duty Free	Carcasses and half -carcasses	04 02 00 21	
Duty Free	Other cuts with bone in	04 02 00 22	
Duty Free	Boneless	00 23 04 02	
Duty Free	Fresh or chilled	04 02 11 50	
Duty Free	Fresh or chilled	50 04 02 21	
	Boneless		
Duty Free	Fresh or chilled	50 04 02 31	
Duty Free	Edible offal of sheep & goats, fresh or chilled	80 06 02 10	
Duty Free	Meat of rabbits or hares fresh or chilled	10 08 02 10	02.08
	Live fish		03.01
Duty Free	Ornamental fish	01 03 00 10	
	Other live fish :		
	trout (Salmo trutta, Oncorhynchus mykiss, Oncorhynchus clarki, Oncorhynchus aguabonita, Oncorhynchus gilae, Oncorhynchus apache & Oncorhynchus chrysogaster		
Duty Free	Breeding	01 03 10 91	
Duty Free	Other	01 03 90 91	
	Eels (Anguilla spp.) :		
Duty Free	Breeding	01 03 10 92	
Duty Free	Other	01 03 90 92	
	Carp :		
Duty Free	Breeding	01 03 10 93	
Duty Free	Other	01 03 90 93	
	Other :		
Duty Free	Breeding	01 03 10 99	
Duty Free	Tilapia nilotica	01 03 20 99	

For additional analytical, marketing, investment and business opportunities information, please contact
Global Investment & Business Center, USA
(202) 546-2103. Fax: (202) 546-3275. E-mail: rusric@erols.com

Duty Free	Other	01 03 90 99	
	Salmonidae, excluding livers and roes :		
Duty Free	Trout fish (Salmo trutta, Oncorhynchus mykiss, Oncorhynchus clarki, Oncorhynchus aguabonita, Oncorhynchus gilae, Oncorhynchus apache & Oncorhynchus chrysogaster)	02 03 00 11	
Duty Free	Pacific salmon fish (Oncorhynchus nerka, Oncorhynchus gorbuscha, Oncorhynchus keta, Oncorhynchus tschawytscha, Oncorhynchus kisutch, Oncorhynchus masou & Oncorhynchus rhodurus), Atlanic salmon (Salmon salar) & Danube salmon (Hucho hucho)	02 03 00 12	
Duty Free	Other	02 03 00 19	
	Flat fish (Pleuronectidae, Bothidae, Cynoglossidae, Soleidae, Scophthalmidae and Citharidae), excluding livers and roes :		
Duty Free	Halibut (Reinhardtius hippoglossoides, Hippoglossus hippoglossus,Hippoglossus stenolepis)	02 03 00 21	
Duty Free	Plaice (Pleuronectes platessa)	02 03 00 22	
Duty Free	Sole (Solea spp.)	02 03 00 23	
Duty Free	Other	02 03 00 29	
	Tunas (of the genus Thunnus) skipjack or stripebellied bonito (Euthynnus (Katsuwonus) pelamis), excluding livers and roes :		
Duty Free	Albacore or longfinned tunas (Thunnus alalunga)	02 03 00 31	
Duty Free	Yellowfin tunas (Thunnus albacares)	02 03 00 32	
Duty Free	Skipjack or stripebellied bonito	02 03 00 33	
Duty Free	Bigeye tunas (Thunnus obesus)	02 03 00 34	
Duty Free	Bluefin tunas (Thunnus thynnus)	02 03 00 35	
Duty Free	Southern bluefin tunas (Thunnus maccoyii)	02 03 00 36	
Duty Free	Other	02 03 00 39	
Duty Free	Herrings (Clupea harengus, Clupea pallasii), excluding livers and roes	02 03 00 40	
Duty Free	Cod (Gadus morhua, Gadus ogac, Gadus macrocephalus), excluding livers and roes.	02 03 00 50	
	Other fish, excluding livers and roes :		
Duty Free	Sardines (Sardina pilchardus, Sardinops spp.), sardinella (Sardinella spp.), brisling or sprats(Sprattus sprattus)	02 03 00 61	
Duty Free	Haddock (Melanogrammus aeglefinus)	02 03 00 62	
Duty Free	Coalfish (Pollachius virens)	02 03 00 63	

For additional analytical, marketing, investment and business opportunities information, please contact
Global Investment & Business Center, USA
(202) 546-2103. Fax: (202) 546-3275. E-mail: rusric@erols.com

	Mackerel (Scomber scombrus, Scomber australasicus, Scomber japonicus)		
Duty Free	Canad	02 03 10 64	
Duty Free	agah	02 03 20 64	
Duty Free	Other	02 03 90 64	
Duty Free	Dogfish & other sharks	02 03 00 65	
Duty Free	Eels (Anguilla spp.)	02 03 00 66	
	Other :		
Duty Free	Hamoor	02 03 10 69	
Duty Free	(sheirii)	02 03 20 69	
Duty Free	(Hamra)	02 03 30 69	
Duty Free	Hamam	02 03 40 69	
Duty Free	Zobedi	02 03 50 69	
Duty Free	Shoomeat (brime)	02 03 60 69	
Duty Free	Nagroor	02 03 70 69	
Duty Free	Bori, Meed, Meah	02 03 80 69	
	Other :		
Duty Free	Safi	02 03 91 69	
Duty Free	Other	02 03 99 69	
Duty Free	Livers & roes	02 03 00 70	
	Crustaceans, whether in shell or not, live, fresh, chilled, frozen, dried, salted or in brine; crustaceans, in shell, cooked by steaming or by boiling in water, whether or not chilled, frozen, dried, salted or in brine; flours, meals and pellets of crustaceans, fit for human consumption .		03.06
	Frozen :		
Duty Free	Rock lobster & other sea crawfish (Palinurus spp., Panulirus spp., Jasus spp.),	11 06 03 00	
Duty Free	Lobsters (Homarus spp.)	12 06 03 00	
Duty Free	Shrimps & prawns	13 06 03 00	
Duty Free	Crabs	14 06 03 00	
Duty Free	Other, including flours, meals & pellets of crustaceans, fit for human consumption.	19 06 03 00	
	Not frozen :		
Duty Free	Rock lobster & other sea crawfish (Palinurus spp., Panulirus	21 06 03 00	

For additional analytical, marketing, investment and business opportunities information, please contact
Global Investment & Business Center, USA
(202) 546-2103. Fax: (202) 546-3275. E-mail: rusric@erols.com

	spp., Jasus spp.)		
Duty Free	Lobsters (Homarus spp.)	22 06 03 00	
Duty Free	Shrimps & prawns	23 06 03 00	
Duty Free	Crabs	24 06 03 00	
Duty Free	Other, including flours, meals & pellets of crustaceans, fit for human consumption.	29 06 03 00	
Duty Free	hatching eggs	00 07 04 11	
Duty Free	Bulbs, tubers, tuberous roots, corms, crowns & rhizomes, dormant.	10 01 06 00	
Duty Free	Bulbs, tubers, tuberous roots, corms, crowns & rhizomes, in growth or in flower; chicory plants & roots	20 01 06 00	
	Unrooted cuttings and slips :		
Duty Free	Grapevines (Grapeslips)	10 02 06 10	
Duty Free	Other	10 02 06 90	
	Trees, shrubs or bushes grafted or nor kinds which bear edible fruits or nuts.		
Duty Free	Palm tree seedling	20 02 06 10	
Duty Free	Other	20 02 06 90	
Duty Free	Seed	01 07 00 10	
Duty Free	Other	01 07 00 90	
Duty Free	Tomatoes, fresh or chilled.	07 00 00 02	07.02
	Onions, shallots, garlic, leeks and other alliaceous vegetables, fresh or chilled		07.03
	Onions and shallots :		
	Onions :		
Duty Free	Onions for food (green or dry rind, fresh or chilled)	03 07 11 10	
Duty Free	Onions (for sowing)	03 07 12 10	
Duty Free	Shallots	03 07 20 10	
Duty Free	Garlic	03 07 00 20	
Duty Free	Leeks & other alliaceous vegetables	03 07 00 90	
	Cabbages, cauliflowers, kohlrabi, kale and similar edible brassicas, fresh or chilled.		07.04
Duty Free	Cauliflowers & headed broccoli	04 07 00 10	
Duty Free	Brussels sprouts	04 07 00 20	
Duty Free	Other	04 07 00 90	
	Lettuce (Lactuca sativa) and chicory (Cichorium spp.).		07.05

For additional analytical, marketing, investment and business opportunities information, please contact
Global Investment & Business Center, USA
(202) 546-2103. Fax: (202) 546-3275. E-mail: rusric@erols.com

	fresh or chilled.		
	lettuce :		
Duty Free	Cabbage lettuce (head lettuce)	05 07 00 11	
Duty Free	Other	05 07 00 19	
	Chicory :		
Duty Free	Witloof chicory (Cichorium intybus var.foliosum)	05 07 00 21	
Duty Free	Other	05 07 00 29	
	Carrots, turnips, salad beetroot, salsify, celeriac, radishes and similar edible roots, fresh or chilled.		07.06
Duty Free	Carrots & turnips	06 07 00 10	
Duty Free	Other	06 07 00 90	
Duty Free	Cucumbers and gherkins, fresh or chilled.	07 07 00 00	07.07
	Leguminous vegetables, shelled or unshelled, fresh or chilled.		07.08
Duty Free	Peas (Pisum sativum)	08 07 00 10	
Duty Free	Beans (Vigna spp., Phaseolus spp.)	08 07 00 20	
	Other leguminous vegetables :		
Duty Free	Beans	08 07 10 90	
Duty Free	Other	08 07 90 90	
	Other vegetables, fresh or chilled.		07.09
Duty Free	Globe artichokes	09 07 00 10	
Duty Free	Asparagus	09 07 00 20	
Duty Free	Aubergines (egg plants)	09 07 00 30	
Duty Free	Celery other than celeriac	09 07 00 40	
	Mushrooms and Truffles:		
Duty Free	Mushrooms of the genus Agaricus	09 07 00 51	
Duty Free	Truffles	09 07 00 52	
Duty Free	Other.	09 07 00 59	
Duty Free	Fruits of the genus Capsicum or of the genus Pimenta	09 07 00 60	
Duty Free	Spinach, New Zealand spinach & orache spinach (garden spinach)	09 07 00 70	
	Other :		
Duty Free	Pumpkins	09 07 10 90	
Duty Free	Marrow	09 07 20 90	
Duty Free	Olives	09 07 30 90	

For additional analytical, marketing, investment and business opportunities information, please contact
Global Investment & Business Center, USA
(202) 546-2103. Fax: (202) 546-3275. E-mail: rusric@erols.com

Duty Free	Okra	09 07 40 90	
Duty Free	Parsley	09 07 50 90	
Duty Free	Coriander	09 07 60 90	
Duty Free	Other	09 07 90 90	
Duty Free	Seedling	31 13 07 10	
	Small red (Adzuki) beans (phaseolus or vigna angularis) :		
Duty Free	Seeding	32 13 07 10	
	Kidney beans, including white pea beans (phaseolus vulgaris) :		
Duty Free	Seed	33 13 07 10	
Duty Free	Bananas, including plantains, fresh or dried	03 08 00 00	08.03
	Dates :		
Duty Free	Fresh	04 08 10 10	
Duty Free	Dried	04 08 20 10	
Duty Free	Stored dates.	04 08 30 10	
Duty Free	Other	04 08 90 10	
	Figs :		
Duty Free	Fresh	04 08 10 20	
Duty Free	Dried	04 08 20 20	
Duty Free	Pineapples	04 08 00 30	
Duty Free	Avocados	04 08 00 40	
	Guavas, mangoes and mangosteens:		
Duty Free	Guavas	04 08 10 50	
Duty Free	Mangoes	04 08 20 50	
Duty Free	Mangosteens	30 50 04 08	
	Citrus fruit fresh or dried		08.05
Duty Free	Oranges	05 08 00 10	
Duty Free	Mandarins (including tangerines & satsumas); clementines, wilkings & similar citrus hybrids	05 08 00 20	
Duty Free	Grapefruit	05 08 00 40	
	Lemons (citrus limon, citrus limonum) and limes (citrus aurantifolia, citrus latifolia)		
Duty Free	Fresh	05 08 10 50	
Duty Free	Dried	05 08 20 50	
Duty Free	Other	05 08 00 90	

For additional analytical, marketing, investment and business opportunities information, please contact
Global Investment & Business Center, USA
(202) 546-2103. Fax: (202) 546-3275. E-mail: rusric@erols.com

	Grapes fresh or dried		08.06
Duty Free	Fresh.	06 08 00 10	
Duty Free	Dried.	06 08 00 20	
	Melons (including watermelons) and papaws (papayas) fresh		08.07
	Melons(including watermelons)		
Duty Free	Watermelons	07 08 00 11	
	Other :		
Duty Free	Melon (muskmelon)	07 08 10 19	
Duty Free	Other	07 08 90 19	
Duty Free	Papaws (papayas)	07 08 00 20	
	Apples, pears and quinces fresh		08.08
Duty Free	Apples	08 08 00 10	
	Pears & quinces:		
Duty Free	Pears	08 08 10 20	
Duty Free	Quinces	08 08 20 20	
	Apricots, cherries, peaches(including nectarines), plums and sloes, fresh		08.09
Duty Free	Apricots	09 08 00 10	
Duty Free	Cherries	09 08 00 20	
Duty Free	Peaches, including nectarines	09 08 00 30	
Duty Free	Plums & sloes	09 08 00 40	
	Other fruit, fresh.		08.10
Duty Free	Strawberries	10 08 00 10	
Duty Free	Raspberries, blackberries, mulberries & loganberries	10 08 00 20	
Duty Free	Black, white or red currants & gooseberries	10 08 00 30	
Duty Free	Cranberries, bilberries & other fruits of the genus Vaccinium	10 08 00 40	
Duty Free	Kiwifruit	10 08 00 50	
Duty Free	Durians	10 08 00 60	
	Other :		
Duty Free	Pomegranate	10 08 10 90	
Duty Free	Medlar	10 08 20 90	
Duty Free	Prickly Pears	10 08 30 90	
Duty Free	Other	10 08 90 90	

For additional analytical, marketing, investment and business opportunities information, please contact
Global Investment & Business Center, USA
(202) 546-2103. Fax: (202) 546-3275. E-mail: rusric@erols.com

	Coffee, not roasted		
Duty Free	Not decaffeinated	01 09 00 11	
Duty Free	Decaffeinated.	01 09 00 12	
	Coffee roasted		
Duty Free	Not decaffeinated	01 09 00 21	
Duty Free	Decaffeinated.	01 09 00 22	
Duty Free	Other	01 09 00 90	
	Tea, whether or not flavoured.		09.02
Duty Free	Green tea (not fermented) in immediate packings of a content not exceeding 3 kg	10 02 09 00	
Duty Free	Other green tea (not fermented)	20 02 09 00	
	Black tea (fermented) and paltry fermented tea, in immediate packing of a content not exceeding 3 kg		
Duty Free	Teabag not exceeding 3 g	10 30 02 09	
Duty Free	Other	30 02 09 90	
Duty Free	Other black tea (fermented) & other partly frmented tea	40 02 09 00	
Duty Free	Cardamoms	08 09 00 30	
	Wheat and meslin		10.01
Duty Free	Durum wheat	01 10 00 10	
	Other :		
Duty Free	Normal wheat.	01 10 10 90	
Duty Free	Thin wheat.	01 10 20 90	
Duty Free	Mixed wheat and rye.	01 10 30 90	
Duty Free	Barley.	03 10 00 00	10.03
	Oats		10.04
Duty Free	Grey oats (or black).	04 10 10 00	
Duty Free	White oats (or yellow).	04 10 20 00	
	Maize (corn)		10.05
Duty Free	Seeds.	05 10 00 10	
	Other :		
Duty Free	Golden corn	05 10 10 90	
Duty Free	White corn	05 10 20 90	
Duty Free	Brown corn	05 10 30 90	
Duty Free	Other	05 10 90 90	

For additional analytical, marketing, investment and business opportunities information, please contact
Global Investment & Business Center, USA
(202) 546-2103. Fax: (202) 546-3275. E-mail: rusric@erols.com

	Rice		10.06
Duty Free	Rice in the husk (paddy or rough)	06 10 00 10	
Duty Free	Husked (brown) rice	06 10 00 20	
Duty Free	Semi-milled or wholly milled rice, whether or not polished or glazed	06 10 00 30	
Duty Free	Broken rice	06 10 00 40	
	Buckwheat millet and canary seed other cereals		10.08
Duty Free	Buckwheat	08 10 00 10	
Duty Free	Millet	08 10 00 20	
Duty Free	Canary seed	08 10 00 30	
Duty Free	Other cereals	08 10 00 90	
	Wheat or meslin flour.		11.01
Duty Free	Wheat	01 11 10 00	
Duty Free	Flour of mixed wheat & rye	01 11 20 00	
	Cereal flours other than of wheat or meslin.		11.02
Duty Free	Rye flour	02 11 00 10	
Duty Free	Maize (corn) flour	02 11 00 20	
Duty Free	Rice flour	02 11 00 30	
	Other :		
Duty Free	Of barley	02 11 10 90	
Duty Free	Of oats	02 11 20 90	
Duty Free	Of sorghum	02 11 30 90	
Duty Free	Of buckwheat	02 11 40 90	
Duty Free	Of millet	02 11 50 90	
Duty Free	Other	02 11 90 90	
	Cereal groats, meal and pellets.		11.03
	Groats and meal :		
	Of wheat :		
Duty Free	Groats	03 11 10 11	
Duty Free	Meal	03 11 20 11	
	Of maize (corn) :		
Duty Free	Groats	03 11 10 13	
Duty Free	Meal	03 11 20 13	
	Of other cereals :		

For additional analytical, marketing, investment and business opportunities
information, please contact
Global Investment & Business Center, USA
(202) 546-2103. Fax: (202) 546-3275. E-mail: rusric@erols.com

Duty Free	Of barley	03 11 10 19	
Duty Free	Of sorghum	03 11 20 19	
Duty Free	Of darnel	03 11 30 19	
Duty Free	Of buck wheat	03 11 40 19	
Duty Free	Of millet	03 11 50 19	
Duty Free	Of other cereals	03 11 90 19	
Duty Free	Pellets	03 11 00 20	
Duty Free	Sugar beet seed	09 12 00 10	
	Seeds of forage plants :		
Duty Free	Lucerne (alfalfa) seed	09 12 00 21	
Duty Free	Clover (Trifolium spp.) seed	09 12 00 22	
Duty Free	Fescue seed	09 12 00 23	
Duty Free	Kentucky blue grass (poa pratensis L) seed	09 12 00 24	
Duty Free	Rye grass (Lolium multiflorum Lam., Lolium perenne L.) seed	09 12 00 25	
Duty Free	Tmothy grass seed	09 12 00 26	
	Other :		
Duty Free	Lupine	09 12 10 29	
Duty Free	Other	09 12 90 29	
Duty Free	Seeds of herbaceous plants cultivated principally for their flowers	09 12 00 30	
	Other :		
	Vegetable seeds :		
Duty Free	Tomatoes	09 12 10 91	
Duty Free	Leeks	09 12 20 91	
Duty Free	Radish	09 12 30 91	
Duty Free	Carrots	09 12 40 91	
Duty Free	Cucumbers	09 12 50 91	
Duty Free	Marrow	09 12 60 91	
Duty Free	Pumpkin	09 12 70 91	
Duty Free	Eggplant seeds	09 12 80 91	
	Other :		
Duty Free	Lettuce	09 12 91 91	
Duty Free	Cress	09 12 92 91	

For additional analytical, marketing, investment and business opportunities
information, please contact
Global Investment & Business Center, USA
(202) 546-2103. Fax: (202) 546-3275. E-mail: rusric@erols.com

Duty Free	Capsicum	09 12 93 91	
Duty Free	Other	09 12 99 91	
Duty Free	Other	09 12 00 99	
	Cane or beet sugar and chemically pure sucrose in solid form		17.01
	Raw sugar not containing added flavouring or colouring matter		
	Cane sugar :		
Duty Free	Raw cane sugar not containing added flavouring or colouring matter	01 17 10 11	
Duty Free	Other	01 17 90 11	
	Beet sugar :		
Duty Free	Raw beet sugar not containing added flavouring or colouring matter	01 17 10 12	
Duty Free	Other	01 17 90 12	
	Other :		
Duty Free	Containing added flavouring or colouring matter	01 17 00 91	
	Other :		
	Refined :		
Duty Free	Crystal sugar	01 17 11 99	
Duty Free	Cube sugar	01 17 12 99	
Duty Free	Powdered sugar	01 17 13 99	
Duty Free	Rock candy (sugar candy), not containing	01 17 20 99	
Duty Free	Chemically pure sucrose	01 17 30 99	
Duty Free	Other	01 17 90 99	
Duty Free	Preparations for infant use based on milk malted milk prepared as substitutes of mothers milk not containing cocoa, put up for retail sale	01 19 10 10	
Duty Free	Preparations for infant use based on milk prepared as substitutes of mothers milk containing5 % cocoa by weight	10 01 19 20	
Duty Free	Other	10 01 19 90	
Duty Free	Sweets, gums and the like(for diabetics) containing synthetic sweetening agents instead of sugar	06 21 70 90	
Duty Free	Oil-cake and other solid residues, whether or not ground or in the form of pellets, resulting from the extraction of soyabean oil .	23 00 00 04	23.04

For additional analytical, marketing, investment and business opportunities information, please contact
Global Investment & Business Center, USA
(202) 546-2103. Fax: (202) 546-3275. E-mail: rusric@erols.com

	Radioactive elements & isotopes & compounds other than those of subheading44 28 .10,44 28 . 20or 44 28 .30; alloys, dispersions (including cermets), ceramic products & mixtures containing these elements, isotopes or compounds, radioactive residues		
Duty Free	For medical use	10 40 44 28	
Duty Free	Other	90 40 44 28	
	Glands and other organs for organotherapeutic uses, dried, whether or not powdered; extracts of glands or other organs or of their secretions for organo – therapeutic uses; heparin and its salts; other human or animal substances prepared for therapeutic or prophylactic uses, not elsewhere specified or included.		30.01
Duty Free	Glands and other organs, dried, whether or not powdered	10 01 30 00	
Duty Free	Extracts of glands or other organs or of their secretions	20 01 30 00	
Duty Free	Other	90 01 30 00	
	Human blood; animal blood prepared for therapeutic, prophylactic or diagnostic uses; antisera and other blood fractions and modified immunological products, whether or not obtained by means of biotechnological processes; vaccines, toxins, cultures of micro-organisms (excluding yeasts) and similar products.		30.02
Duty Free	Antisera and other blood fractions and modified immunological products, whether or not obtained by means of biotechnological processes	10 02 30 00	
Duty Free	Vaccines for human medicine	20 02 30 00	
Duty Free	Vaccines for veterinary medicine	30 02 30 00	
	Other :		
Duty Free	Sacs toxinse	90 02 30 10	
Duty Free	Recein	20 90 02 30	
Duty Free	Other	90 02 30 90	
	Medicaments (excluding goods of heading30 .02,30 . 05or30 . 06) consisting of two or more constituents which have been mixed together for therapeutic or prophylactic uses, not put up in measured doses or in forms or packings for retail sale.		30.03
Duty Free	Containing penicillins or derivatives thereof, with a penicillanic acid structure, or streptomycins or their derivatives	10 03 30 00	
Duty Free	Containing other antibiotics	20 03 30 00	
	Containing hormones or other products of heading29 . 37but not containing antibiotics :		

For additional analytical, marketing, investment and business opportunities information, please contact
Global Investment & Business Center, USA
(202) 546-2103. Fax: (202) 546-3275. E-mail: rusric@erols.com

Duty Free	Containing insulin	31 03 30 00	
Duty Free	Other	39 03 30 00	
Duty Free	Containing alkaloids or derivatives thereof but not containing hormones or other products of heading29 . 37antibiotics	40 03 30 00	
Duty Free	Other	90 03 30 00	
	Medicaments (excluding goods of heading30 .02,30 . 05or30 . 06) consisting of mixed or unmixed products for therapeutic or prophylactic uses, put up in measured doses (including those in the form of transdermal administration systems or in forms or packing for retails sale.		30.04
Duty Free	Containing penicillin or derivatives thereof, with a penicillanic acid structure, or streptomycins or their derivatives	10 04 30 00	
Duty Free	Containing other antibiotics	20 04 30 00	
	Containing hormones or other products of heading29 . 37but not containing antibiotics:		
Duty Free	Containing insulin	31 04 30 00	
Duty Free	Containing corticosteroid hormones, their derivatives and structural analogues	32 04 30 00	
Duty Free	Other	39 04 30 00	
Duty Free	Containing alkaloids or derivatives thereof but not containing hormones, other products of heading29 . 37or antibiotics	40 04 30 00	
Duty Free	Other medicaments containing vitamins or other products of heading 29.36	50 04 30 00	
	Other medicinal		
Duty Free	solutions	90 04 30 10	
Duty Free	Other	90 04 30 90	
Duty Free	Adhesive dressings & other articles having an adhesive layer	10 05 30 00	
	Other :		
Duty Free	Medical cotton.	90 05 30 10	
	Wadding, gauze, bandages & similar articles		
Duty Free	Impregnated or coated with pharmaceutical substances	90 05 30 21	
Duty Free	Wadding, gauze, bandages & similar articles, not impregnated or coated with pharmaceutical substances but up for retail sale without repacking, or packed or label affixed to be exclusively used in hospital, health departments, emergency, for medical or surgical use	90 05 30 22	
Duty Free	Other	90 05 30 90	
Duty Free	Sterile surgical catgut for surgical wound closure.	10 06 30 10	

For additional analytical, marketing, investment and business opportunities information, please contact
Global Investment & Business Center, USA
(202) 546-2103. Fax: (202) 546-3275. E-mail: rusric@erols.com

Duty Free	Sterile laminaria.	10 06 30 20	
Duty Free	Sterile absorbable surgical or dental haemostatics.	10 06 30 30	
Duty Free	Sterile tissue adhesives for surgical wound closure.	10 06 30 40	
Duty Free	Bloodgrouping reagents.	20 06 30 00	
Duty Free	Opacifying preparations for Xray examinations; diagnostic reagents designed to be administered to the patient.	30 06 30 00	
Duty Free	Dental cements & other dental fillings; bone reconstruction cements.	40 06 30 00	
Duty Free	Firstaid boxes & kits.	50 06 30 00	
Duty Free	Chemical contraceptive preparations based on hormones, on other products of heading 29 . 37or on spermicides.	60 06 30 00	
Duty Free	Gel preparations designed to be used in human or veterinary medicine as a lubricant for parts of the body for surgical operations or physical examinations or as a coupling agent between the body & medical instruments.	70 06 30 00	
Duty Free	Chemical elements doped for use in electronics, in the form of discs, wafers or similar forms; chemical compounds doped for use in electronics.	00 18 38 00	38.18
Duty Free	Diagnostic or laboratory reagents on a backing, prepared diagnostic or laboratory reagents whether or not on a backing, other than those of heading30 . 02or 30 .06; certified reference materials.	00 22 38 00	38.22
	Printed books, brochures, leaflets and similar printed matter or not in single sheets.		49.01
	- In single sheets, whether or not folded :		
Duty Free	Serial numbers cards, containing Questions or answers, information general educational	01 49 10 10	
Duty Free	Other	01 49 90 10	
	Other :		
Duty Free	Dictionaries and encyclopaedias, and serial instalments thereof	01 49 00 91	
	Other :		
Duty Free	Books, booklets & pamphlets, consisting essentially of textual matter of any kind, printed	01 49 10 99	
Duty Free	Books, booklets & pamphlets, in Braille or shorthand.	01 49 20 99	
Duty Free	School and university books	01 49 30 99	
Duty Free	Museums & public libraries indexes.	01 49 40 99	
Duty Free	Children's picture books where pictures does not form the principal interest.	01 49 50 99	

For additional analytical, marketing, investment and business opportunities information, please contact
Global Investment & Business Center, USA
(202) 546-2103. Fax: (202) 546-3275. E-mail: rusric@erols.com

Duty Free	Newspapers, journals & periodical bound otherwise then in paper, & sets of newspapers, journals or periodicals comprising more than one number under a single cover whether or not containing advertising materials.	01 49 60 99	
Duty Free	Other	01 49 90 99	
	Newspapers journals and periodicals whether or not illustrated or containing advertising material		49.02
	Appearing at least four times a week		
Duty Free	Newspapers	02 49 10 10	
Duty Free	Magazines	02 49 20 10	
Duty Free	Other	02 49 90 10	
	Other :		
Duty Free	Newspapers	02 49 10 90	
Duty Free	Magazines	02 49 20 90	
Duty Free	Periodicals	02 49 30 90	
Duty Free	Other	02 49 90 90	
	Children's picture, drawing or colouring books.		49.03
Duty Free	Drawing & painting books for children.	00 03 49 10	
Duty Free	Picture bound pages for children.	00 03 49 20	
Duty Free	Other	00 03 49 90	
	Maps and hydrographic or similar charts of all kinds, including atlases, wall maps, topographical plans and globes, printed		49.05
Duty Free	Globes	10 05 49 00	
	Other :		
Duty Free	In book form	91 05 49 00	
Duty Free	Other	99 05 49 00	
	Unused posted, revenue or similar stamps of current or new issue in the country in which they have, or will have, a recognized face value;		49.07
Duty Free	Unused postage stamps of current issue in the country in which they have, or will have a recognised face value	00 07 49 11	
Duty Free	Revenue stamp	00 07 49 12	
Duty Free	Unused postage	00 07 49 19	
Duty Free	Papers, cards or envelopes impressed with stamps.	00 07 49 20	
	Banknotes :		
Duty Free	Banknotes in circulation	00 07 49 31	

For additional analytical, marketing, investment and business opportunities
information, please contact
Global Investment & Business Center, USA
(202) 546-2103. Fax: (202) 546-3275. E-mail: rusric@erols.com

Duty Free	Banknotes not yet in legal circulation	00 07 49 32	
Duty Free	Travelers checks.	00 07 49 40	
Duty Free	Negotiable ratified checks.	00 07 49 50	
Duty Free	Stocks, shares, bond certificates & the like, numbered & signed.	00 07 49 60	
Duty Free	Stocks, shares, bond certificates & the like intended for use.	00 07 49 70	
Duty Free	Cheque forms	00 07 49 80	
Duty Free	Other	00 07 49 90	
Duty Free	Silver Powder	06 71 00 10	
Duty Free	Ingot of silver	06 71 10 91	
Duty Free	Other	06 71 90 91	
Duty Free	Semimanufactured	06 71 00 92	
Duty Free	Powder	08 71 00 11	
Duty Free	Ingot of gold	08 71 10 12	
Duty Free	Other	08 71 90 12	
Duty Free	Other semi – manufactured forms	08 71 00 13	
Duty Free	Monetary	08 71 00 20	
	Platinum		
	Unwrought or in powder :		
Duty Free	Ingot	10 71 10 11	
Duty Free	Other	10 71 90 11	
Duty Free	Other	10 71 00 19	
	Palladium :		
Duty Free	Unwrought or in powder form	00 21 10 71	
Duty Free	Other	00 29 10 71	
	Rhodium :		
Duty Free	Unwrought or in powder form	00 31 10 71	
Duty Free	Other	00 39 10 71	
	Iridium, osmium and ruthenium :		
Duty Free	Unwrought or in powder form	00 41 10 71	
Duty Free	Other	00 49 10 71	
Duty Free	Coin (other than gold coin), not being legal tender	00 10 18 71	
Duty Free	Other	00 90 18 71	
Duty Free	Filters for blood purifications	10 29 21 84	

For additional analytical, marketing, investment and business opportunities information, please contact
Global Investment & Business Center, USA
(202) 546-2103. Fax: (202) 546-3275. E-mail: rusric@erols.com

	Carriages for disabled persons, whether or not motorised or otherwise mechanically propelled		87.13
Duty Free	Not mechanically propelled	00 10 13 87	
Duty Free	Other	00 90 13 87	
Duty Free	Of carriages for disabled persons	00 20 14 87	
	Other aircraft (for example, helicopters, aeroplanes): spacecraft (including satellites) and suborbital and spacecraft launch vehicles		88.02
	Helicopters:		
Duty Free	Of an unladen weight not exceeding2 , 000kg	11 02 88 00	
Duty Free	Of an unladen weight exceeding2 , 000kg	12 02 88 00	
Duty Free	Aeroplanes and other aircraft, of an unladen weight exceeding2 , 000kg	20 02 88 00	
Duty Free	Aeroplanes and other aircraft, of an unladen weight exceeding2 ,000kg but not exceeding15 , 000 kg	30 02 88 00	
Duty Free	Aeroplanes and other aircraft, of an unladen weight exceeding15 , 000kg	40 02 88 00	
Duty Free	Spacecraft (including satellites) and suborbital and spacecraft launch vehicles	60 02 88 00	
	Cruise ships, excursion boats, ferryboats, cargo ship, barges and similar vessels for the transport of persons or goods.		89.01
Duty Free	Cruise ships, excursion boats and similar vessels principally designed for the transport of persons; ferryboats of all kinds	10 01 89 00	
Duty Free	Tankers	20 01 89 00	
Duty Free	Refrigerated vessels, other than those of subheading8901 .20	30 01 89 00	
Duty Free	Other vessels for the transport of goods and other vessels for the transport of both persons and goods	90 01 89 00	
Duty Free	Fishing vessels; factory ships and other vessels for processing or preserving fishery products.	00 02 89 00	89.02
Duty Free	Tugs and pusher craft	00 00 04 89	89.04
	Lightvessels, firefloats, dredgers, floating cranes, and other vessels the navigability of which is subsidiary to their main function; floating docks; floating or submersible drilling or production platforms.		89.05
Duty Free	Dredgers	10 05 89 00	
Duty Free	Floating or submersible drilling or production platforms	20 05 89 00	
	Other		
Duty Free	Firefloats	90 05 89 10	

For additional analytical, marketing, investment and business opportunities information, please contact
Global Investment & Business Center, USA
(202) 546-2103. Fax: (202) 546-3275. E-mail: rusric@erols.com

Duty Free	Light vessels		90 05 89 20	
Duty Free	Other		90 05 89 90	
	Other vessels, including warships and lifeboats other than rowing boats. (1)			89.06
Duty Free	Warships		10 06 89 00	
	Other :			
Duty Free	War vessels & boats, of all kinds including lifeboats		90 06 89 10	
Duty Free	Other		90 06 89 90	
	Other floating structures (for example, rafts, tanks, coffer-dams, landing-stages, buoys and beacons)			89.07
Duty Free	Inflatable rafts		10 07 89 00	
Duty Free	Other		90 07 89 00	
Duty Free	Vessels and other floating structures for breaking up .		00 08 89 00	89.08

STRATEGIC CONTACTS

AMERICAN EMBASSY ABU DHABI CONTACTS

UAE Country dialing code: 971.

Embassy: 971-2-443 6691   FAX: 971-2-443 5441
After Hours Post One: 971-2-443 4457

Other Embassy Numbers

AGENCY	TELEPHONE	FAX
Apache Field Office:	**971-2-441 5033**	**971-2-441 4088**
Apache Taft:	**971-2-445 1341**	**971-2-443 4171**
Commerical Section:	**971-2-627 3666**	**971-2-627 1377**
Consular:	**971-2-443 6691**	**971-2-443 5786**
Defense Attache:	**971-2-443 6962**	**971-2-445 3098**
Hawk Field Office:	**971-2-443 4141**	**971-2-443 4171**
Marine House:	**971-2-443 4842**	
Port Liaison Element:	**971-2-443 5058**	**971-2-443 3756**
Public Affairs Office:	**971-2-443 6567**	**971-2-443 4802**
United States Liaison Office:	**971-2-443 4192**	**971-2-443 4604**
United States Geological Survey:	**971-3-612544**	**971-3-612606**

MINISTRIES CONTACTS INFORMATION

1	▶**Ministry of Finance & Industry**		
	AbuDhabi	Tel: 971-2-	Fax:971-2-6768414 P O Box 433

For additional analytical, marketing, investment and business opportunities information, please contact
Global Investment & Business Center, USA
(202) 546-2103. Fax: (202) 546-3275. E-mail: rusric@erols.com

		6726000		
	Dubai	Tel: 971-4-3939000	Fax:971-4-3939738	P.O.Box 1565
	Email	mofi@uae.gov.ae		
	HomePage	www.uae.gov.ae/mofi		
2	**▸Ministry of Electricity & Water**			
	AbuDhabi	Tel: 971-2-6274222	Fax:971-2-6269738	P.O.Box 629
	Dubai	Tel: 971-4-2322000	Fax:971-4-2622555	P.O.Box 99979
3	**▸Ministry of Education and Youth**			
	AbuDhabi	Tel: 971-2-6213800	Fax:971-2-6313778	P.O.Box 295
	Dubai	Tel: 971-4-2994053	Fax:971-4-2994535	P.O.Box 3962
	Email			
	HomePage	http://education.gov.ae/		
4	**▸Ministry of Foreign Affairs**			
	AbuDhabi	Tel: 971-2-6652200	Fax:971-2-6668015	P.O.Box 1
	Dubai	Tel: 971-4-2221144		
	Email	mofa@uae.gov.ae		
5	**▸Ministry of Petroleum & Mineral Resources**			
	AbuDhabi	Tel: 971-2-6651810	Fax:971-2-6664573	P.O.Box 59 Telex:22544
	Email	mopmr@uae.gov.ae		
6	**▸Ministry of Planning**			
	AbuDhabi	Tel: 971-2-6271100	Fax:971-2-6269942	P.O.Box 904
	Email	mop@uae.gov.ae		
	HomePage	www.uae.gov.ae/mop		
7	**▸Ministry of Higher Education and Scientific Research**			
	AbuDhabi	Tel: 971-2-6428000	Fax:971-2-6427262	P.O.Box 45253
	Email	mohe@uae.gov.ae		
	HomePage	www.uae.gov.ae/mohe		
8	**▸Ministry of Labour and Social Affairs**			

For additional analytical, marketing, investment and business opportunities
information, please contact
Global Investment & Business Center, USA
(202) 546-2103. Fax: (202) 546-3275. E-mail: rusric@erols.com

	AbuDhabi Tel: 971-2-6671700 Fax:971-2-6665889 P.O.Box 809 Dubai Tel: 971-4-2691666 Fax:971-4-2668967 P.O.Box 4409 HomePage
9	▶**Ministry of Public Works & Housing** AbuDhabi Tel: 971-2-6651778 Fax:971-2-6665598 P.O.Box 878 Dubai Tel: 971-4-2693900 Fax:971-4-2692931 P.O.Box 1828 Email mpwh@uae.gov.ae

10	▶**Ministry of Justice, Islamic Affairs and Awqaf** AbuDhabi Tel: 971-2-6814000 Fax:971-2-6810680 P.O.Box 260 Dubai Tel: 971-4-2825999 Fax:971-4-2825121 P.O.Box 1682
11	▶**Ministry of Agriculture & Fisheries** AbuDhabi Tel: 971-2-6662781 Fax:971-2-6654787 P.O.Box 213 Dubai Tel: 971-4-2228161 Fax:971-4-2232781 P.O.Box 1509 Email maf@uae.gov.ae HomePage www.uae.gov.ae/maf
12	▶**Ministry of Economy & Commerce** AbuDhabi Tel: 971-2-6265000 Fax:971-2-6215339 P.O.Box 901 Email moec@uae.gov.ae HomePage www.uae.gov.ae/moec
13	▶**Ministry of Information & Culture** AbuDhabi Tel: 971-2-4453000 Fax:971-2-4452504 P.O.Box 17 Email mic@uae.gov.ae HomePage
14	▶**Ministry of Interior** AbuDhabi Tel: 971-2-4414666 Fax:971-2-4414938 P.O.Box 398 Email

For additional analytical, marketing, investment and business opportunities
information, please contact
Global Investment & Business Center, USA
(202) 546-2103. Fax: (202) 546-3275. E-mail: rusric@erols.com

15	**▶Ministry of Communication** AbuDhabi Tel: 971-2-6651900 Fax:971-2-6651691 P.O.Box 900 Dubai Tel: 971-4-2953330
16	**▶Ministry of Health** AbuDhabi Tel: 971-2-6330000 Fax:971-2-6726000 P.O.Box 848 Dubai Tel: 971-4-3348000 Email moh@uae.gov.ae HomePage www.uae.gov.ae/moh
17	**▶Ministry of Defence** AbuDhabi Tel: 971-2-4461300 Fax:971-2-4463286 P.O.Box 46616 Dubai Tel: 971-4-2611111 Fax:971-4-2621387 Email HomePage
18	**▶Ministry of State for Cabinet Affairs** AbuDhabi Tel: 971-2-6811106 Fax:971-2-6812968 Email moca@uae.gov.ae HomePage www.uae.gov.ae/moca

SELECTED GOVERNMENT & BUSINESS CONTACTS

Abu Dhabi: Senior Commercial Officer - Tapan Banerjee
Tel: (971-2) 273666, Fax: (971-2) 271377.
Dubai: Commercial Officer - David Rundell
Tel: (971-4) 313584, Fax: (971-4) 313121

Washington D.C.:
U.A.E. Desk Officer: David Guglielmi Tel:(202)482-5545;Fax: (202)
482-0878; Flash Fax:(202) 482-1064
Acting Regional Director: Jenelle Matheson
Associate Regional Director: Danny DeVito
Tel: (202) 482-4836, Fax: (202) 482-5179

ATO Contact Information

Agricultural Trade Office
P.O.Box 9343
Dubai, U.A.E.
Tel: (971-4) 314-063, Fax: (971-4) 314-998
E-mail: atodubai@emirates.net.ae

**For additional analytical, marketing, investment and business opportunities
information, please contact
Global Investment & Business Center, USA
(202) 546-2103. Fax: (202) 546-3275. E-mail: rusric@erols.com**

Contact: Edwin Porter, Regional Director
(Covers: Bahrain, Kuwait, Oman, Qatar and U.A.E.

COUNTRY CONTACTS

The UAE Ministry of Agriculture and Fisheries
Contact: H.E. Saeed Raqabani
Title: Minister
P.O.Box 1509
Dubai, United Arab Emirates
Tel: (9714) 228-161
Fax: (9714) 232-781

USDA CONTACT INFORMATION

Trade Assistance and Promotion Office (TAPO)
Foreign Agricultural Service (FAS)
U.S. Department of Agriculture
Ag Box 1052
Washington, D.C. 20250-1052
Tel: 202-720-7420
Fax: 202-690-4374

The FAS home page address on Internet is
http://www.fas.usda.gov

UAE EMBASIES

ADDRESS	TELEPHONE	FAX
UNITED ARAB EMIRATES EMBASSY (Ottawa) World Exchange Plaza - Suite 1800 45 O'Conner Street Ottawa, Ontario K1P 1A4	+1-613-565-7272	+1-613-565-8007
UNITED NATIONS ORGANIZATION (New York) 747 Third 36th Floor, New York N.Y 10017 USA	+1-371-4808182	+1-371-3195433
UNITED ARAB EMIRATES EMBASSY (Beirut) Al Janah - Ramlah Al Bayda, Opposite to Edin Rock, Lebanon	+961-1- 857000 to 6	+961-1-857009
UNITED ARAB EMIRATES EMBASSY (Cairo) 4 Ebn Senaa Street Al Jezaa, Egypt	+20-2-5706750	+20-2-5700844
UNITED ARAB EMIRATES EMBASSY (Kuwait) AL Daiyah-Al Estqlal Street-Embassy City, Kuwait	+965-2526356	+965-2526382

**For additional analytical, marketing, investment and business opportunities information, please contact
Global Investment & Business Center, USA
(202) 546-2103. Fax: (202) 546-3275. E-mail: rusric@erols.com**

UNITED ARAB EMIRATES EMBASSY (Islamabad) PO BOX: 1111 Plot No.1-22, University Road, Diplomatic Enclave Islamabad, Pakistan	+92-51-206738	+93-51-279063
UNITED ARAB EMIRATES CONSULATE (Karachi) PO BOX: 8523, 84-Clifton, Shahrahe-Iran, Karachi, Pakistan	+92-21-5874606	+92-21-5874387
UNITED ARAB EMIRATES EMBASSY (London) 30 Princes Gate, London SW 7 1PT, England	+44-207-5811281	+44-207-5819616
UNITED ARAB EMIRATES EMBASSY (Sana'h) PO BOX: 2250 Sana'h-Al Daery Al Janobi, Yemen	+967-1-266057	+967-1-248779
UNITED ARAB EMIRATES EMBASSY (New Delhi) EP-12, Chander Gupta Marg, Chanakyapuri, New Delhi-110021, India	+91-11-6872937	+91-11-6877648
UNITED ARAB EMIRATES CONSULATE (Bombay) PO.BOX: 6104, Bungalow No, 7 Jolly Marker Apt No. 1, Cuffe Parade, Colaba, Bombay-400005, India	+91-22-2189653	+91-22-2181162
UNITED ARAB EMIRATES EMBASSY (Al Khartoum) PO BOX: 1225 Al Emaraat Area 3 Street, Khartoum, Sudan	+249-11-471094	+249-11-471110
UNITED ARAB EMIRATES EMBASSY (Paris) 3, Rue Delota 75116, Paris, France	+33-1-45539404	+33-1-47556104
UNITED ARAB EMIRATES EMBASSY (Damascus) PO BOX: 33787 Al Mahdi Bin Barakah -Abu Rumana, Damascus, Syria	+963-11-3339643	+963-11-3320177
UNITED ARAB EMIRATES EMBASSY (Tehran) PO BOX: 19395/4616, Walli Aser Street-Waheed Dstkrdi No.355, Iran	+98-21-8788515	+98-21-8884250

For additional analytical, marketing, investment and business opportunities
information, please contact
Global Investment & Business Center, USA
(202) 546-2103. Fax: (202) 546-3275. E-mail: rusric@erols.com

UNITED ARAB EMIRATES CONSULATE (Bandar Abases) PO BOX: 79145/3473 Bandar abases, Shahid Naser Street-Opposite Shahid Shareati Hospital, Bandar Abases, Iran	+98-761-38712	+98-761-37446
UNITED ARAB EMIRATES EMBASSY (Tripoli) PO BOX: 3996, Qarqaresh -Abu Al Nawias, Tripoli, Libya	+218-21-4832597	+218-21-4832598
UNITED ARAB EMIRATES EMBASSY (Amman) PO BOX: 2623 Oman Mountain-Floor One, Jawdat Rashid Shmma Street- Oman Mountain, Amman, Jordan	+962-6-5934782	+962-6-5933888
UNITED ARAB EMIRATES EMBASSY (Muscat) PO.BOX: 551 NO 111 Al Seeb, Al Khouar, Muscat, Oman	+968-602531	+968-604182
UNITED ARAB EMIRATES EMBASSY (Rabat) PO BOX: 478, 11 Al Alwayeen Street-Rabat, Rabat, Morocco	+212-7-730976	+212-7-724145
UNITED ARAB EMIRATES EMBASSY (Tokyo) Tokyo 150-10 Nanpeidai-Cho, Shibuya-Ku, Tokyo, Japan	+81-3-54890814	+81-3-54890813
UNITED ARAB EMIRATES EMBASSY (Washington) 1255 22nd St., N.W.Suite 700-Washington D.C 20037, USA	+1-202-955-7999	+1-202-3377029
UNITED ARAB EMIRATES EMBASSY (Tunis) PO BOX 1002 , 9 Ashtrat - Al Balvideer 1002, Tunis, Tunisia	+216-1-785463	+216-1-783507
UNITED ARAB EMIRATES EMBASSY (Algiers) PO BOX 165, 14 Mohamed Drarini Street Hidara-Algiers, Algeria	+213-2-692081	+213-2-693770
UNITED ARAB EMIRATES EMBASSY (Riyadh) PO.BOX: 94385-11693 Riyadh, Abu Baker Al Krkhe Area- Amro bin Omiyah Street, Riyadh, Saudi Arabia	+966-1-4881227	+966-1-4827504

For additional analytical, marketing, investment and business opportunities information, please contact
Global Investment & Business Center, USA
(202) 546-2103. Fax: (202) 546-3275. E-mail: rusric@erols.com

UNITED ARAB EMIRATES CONSULATE (Jeddah) Osman Bin Affan Street- Al Sharqiya- Jeddah, Saudi Arabia	+966-2-6511557	+966-2-6513246
UNITED ARAB EMIRATES EMBASSY (Bonn) Erste Fahrgasse 6-54113 Bonn, Germany	+49-228-267070	+49-228-2670715
UNITED ARAB EMIRATES CONSULATE (Munich) Ismaning Str.21 81675 Munich, Germany	+49-89-419770	+49-89-4177177
UNITED ARAB EMIRATES EMBASSY (Vienna) Peter Jordan St. 66A/1190 Vienna, Austria	+43-1-3681455	+43-1-3683240
UNITED ARAB EMIRATES EMBASSY (Geneva) UAE Permanent Mission, 58, Rue Moillebeau 1209 Geneva, Switzerland	+41-22-7334338	+41-22-7345562
UNITED ARAB EMIRATES EMBASSY (Brussels) 73 Avenue Fr. Roosevelt-1050 Brussels, Belgium	+32-2-6406000	+32-2-6462473
UNITED ARAB EMIRATES EMBASSY (Madrid) C/Capitan Haya, 40 Madrid 28020 Madrid, Spain	+34-91-5701001	+34-91-5717148
UNITED ARAB EMIRATES EMBASSY (Dhaka) House No.41 Road no.113 Gulshan Model Town Dhaka, Bangladesh	+88-2-9882277	+88-2-883225
UNITED ARAB EMIRATES EMBASSY (Roma) Via Della Camilluccia,551-00135 Roma, Italy	+39-6-363006100	+39-6-36306155
UNITED ARAB EMIRATES EMBASSY (Angora) Mahmut Yesari Sokak No.10 Cankaya, Ankara	+90-312-4408413	+90-312-4389854
UNITED ARAB EMIRATES CONSULATE (Istanbul) PO.BOX 105, Ali Zeren Sokak No.7 Lievent Istanbul, Turkey	+90-212-2782062	+90-212-2780570
UNITED ARAB EMIRATES EMBASSY (Seoul) 5-5 Hanam- Dong,Young San-Ku, Seoul, Korea	+82-2-7903235	+82-2-7903239

For additional analytical, marketing, investment and business opportunities information, please contact
Global Investment & Business Center, USA
(202) 546-2103. Fax: (202) 546-3275. E-mail: rusric@erols.com

UNITED ARAB EMIRATES EMBASSY (Beijing) TA Yuan Bidg,1-9-1 Beijing(100600), 1-9-1 TA Yuan Diplomatic Office Bldg, Beijing, China	+86-10-65323024	+86-10-65985089
UNITED ARAB EMIRATES EMBASSY (Moscow) Ulcfa Palme St. r.4y/ Moscow, Russia	+7-95-2344060	+7-95-2344070
UNITED ARAB EMIRATES EMBASSY (Manila) 2nd Floor,Renaissance Bldg,215 Salcedo St. Legaspi Village Metro Manila City, Philippines	+63-2-8173906	+63-2-8189763
UNITED ARAB EMIRATES EMBASSY (Brasilia) Shis Qi 05 Chacara 18, Brasilia-DF CEP:70486-901, Brazil	+55-61-248-0973	+55-61-2487543
UNITED ARAB EMIRATES EMBASSY (Jakarta) PO.BOX 4859,Jakarta 12048, Ji.Singaraja Blok C- 4,Kav16-17,Kuningan Timur Jakarta, Indonesia	+61-21-5206528	+62-21-5206526
UNITED ARAB EMIRATES EMBASSY (Doha) PO.BOX 3099, 32 Al Murkiya St. Northern Kalifa City, Doha, Qatar	+974-882836	+974-822841
UNITED ARAB EMIRATES EMBASSY (Manama) PO.BOX 26505, 4007 St. 340 Al Manama, Bahrain	+973-723737	+973-727343
UNITED ARAB EMIRATES EMBASSY (Nouakchott) PO.BOX 6824 Nouakchott, Tafrig Zinaa area 401 Res. Nouakchott, Mauritania	+222-251098	+222-50992
UNITED ARAB EMIRATES EMBASSY (Kuala Lumpur) 12 Jalan Keranji 2 Off Kedondong-55000 Kuala Lumpur, Malaysia	+60-3-4535221	+60-3-4535220
UNITED ARAB EMIRATES EMBASSY (Pretoria) PO.BOX Arcadia 0007-57090, 980-Park Street Arcadia 0083, Pretoria South Africa	+27-12-3427736	+27-12-3427738

UNITED ARAB EMIRATES EMBASSY (Canberra) PO.BOX 173 Ggarran Act 2605, 36 Culgoa Circuit, O Malley Act 2606 Canberra, Australia	+61-6-2868802	+61-6-2869077
UNITED ARAB EMIRATES EMBASSY (Bangkok) 82 Seng Thong Thong Thani Bldg. 32ed Floor Sathorn Nua Road Bangkok 10500, Thailand	+66-2-6399820	+66-2- 6399818

IMPORTANT CONTACTS IN UAE

NEWSPAPERS:

English Newspapers

Gulf News
P.O. Box 6519, Dubai, U.A.E.
Tel. 971-4-447100, Fax. 971-4-441627
Contact Mr. Francis Matthew, Editor

Khaleej Times
P.O. Box 11243, Dubai, U.A.E.
Tel. 971-4-382400, Fax. 971-4-382238
Contact: Mr. Nihal Singh, Chief Editor

Emirates News
P.O. Box 791, Abu Dhabi, U.A.E.
Tel. 971-2-451446, Fax. 971-2-453662
Contact: Mr. Peter Hellyer, Managing Editor

The Gulf Today
P.O. Box 30, Sharjah, U.A.E.
Tel. 971-6-591919, Fax. 971-6-532737
Contact: Mr.Dilip Padgaonkar, Editor

Arabic Newspapers

Al Khaleej
P.O. Box 30, Sharjah, U.A.E.
Tel. 971-6-598777, Fax. 971-6-598547
Contact: Mr. Ghassan Tahboub, Managing Editor

Al Bayan
P.O. Box 2710, Dubai, U.A.E.
Tel. 971-4-444400, Fax. 971-4-447846
Contact: Mr. Khaled Mohammed, Editor

Al Ittihad

For additional analytical, marketing, investment and business opportunities information, please contact
Global Investment & Business Center, USA
(202) 546-2103. Fax: (202) 546-3275. E-mail: rusric@erols.com

P.O. Box 791, Abu Dhabi, U.A.E.
Tel. 971-2-455555, Fax. 971-2-451653
Contact: Mr. Obeid Sultan, Managing Editor

Al Fajer
P.O. Box 505, Abu Dhabi, U.A.E.
Tel. 971-2-488300, Fax. 971-2-484326
Contact: Mr. Obeid Al Mazroui, Chief Editor

FOREIGN EMBASSIES

ORGANISATION	CONTACT INFORMATION	TELEPHONE	FAX
Afghanistan,Embassy of the Islamic State	POB 5687, Abu Dhabi	+971 (2) 6661244	+971 (2) 6655310
Algerian Democratic Republic, Embassy Of the People's	POB 3070, Abu Dhabi	+971 (2) 4448943	+971 (2) 4447068
Argentina, Embassy	POB 3325, Abu Dhabi	+971 (2) 4436838	+971 (2) 4431392
Australian Consulate	POB 9303, Dubai	+971 (4) 3313444	+971 (4) 3314812
Austrian Embassy	POB 3095, Abu Dhabi	+971 (2) 6267755	+971 (2) 6267133
Bahrain, Embassy	POB 3367, Abu Dhabi	+971 (2) 6312200	+971 (2) 6311202
Bangladesh, Embassy	POB 2504, Abu Dhabi	+971 (2) 4465100	+971 (2) 4464733
Belgian Embassy	POB 3686, Abu Dhabi	+971 (2) 6319449	+971 (2) 6319353
Belize, Embassy	POB 43432, Abu Dhabi	+971 (2) 6333554	+971 (2) 6330429
Bosnia and Harzegovina, Embassy of the Republic	POB 43362, Abu Dhabi	+971 (2) 6745524	+971 (2) 6746619
Brazil, Embassy of	POB 3027, Abu Dhabi	+971 (2) 6665352	+971 (2) 6654559
British Embassy	POB 65, Dubai	+971 (4) 3521070	+971 (4) 3525750
Brunei, Embassy of	POB 5836, Abu Dhabi	+971 (2) 4491100	+971 (2) 4491567
Canadian Consulate	POB 52472, Dubai Juma Al Majid Building, Suite 708 Khalid Ibn Al Waleed St.	+971 (4) 3521717	+971 (4) 3517722
Canadian Embassy	Villa 440 26th Street (Near Bateen Co-op) between French and German	+971 (2) 4456969	+971 (2) 4458787

For additional analytical, marketing, investment and business opportunities information, please contact
Global Investment & Business Center, USA
(202) 546-2103. Fax: (202) 546-3275. E-mail: rusric@erols.com

	Embassies; near Delma Street)		
China, Consulate General of the People's Republic	POB 9348, Dubai	+971 (4) 3984357	+971 (4) 3983078
China(Taiwan), the Commercial Office	POB 3059, Dubai	+971 (4) 3358177	+971 (4) 3358180
Croation Embassy	POB 3367, Abu Dhabi	+971 (2) 6311700	+971 (2) 6311202
Czech Republic, Embassy	POB 27009, Abu Dhabi	+971 (2) 6782800	+971 (2) 6795716
Egypt, Consulate	POB 2575, Dubai	+971 (4) 3971122	+971 (4) 3971033
Eritrea, Embassy of	POB 2597, Abu Dhabi	+971 (2) 6331838	+971 (2) 6346451
Finland, Office of the Honorary Consul	POB 1042, Dubai	+971 (4) 2823338	+971 (4) 2823041
France, Consulate	POB 3314, Dubai	+971 (4) 3329040	+971 (4) 3328033
Germany, Consulate General of the Federal Republic	POB 2247, Dubai	+971 (4) 3523352	+971 (4) 3528138
Greece, Embassy	POB 5483, Abu Dhabi	+971 (2) 6654847	+971 (2) 6656008
Hungary, Embassy	POB 44450, Abu Dhabi	+971 (2) 6660107	+971 (2) 6667877
India, Consulate General	POB 737, Dubai	+971 (4) 3971222	+971 (4) 3970453
Indonesia, Embassy of the Republic	POB 7256, Abu Dhabi	+971 (2) 4454448	+971 (2) 4455453
Iran, Consulate General of the Islamic Republic	POB 2832, Dubai	+971 (4) 3521150	+971 (4) 3512069
Italy, Consulate General	POB 24910, Dubai	+971 (4) 3314167	+971 (4) 3317469
Japan, Consulate	POB 9336, Dubai	+971 (4) 3319191	+971 (4) 3319292
Jordan, Consulate General of the Hashemite Kingdom	POB 2787, Dubai	+971 (4) 3970500	+971 (4) 3971675
Kenya, Embassy	POB 3854, Abu Dhabi	+971 (2) 6666300	+971 (2) 6652827
Korea, Embassy	POB 3270, Abu Dhabi	+971 (2) 4435337	+971 (2) 4435348

For additional analytical, marketing, investment and business opportunities information, please contact
Global Investment & Business Center, USA
(202) 546-2103. Fax: (202) 546-3275. E-mail: rusric@erols.com

Kuwait, Consulate General of the State of	POB 806, Dubai	+971 (4) 2284111	+971 (4) 2232024
Lebanon, Consulate	POB 7800, Dubai	+971 (4) 3977450	+971 (4) 3977431
Libyan Arab Jamahiriya, Embassy of Great Socialist People's	POB 5739, Abu Dhabi	+971 (2) 4450030	+971 (2) 4450033
Malaysia, Consulate General of	POB 4598, Dubai	+971 (4) 3355528	+971 (4) 3352220
Mauritania, Embassy of the Islamic Republic	POB 2714, Abu Dhabi	+971 (2) 4462724	+971 (2) 4465772
Morocco, Embassy of the Kingdom of	POB 4066, Abu Dhabi	+971 (2) 4433973	+971 (2) 4433917
Pakistan, Consulate General of the State	POB 340, Dubai	+971 (4) 3970412	+971 (4) 3971975
Palestine, Consulate General of the State	POB 22132, Dubai	+971 (4) 2681618	+971 (4) 2687084
Panama, Consulate	POB 2121, Dubai	+971 (4) 6263366	+971 (4) 6263315
Philippines, Embassy	POB 3215, Abu Dhabi	+971 (2) 6345664	+971 (2) 6313559
Polish Republic, Embassy of the	POB 2334, Abu Dhabi	+971 (2) 4465200	+971 (2) 4465967
Qatar, Consulate	POB 1877, Dubai	+971 (4) 3982888	+971 (4) 3983555
Rumania, Consulate	POB 1404, Dubai	+971 (4) 3940580	+971 (4) 3940992
Royal Danish Consulate	POB 2988, Dubai	+971 (4) 2227699	+971 (4) 2223575
Royal Netherlands Consulate	POB 7726, Dubai	+971 (4) 3528700	+971 (4) 3510502
Royal Norwegian Consulate	POB 8612, Dubai	+971 (4) 3533833	+971 (4) 3533915
Royal Swedish Consulate General	POB 9219, Dubai	+971 (4) 3457716	+971 (4) 3452439
Royal Thai Consulate	POB 51844, Dubai	+971 (4) 3492863	+971 (4) 3490932
Russian Federation Embassy of the	POB 8211, Abu Dhabi	+971 (2) 6721797	+971 (2) 6788731
Saudi Arabia, Royal Consulate General of	POB 1876, Dubai	+971 (4) 2663383	+971 (4) 2662524

For additional analytical, marketing, investment and business opportunities information, please contact
Global Investment & Business Center, USA
(202) 546-2103. Fax: (202) 546-3275. E-mail: rusric@erols.com

Slovak Republic, Embassy	POB 3382, Abu Dhabi	+971 (2) 6321674	+971 (2) 6315839
Somalia, Consulate	POB 23900, Dubai	+971 (4) 2223030	+971 (4) 2274570
South Africa, Embassy	POB 29446, Abu Dhabi	+971 (2) 6316700	+971 (2) 6333909
Spain, Embassy	POB 46474, Abu Dhabi	+971 (2) 6269544	+971 (2) 6274978
Sri Lanka, Consulate	POB 51528, Dubai	+971 (4) 3986279	+971 (4) 3984687
Sudan, Embassy	POB 4027, Abu Dhabi	+971 (2) 6666788	+971 (2) 6654231
Sultanate of Oman	POB 1898, Dubai	+971 (4) 3515000	+971 (4) 3552226
Switzerland, Consulate	POB 9300, Dubai	+971 (4) 3313542	+971 (4) 3313679
Syria, Consulate General	POB 7801, Dubai	+971 (4) 2663354	+971 (4) 2698277
Tunisia, Embassy	POB 4166, Abu Dhabi	+971 (2) 6661331	+971 (2) 6660707
Turkish Consulate	POB 9221, Dubai	+971 (4) 3314788	+971 (4) 3371371
Ukraine, Embassy	POB 45714, Abu Dhabi	+971 (2) 6327586	+971 (2) 6327506
United States of America, Consulate	POB 9343, Dubai	+971 (4) 3313115	+971 (4) 3313121
Uzbekistan, Consulate	POB 53432, Dubai	+971 (4) 3387474	+971 (4) 3383234
Yemen, Consulate	POB 1947, Dubai	+971 (4) 3970131	+971 (4) 3972901

BANKS

BANK	ADDRESS	TEL	FAX	LOCATION
ABN Amro Bank	POB 1971	5594900	5591009	Abdul Aziz Al Majid Bldg King Faisal Street
Abu Dhabi Commercial Bank	POB 4377	5737000	5725331	Main Branch, Al Mina Street
Abu Dhabi Commercial Bank	POB 23657	5336600	5321285	Branch, Industrial Area

For additional analytical, marketing, investment and business opportunities information, please contact
Global Investment & Business Center, USA
(202) 546-2103. Fax: (202) 546-3275. E-mail: rusric@erols.com

ANZ Grindlays Bank	POB 357	5359998	5357046	Al Boorj Avenue
Arab Bank	POB 130	5613994	5617182	Al Arouba Street
Bank Melli Iran	POB 459	5522510	5350565	Al Boorj Avenue
Bank of Baroda	POB 1671	5354231	5543025	Al Arouba Street
Bank of Sharjah	POB 1394	5352111	5350323	Al Boorj Avenue
Sharjah Banque Banorabe	POB 5803	5736100	5736080	King Faisal Street
Banque Du Caire	POB 254	5522946	5365427	HH Sheikh Mohammed Al Qassimi Building, Al Arouba Street
Banque Libanaise pour Le Commerce (France)	POB 1953	5724561	5727843	Al Boorj Avenue
British Bank of the Middle East (BBME)	POB 25	5537222	5537880	Abdul Aziz Al Majid Bldg King Faisal Street
Central Bank of the UAE	POB 645	5592592	5593977	Abu Shagara Area, Opp. Immigration Building
Citibank	POB 346	5722533	5373378	Al Wahda Street, close to Safestway Super Market
Dubai Islamic Bank	POB 1409	5726444	5727555	Al Qassimia, King Abdulaziz Road
Emirates Bank International	POB 25090	5733300	5730077	Al Qassimia, Old Airport Road
Habib Bank AG Zurich	POB 1166	5354468	5379958	Al Boorj Avenue
Mashreq Bank	POB 2082	5351366	5372903	Al Boorj Avenue
Middle East Bank	POB 5169	5356166	5356498	Al Boorj Avenue
National Bank of Sharjah - Main Branch E-Mail : nbsmail@emirates.net.ae	POB 4	5547745	5543483	Al Boorj Avenue
National Bank of Sharjah - King Faisal Street Branch	POB 4	5591323	5594495	Hamrain Building
National Bank of Sharjah - SAIF Zone Branch	POB 4	5571282	5571595	SAIF Zone

National Bank of Sharjah - Khor Fakkan Branch	POB 10308	(9)2385735	(9)2387475	Corniche Road
National Bank of Sharjah - Dibba Branch	POB 12005	(9)2444295	(9)2443549	Corniche Road
Standard Chartered Bank	POB 5	5357788 or 800 4949 (Toll free)	5543604	Al Boorj Avenue
United Arab Bank E-Mail : uarab@emirates.net.ae	POB 881	5354111	5374965	Al Wahda Street
United Bank Limited	POB 669	5529974	5350880	Al Boorj Avenue

IMPORTANT CONTACTS

The American Business Group of Abu Dhabi
P.O. Box 43710, Abu Dhabi, UAE
Tel: 971-2-262086; Fax: 971-2-262087
Contact: Mr. Christopher Miller, President

Dubai Business Council
P.O. Box 9281, Dubai, U.A.E.
Tel: 971-4-314735; Fax: 971-4-314227
Contact: Hamdi Osman, President

Presidential Court of the U.A.E.
P.O. Box 280 Abu Dhabi, U.A.E.
Tel: 971-2-652000, Fax: 971-2-653855
Chamberlain: Shaykh Suroor Bin Mohamed Al Nahyan
Office Director: Sultan Al Rumaithy

Court of the Crown Prince of Abu Dhabi
(Shaykh Khalifa Bin Zayid Al Nahyan)
P.O. Box 124, Abu Dhabi, U.A.E.
Tel: 971-2-652265, Fax: 971-2-650505/650065
Chairman: Shaykh Sultan Bin Khalifa Al Nahyan

Ministry of Agriculture and Fisheries
P.O. Box 1509
Dubai, UAE
Tel: 971-2-228161, Fax: 971-2-232781
Minister: H.E. Saeed Raqabani

U.A.E. Armed Forces General Headquarters (GHQ)
P.O. Box 309/2, Abu Dhabi, U.A.E.
Tel: 971-2-444222/666555, Fax: 971-2-415890/415222

Chief of Staff: H.H. Shaykh Mohamed Bin Zayid Al Nahyan

UAE Armed Forces Directorate of General Purchasing
GHQ, P.O. Box 2501, Abu Dhabi, UAE
Tel: 971-2-415300/415301, Fax: 971-2-415687
Deputy Director: Colonel Obaid Al-Ketbi

Ministry of Communications
P.O. Box 900, Abu Dhabi, U.A.E.
Tel: 971-2-651900, 971-2-651691
Minister: Ahmed Humair Al Tayer

Directorate of Civil Aviation
P.O. Box 6558, Abu Dhabi, U.A.E.
Tel: 971-2-447666, Fax: 971-2-4054485
Director General: Mohammed Ghanem Al Ghaith

Abu Dhabi Department of Civil Aviation
P.O. Box: 20, Abu Dhabi, U.A.E.
Tel: 971-2-757500, Fax: 971-2-757285
Chairman: H.H. Shaykh Hamdan Bin Mubarak Al Nahyan

Dubai Civil Aviation Dept.
P.O. Box 2525, Dubai, U.A.E.
Tel: 971-4-2062727, Fax: 971-4-244074
Director General: Mohi-Din Binhendi

Ministry of Economy and Commerce
P.O. Box 901, Abu Dhabi, U.A.E.
Tel: 971-2-265000, Fax: 971-2-260000
Minister: H.H. Shaykh Fahim Bin Sultan Al Qassimi

For additional analytical, marketing, investment and business opportunities information, please contact
Global Investment & Business Center, USA
(202) 546-2103. Fax: (202) 546-3275. E-mail: rusric@erols.com

Ministry of Electricity and Water
P.O. Box 629, Abu Dhabi, U.A.E.
Tel: 971-2-274222, Fax: 971-2-269738
Minister: Humaid Bin Nasser Al Owais

Water and Electricity Department of Abu
Dhabi
P.O. Box 219, Abu Dhabi, U.A.E.
Tel: 971-2-971-2-721500, Fax: 971-2-784033/769908
Chairman: H.H. Shaykh Dheyaab Bin Zaid Al
Nahyan

Ministry of Health
P.O. Box 848, Abu Dhabi, U.A.E.
Tel: 971-2-330000,331000, Fax: 971-2-215422
Minister: Hamad Abdul Rahman Al Midfa

Ministry of Labor and Social Affairs
P.O. Box 809, Abu Dhabi, U.A.E.
Tel: 971-2-671700, Fax: 971-2-665889
Minister: Mattar Humaid Al Tayer

Ministry of Petroleum and Mineral Resources
P.O. Box 59, Abu Dhabi, U.A.E.
Tel: 971-2-672007, Fax: 971-2-663414
Minister: Obeid Bin Saeed Al Nasseri

Ministry of Planning
P.O. Box 904, Abu Dhabi, U.A.E.
Tel: 971-2-269949, Fax: 971-2-269942
Minister: H.H.Sh. Humaid Bin Ahmed Al
Moalla

Abu Dhabi Finance Department
P.O. Box 246, Abu Dhabi, U.A.E.
Tel: 971-2-651500, Fax: 971-2-665240
Chairman: Mohamed Habroosh Al Suweidi

Abu Dhabi Municipality
P.O. Box: 263, Abu Dhabi, U.A.E.
Tel: 971-2-788888, Fax: 971-2-774919
Chairman: Shaykh Mohamed Bin Butti

Abu Dhabi Chamber of Commerce & Industry
P.O. Box 662, Abu Dhabi, U.A.E.
Tel: 971-2-214000, Fax: 971-2-215867
Director General: Mohammed Omar Abdulla

Abu Dhabi General Industry Corporation
P.O. Box 4499, Abu Dhabi, U.A.E.

Tel: 971-2-214900, Fax: 971-2-325034
Chairman: h.H. Shaykh Engr. Hamad Bin
Tahnoon Al Nahyan

Dubai Chamber of Commerce & Industry
P.O. Box 1457, Dubai, U.A.E.
Tel: 971-4-280000, Fax: 971-4-211646
Director General: Abdul Rahman G. Al
Mutaiwee

Abu Dhabi Immigration & Naturalization
Department
P.O. Box 29444, Abu Dhabi, U.A.E.
Tel: 971-2-462244, Fax: 971-2-461621
Director: Mohammed Badr Al Hameli

Abu Dhabi Public Works Department
P.O. Box 3, Abu Dhabi, U.A.E.
Tel: 971-2-434111, Fax: 971-2-434338
Chairman: H.H. Shaykh Sultan Bin Zayid Al
Nahyan

Abu Dhabi Commercial Buildings and Social
Services Dept.
(The "Khalifa Committee")
P.O. Box: 3564, Abu Dhabi, U.A.E.
Tel: 971-2-310000, Fax: 971-2-310032
Chairman: Saif Bin Ahmed Jaber Al Hamili

Abu Dhabi Town Planning Dept.
P.O. Box 862, Abu Dhabi, U.A.E.
Tel:971-2-780000, Fax: 971-2-786716
Undersecretary: Engr. Mohammed Abdullah
Al Suwaidi

Abu Dhabi Purchasing Department
P.O. Box 838, Abu Dhabi, U.A.E.
Tel: 971-2-212700, Fax: 971-2-343696
Chairman: Khalfan Ghaith Al Moheirbie

Abu Dhabi National Oil Company (ADNOC)
P.O. Box 898, Abu Dhabi, U.A.E.
Tel: 6020000, Fax: 971-2-6023389
General Manager: Yousef Bin Omayr Bin
Yousef

Abu Dhabi Investment Authority (ADIA)
P.O. Box 3600, Abu Dhabi, U.A.E.
Tel: 971-2-266500, Fax: 971-2-274605
Managing Director: H.H. Shaikh Ahmed Bin
Zayed Al Nahyan

**For additional analytical, marketing, investment and business opportunities
information, please contact
Global Investment & Business Center, USA
(202) 546-2103. Fax: (202) 546-3275. E-mail: rusric@erols.com**

Abu Dhabi Marine Operating Company
(ADMA-OPCO)
P.O. Box 303, Abu Dhabi, U.A.E.
Tel: 971-2-6060000, Fax: 971-2-266005
General Manager: Mr. Bcconaer

Abu Dhabi Company for Onshore Oil
Operations (ADCO)
P.O. Box 270, Abu Dhabi
Tel: 971-2-6040000, Fax: 971-2-669785
General Manager: Kevin Dunn

World Trade Center Abu Dhabi
P.O. Box 33399
Abu Dhabi, UAE
Tel. 971-2-328555
Fax. 971-2-328855
email wtcad@emirates.net ae
Mr. Ousama Gahnnoum, General Manager

Dubai Port Authority
P.O. Box 17000, Dubai, U.A.E.
Tel: 971-4-815000, Fax: 971-4-816093
Chairman: Sultan Bin Sulayem

Dubai Municipality
P.O. Box 67, Dubai, U.A.E.
Tel: 971-4-215555, Fax: 971-4-
222424/246666
Director: Qassim Sultan

Dubai Petroleum Company (DPC)
P.O. Box 2222, Dubai, U.A.E.
Tel: 971-4-442990, Fax: 971-4-4062200
President: Sigmund Cornelius

U.S. Agricultural Trade Office (ATO), P.O.
Box 9343, Dubai,
United Arab Emirates, Tel: 971-4-314063,
Fax: 971-4-314998

SELECTED BUSINESS CONTACTS

Ministry of Information & Culture
PO Box 17, Abu Dhabi, UAE
Tel: (2) 453 000 *or* 452 922 *or* 454 766. Fax: (2) 452 504.

Government of Dubai Department of Tourism & Commerce Marketing
Albwardy Building 2, PO Box 594, Dubai, UAE
Tel: (4) 230 000. Fax: (4) 511 711.
E-mail: info@dctpb.gov.ae
Web site: http://www.dubaitourism.com

Embassy of the United Arab Emirates
30 Prince's Gate, London SW7 1PT
Tel: (0171) 581 1281. Fax: (0171) 581 9616.
E-mail: 101746.1630@compuserve.com

Opening hours: 0900-1500 Monday to Friday.

Consulate of the United Arab Emirates
48 Prince's Gate, London SW7 1PT
Tel: (0171) 589 3434. Fax: (0171) 581 9616.

Opening hours: 0900-1500 Monday to Friday; 0930-1300 Monday to Friday (visa section).

Government of Dubai Department of Tourism & Commerce Marketing
First Floor, 125 Pall Mall, London SW1Y 5EA
Tel: (0171) 839 0580. Fax: (0171) 839 0582.
Opening hours: 0900-1730 Monday to Friday.

For additional analytical, marketing, investment and business opportunities
information, please contact
Global Investment & Business Center, USA
(202) 546-2103. Fax: (202) 546-3275. E-mail: rusric@erols.com

British Embassy
PO Box 248, Abu Dhabi, UAE
Tel: (2) 326 600 *or* 321 364. Fax: (2) 341 744 *or* 318 138 *or* 345 968 (consular section).

Embassy also in: Dubai (tel: (4) 521 070).

Embassy of the United Arab Emirates
Suite 700, 1255 22nd Street NW, Washington DC 20037
Tel: (202) 955 7999. Fax: (202) 337 7029 (consular section).
E-mail: info@tridentpress.ie
Web site: http://www.the-emirates.com

Also deals with enquiries from Canada.

Embassy of the United States of America
Postal address: PO Box 4009, Abu Dhabi, UAE
Street address: Al-Sudan Street, Abu Dhabi, UAE
Tel: (2) 436 691. Fax: (2) 435 441
E-mail: usisamem@emirates.net.ae
Web site: http://www.usembabu.gov.ae

Consulate General in: Dubai (tel: (4) 313 115).

The Canadian Embassy
Postal address: PO Box 4009, Al-Sudan Street, Abu Dhabi, UAE
Street address: Villa 440, 26th Street, Abu Dhabi, UAE
Tel: (2) 456 969. Fax: (2) 458 787.
E-mail: canada@emirates.net.ae
Consulate in: Du

MAJOR ARABIC BANKS

ALGERIA

BANQUE ALGERIENNE DE DEVELOPPEMENT
12 Boulevard Colonel Amirouche
Algiers, Algeria
tel: (213) 2-738950
fax: (213) 2-746256
Director General: Mohamed Kerkebane

BANQUE ALGERIENNE DE DEVELOPPEMENT RURAL (BADR)
17 Boulevard Colonel Amirouche
Algiers, Algeria
tel: (213) 647264

BANQUE CENTRALE D'ALGERIE
8 Avenue Franklin Roosevelt, 16000
Algiers, Algeria
tel: (213)2-647 264
fax: (213) 2-552428
Governor: Abderahmane Hadj Nacer

BANQUE EXTERIEURE D'ALGERIE
1 Rue du Docteur Lucien Raynaud
Algiers, Algeria
Tel: (213) 2-711252
Fax: (213) 2-639334
President: Mohamed Nour Eddine Kerras

BANQUE NATIONALE D'ALGERIA
8 Boulevard Che Guevara
Algiers, Algeria
Tel: (213) 2-714719
Fax: (213) 2-712422
General Manager: A. F. Benmalek

BAHRAIN

ARAB BANKING CORPORATION
PO Box 5698
Manama, Bahrain
tel: (973) 532235
fax: (973) 533163
Chairman: Abdulmohsen Y Al Hunaif

For additional analytical, marketing, investment and business opportunities
information, please contact
Global Investment & Business Center, USA
(202) 546-2103. Fax: (202) 546-3275. E-mail: rusric@erols.com

GULF INTERNATIONAL BANK
PO Box 1017
Manama, Bahrain
tel: (973) 534000
fax: (973) 522633
Chairman: HE Ibrahim Abdul Karim

NATIONAL BANK OF BAHRAIN
PO Box 106
Manama, Bahrain
tel: (973) 258800
fax: (973) 228998/211307
Chairman: Ahmed Ali Kanoo

INVESTCORP
PO Box 5340
Manama, Bahrain
tel: (973) 532000
fax: (973) 530816

BAHRAIN INTERNATIONAL BANK
PO Box 5016
Manama, Bahrain
tel: (973) 534545
fax: (973) 535141
Chairman: Faisal Yousef Al Marzouk

AL AHLI BANK
PO Box 5941
Manama, Bahrain
tel: (973) 224333
fax: (973) 224322
Chairman: Mohammad Yousef Jalal

BAHRAIN MIDDLE EAST BANK
PO Box 797
Manama, Bahrain
tel: (973) 532-345
fax: (973) 530-526
Chairman: HE Abdul Rahman Salem Al-Ateeqi

TRANS ARABIAN INVESTMENT BANK (TAIB)
PO Box 20485
Manama, Bahrain
tel: (973) 533-334
fax: (973) 533-174
Chairman: Abdulrahman Al Jeraisy

EGYPT

NATIONAL BANK OF EGYPT
PO Box 11611
Cairo, Egypt
tel: (20) 2-5749101
fax: (20) 2-5746858
Chairman: Mahmoud Abdel Aziz

BANQUE MISR
151 Mohamed Farid Street
Cairo, Egypt
tel: (20) 2-3911159
fax: (20) 2-3919779
Chairman: Essam El Din Ahmady

BANQUE DU CAIRE
PO Box 2335
Cairo, Egypt
tel: (20) 2-3548323
fax: (20) 2-350616
Chairman: Mohamed Abdo El Fath

BANK OF ALEXANDRIA
49 Kasr El Nil Street
Cairo, Egypt
tel: (20) 2-3921481
fax: (20) 2-3900940
Chairman: Ismail Hassan Mohamed

COMMERCIAL INTERNATIONAL BANK
PO Box 2430
Cairo, Egypt
tel: (20) 2-5703043
fax: (20) 2-5702691

IRAQ

RAFIDAIN BANK
PO Box 11360
Baghdad, Iraq
tel: (964) 1-4158642
Chairman: Tarik H Al Khateeb

RASHID BANK
7177 Haifa Street
Baghdad, Iraq
tel: (964) 1-5388550
President: A Majid H Al Ani

JORDAN

ARAB BANK
PO Box 950544
Amman, Jordan
tel: (962) 6-5607231/6-5607115
fax: (962) 6-5606793/6-560683
Chairman: Abdulmajeed A H Shoman

JORDAN NATIONAL BANK
PO Box 1578
Amman, Jordan
tel: (962) 6-642391
fax: (962) 6-628809
Chairman: HE Abdulkader Tash

For additional analytical, marketing, investment and business opportunities
information, please contact
Global Investment & Business Center, USA
(202) 546-2103. Fax: (202) 546-3275. E-mail: rusric@erols.com

CAIRO AMMAN BANK
PO Box 715
Amman, Jordan
tel: (962) 6-639321
fax: (962) 6-639328
Chairman: Khalil Talhouni

BANK OF JORDAN
PO Box 2140
Amman, Jordan
tel: (962) 5-644327
fax: (962) 5-656642
Chairman: Tawfiq Fakhoury

HOUSING BANK
PO Box 7693
Amman, Jordan
tel: (962) 5-667126
fax: (962) 5-678121
Chairman: Zuhair Khouri

JORDAN KUWAIT BANK
PO Box 9776
Amman, Jordan
tel: (962) 5-688814
fax: (962) 5-687452
Chairman: Sufian I Yasin Sartwai

JORDAN GULF BANK
PO Box 9989
Amman 11191, Jordan
tel: (962) 4-603931
fax: (962) 6-664110
Chairman: Awartani F Zuhair

ARAB JODAN INVESTMENT BANK
PO Box 8797
Amman, Jordan
tel: (962) 6-507126/7
fax: (962) 6-681482
Chairman: Abdul Kader Qadi

KUWAIT

NATIONAL BANK OF KUWAIT
PO Box 95
Safat 13001, Kuwait
tel: (965) 2422011
fax: (965) 2431888
Chairman: Mohamed Abdul Rahman Al Bahar

GULF INVESTMENT CORPORATION
PO Box 3402
Safat 13035, Kuwait
tel: (965) 2431911
fax: (965) 2448894/2408006

Chairman: HE Sheikh Mohammed Bin Khalifa Al Thani

THE GULF BANK
PO Box 3200
Safat 13032, Kuwait
tel: (965) 2449501
fax: (965) 2424605
Chairman: Ali Mishari Al Hilal Al Mutairi

KUWAIT FINANCE HOUSE
PO Box 24989
Safat 12110, Kuwait
tel: (965)2445050
fax: (965) 2455135
Chairman: Bader Abdul Mohsen Al Mukhaizeem

ALAHLI BANK OF KUWAIT
PO Box 1387
Safat 13014, Kuwait
tel: (965) 2400900
fax: (965) 2424557
Chairman: Morad Yousuf Behbehani

COMMERCIAL BANK OF KUWAIT
PO Box 2861
Safat 13029, Kuwait
tel: (965) 2411001
fax: (965) 2450150
Chairman: Hamad Abdul Latif Al Hamad

BURGAN BANK
PO Box 5389
Safat 13054, Kuwait
tel: (965) 2439000
fax: (965) 2461148
Chairman: Sheikh Ahmed Abdullah Al Ahmed Al Sabah

BANK OF KUWAIT & THE MIDDLE EAST
PO Box 71
Safat 13001, Kuwait
tel: (965) 2461428
fax: (965) 2461430
Chairman: Saleh Mubarak Al Falah

LEBANON

BANQUE DU LIBAN ET D'OUTRE MER
PO Box 1912-11
Beirut, Lebanon
tel: (961) 1-346290
fax: (961) 1-602247
Chairman: Mrs. Boutros El Khoury

For additional analytical, marketing, investment and business opportunities
information, please contact
Global Investment & Business Center, USA
(202) 546-2103. Fax: (202) 546-3275. E-mail: rusric@erols.com

BANQUE AUDI
PO Box 11-2560
Beirut, Lebanon
tel: (961) 1-200250
fax: (961) 1-200955
Chairman: Georges W. Audi

BANQUE LIBANO-FRANCAISE
PO Box 11-808
Beirut, Lebanon
tel: (961) 1-340350
fax: (961) 1-340355
Chairman: Farid Ratelael

FRANSABANK
PO Box 11-0393
Beirut, Lebanon
tel: (961) 1-345572
Chairman: Adnan Kasser

BYBLOS BANK
PO Box 11-5605
Beirut, Lebanon
tel: (961) 1-898200
fax: (961) 1-898209
Chairman: Dr. Francois S. Bassil

LIBYA

ARAB BANKING CORPORATION
PO Box 3578
Tripoli, Libya
tel: (218) 21-3350227/3350220
fax: (218) 21-3350229
Chief Representitive: Ali Dahmani

CENTRAL BANK OF LIBYA
PO Box 1103
Tripoli, Libya
tel: (218) 21-33591
Governor: Abdulhafid Mahmoud Zlitni

MAURITANIA

BANQUE CENTRALE DE MAURITANIE
PO Box 623
Nouakchott, Mauritania
tel: (222) 2-52206
fax: (222) 2-52759
Chairman: Ahmed Ould Zeid

MOROCCO

ARAB BANK MAROC
PO Box 13810
Casablanca, Morocco

tel: (212) 2-223152
fax: (212) 2-200233
President: Hadj Abderahmane Bouftas

BANQUE COMERCIALE DU MAROC
PO Box 141
Casablanca, Morocco
tel: (212) 2-224169
fax: (212) 2-226982
President: Abd Al Aziz Alami

CREDIT DU MAROC SA
PO Box 13579
Casablanca, Morocco
tel: (212) 2-477000
fax: (212) 2-277127
Chairman: Jawad Ben Brahim

CREDIT POPULAIRE DU MAROC
PO Box 10622
Casablanca, Morocco
tel: (212) 2-202533/89
fax: (212) 2-222699
Chairman: Abd Al-Latif Laraki

WAFABANK

163 Avenue Hassan II
Casablanca 01, Morocco
tel: (212) 2-224105
fax: (212) 2-266202

OMAN

BANK MUSCAT AL AHLI AL OMAN
PO Box 134
Ruwi 112, Oman
tel: (968) 784776
fax: (968) 784056
Chairman: HE Sheikh Zaher Bin hamad Al Harthy

NATIONAL BANK OF OMAN
PO Box 3751
Ruwi 112, Oman
tel: (968) 708894
fax: (968) 707781
Chairman: HE Khalfan Bin Nasser Al Wohaibi

BANK OF OMAN, BAHRAIN & KUWAIT
PO Box 1708
Ruwi 112, Oman
tel: (968) 701532/701528
fax: (968) 705607
Chairman: HE Mohsin Haidar Darwish

For additional analytical, marketing, investment and business opportunities
information, please contact
Global Investment & Business Center, USA
(202) 546-2103. Fax: (202) 546-3275. E-mail: rusric@erols.com

OMAN INTERNATIONAL BANK
PO Box 1727
Ruwi 112, Oman
tel: (968) 682500
fax: (968) 682800
Chairman: HE Dr. Omar Bin Abdul Muniem Al Zuwawi

BANK DHOFAR AL-OMANI AL-FRANSI
PO Box 1507
Ruwi 112, Oman
tel: (968) 790466/790467
fax: (968) 797246
Chairman: Eng. Abdulhafidh Salim Rjab Al Aujaili

COMMERCIAL BANK OF OMAN
PO Box 1696
Ruwi 112, Oman
tel: (968) 793226
fax: (968) 793229
Chairman: HE Amer Bin Shuwain

OMAN ARAB BANK
PO Box 2010
Ruwi 112, Oman
tel: (968) 700161/700162
fax: (968) 797736

QATAR

QATAR NATIONAL BANK
PO Box 1002
Doha, Qatar
tel: (974) 413511
fax: (974) 413753
Chairman: HE Sheikh Abdul Aziz bin Khalifa Althani

QATAR INTERNATIONAL ISLAMIC BANK
PO Box 3211
Doha, Qatar
tel: (974) 436776
fax: (974) 444101
Chairman: Abdul Rahman Bin Abdullah Al Mahmood

SAUDI ARABIA

NATIONAL COMMERCIAL BANK
PO Box 3555
Jeddah 21481, Saudi Arabia
tel: (966) 2-6446644
fax: (966) 2-6433282
General Manager: Salim Ahmed Bin Mahfouz

RIYAD BANK
PO Box 22622

Riyadh 11416, Saudi Arabia
tel: (966) 1-4013030
fax: (966) 1-4042707
Chairman: Sheikh Ismail Abou Dawood

SAUDI AMERICAN BANK
PO Box 833
Riyadh 11421, Saudi Arabia
tel: (966) 1-4774770
fax: (966) 1-4774770
Chairman: Abdul Aziz Bin Hamad Al Gosaibi

ARAB NATIONAL BANK
PO Box 56921
Riyadh 11564, Saudi Arabia
tel: (966) 1-4029000
fax: (966) 1-4027747
Chairman: Rasheed Abdulrahman Al Rasheed

AL RAJHI BANKING & INVESTMENT CORPORATION
PO Box 28
Riyadh 11511, Saudi Arabia
tel: (966) 1-4054244
fax: (966) 1-4052950
Chairman: Sheikh Saleh Ibn Abdul Aziz Alrajhi

SAUDI BRITISH BANK
PO Box 9084
Riyadh 11413, Saudi Arabia
tel: (966) 1-4050677
fax: (966) 1-4050660
Chairman: Hisham A Alireza

AL BANK AL SAUDI AL FRANSI
PO Box 56006
Riyadh 11554, Saudi Arabia
tel: (966) 1-4042222
fax: (966) 1-4042311
Chairman: Sheikh Ibrahim Al Touq

SAUDI CAIRO BANK
PO Box 11222
Jeddah 21453, Saudi Arabia
tel: (966) 2-6608820
fax: (966) 2- 6608820 ext. 338
Chairman: Wahib Bin Zagr

SAUDI HOLLANDI BANK
PO Box 1467
Riyadh 11431, Saudi Arabia
tel: (966) 1-4067888
fax: (966) 1-4031104
Chairman: Sulaiman A R Al Sulaiman

UNITED SAUDI COMMERCIAL BANK
PO Box 25895

For additional analytical, marketing, investment and business opportunities information, please contact
Global Investment & Business Center, USA
(202) 546-2103. Fax: (202) 546-3275. E-mail: rusric@erols.com

Riyadh 11476, Saudi Arabia
tel: (966) 1-4784200
fax: (966) 1-4783197
Chairman: HRH Prince Al Waleed Bin Talal Bin
Abdulaziz Al Saud

SAUDI INVESTMENT BANK
PO Box 3533
Riyadh 11481, Saudi Arabia
tel: (966) 1-4778433
fax: (966) 1-4776781
Chairman: Dr. Abdulaziz O'Hali

BANK AL-JAZIRA
PO Box 5859
Riyadh 11432, Saudi Arabia
tel: (966) 1-4036344/401636
fax: (966) 1-4036344

SYRIA

CENTRAL BANK OF SYRIA
PO Box 2254
Damascus, Syria
tel: (963) 11-224800

COMMERCIAL BANK OF SYRIA
PO Box 933
Damascus, Syria
tel: (963) 11-218890
fax: (963) 11-228524
Chairman: Riad Hakim

TUNISIA

BANQUE NATIONALE AGRICOLE (BNA)
Rue Hedi Novira
1000 Tunis, Tunisia
tel: (216) 1-833104
fax: (216) 1-835950
Chairman: Habib Nafir

BANQUE INTERNATIONALE ARABE DE TUNISIE (BIAT)
BP 520
Tunis Cedex, Tunisia
tel: (216) 1-340719
fax: (216) 1-340680
President: Mokhtar Fhakhfakh

ARAB TUNISIAN BANK (ATB)
Rue de la Monnaie
1001 Tunis, Tunisia
tel: (216) 1-351155
fax: (216) 1-342852
Chairman: Hatem Kchouk

U.A.E.

NATIONAL BANK OF ABU DHABI
PO Box 4
Abu Dhabi, U.A.E.
tel: (971) 2-668000
fax: (971) 2-655329
Chairman: HE Mohammed Habroush Al Suwaidi

NATIONAL BANK OF DUBAI
PO Box 777
Dubai, U.A.E.
tel: (971) 4-267000
fax: (971) 4-268939
Chairman: Sultan Ali Al Owais

EMIRATES BANK INTERNATIONAL
PO Box 2923
Dubai, U.A.E.
tel: (971) 4-256256
fax: (971) 4-268005
Chairman: HE Ahmed Humaid Al Tayer

MASHREQ BANK
PO Box 1250
Dubai, U.A.E.
tel: (971) 4-229131
fax: (971) 4-226061
Chairman: Saif Ahmed Al Guhair

ARAB BANK FOR INVESTMENT & FOREIGN TRADE
PO Box 46733
Abu Dhabi, U.A.E.
tel: (971) 2-721900
fax: (971) 2-777550
Chairman: Dr. Abdul Hafid M. Zlitni

COMMERCIAL BANK OF DUBAI
PO Box 2668
Dubai, U.A.E.
tel: (971) 4-523355
fax: (971) 4-520444
Chairman: HE Ahmed Humaid Al Tayer

INVESTMENT BANK FOR TRADE AND FINANCE (INVESTBANK)
PO Box 2875
Abu Dhabi, U.A.E.
tel: (971) 2-794594
fax: (971) 2-795592
Chairman: HH Sheikh Saqr Bin Mohammad Al Qassami

YEMEN

For additional analytical, marketing, investment and business opportunities
information, please contact
Global Investment & Business Center, USA
(202) 546-2103. Fax: (202) 546-3275. E-mail: rusric@erols.com

ARAB BANK LTD
PO Box 475
Sanaa, Yemen
tel: (967) 1-276585
fax: (967) 1-276583
Manager: Abdul Mahdi Alawi

BANK INDOSUEZ
PO Box 651
Sanaa, Yemen
tel: (967) 1-272801/2/3
fax: (967) 1-274161
General Manager: Manuel Garcia-Ligero

COOPERATIVE BANK OF YEMEN
PO Box 2015
Sanaa, Yemen

tel: (967) 1-207327
fax: (967) 1-203714
Chairman: Abdallah Al Barakani

INTERNATIONAL BANK OF YEMEN
PO Box 2847
Sanaa, Yemen
tel: (967) 1-272920/112/314
fax: (967) 1-274127
General Manager: Mohammedmian Soomro

NATIONAL BANK OF YEMEN
PO Box 19839
Aden, Yemen
tel: (967) 1-275373
fax: (967) 1-273311

AIRLINES SERVING THE ARAB WORLD

AIRLINE	PHONE NUMBER
AEROFLOT	USA tel: (800) 995-5555
AIR ALGERIA	Algiers tel: (213) 2-74 24 28 fax: (213) 2- 74 44 25
AIR CANADA	USA tel: (800) 776-3000
AIR FRANCE	USA tel: (800) 237-2747
ALITALIA	USA tel: (800) 221-4745
AUSTRIAN AIR	USA tel: (800) 843-0002
BRITISH AIRWAYS (BA)	USA tel: (800) 247-9297
EGYPTAIR	Cairo tel: (20) 2-3902444 fax: (20) 2-3901557 USA tel: (800) 334-6787
EMIRATES	Dubai tel: (971) 4-223698 fax: (971) 4-214560 USA tel: (800) 777-3999
GULF AIR	Bahrain tel: (973) 531166 fax: (973) 330466 USA tel: (800) 553-2824
IRAQI AIRWAYS CO	Baghdad tel: (964) 555 9999
JAMAHIRIYA LIBYAN ARAB AIRLINES	Tripoli tel: (218) 21-602083
KLM	USA tel: (800) 374-7747
KUWAIT AIRWAYS (KAC)	Kuwait tel: (965) 4740166 fax: (965) 4314726

For additional analytical, marketing, investment and business opportunities
information, please contact
Global Investment & Business Center, USA
(202) 546-2103. Fax: (202) 546-3275. E-mail: rusric@erols.com

	USA tel: (800) 458-9248
LUFTHANSA	USA tel: (800) 645-3880
MIDDLE EAST AIRLINES (MEA)	Beirut tel: (961) 1-316316 USA tel: (800) 664-7310
OLYMPIC AIRWAYS	USA tel: (800) 223-1226
QANTAS	USA tel: (800) 227-4500
ROYAL AIR MAROC	Casablanca tel: (212) 2-91200 fax: (212) 2-912397 USA tel: (800) 344-6726
ROYAL JORDANIAN AIRLINE	Amman tel: (962) 672872 fax: (962) 672527 USA tel: (800) 223-0470
SABENA	USA tel: (800) 873-3900
SAS	USA tel: (800) 221-2350
SAUDIA-SAUDI ARABIAN AIRLINES	Jeddah tel: (966) 2-686 0000 fax: (966) 2-686 4552 USA tel: (800) 457-8329
SWISS AIR	USA tel: (800) 221-4750
SYRIAN ARAB AIRLINES	Damascus tel: (963) 11-232154
TUNIS AIR	Tunis tel: (216) 1-700 100 fax: (216) 1-700 754
TURKISH AIRWAYS	USA tel: (800) 874-8875
TWA	USA tel: (800) 221-2000
UNITED AIRLINES	USA tel: (800) 241-6522
YEMEN AIRWAYS	Sanaa tel: (967) 1-232389

NUMBER OF COMPANIES BY SECTOR

Activities	Est.No	Labor	Investment-Dh
Manufacture of Food	158	15054	1882177577
Manufacture of Tobacco Products	1	66	7300000
Manufacture of Textiles	33	2591	365899631
Manufacture of Wearing Apparel	141	26091	129283278
Manufacture of Leather Products	15	908	48275491
Manufacture of Wood and Wood Products	24	1704	30645877
Manufacture of Paper and Paper Products	56	3247	388989622

For additional analytical, marketing, investment and business opportunities
information, please contact
Global Investment & Business Center, USA
(202) 546-2103. Fax: (202) 546-3275. E-mail: rusric@erols.com

Publishing and Printing	61	5551	333176492
Manufacture of Refined Petroleum Products	20	1155	327485123
Manufacture of Chemicals & Chemical Products	131	6518	761533325
Manufacture of Rubber and Plastic Products	139	9033	549830598
Manufacture of Non-metallic Mineral Products	255	21293	4249071284
Basic Metals	40	5056	3332322795
Manufacture of Fabricated Metal Products	281	29510	1094608426
Manufacture of Machinery Equipment	37	3393	110547029
Manufacture of Office Accounting & computing Machinery	1	12	650000
Manufacture of Electric Machinery Apparatus	44	2051	98652857
Manufacture of Scientific & Professional Instruments	1	28	550000
Manufacture of Motor Vehicles, Trailers & Semi Products	18	820	30005550
Manufacture of Other Transport Equipment's	34	1839	278946518
Manufacture of Furniture Manufacturing N.E.C.	158	7955	326607798
Recycling	1	13	1000000
Manufacture of Handicrafts	46	1646	24674547
Total	**1695**	**145534**	**14372233818**

IMPORTANT CONTACTS

DEPARTMENT OF TOURISM AND COMMERCE MARKETING

The Department is responsible for the promotion of Dubai as a major regional and international centre of business and tourism. Its activities include trade fair participation and organisation, inward and outward missions, seminars and presentations, special events, information services, advertising, publications and media relations.

In addition to its responsibilities for promoting trade, investment and tourism, the Department is the primary planning, regulating, licensing and development authority for all matters relating to tourism in the emirate.

Head Office:
Department of Tourism and Commerce Marketing
PO Box 594
Dubai, United Arab Emirates
Telephone: (971) (4) 2230000
Telefax: (971) (4) 2230022
Internet: http://dubaitourism.co.ae
Telex: 46182 DCTPB EM

DEPARTMENT OF ECONOMIC DEVELOPMENT

For additional analytical, marketing, investment and business opportunities information, please contact
Global Investment & Business Center, USA
(202) 546-2103. Fax: (202) 546-3275. E-mail: rusric@erols.com

Established in 1992, the Department has wide ranging responsibility for the emirate's economic development and plays a leading role in the formulation of economic and commercial policy. It is also responsible for the regulation of companies and for maintaining the emirate's commercial register. The Department has authority over the granting of trade licences.

Department of Economic Development
PO Box 13223, Dubai, U.A.E.
Telephone: () (4) 2229922. Telefax: (971) (4) 2225577

DUBAI CHAMBER OF COMMERCE AND INDUSTRY

Established in 1965, the Chamber is responsible for organising and protecting commercial and industrial activities and for promoting trade and business cooperation both within the UAE and internationally. Its work falls under the following broad headings: foreign relations, registration and documentation, industrial affairs, administration and finance, and legal affairs.

Dubai Chamber of Commerce and Industry
PO Box 1457, Dubai, U.A.E.
Telephone: (971) (4) 2280000. Telefax: (971) (4) 2211646

DUBAI MUNICIPALITY

The Municipality has extensive responsibilities covering both the provision of essential civic services and for the planning and development of the emirate's infrastructure.

Dubai Municipality
PO Box 67, Dubai, U.A.E.
Telephone: (971) (4) 2215555. Telefax: (971) (4) 2246666

JEBEL ALI FREE ZONE AUTHORITY

Established in 1985, the Authority is charged with supervision of the Free Zone. Its responsibilities include issuing rules and licences to companies wishing to operate in Jebel Ali. It is also active in developing the infrastructure within the zone and for providing a wide range of services and administrative support, including personnel recruitment, for companies in the Free Zone.

Jebel Ali Free Zone Authority
PO Box 17000, Dubai, U.A.E.
Telephone: (971) (4) 8815000. Telefax: (971) (4) 8816093

DUBAI PORTS AUTHORITY

Dubai Ports Authority, the operator of Port Rashid and Jebel Ali Port, is the largest operation of its kind in the Gulf. In 1997, DPA handled 36.0 million tonnes of cargo. Its throughput of 2.60 million TEUs makes it one of the top ten container ports in the world.

Dubai Ports Authority
PO Box 2149. Dubai, U.A.E.
Telephone: (971) (4) 3451545. Telefax: (971) (4) 3452002

For additional analytical, marketing, investment and business opportunities information, please contact
Global Investment & Business Center, USA
(202) 546-2103. Fax: (202) 546-3275. E-mail: rusric@erols.com

DUBAI AIRPORT FREE ZONE

The Department of Civil Aviation has established a new free zone at Dubai International Airport. Offering the same package of incentives as the Jebel Ali Free Zone, it will focus on attracting high tech investors and companies using air freight.

Dubai Airport Free Zone
PO Box 2525, Dubai, U.A.E.
Telephone: (971) (4) 2027000. Telefax: (971) (4) 2995500

DUBAI WORLD TRADE CENTRE (L.L.C.)

The Dubai World Trade Centre complex incorporates the leading exhibition and conference venue in the Middle East, hosting some 60 major international events each year. Total exhibition space amounts to 37,000 sq.m.

Dubai World Trade Centre (L.L.C.)
PO Box 9292, Dubai, U.A.E.
Telephone: (971) (4) 3321000. Telefax: (971) (4) 3318034

INDUSTRIAL STATISTICS

MANUFACTURING ACTIVITIES IN UAE

Activities	Est. No	Labor	Investment- million -Dh
Manufacture of Food	199	19602	3064
Manufacture of Tobacco Products	1	73	8
Manufacture of Textiles	52	3628	509
Manufacture of Wearing Apparel	148	27277	255
Manufacture of Leather Products	18	1004	51
Manufacture of Wood and Wood Products	41	3315	169
Manufacture of Paper and Paper Products	64	3763	576
Publishing and Printing	80	6697	484
Manufacture of Refined Petroleum Products	26	1385	466
Manufacture of Chemicals & Chemical Products	176	8752	1374
Manufacture of Rubber and Plastic Products	181	10042	1156
Manufacture of Non-metallic Mineral Products	302	27600	5922
Basic Metals	46	5823	6410
Manufacture of Fabricated Metal Products	361	33793	1889
Manufacture of Machinery Equipment	52	4017	265
Manufacture of Office Accounting & computing Machinery	2	43	12
Manufacture of Electric Machinery Apparatus	71	3162	167
Manufacture of Motor Vehicles, Trailers & Semi Products	28	1764	131

For additional analytical, marketing, investment and business opportunities information, please contact
Global Investment & Business Center, USA
(202) 546-2103. Fax: (202) 546-3275. E-mail: rusric@erols.com

Manufacture of Other Transport Equipment's	38	2306	256
Manufacture of Furniture Manufacturing N.E.C.	216	10763	477
Recycling	2	16	2
Manufacture of Handicrafts	49	1435	27
Total	2153	176260	23670

NUMBER OF ESTABLISHMENTS, LABOR, AND INVESTMENT IN ALL EMIRATES

Activities	Est. No	Labor	Investment million—Dh
ABU DHABI	220	25140	3532
DUBAI	793	61071	12730
AL SHARJAH	685	51313	2845
AJMAN	301	23567	779
RAS AL KHIMAH	76	10045	2787
UMM AL QUWAIN	44	2376	351
AL FUJAIRAH	34	2748	646
Total	2153	176260	23670

NUMBER OF ESTABLISHMENTS, LABOR, AND INVESTMENT IN ABU DHABI

Activities	Est. No	Labor	Investment- million -Dh
Manufacture of Food	19	3647	944
Manufacture of Tobacco Products	0	0	0
Manufacture of Textiles	1	149	20
Manufacture of Wearing Apparel	9	1466	17
Manufacture of Leather Products	1	287	30
Manufacture of Wood and Wood Products	1	230	4
Manufacture of Paper and Paper Products	8	360	102
Publishing and Printing	7	290	37
Manufacture of Refined Petroleum Products	5	285	230
Manufacture of Chemicals & Chemical Products	25	1009	211
Manufacture of Rubber and Plastic Products	23	1453	249
Manufacture of Non-metallic Mineral Products	48	4192	916
Basic Metals	4	360	26
Manufacture of Fabricated Metal Products	43	8583	383
Manufacture of Machinery Equipment	6	1276	76

For additional analytical, marketing, investment and business opportunities information, please contact
Global Investment & Business Center, USA
(202) 546-2103. Fax: (202) 546-3275. E-mail: rusric@erols.com

Manufacture of Office Accounting & computing Machinery	0	0	0
Manufacture of Electric Machinery Apparatus	8	209	19
Manufacture of Motor Vehicles, Trailers & Semi Products	5	571	63
Manufacture of Other Transport Equipment's	3	548	181
Manufacture of Furniture Manufacturing N.E.C.	4	225	24
Recycling	0	0	0
Manufacture of Handicrafts	0	0	0
Total	220	25140	3532

NUMBER OF ESTABLISHMENTS, LABOR, AND INVESTMENT IN DUBAI

Activities	Est. No	Labor	Investment- million -Dh
Manufacture of Food	91	8795	1400
Manufacture of Tobacco Products	0	0	0
Manufacture of Textiles	11	1092	162
Manufacture of Wearing Apparel	4	2355	44
Manufacture of Leather Products	4	285	11
Manufacture of Wood and Wood Products	17	1495	77
Manufacture of Paper and Paper Products	26	1930	352
Publishing and Printing	34	3540	221
Manufacture of Refined Petroleum Products	5	317	111
Manufacture of Chemicals & Chemical Products	61	3078	552
Manufacture of Rubber and Plastic Products	52	2925	477
Manufacture of Non-metallic Mineral Products	108	8427	1600
Basic Metals	22	3697	6270
Manufacture of Fabricated Metal Products	167	14550	991
Manufacture of Machinery Equipment	20	1007	108
Manufacture of Office Accounting & computing Machinery	1	31	11
Manufacture of Electric Machinery Apparatus	35	1762	105
Manufacture of Motor Vehicles, Trailers & Semi Products	12	759	54
Manufacture of Other Transport Equipment's	14	869	30

For additional analytical, marketing, investment and business opportunities information, please contact
Global Investment & Business Center, USA
(202) 546-2103. Fax: (202) 546-3275. E-mail: rusric@erols.com

Manufacture of Furniture Manufacturing N.E.C.	82	3681	145
Recycling	1	3	1
Manufacture of Handicrafts	16	473	8
Total	793	61071	12730

NUMBER OF ESTABLISHMENTS, LABOR, AND INVESTMENT IN AL- SHARJAH

Activities	Est. No	Labor	Investment- million -Dh
Manufacture of Food	48	4648	347
Manufacture of Tobacco Products	0	0	0
Manufacture of Textiles	25	1665	303
Manufacture of Wearing Apparel	52	10164	102
Manufacture of Leather Products	6	148	3
Manufacture of Wood and Wood Products	17	1010	32
Manufacture of Paper and Paper Products	15	847	83
Publishing and Printing	31	2319	136
Manufacture of Refined Petroleum Products	6	542	97
Manufacture of Chemicals & Chemical Products	61	2953	222
Manufacture of Rubber and Plastic Products	66	4267	371
Manufacture of Non-metallic Mineral Products	75	4967	344
Basic Metals	13	1337	75
Manufacture of Fabricated Metal Products	95	7543	315
Manufacture of Machinery Equipment	22	1644	70
Manufacture of Office Accounting & computing Machinery	0	0	0
Manufacture of Electric Machinery Apparatus	23	1009	33
Manufacture of Motor Vehicles, Trailers & Semi Products	5	287	11
Manufacture of Other Transport Equipment's	6	189	15
Manufacture of Furniture Manufacturing N.E.C.	100	5339	273
Recycling	0	0	0
Manufacture of Handicrafts	19	435	13
Total	685	51313	2845

For additional analytical, marketing, investment and business opportunities information, please contact
Global Investment & Business Center, USA
(202) 546-2103. Fax: (202) 546-3275. E-mail: rusric@erols.com

NUMBER OF ESTABLISHMENTS, LABOR, AND INVESTMENT IN AJMAN

Activities	Est. No	Labor	Investment- million -Dh
Manufacture of Food	20	771	90
Manufacture of Tobacco Products	1	73	8
Manufacture of Textiles	13	596	22
Manufacture of Wearing Apparel	70	12786	89
Manufacture of Leather Products	6	257	6
Manufacture of Wood and Wood Products	4	468	52
Manufacture of Paper and Paper Products	11	503	21
Publishing and Printing	4	281	18
Manufacture of Refined Petroleum Products	8	176	8
Manufacture of Chemicals & Chemical Products	19	399	69
Manufacture of Rubber and Plastic Products	29	1004	31
Manufacture of Non-metallic Mineral Products	27	1067	115
Basic Metals	3	146	18
Manufacture of Fabricated Metal Products	36	2551	174
Manufacture of Machinery Equipment	2	33	2
Manufacture of Office Accounting & computing Machinery	1	12	1
Manufacture of Electric Machinery Apparatus	2	83	4
Manufacture of Motor Vehicles, Trailers & Semi Products	5	137	2
Manufacture of Other Transport Equipment's	10	620	26
Manufacture of Furniture Manufacturing N.E.C.	23	1246	21
Recycling	0	0	0
Manufacture of Handicrafts	7	358	2
Total	301	23567	779

NUMBER OF ESTABLISHMENTS, LABOR, AND INVESTMENT IN RAS-AL KHIMAH

Activities	Est. No	Labor	Investment- million -Dh
Manufacture of Food	10	933	223
Manufacture of Tobacco Products	0	0	0
Manufacture of Textiles	1	109	1

For additional analytical, marketing, investment and business opportunities information, please contact
Global Investment & Business Center, USA
(202) 546-2103. Fax: (202) 546-3275. E-mail: rusric@erols.com

Manufacture of Wearing Apparel	2	166	2
Manufacture of Leather Products	0	0	0
Manufacture of Wood and Wood Products	0	0	0
Manufacture of Paper and Paper Products	2	55	14
Publishing and Printing	3	225	65
Manufacture of Refined Petroleum Products	1	61	10
Manufacture of Chemicals & Chemical Products	4	1112	303
Manufacture of Rubber and Plastic Products	2	35	3
Manufacture of Non-metallic Mineral Products	22	6442	2108
Basic Metals	3	183	20
Manufacture of Fabricated Metal Products	10	245	12
Manufacture of Machinery Equipment	1	33	7
Manufacture of Office Accounting & computing Machinery	0	0	0
Manufacture of Electric Machinery Apparatus	0	0	0
Manufacture of Motor Vehicles, Trailers & Semi Products	1	10	1
Manufacture of Other Transport Equipment's	4	66	3
Manufacture of Furniture Manufacturing N.E.C.	3	201	11
Recycling	0	0	0
Manufacture of Handicrafts	7	169	4
Total	76	10045	2787

NUMBER OF ESTABLISHMENTS, LABOR, AND INVESTMENT IN UMM AL QUWAIN

Activities	Est. No	Labor	Investment- million -Dh
Manufacture of Food	6	550	20
Manufacture of Tobacco Products	0	0	0
Manufacture of Textiles	1	17	1
Manufacture of Wearing Apparel	0	0	0
Manufacture of Leather Products	0	0	0
Manufacture of Wood and Wood Products	2	112	4
Manufacture of Paper and Paper Products	1	42	2
Publishing and Printing	0	0	0

For additional analytical, marketing, investment and business opportunities information, please contact
Global Investment & Business Center, USA
(202) 546-2103. Fax: (202) 546-3275. E-mail: rusric@erols.com

Manufacture of Refined Petroleum Products	1	4	10
Manufacture of Chemicals & Chemical Products	5	194	12
Manufacture of Rubber and Plastic Products	5	133	9
Manufacture of Non-metallic Mineral Products	10	887	281
Basic Metals	1	100	1
Manufacture of Fabricated Metal Products	6	218	4
Manufacture of Machinery Equipment	0	0	0
Manufacture of Office Accounting & computing Machinery	0	0	0
Manufacture of Electric Machinery Apparatus	1	38	3
Manufacture of Motor Vehicles, Trailers & Semi Products	0	0	0
Manufacture of Other Transport Equipment's	1	14	1
Manufacture of Furniture Manufacturing N.E.C.	3	54	2
Recycling	1	13	1
Manufacture of Handicrafts	0	0	0
Total	44	2376	351

Number of Establishments, Labor, and Investment in Al- Fujairah

Activities	Est. No	Labor	Investment- million -Dh
Manufacture of Food	5	258	40
Manufacture of Tobacco Products	0	0	0
Manufacture of Textiles	0	0	0
Manufacture of Wearing Apparel	1	340	1
Manufacture of Leather Products	1	27	1
Manufacture of Wood and Wood Products	0	0	0
Manufacture of Paper and Paper Products	1	26	2
Publishing and Printing	1	42	7
Manufacture of Refined Petroleum Products	0	0	0
Manufacture of Chemicals & Chemical Products	1	7	5
Manufacture of Rubber and Plastic Products	4	225	16
Manufacture of Non-metallic Mineral Products	12	1618	558

For additional analytical, marketing, investment and business opportunities information, please contact
Global Investment & Business Center, USA
(202) 546-2103. Fax: (202) 546-3275. E-mail: rusric@erols.com

Basic Metals	0	0	0
Manufacture of Fabricated Metal Products	4	103	10
Manufacture of Machinery Equipment	1	24	2
Manufacture of Office Accounting & computing Machinery	0	0	0
Manufacture of Electric Machinery Apparatus	2	61	3
Manufacture of Motor Vehicles, Trailers & Semi Products	0	0	0
Manufacture of Other Transport Equipment's	0	0	0
Manufacture of Furniture Manufacturing N.E.C.	1	17	1
Recycling	0	0	0
Manufacture of Handicrafts	0	0	0
Total	34	2748	646

BASIC TITLES FOR UAE

IMPORTANT!
All publications are updated annually!
Please contact IBP, Inc. at ibpusa3@gmail.com for the latest ISBNs and additional information

TITLE
UAE A "Spy" Guide - Strategic Information and Developments
UAE A Spy" Guide"
UAE Banking & Financial Market Handbook
UAE Banking & Financial Market Handbook
UAE Business and Investment Opportunities Yearbook
UAE Business and Investment Opportunities Yearbook
UAE Business and Investment Opportunities Yearbook Volume 1 Strategic Information and Opportunities
UAE Business and Investment Opportunities Yearbook Volume 2 Leading Export-Import, Business, Investment Opportunities and Projects
UAE Business Intelligence Report - Practical Information, Opportunities, Contacts
UAE Business Intelligence Report - Practical Information, Opportunities, Contacts
UAE Business Law Handbook - Strategic Information and Basic Laws
UAE Business Law Handbook - Strategic Information and Basic Laws
UAE Business Law Handbook - Strategic Information and Basic Laws
UAE Business Law Handbook - Strategic Information and Basic Laws
UAE Business Success Guide - Basic Practical Information and Contacts
UAE Company Laws and Regulations Handbook
UAE Company Laws and Regulations Handbook - Strategic Information and Basic Laws
UAE Constitution and Citizenship Laws Handbook - Strategic Information and Basic Laws
UAE Country Study Guide - Strategic Information and Developments
UAE Country Study Guide - Strategic Information and Developments
UAE Country Study Guide - Strategic Information and Developments Volume 1 Strategic Information and Developments

For additional analytical, marketing, investment and business opportunities information, please contact
Global Investment & Business Center, USA
(202) 546-2103. Fax: (202) 546-3275. E-mail: rusric@erols.com

TITLE
UAE Criminal Laws, Regulations and Procedures Handbook - Strategic Information, Regulations, Procedures
UAE Customs, Trade Regulations and Procedures Handbook
UAE Customs, Trade Regulations and Procedures Handbook
UAE Diplomatic Handbook - Strategic Information and Developments
UAE Diplomatic Handbook - Strategic Information and Developments
UAE Ecology & Nature Protection Handbook
UAE Ecology & Nature Protection Handbook
UAE Ecology & Nature Protection Laws and Regulation Handbook
UAE Economic & Development Strategy Handbook
UAE Economic & Development Strategy Handbook
UAE Electoral, Political Parties Laws and Regulations Handbook - Strategic Information, Regulations, Procedures
UAE Energy Policy, Laws and Regulation Handbook Vol 1
UAE Energy Policy, Laws and Regulations Handbook
UAE Energy Policy, Laws and Regulations Handbook Vol 2
UAE Export-Import Trade and Business Directory
UAE Export-Import Trade and Business Directory
UAE Fishing and Aquaculture Industry Handbook - Strategic Information, Regulations, Opportunities
UAE Foreign Policy and Government Guide
UAE Foreign Policy and Government Guide
UAE Government and Business Contacts Handbook
UAE Government and Business Contacts Handbook
UAE Healthcare Sector Organization, Management and Payment Systems Handbook - Strategic Information, Programs and Regulations
UAE Immigration Laws and Regulations Handbook - Strategic Information and Basic Laws
UAE Industrial and Business Directory
UAE Insolvency (Bankruptcy) Laws and Regulations Handbook - Strategic Information and Basic Laws
UAE Internet and E-Commerce Investment and Business Guide - Strategic and Practical Information: Regulations and Opportunities
UAE Internet and E-Commerce Investment and Business Guide - Strategic and Practical Information: Regulations and Opportunities
UAE Investment & Business Guide
UAE Investment & Business Guide
UAE Investment and Business Guide - Strategic and Practical Information
UAE Investment and Business Guide - Strategic and Practical Information
UAE Investment and Business Guide Volume 2 Business, Investment Opportunities and Incentives
UAE Investment and Business Profile - Basic Information and Contacts for Succesful investment and Business Activity
UAE Investment and Trade Laws and Regulations Handbook
UAE Investment, Trade Strategy and Agreements Handbook - Strategic Information and Basic Agreements
UAE Labor Laws and Regulations Handbook - Strategic Information and Basic Laws
UAE Land Ownership and Agriculture Laws Handbook
UAE Mineral & Mining Sector Investment and Business Guide - Strategic and Practical Information
UAE Mineral & Mining Sector Investment and Business Guide - Strategic and Practical Information
UAE Mining Laws and Regulations Handbook
UAE Oil & Gas Sector Business & Investment Opportunities Yearbook
UAE Oil & Gas Sector Business & Investment Opportunities Yearbook
UAE Oil and Gas Exploration Laws and Regulation Handbook

For additional analytical, marketing, investment and business opportunities information, please contact
Global Investment & Business Center, USA
(202) 546-2103. Fax: (202) 546-3275. E-mail: rusric@erols.com

TITLE
UAE Recent Economic and Political Developments Yearbook
UAE Recent Economic and Political Developments Yearbook
UAE Recent Economic and Political Developments Yearbook
UAE Ruler Handbook
UAE Ruler Handbook
UAE Starting Business (Incorporating) in....Guide
UAE Tax Guide Volume 1 Strategic Information and Basic Regulations
UAE Taxation Laws and Regulations Handbook
UAE Telecom Laws and Regulations Handbook
UAE Telecommunication Industry Business Opportunities Handbook
UAE Telecommunication Industry Business Opportunities Handbook
UAE Transportation Policy and Regulations Handbook
United Arab Emirates: Recent Economic Developments Yearbook
UAE Stock, Financial Market Laws and Regulations Handbook - Strategic Information and Basic Laws
UAE: Abu Dhabi Stock Exchange Trading and Financial Operation Guide - Practical Information and Regulations
UAE Construction Companies Handbook - Strategic Information and Contacts
UAE Electronics, Computers and Information Technology Industry Handbook - Strategic Information and Contacts
UAE Free Economic Zones Handbook
UAE Free Economic Zones Handbook
UAE Import Tariffs Handbook
UAE Largest Importers Directory - Strategic Information and Contacts
UAE Medical and Pharmaceutical Industry Handbook - Strategic Information and Contacts
UAE Oil, Gas Exploration Industry Business and Investment Contacts Handbook
UAE Stock Market Business Laws and Regulations Handbook
UAE Transportation Sector Handbook - Strategic Information and Contacts

**For additional analytical, marketing, investment and business opportunities
information, please contact
Global Investment & Business Center, USA
(202) 546-2103. Fax: (202) 546-3275. E-mail: rusric@erols.com**

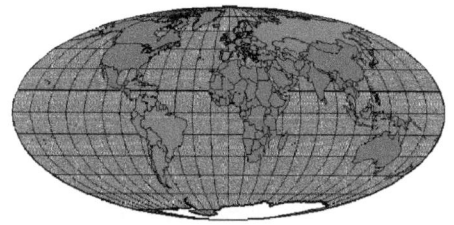

WORLD BUSINESS LAW HANDBOOKS LIBRARY

World Business Information Catalog, USA: http://www.ibpus.com

Email: ibpusa3@gmail.com

Price: $99.95 Each

TITLE
Abkhazia (Republic of Abkhazia) Business Law Handbook Volume 1 Strategic Information and Basic Laws
Afghanistan Business Law Handbook Volume 1 Strategic Information and Basic Laws
Aland Business Law Handbook Volume 1 Strategic Information and Basic Laws
Albania Business Law Handbook Volume 1 Strategic Information and Basic Laws
Algeria Business Law Handbook Volume 1 Strategic Information and Basic Laws
Andorra Business Law Handbook Volume 1 Strategic Information and Basic Laws
Angola Business Law Handbook Volume 1 Strategic Information and Basic Laws
Anguilla Business Law Handbook Volume 1 Strategic Information and Basic Laws
Antigua and Barbuda Business Law Handbook Volume 1 Strategic Information and Basic Laws
Antilles (Netherlands) Business Law Handbook Volume 1 Strategic Information and Basic Laws
Argentina Business Law Handbook Volume 1 Strategic Information and Basic Laws
Armenia Business Law Handbook Volume 1 Strategic Information and Basic Laws
Aruba Business Law Handbook Volume 1 Strategic Information and Basic Laws
Australia Business Law Handbook Volume 1 Strategic Information and Basic Laws
Austria Business Law Handbook Volume 1 Strategic Information and Basic Laws
Azerbaijan Business Law Handbook Volume 1 Strategic Information and Basic Laws
Bahamas Business Law Handbook Volume 1 Strategic Information and Basic Laws
Bahrain Business Law Handbook Volume 1 Strategic Information and Basic Laws
Bangladesh Business Law Handbook Volume 1 Strategic Information and Basic Laws
Barbados Business Law Handbook Volume 1 Strategic Information and Basic Laws
Belarus Business Law Handbook Volume 1 Strategic Information and Basic Laws
Belgium Business Law Handbook Volume 1 Strategic Information and Basic Laws
Belize Business Law Handbook Volume 1 Strategic Information and Basic Laws
Benin Business Law Handbook Volume 1 Strategic Information and Basic Laws
Bermuda Business Law Handbook Volume 1 Strategic Information and Basic Laws
Bhutan Business Law Handbook Volume 1 Strategic Information and Basic Laws
Bolivia Business Law Handbook Volume 1 Strategic Information and Basic Laws
Bosnia and Herzegovina Business Law Handbook Volume 1 Strategic Information and Basic Laws
Botswana Business Law Handbook Volume 1 Strategic Information and Basic Laws
Brazil Business Law Handbook Volume 1 Strategic Information and Basic Laws
Brunei Business Law Handbook Volume 1 Strategic Information and Basic Laws
Bulgaria Business Law Handbook Volume 1 Strategic Information and Basic Laws
Burkina Faso Business Law Handbook Volume 1 Strategic Information and Basic Laws
Burundi Business Law Handbook Volume 1 Strategic Information and Basic Laws
Cambodia Business Law Handbook Volume 1 Strategic Information and Basic Laws
Cameroon Business Law Handbook Volume 1 Strategic Information and Basic Laws
Canada Business Law Handbook Volume 1 Strategic Information and Basic Laws

For additional analytical, business and investment opportunities information,
Please contact Global Investment & Business Center, USA
at (202) 546-2103. Fax: (202) 546-3275. E-mail: ibpusa3@gmail.com

TITLE
Cape Verde Business Law Handbook Volume 1 Strategic Information and Basic Laws
Cayman Islands Business Law Handbook Volume 1 Strategic Information and Basic Laws
Central African Republic Business Law Handbook Volume 1 Strategic Information and Basic Laws
Chad Business Law Handbook Volume 1 Strategic Information and Basic Laws
Chile Business Law Handbook Volume 1 Strategic Information and Basic Laws
China Business Law Handbook Volume 1 Strategic Information and Basic Laws
Colombia Business Law Handbook Volume 1 Strategic Information and Basic Laws
Comoros Business Law Handbook Volume 1 Strategic Information and Basic Laws
Congo Business Law Handbook Volume 1 Strategic Information and Basic Laws
Congo, Democratic Republic Business Law Handbook Volume 1 Strategic Information and Basic Laws
Cook Islands Business Law Handbook Volume 1 Strategic Information and Basic Laws
Costa Rica Business Law Handbook Volume 1 Strategic Information and Basic Laws
Cote d'Ivoire Business Law Handbook Volume 1 Strategic Information and Basic Laws
Croatia Business Law Handbook Volume 1 Strategic Information and Basic Laws
Cuba Business Law Handbook Volume 1 Strategic Information and Basic Laws
Cyprus Business Law Handbook Volume 1 Strategic Information and Basic Laws
Czech Republic Business Law Handbook Volume 1 Strategic Information and Basic Laws
Denmark Business Law Handbook Volume 1 Strategic Information and Basic Laws
Djibouti Business Law Handbook Volume 1 Strategic Information and Basic Laws
Dominica Business Law Handbook Volume 1 Strategic Information and Basic Laws
Dominican Republic Business Law Handbook Volume 1 Strategic Information and Basic Laws
Ecuador Business Law Handbook Volume 1 Strategic Information and Basic Laws
Egypt Business Law Handbook Volume 1 Strategic Information and Basic Laws
El Salvador Business Law Handbook Volume 1 Strategic Information and Basic Laws
Equatorial Guinea Business Law Handbook Volume 1 Strategic Information and Basic Laws
Eritrea Business Law Handbook Volume 1 Strategic Information and Basic Laws
Estonia Business Law Handbook Volume 1 Strategic Information and Basic Laws
Ethiopia Business Law Handbook Volume 1 Strategic Information and Basic Laws
Falkland Islands Business Law Handbook Volume 1 Strategic Information and Basic Laws
Faroes Islands Business Law Handbook Volume 1 Strategic Information and Basic Laws
Fiji Business Law Handbook Volume 1 Strategic Information and Basic Laws
Finland Business Law Handbook Volume 1 Strategic Information and Basic Laws
France Business Law Handbook Volume 1 Strategic Information and Basic Laws
Gabon Business Law Handbook Volume 1 Strategic Information and Basic Laws
Gambia Business Law Handbook Volume 1 Strategic Information and Basic Laws
Georgia Business Law Handbook Volume 1 Strategic Information and Basic Laws
Germany Business Law Handbook Volume 1 Strategic Information and Basic Laws
Ghana Business Law Handbook Volume 1 Strategic Information and Basic Laws
Gibraltar Business Law Handbook Volume 1 Strategic Information and Basic Laws
Greece Business Law Handbook Volume 1 Strategic Information and Basic Laws
Greenland Business Law Handbook Volume 1 Strategic Information and Basic Laws
Grenada Business Law Handbook Volume 1 Strategic Information and Basic Laws
Guam Business Law Handbook Volume 1 Strategic Information and Basic Laws
Guatemala Business Law Handbook Volume 1 Strategic Information and Basic Laws
Guernsey Business Law Handbook Volume 1 Strategic Information and Basic Laws
Guinea Business Law Handbook Volume 1 Strategic Information and Basic Laws

For additional analytical, business and investment opportunities information,
Please contact Global Investment & Business Center, USA
at (202) 546-2103. Fax: (202) 546-3275. E-mail: ibpusa3@gmail.com

TITLE
Guinea-Bissau Business Law Handbook Volume 1 Strategic Information and Basic Laws
Guyana Business Law Handbook Volume 1 Strategic Information and Basic Laws
Haiti Business Law Handbook Volume 1 Strategic Information and Basic Laws
Honduras Business Law Handbook Volume 1 Strategic Information and Basic Laws
Hungary Business Law Handbook Volume 1 Strategic Information and Basic Laws
Iceland Business Law Handbook Volume 1 Strategic Information and Basic Laws
India Business Law Handbook Volume 1 Strategic Information and Basic Laws
Indonesia Business Law Handbook Volume 1 Strategic Information and Basic Laws
Iran Business Law Handbook Volume 1 Strategic Information and Basic Laws
Iraq Business Law Handbook Volume 1 Strategic Information and Basic Laws
Ireland Business Law Handbook Volume 1 Strategic Information and Basic Laws
Israel Business Law Handbook Volume 1 Strategic Information and Basic Laws
Italy Business Law Handbook Volume 1 Strategic Information and Basic Laws
Jamaica Business Law Handbook Volume 1 Strategic Information and Basic Laws
Japan Business Law Handbook Volume 1 Strategic Information and Basic Laws
Jersey Business Law Handbook Volume 1 Strategic Information and Basic Laws
Jordan Business Law Handbook Volume 1 Strategic Information and Basic Laws
Kazakhstan Business Law Handbook Volume 1 Strategic Information and Basic Laws
Kenya Business Law Handbook Volume 1 Strategic Information and Basic Laws
Kiribati Business Law Handbook Volume 1 Strategic Information and Basic Laws
Korea, North Business Law Handbook Volume 1 Strategic Information and Basic Laws
Korea, South Business Law Handbook Volume 1 Strategic Information and Basic Laws
Kosovo Business Law Handbook Volume 1 Strategic Information and Basic Laws
Kurdistan Business Law Handbook Volume 1 Strategic Information and Basic Laws
Kuwait Business Law Handbook Volume 1 Strategic Information and Basic Laws
Kyrgyzstan Business Law Handbook Volume 1 Strategic Information and Basic Laws
Laos Business Law Handbook Volume 1 Strategic Information and Basic Laws
Latvia Business Law Handbook Volume 1 Strategic Information and Basic Laws
Lebanon Business Law Handbook Volume 1 Strategic Information and Basic Laws
Lesotho Business Law Handbook Volume 1 Strategic Information and Basic Laws
Liberia Business Law Handbook Volume 1 Strategic Information and Basic Laws
Libya Business Law Handbook Volume 1 Strategic Information and Basic Laws
Liechtenstein Business Law Handbook Volume 1 Strategic Information and Basic Laws
Lithuania Business Law Handbook Volume 1 Strategic Information and Basic Laws
Luxembourg Business Law Handbook Volume 1 Strategic Information and Basic Laws
Macao Business Law Handbook Volume 1 Strategic Information and Basic Laws
Macedonia Business Law Handbook Volume 1 Strategic Information and Basic Laws
Madagascar Business Law Handbook Volume 1 Strategic Information and Basic Laws
Madeira Business Law Handbook Volume 1 Strategic Information and Basic Laws
Malawi Business Law Handbook Volume 1 Strategic Information and Basic Laws
Malaysia Business Law Handbook Volume 1 Strategic Information and Basic Laws
Maldives Business Law Handbook Volume 1 Strategic Information and Basic Laws
Mali Business Law Handbook Volume 1 Strategic Information and Basic Laws
Malta Business Law Handbook Volume 1 Strategic Information and Basic Laws
Man Business Law Handbook Volume 1 Strategic Information and Basic Laws
Marshall Islands Business Law Handbook Volume 1 Strategic Information and Basic Laws

For additional analytical, business and investment opportunities information,
Please contact Global Investment & Business Center, USA
at (202) 546-2103. Fax: (202) 546-3275. E-mail: ibpusa3@gmail.com

TITLE
Mauritania Business Law Handbook Volume 1 Strategic Information and Basic Laws
Mauritius Business Law Handbook Volume 1 Strategic Information and Basic Laws
Mayotte Business Law Handbook Volume 1 Strategic Information and Basic Laws
Mexico Business Law Handbook Volume 1 Strategic Information and Basic Laws
Micronesia Business Law Handbook Volume 1 Strategic Information and Basic Laws
Moldova Business Law Handbook Volume 1 Strategic Information and Basic Laws
Monaco Business Law Handbook Volume 1 Strategic Information and Basic Laws
Mongolia Business Law Handbook Volume 1 Strategic Information and Basic Laws
Montserrat Business Law Handbook Volume 1 Strategic Information and Basic Laws
Montenegro Business Law Handbook Volume 1 Strategic Information and Basic Laws
Morocco Business Law Handbook Volume 1 Strategic Information and Basic Laws
Mozambique Business Law Handbook Volume 1 Strategic Information and Basic Laws
Myanmar Business Law Handbook Volume 1 Strategic Information and Basic Laws
Nagorno-Karabakh Republic Business Law Handbook Volume 1 Strategic Information and Basic Laws
Namibia Business Law Handbook Volume 1 Strategic Information and Basic Laws
Nauru Business Law Handbook Volume 1 Strategic Information and Basic Laws
Nepal Business Law Handbook Volume 1 Strategic Information and Basic Laws
Netherlands Business Law Handbook Volume 1 Strategic Information and Basic Laws
New Caledonia Business Law Handbook Volume 1 Strategic Information and Basic Laws
New Zealand Business Law Handbook Volume 1 Strategic Information and Basic Laws
Nicaragua Business Law Handbook Volume 1 Strategic Information and Basic Laws
Niger Business Law Handbook Volume 1 Strategic Information and Basic Laws
Nigeria Business Law Handbook Volume 1 Strategic Information and Basic Laws
Niue Business Law Handbook Volume 1 Strategic Information and Basic Laws
Northern Cyprus (Turkish Republic of Northern Cyprus) Business Law Handbook Volume 1 Strategic Information and Basic Laws
Northern Mariana Islands Business Law Handbook Volume 1 Strategic Information and Basic Laws
Norway Business Law Handbook Volume 1 Strategic Information and Basic Laws
Oman Business Law Handbook Volume 1 Strategic Information and Basic Laws
Pakistan Business Law Handbook Volume 1 Strategic Information and Basic Laws
Palau Business Law Handbook Volume 1 Strategic Information and Basic Laws
Palestine (West Bank & Gaza) Business Law Handbook Volume 1 Strategic Information and Basic Laws
Panama Business Law Handbook Volume 1 Strategic Information and Basic Laws
Papua New Guinea Business Law Handbook Volume 1 Strategic Information and Basic Laws
Paraguay Business Law Handbook Volume 1 Strategic Information and Basic Laws
Peru Business Law Handbook Volume 1 Strategic Information and Basic Laws
Philippines Business Law Handbook Volume 1 Strategic Information and Basic Laws
Pitcairn Islands Business Law Handbook Volume 1 Strategic Information and Basic Laws
Poland Business Law Handbook Volume 1 Strategic Information and Basic Laws
Polynesia French Business Law Handbook Volume 1 Strategic Information and Basic Laws
Portugal Business Law Handbook Volume 1 Strategic Information and Basic Laws
Qatar Business Law Handbook Volume 1 Strategic Information and Basic Laws
Romania Business Law Handbook Volume 1 Strategic Information and Basic Laws
Russia Business Law Handbook Volume 1 Strategic Information and Basic Laws
Rwanda Business Law Handbook Volume 1 Strategic Information and Basic Laws
Sahrawi Arab Democratic Republic Volume 1 Strategic Information and Developments

For additional analytical, business and investment opportunities information,
Please contact Global Investment & Business Center, USA
at (202) 546-2103. Fax: (202) 546-3275. E-mail: ibpusa3@gmail.com

TITLE
Saint Kitts and Nevis Business Law Handbook Volume 1 Strategic Information and Basic Laws
Saint Lucia Business Law Handbook Volume 1 Strategic Information and Basic Laws
Saint Vincent and The Grenadines Business Law Handbook Volume 1 Strategic Information and Basic Laws
Samoa (American) A Business Law Handbook Volume 1 Strategic Information and Basic Laws
Samoa (Western) Business Law Handbook Volume 1 Strategic Information and Basic Laws
San Marino Business Law Handbook Volume 1 Strategic Information and Basic Laws
Sao Tome and Principe Business Law Handbook Volume 1 Strategic Information and Basic Laws
Saudi Arabia Business Law Handbook Volume 1 Strategic Information and Basic Laws
Scotland Business Law Handbook Volume 1 Strategic Information and Basic Laws
Senegal Business Law Handbook Volume 1 Strategic Information and Basic Laws
Serbia Business Law Handbook Volume 1 Strategic Information and Basic Laws
Seychelles Business Law Handbook Volume 1 Strategic Information and Basic Laws
Sierra Leone Business Law Handbook Volume 1 Strategic Information and Basic Laws
Singapore Business Law Handbook Volume 1 Strategic Information and Basic Laws
Slovakia Business Law Handbook Volume 1 Strategic Information and Basic Laws
Slovenia Business Law Handbook Volume 1 Strategic Information and Basic Laws
Solomon Islands Business Law Handbook Volume 1 Strategic Information and Basic Laws
Somalia Business Law Handbook Volume 1 Strategic Information and Basic Laws
South Africa Business Law Handbook Volume 1 Strategic Information and Basic Laws
Spain Business Law Handbook Volume 1 Strategic Information and Basic Laws
Sri Lanka Business Law Handbook Volume 1 Strategic Information and Basic Laws
St. Helena Business Law Handbook Volume 1 Strategic Information and Basic Laws
St. Pierre & Miquelon Business Law Handbook Volume 1 Strategic Information and Basic Laws
Sudan (Republic of the Sudan) Business Law Handbook Volume 1 Strategic Information and Basic Laws
Sudan South Business Law Handbook Volume 1 Strategic Information and Basic Laws
Suriname Business Law Handbook Volume 1 Strategic Information and Basic Laws
Swaziland Business Law Handbook Volume 1 Strategic Information and Basic Laws
Sweden Business Law Handbook Volume 1 Strategic Information and Basic Laws
Switzerland Business Law Handbook Volume 1 Strategic Information and Basic Laws
Syria Business Law Handbook Volume 1 Strategic Information and Basic Laws
Taiwan Business Law Handbook Volume 1 Strategic Information and Basic Laws
Tajikistan Business Law Handbook Volume 1 Strategic Information and Basic Laws
Tanzania Business Law Handbook Volume 1 Strategic Information and Basic Laws
Thailand Business Law Handbook Volume 1 Strategic Information and Basic Laws
Timor Leste (Democratic Republic of Timor-Leste) Business Law Handbook Volume 1 Strategic Information and Basic Laws
Togo Business Law Handbook Volume 1 Strategic Information and Basic Laws
Tonga Business Law Handbook Volume 1 Strategic Information and Basic Laws
Trinidad and Tobago Business Law Handbook Volume 1 Strategic Information and Basic Laws
Tunisia Business Law Handbook Volume 1 Strategic Information and Basic Laws
Turkey Business Law Handbook Volume 1 Strategic Information and Basic Laws
Turkmenistan Business Law Handbook Volume 1 Strategic Information and Basic Laws
Turks & Caicos Business Law Handbook Volume 1 Strategic Information and Basic Laws
Tuvalu Business Law Handbook Volume 1 Strategic Information and Basic Laws
Uganda Business Law Handbook Volume 1 Strategic Information and Basic Laws
Ukraine Business Law Handbook Volume 1 Strategic Information and Basic Laws

For additional analytical, business and investment opportunities information,
Please contact Global Investment & Business Center, USA
at (202) 546-2103. Fax: (202) 546-3275. E-mail: ibpusa3@gmail.com

TITLE
United Arab Emirates Business Law Handbook Volume 1 Strategic Information and Basic Laws
United Kingdom Business Law Handbook Volume 1 Strategic Information and Basic Laws
United States Business Law Handbook Volume 1 Strategic Information and Basic Laws
Uruguay Business Law Handbook Volume 1 Strategic Information and Basic Laws
Uzbekistan Business Law Handbook Volume 1 Strategic Information and Basic Laws
Vanuatu Business Law Handbook Volume 1 Strategic Information and Basic Laws
Vatican City (Holy See) Business Law Handbook Volume 1 Strategic Information and Basic Laws
Venezuela Business Law Handbook Volume 1 Strategic Information and Basic Laws
Vietnam Business Law Handbook Volume 1 Strategic Information and Basic Laws
Virgin Islands, British Business Law Handbook Volume 1 Strategic Information and Basic Laws
Wake Atoll Business Law Handbook Volume 1 Strategic Information and Basic Laws
Wallis & Futuna Business Law Handbook Volume 1 Strategic Information and Basic Laws
Western Sahara Business Law Handbook Volume 1 Strategic Information and Basic Laws
Yemen Business Law Handbook Volume 1 Strategic Information and Basic Laws
Zambia Business Law Handbook Volume 1 Strategic Information and Basic Laws
Zimbabwe Business Law Handbook Volume 1 Strategic Information and Basic Laws

For additional analytical, business and investment opportunities information,
Please contact Global Investment & Business Center, USA
at (202) 546-2103. Fax: (202) 546-3275. E-mail: ibpusa3@gmail.com

Lightning Source UK Ltd.
Milton Keynes UK
UKHW050648096122
396802UK00001B/10

9 781514 502198